BLACK PANTHER WOMAN

BLACK POWER SERIES
General Editors: Ibram X. Kendi and Ashley D. Farmer

Black Panther Woman

The Political and Spiritual Life of Ericka Huggins

Mary Frances Phillips

NEW YORK UNIVERSITY PRESS

New York

NEW YORK UNIVERSITY PRESS
New York
www.nyupress.org

Library of Congress Cataloging-in-Publication Data
Names: Phillips, Mary Frances, author.
Title: Black Panther woman : the political and spiritual life of Ericka Huggins /
Mary Frances Phillips.
Other titles: Political and spiritual life of Ericka Huggins
Description: New York : New York University Press, [2024] | Series: Black power |
Includes bibliographical references and index.
Identifiers: LCCN 2024007780 (print) | LCCN 2024007781 (ebook) |
ISBN 9781479802937 (hardback) | ISBN 9781479802944 (ebook other) |
ISBN 9781479802951 (ebook)
Subjects: LCSH: Huggins, Ericka. | Black Panther Party—Biography. | African American
feminists—Biography. | Feminist spirituality—United States—History—20th century. |
African American women political activists—Biography. | Human rights workers—United
States—Biography. | Black power—United States—History—20th century. | Sister Love
Collective. | Political activists—United States—Biography.
Classification: LCC E185.615 .H8447 2024 (print) | LCC E185.615 (ebook) | DDC
323.11960730092 b—dc23/eng/20240809
LC record available at https://lccn.loc.gov/2024007780
LC ebook record available at https://lccn.loc.gov/2024007781

This book is printed on acid-free paper, and its binding materials are chosen for strength
and durability. We strive to use environmentally responsible suppliers and materials to the
greatest extent possible in publishing our books.

Manufactured in the United States of America

Also available as an ebook

CONTENTS

FOREWORD

CHARLENE A. CARRUTHERS

Sisterly love is not a small or insignificant matter. I know this because Black women have saved my life, over and over again. Loving and being loved by Black women has saved my life, over and over again. Whether it was bonding while sitting in a jail together after a civil disobedience direct action or sharing a meal on a Sunday afternoon, sisterhood has sustained me throughout more moments than I can recount. This love is not new or limited to my own experiences. Sisterly love spans generations and geographies. The histories of such love reside in Black women's poetry, film, novels, and auto/biographies. Sisterly love is necessary for our collective survival. To the provocation "Are you sure . . . you want to be well?" posed by Black feminist cultural worker Toni Cade Bambara's character Minnie Ransom in her novel *The Salt Eaters*, I say yes. I want to be well even though wholeness, as Minnie wisely notes, "is no trifling matter." Sisterly love is necessary for my spirit to thrive and for me to be well.

But how can any of us be well in a world where small groups of people leverage white supremacist, patriarchal, and capitalist power to generate suffering and precarity for the majority? *Black Panther Woman* narrates how Ericka Huggins has been on a journey to do just that throughout her life. Beginning in her childhood home in Washington, DC, and continuing throughout her leadership in the Black Panther Party, Ericka Huggins practiced an ethic of love even while being held alongside other incarcerated women as a political prisoner. It was then that she committed to a life's work of spiritual wellness, which in turn fortified her as a political leader, educator, spiritual worker, and mother.

In researching and writing this epic history of Ericka Huggins's life, author Mary Frances Phillips strengthens the Black radical tradition of telling more complete stories in service of crafting more complete solutions. Phillips's method and the resulting historical narrative in *Black Panther Woman* required in-depth archival research along with extensive interwoven oral history interviews where what Black feminist historian Ula Y. Taylor calls "personal, political, and professional" are intertwined. Through method and narrative, *Black Panther Woman* adds to the Black radical tradition's collection of cultural, intellectual, action-oriented labor that disrupts (and recreates) social, political, economic, and cultural norms that originate in anti-colonial and anti-slavery struggles.

Many historians, including myself, stay away from the heavy task of writing about the living. I often venture several centuries back in time to glean insight on our present-day conditions. While this does not allow me to escape from the horrors of colonialism and chattel slavery present in archives or my responsibility to endeavor to tell the truth, it creates a distance that allows me to give room for stories to be told in our ancestors' terms. There is also an element of risk that is lessened when my subjects are dead. While the dead are not wholly absent in my life, they are less likely to send ungracious emails or drag me on social media! Still, I know that being a historian of Black life renders a degree of power and a heap of responsibility to do well by the stories I tell about the past. Many of the individuals and the communities Ericka Huggins is accountable to are very much still alive across these pages in the world as I write these opening words. Huggins is not a vestige of the past, and neither are the problems she began to struggle against in the 1960s. Cultivating a Black liberation movement that values and centers the spirit is needed right now. She understood this in 1970 as she served nearly eighteen months in solitary confinement in the Connecticut Correctional Institution in Niantic, and she continues to understand it today as she cultivates her own spiritual wellness while supporting others in doing the same. Practicing spiritual wellness, as bell hooks teaches us in her book *All about Love: New Visions*, must go beyond the individual and be practiced in "the context of community."

Readers, I encourage you to ask yourselves about your own wellness and the wellness of the communities you belong to as you read *Black Panther Woman*. Do you want to be well? For those of us living in the belly of the beast that is the United States of America, we must ask those appointed and elected into leadership across all institutions, Do they want us to want to be well? Do they act as though they want us, or even themselves, to be well? If not, they must go. We must develop ourselves and support others in developing themselves into good stewards in the world. We deserve nothing less than transformation for the sake of our collective liberation, the wellness of the planet, and full dignity for future generations.

Introduction

As historians follow a trail of documents to evaluate the
claims of an alleged experience, we should also think and
theorize from these same documents not only to recover
voices but also to disrupt those canonical discourses that
have too often rendered African American women invisible.
—Ula Y. Taylor

In quick succession, I was barraged with questions. "Where are you
located? Why are you choosing this topic? I'm assuming you're an African American woman?"[1] One after the other, the questions derailed me.
I came to this experience as the interviewer, and yet, during my first
conversation with Black Panther Party veteran, educator, poet, human
rights activist, and former political prisoner Ericka Cozette (Jenkins)
Huggins in 2010, I quickly learned that I was the interviewee. I soon
discovered that this was not a typical researcher-subject relationship
(if one exists). In our interview process, Ericka would interview me as
much as I interviewed her; but in the moment, I was taken aback. I was
the scholar. She was the subject. And yet, here I was explaining that I
was a Black woman and daughter of Detroit, Michigan, passionate about
centering Black Panther Party (BPP) women as frontline revolutionaries who intellectually contributed to Black Power theory. From this
first interview, I knew that my place of origin, interest in BPP women,
and racial background mattered in ways I had not considered. Neither
one of us could relinquish for the sake of objectivity or scholarship our
race, womanhood, or values. I had met my research subject, but more
importantly, I met who would become my revolutionary teacher. Ericka
offered historical context for our conversations, rooting our engage-
ments in the racial system of US slavery and the history of civil rights
women. She recommended books on the BPP for me to read and sometimes invited me to events on BPP women. As it turns out, she was not

1

a research subject but a guide. What I had conceived of as interviews became conversations. Together, we weaved our dialogue, one that preserved our identities while simultaneously being open to critique and hard questions. These conversations revealed the convergence of Ericka's social justice and spirituality, prompting me as the scholar-interlocutor to reconsider my preconceived notions of scholarship. To effectively capture the richness of Ericka's story, this book required an entirely different scholarly approach—one that called for my active engagement and self-reflection alongside Ericka as I focused on what I call spiritual wellness.

Spiritual wellness encompasses a comprehensive framework that intertwines self-care and community care, operating on a scale from the local to the global, from everyday practices to revolutionary change. This book's primary intervention lies in an examination of Ericka's profound practice of spiritual wellness. I define spiritual wellness as Black feminist practice that interweaves community and self-affirming acts of care. Ericka engaged in spiritual wellness by practicing yoga and meditation, composing letters, writing poetry, and making community connections during her two-year imprisonment in the late 1960s. These spirit-based acts of service were forged to ward off the visceral and psychological impacts of racial oppression. While Ericka's experience with state and federal violence, particularly her 1969 Connecticut arrest, catalyzed this lifelong spiritual wellness journey, seeds of this journey were sown early on in her childhood.

Ericka began raising her political consciousness at an early age. She was born on January 5, 1948, in Washington, DC, in a working-class family. When she attended the March on Washington on August 28, 1963, as a fifteen-year-old girl, against her parents' wishes, Ericka reached a turning point in her young life and vowed that she would serve humanity.[2] Later, while attending college at Lincoln University, a historic Black university, she read a *Ramparts* magazine article on criminal charges levied against Huey P. Newton, BPP co-founder and minister of defense.[3] Upon reading the story, Ericka and her partner, John, decided to leave college in the fall of 1967, move to California, and join the BPP. The BPP was one of the best-known and most misunderstood organizations during the Black Power movement. Founded in Oakland, California, in 1966, the BPP functioned as a grassroots political coalition-building organization and served as a political home for Ericka from 1967 to 1981.

Black Panther activism is a practice of care and belonging to empower communities. In theory and practice, the BPP's mission was fundamentally concerned with communal care and restorative justice. The Black Panther Party provided Black communities with resources, education, and tools to survive and thrive. As a predominantly Black American group that built coalitions in the United States, the BPP was not anti-white.[4] It met the changing needs of Black and poor communities nationwide through social service initiatives. As outlined in its Ten-Point Platform and Program, community programs sought to remedy the effects of racism and capitalism on Black communities as they related to unemployment, housing discrimination, inadequate education, and legal and state violence. In the early 1970s Huey employed the phrase "survival pending revolution" to describe the Ten-Point Platform and Program and its emphasis on increased community engagement.[5] Its efforts sustained local communities by providing access to necessary resources such as food, education, health care, employment, housing, and judicial support services.[6] Huey expounded, "Until we can achieve that total transformation, we must exist. To exist, we must survive; therefore, we need a survival kit: the Ten-Point Program."[7] The "Survival Kit" characterized the soul of the BPP's programs. The BPP was critical to Ericka's political consciousness-raising surrounding the fight for Black liberation and equality.

Ericka's Arrest

"I thought we were going to be killed," Ericka recalled, when on the evening of January 17, 1969, FBI Counterintelligence Program (COINTELPRO) agents murdered her husband, John Huggins, and her comrade Alprentice "Bunchy" Carter on the University of California, Los Angeles (UCLA) campus.[8] Ericka was only twenty-one years old and postnatal when the state murdered her husband. Home alone the day of the shooting, Ericka noticed the police stationed outside the Black Panthers' two-level apartment. Despite having just learned of the shootings of her husband and friend in cold blood, her concern instinctively shifted to her three-week-old daughter, Mai. Due to heavy police surveillance, Ericka feared for Mai's life. After the rest of the Black Panthers returned to the apartment without John and Bunchy, Ericka recalled,

"I rolled her [Mai] up in a big winter coat and gently placed her under a bed and said goodbye to her." Loud noise and chaos filled the apartment. The police shouted demands, ordering Ericka and her fellow Black Panthers to come down the stairs. Cautiously, she removed Mai from under the bed. With a coat wrapped around Mai, Ericka descended the porch steps.

> "Hold her up so I can see her," one of the police officers demanded. He then pointed his gun directly at Mai.
> "This is a baby! Put the gun away," she pleaded.
> "The baby might have a gun," the officer retorted, scoffing at her concern.[9]

Ericka lifted the coat to prove that she was holding a baby, leaving Mai's two small feet to dangle. The police took Ericka with her baby and the rest of the Black Panthers into custody. Trusted friends picked up Mai, and the police transferred Ericka from the Los Angeles Seventy-Seventh Street police precinct to the Sybil Brand Institute for Women. She was released eight hours later.[10] The police officers' inhumanity resulted in state violence that spared no age or gender.

The murder of Ericka's husband, her subsequent incarceration, her separation from her newborn, and her determination to fight back against a police state propelled her forward. The misogyny of COINTEL-PRO, political repression, and police brutality directly impacted women in the BPP. Indeed, as a young woman, new breastfeeding mother, and social activist, Ericka confronted the terror of law enforcement hours after the murder of her husband. Just two days after her release from Sybil Brand, she was on the other side of the country, roughly three thousand miles away, accompanied by her infant. The journey was to lay John to rest in his hometown of New Haven, Connecticut. At the request of the local Black community, she subsequently opened a BPP chapter.[11] However, before Ericka could settle into her new life, the State of Connecticut slapped her with multiple felony charges only four months after losing John. The state prosecution accused her of kidnapping, murder, and conspiracy to commit the murder of fellow Black Panther Alex Rackley. The police arrested her and sent her to the Connecticut Correctional Institution for Women in Niantic (also known simply as Niantic).[12] After she spent sixty hours in medical segregation upon intake, correctional officers placed her in administrative isolation.[13] But Ericka was not alone. She joined other BPP women, including Frances Elsie Carter, Margaret "Peggy" Hudgins, Rose Marie Smith, Maude Louis Francis, and Jeannie Wilson in administrative segregation, all of them serving time in connection with the death of Alex Rackley.[14] Because Maude Louis Francis and Jeannie Wilson were minors, they were sent to juvenile detention not long after they entered Niantic in 1969.[15] In administrative segregation, Ericka, Frances, Peggy, and Rose had freedom of movement within a segregated wing.

The Imprisonment Years

Throughout their imprisonment, these women endured a range of abuses and horrific treatment. Prison officials censored their mail, stripped them of their reading materials, and frequently denied them adequate medical services, including prenatal care. The women were even subjected to physical attacks by prison officials, resulting in serious injury and emotional distress. Nevertheless, despite the cruel treatment inflicted by correctional officers, the young Black Panther Party women courageously engaged in various acts of resistance. These experiences led Ericka to forge connections with and advocate for the humanity of fellow prisoners, including her compatriots (other Black Panther women political prisoners incarcerated with her) and supporters on the outside, fostering a sense of community. She prioritized the importance of community care and self-care in her own life. For example, the prisoners staged food strikes and fought back against violence at the hands of the officers. Ericka often thwarted the intrusive attempts by prison officials to conduct body searches on her.[16] She also refused medicine and maintained time-stamped written documentation of medications distributed to them.[17] She challenged authority and consistently interrogated prison officials, periodically requesting written documentation of the rules they attempted to enforce.[18] The State of Connecticut eventually released all the other women in 1970 except for Ericka, who remained in administrative segregation—a shared ward with individual cell rooms—and then was later moved to solitary confinement, a small single room. In total, she served nearly eighteen months in administrative segregation and solitary confinement combined.[19] Correctional officers placed Ericka in the general population only after her attorneys filed a complaint in the Connecticut District Court seeking declaratory and injunctive relief to declare the actions taken by authorities illegal and to prevent continued violations of her constitutional rights.[20] She continued to question unfair orders by prison officials in the general population. Following her two-year incarceration, a mistrial was declared, her charges were dismissed, and she was released in 1971.

Spiritual Wellness

Black Panther Woman delves into the embodiment of Ericka's political and spiritual ethics, which shaped her journey of social change from childhood to her release from prison in 1971. The book concludes at that point because it highlights the transformative power of her spiritual practice, which took root in the unlikeliest of places, prison. Despite being physically confined, Ericka discovered the means to nurture a liberated mind and employ spiritual wellness practices, including meditation, letter writing, the composition of poetry and prose, women-centered community-building initiatives, and yoga. These practices helped sustain her and also prevent further injury. Spiritual wellness intertwines with political actions aimed at achieving people's liberation, forming an ethical framework that centers a particular way of being in the world. It also encompasses the intentional internal work that constitutes Ericka's wellness practices. Spiritual wellness borrows from Eastern philosophy while incorporating the unique perspectives and experiences of Black women. In this way, while spiritual wellness is universal in its pursuit, it is particularly meaningful for Black women as it names the critical importance of Black identity and liberation. It also moves beyond the confines of race, gender, and sexual identity categories to embrace the interconnectedness of all intersectional identities. Spiritual wellness consists of six tenets:

1. Spiritual wellness is about meaning making. Specifically, it is about finding meaning in all contexts.
2. It facilitates alignment among established core values through specific practices.

3. It is a way for Black women to feel whole in a white supremacist world that dehumanizes them, particularly within a prison system that treats Black women as less than human.

4. It is a response and resilience strategy, a coping mechanism developed in response to an inhospitable world.

5. It is an alternative to violence, uplifting love, connection, and emotional regulation.

6. It is a mechanism for creating space within oneself even when the world is in chaos.

By tracing Ericka's life and focusing on her time in prison with other BPP members, *Black Panther Woman* unearths how Ericka navigated the complexity of seeking liberation in a society that failed Black people. Her journey helps us to understand how and why liberation dreams change over time and the entanglement of patriarchy, domination, feminism, and women's empowerment. As I recount and analyze Ericka's experiences, the reader will encounter how her revolutionary daily life disrupts and, at times, follows male leadership. *Black Panther Woman* is a story that contextualizes the white supremacist violence as an offshoot of patriarchy. Ultimately, this book is about how Ericka learned to live a life dedicated to empowering Black people, including herself, through healing practices.

I examine Ericka's self-care practice to argue that Black feminist wellness combats white supremacist state violence and dehumanization by promoting personal and community well-being. Ericka's wellness practice stems from the Black feminist praxis that connects the personal to the political. I argue that her self-care and community care reframes this in such a way as to make the spiritual into the political. My use of the term "political" refers capaciously to social and cultural frameworks that center justice and equity, not merely formal political governance. Black women's everyday personal and spiritual experiences are deeply connected to histories of fighting oppression and injustice. Black feminist scholars Frances Beale, Patricia Hill Collins, Beverly Guy-Sheftall, and others have set out core tenets of Black feminism as an ideology that are foundational to the field.[21] In its diversity, Black feminism affirms that our experiences are shaped by multiple oppressions that impact our various identities, that we have to work simultaneously on racial and gender equality, and that ultimately the impetus for liberatory politics is rooted in our daily lives.[22] Ericka's experience of imprisonment and patriarchal violence, her drive to be mentally and spiritually healthy for her child, and her desire to continue the larger Black liberatory project are part of a spiritual process that informs her prison activism. This fuels her ongoing work to maintain practices of meditation, yoga, creative expression, and community education within and beyond the prison walls. Post-prison, she extended her practices by becoming a vegetarian and later a vegan.

Her personal actions are not just about her individual survival; they also offer her community an alternate way of being in the world. In so doing, she embodies the idea that sisterhood and love are political. I use "sisterhood" to denote close friendships among women, attachments defined by mutual care, support, and interdependence. I rely on a definition of Black love to shape my explanation of affective relations as political actions. Black love, as bell hooks reminds us, ought to be expressed interpersonally, in politics, and within movements for justice.[23] Love here "is not just about what Black people do, but what we work to undo."[24] Ericka's Black love ethic is connected to her spirit-based actions. Such actions shape her wellness practices and are central to Black feminist politics.

Ericka's feminist politics crystalized in prison not through her reading of feminist theory but through the practical measures she established to preserve her life and the lives of other women living in an unjust carceral environment. In 2018, on a panel for the National Women's Studies Association, Ericka publicly announced, "What made me the feminist I am today? Well, two years in prison really solidified it for me."[25] Ericka became an ally for the women imprisoned with her. She described key aspects of an ally as someone who "not only has your back but your front, your side, your heart, your everything. They do their inner work."[26] Ericka cultivated her "inner work" through yoga and meditation while simultaneously engaging in forms of resistance such as her prison writings, which included letter writing, prose, and poetry, literary traditions within the Black freedom struggle. She understood that her spiritual practices, which started as self-survival and revelation, placed her in a stronger position to better serve others. This awareness marked a shift for Ericka in coming into a praxis of spirit within a politicized context.

In our conversations, Ericka stated that the BPP lacked a "spiritual container," meaning that spiritual work was underdeveloped, yet crucial for the BPP.[27] Overwhelmed with sorrow at the murder of comrades from mob state terror and the constant FBI surveillance and attacks, some BPP members were walking around wounded and traumatized. Spiritual practices served as a kind of grief work or therapy. Black Panther activists who engaged in life-giving activities, including Ericka's engagement in yoga and meditation, Angela Y. Davis's practice in calisthenics and karate, and Mutulu Shakur's work in acupuncture, demonstrate that there was a wellness practice among some.[28] It was not until 1973 that the Black Panthers sought to fill the spiritual gap in the organization with the establishment of Son of Man Temple, a community program and nontraditional church focused on spirituality in Oakland, California.[29] The wellness movement offers a broader way of understanding the Black Power movement.

Ericka's practices were rooted in spirituality rather than in specific religious dogma and organized religion. I employ William R. Miller and Carl E. Thoresen's definition of religions as "differentiated by particular beliefs and practices, requirements of membership, and modes of social organization."[30] Without religious order and practices, according to Miller and Thoresen, spirituality is "understood to transcend ordinary physical limits of time and space, matter and energy."[31] Ericka turned to spirituality, not religion, for guidance and direction. Spirit and care fueled her activist modalities as she engaged in spiritual work within the context of the women's liberation movement.[32] Radicalized women of color tap into spiritual wellness to survive their distinct oppression. Spiritual wellness is not self-care in an individualist, capitalist sense. Rather, it is a constant engagement in a healing practice of self-improvement and community-based people power. As soul work, spiritual wellness is not only about the presence of care but is also attached to an ethical commitment to challenging oppression and white supremacy, and moves us toward collective liberation.

Ericka serves as a case study for spiritual wellness because she intentionally engaged in healing work to protect herself and remain at peace. It was in prison that Ericka came to understand the mind-body connection. Resistant anti-racist activism, like that practiced by Ericka and others, including Angela Y. Davis, Assata Shakur, and Mutulu Shakur, is predicated on resisting the demoralizing violence of white supremacist rule in the United States. BPP activist work lends purpose to the struggle against racism, but it does not solve the problem of demoralization that comes with existing as a marginalized human being in a racist society. Accordingly, just as social, political, and economic empowerment is key to the Black freedom movement, so too is spiritual uplift. Unlike the practices of some of the most famous civil rights activists, Ericka's practices are not informed by Christian ethos.[33]

Her spirit-affirming practices were important in manifesting what she calls "spiritual maturity." Ericka interprets spiritual maturity as a form of consciousness that challenges the oppressive socialization of white patriarchal society and prioritizes introspection, reflection, and self-analysis. My use of "spiritual wellness" reflects Ericka's conscious practices to achieve spiritual maturity, including meditating, writing poetry, and forming women-centered groups (among other activities). I identify Ericka's striving toward spiritual maturity as a more advanced manifestation of her growth. Her movement into spiritual maturity allowed her to notice the deficits in the spiritual work that she needed to do for herself, understand how she could sustain herself in wellness, and act on behalf of others to meet their material and political needs. Ericka gives us insight into how transformative personal and collective politics grow and take shape. Her concept of spiritual maturity demonstrates for me how Black Power activism could blend political and economic self-determination with physical and spiritual well-being. I posit that scholarly awareness of the relationship between the mind, body, and spirit and their importance to activist work in the Black Power movement will encourage BPP scholars to holistically evaluate the Black Panther Party's own mantra to "Serve the people body and soul."[34]

Black Panther Woman explores the survival of women in prison, primarily through the story of Ericka's compelling life. I historically document women's prison organizing and collective care strategies by Black Panther women to oppose carceral violence. This book reframes the prevailing male-centered discourse surrounding political prisoners and redirects attention toward the experiences of a queer Black mother. Through this shift, the struggles with the state come into sharp focus.

In the stories that make up *Black Panther Woman*, I argue that Ericka's spirit-affirming actions serve as forms of resistance critical not only to her preservation but to that of other women prisoners. The fact that anyone came out of Niantic prison alive and emotionally intact is a testament to their unwavering determination to live, asserting their fundamental right to exist and function as all human beings should. The story of the BPP women exemplifies that surviving prison was a near-impossible feat without the crucial support and tireless advocacy of others. They depended on family members to care for their children and on one another for their mental and spiritual well-being. The profound physical and emotional tolls extended far beyond the prison walls, deeply affecting their families and friendships. I record the self-care and community care practices that Ericka and the other BPP women cultivated in prison. In so doing, I attend to the often ignored resiliency required for women, especially mothers, to navigate the prison system to illustrate another aspect of BPP women organizing within the prison context.

Indeed, Ericka's holistic strategies of self-preservation during her incarceration exemplify the critical role of spiritual growth and its interconnections with social activism. Through an investment in care-based work, Ericka promoted social change as a BPP member inside and outside prison walls. I center the underexamined role of spiritual practice at the heart of that work, thus expanding how scholars have conceptualized activist labor. I delve into Ericka's journey to create the kind of life she envisioned in her quest for the liberation of oppressed communities. Robin D. G. Kelley reminds us that "struggle is par for the course when our dreams go into action"; for Ericka and the women around her, that "action" validated the spirit.[35]

New Directions

Black Panther Woman builds on and modifies Black Power history to capture a more diverse portrait of the varied practices of love and care and their relationship to the body; these wellness practices offer a counterbalance to the pervasive disruption that white supremacist violence causes.[36] Spiritual wellness is a direct response to the violence of white supremacy. In my discussion of white supremacy, I borrow Akiba Solomon and Kenrya Rankin's definition: the "political, cultural and economic system premised on the subjugation of people who are not White."[37] White supremacy is enforced by land theft and physical, mental, and spiritual violence.[38] It shapes and compounds other oppressive structures such as patriarchy. Because white supremacist violence shapes all institutions, including those that seek to dismantle it, the violence that people associate with the Black Panthers was both real and imagined; the Black Panthers were targets of violence and killed by the police. Throughout my conversations with Ericka, she grappled with the BBP leadership's replication of violent behavior, and how her role in the BPP contributed to the ebbs and flows of her spiritual journey.

Black Panther Woman makes three major interventions in the historiography on the BPP, the Black Power movement, and the Black freedom struggle: First, it fills a gap in the scholarship by focusing on non-Christian spiritual work.[39] Second, Ericka's saga allows us to discern the fullness of the carceral lives of Black women political prisoners and their resistance, adding another layer to our understanding of BPP women's organizing. Third, this work continues to advance our knowledge of deep state repression through COINTELPRO by documenting the illegal surveillance of and violence against Black women political activists by the FBI.

How women members experienced the BPP varied from chapter to chapter. The stellar work of historians Robyn C. Spencer-Antoine, Tracye A. Matthews, Ashley D. Farmer, Angela D. LeBlanc-Ernest, Ula Y. Taylor, and Keisha N. Blain has recovered the many experiences and contributions of women's BPP membership, Black feminism, and Black radicalism in relationship to US Black nationalism.[40] Less commonly explored by both popular and academic depictions of the Black Panthers is how BPP activists like Ericka believed that they needed restorative care in order to thrive. *Black Panther Woman* adds to their intellectual offerings. Although Black feminist historians' scholarship evidences the expansive history of BPP women, Hollywood and popular culture representations often continue to depict a male-dominated BPP. In popular depictions of the movement, the Black Panthers' armed ideology has been both romanticized and demonized. I offer a closer look at how this idea overwhelms and obscures the various approaches that emerged from BPP struggles to demonstrate Ericka's role in the Black freedom struggle. In doing this, this book reshapes the public memory of the

BPP from a story about police, criminality, and hate and recasts it to center Black women's prison organizing, resistance, and collision with law enforcement.

Ericka is a high-ranking yet understudied figure in the BPP. Her journey foregrounds the fact that acts of wellness organized the lives of some Black Panthers and help us to redefine the movement for the present generation engaged in self-care and holistic health. The work of spiritual wellness and Black Power as a space of care represents one version of Black Power, not a default approach of the Black Panther Party. Ericka deepens our perception of women's relationship building across the carceral state and the identity politics of the period. But she also transforms our understanding and knowledge of the BPP and Black Power. Her employment of a restorative praxis of wellness offers theoretical tools to better facilitate the liberation of the oppressed under state correctional control.

Although some Black Panther women have written well-known autobiographies, until now, scholars have not undertaken a biography of a Black Panther woman. In bringing women's narratives to the forefront of contemporary history, *Black Panther Woman* joins a growing group of biographies of Black women radicals to broaden the discourse on Black women's history during the civil rights and Black Power movement.[41] Indeed, my monograph taps into a growing demand for portraits of Black women activists. By reframing the historical record in a way that grants agency to women subjects often marginalized in the Black radical protest movement, I advance these biographic treatments by demonstrating how the organizing activities and strategies of Black women radicals pushed the theoretical boundaries of Black Power ideology and practice.

The Sister Love Collective

While in prison, Ericka co-founded the feminist women's Sister Love Collective in 1970. The collective was defined in opposition to white supremacy and capitalism and created to help women survive the daily horrors of prison. Ericka drew upon the BPP's practice of community engagement and modeled historic women's organizational work that followed the tradition of putting women at the center of care. The Black Panther practice of "serving the people body and soul" functioned as the driving force for Sister Love.[42]

With the rise of the Sister Love Collective, Ericka applied the same political practice that she had learned earlier as a Black Panther in her community work in Los Angeles and Oakland. She credits the needs-based orientation of her political work as "one of the reasons why Sister Love worked" for imprisoned women.[43] Her work in prison unknowingly advanced Huey P. Newton's 1971 concept of intercommunalism, a political framework for understanding self-determination and the power of communities, as described in his remarks at Yale University the same year as her prison release.[44] Huey called attention to the abuses of exploited and oppressed communities by "the empire of the United States" and a desire by these communities "to determine their own destinies."[45] Intercommunalists believed in a world free of borders, one in which communities share resources. In practice, intercommunalism enabled communities to thrive and exist on their own terms. Moreover, the recognition of social identities plays a crucial role in intercommunalism, as exemplified by the powerful demonstration of the Sister Love Collective women captives to produce and distribute resources not provided by the carceral state. While incarceration shaped the needs of the community, race also served as a means of fostering solidarity. The cross-racial coalition of the women in the Sister Love Collective and their gendered modes of resistance produced social change. In this way, Sister Love refashioned intercommunalism to include a Black feminist and working-class consciousness.

The Sister Love Collective embodied political consciousness through acts of personal care alongside the exchange of reflections, memories, thoughts, and ideas. Women conversed and offered a listening ear as they shared their joys, troubles, and worries through tears, hugs, smiles, and humor. Conversations ranged from the micro to the macro, from family, friends, legal woes, trial updates, prison life, culture, and politics, to liberation for those incarcerated and freedom for all. Their survival rested on Black feminist practices such as consciousness-raising and collective revolutionary care work.

The utility of a collective structure in Sister Love mirrored Black feminist organizations such as the Third World Women's Alliance (TWWA).[46] According to Kimberly Springer, "The organization operated under the inherited philosophy of participatory democracy that encouraged members to work in all facets of the organization, including

decision making."[47] Like the TWWA, Sister Love encouraged nonhierar-
chical organizing and enabled all women to contribute ideas. It involved
collectivist thinking among women to repair Niantic. The TWWA argued that differences of culture, race, and ethnicity were essential to the
conversation about how to fight capitalistic exploitation in communities of color.[48] Similarly, racial differences operated in Sister Love as a
source of strength to build solidarity and collective consciousness within
Niantic.

Queer Black Feminism

Ericka's lived experiences intersect with feminism, spirituality, sexuality, political repression, and urban education. Ericka embraced what we
might call today queer Black feminism informed by spirituality, in that
she believed in a world of gender equity as expressed in her political
activism, poetry, intimate personal relations, and radical reimagining of
the world. While Ericka has a fraught relationship with labels because
she does not feel that she fits within their confinement, she leans most
toward the term "queer." Cultural scholar José Esteban Muñoz explains
that "queerness is essentially about the rejection of a here and now and
an insistence on potentiality or concrete possibility for another world."[49]
Muñoz's definition corresponds with Ericka's in that it isn't about sexual
identity necessarily nor the inhabitation of a label. Rather, it is about a
future orientation toward a world that enables the survival of those who
have been marginalized. Ericka refuses the "here and now" and imagines a
queer future—queer in the sense of a flourishing of possibilities for spiritual life.[50] Her queer identity laced with her spiritual practices boldly
ushered in compassion, tenderness, and empowering love. Ericka per-
sonifies what transnational feminist scholar Carole Boyce Davies refers
to as "a radical black subject" in that her political activism "constitutes
itself as resisting the particular dominating disciplines, systems, and log-
ics of a given context," evident in her location outside prevailing white
(and Black) heteronormative radical and mainstream spaces.[51]

Ericka's membership offers a window into the world that the Black
Panthers struggled to create for themselves and their communities,
which inspires us to think differently about possibilities for the future.
Ericka unapologetically emblematizes what historian Robin D. G. Kelley

describes in *Freedom Dreams* as the ability "to imagine something different, to realize that things need not always be this way."[52] Her story shows
how "it is that imagination, that effort to see the future in the present"
that the Black Panthers positioned as the heartbeat of their practice.[53] As
a Black Panther, she created new possibilities, experimented with theory
and practice, built institutions, took risks, and created an alternative way
of living life on her own terms. She modeled these aspects in a multitude
of ways across time and space.

Writing on the Living

This book also makes an intervention in Black women's biography
and methodology. To research and write a personal feminist political biography of Ericka, I employed an interdisciplinary methodology
that combines deep and creative archival research with oral history
and sustained conversation. This book is my rendition of Ericka's life
as a political prisoner, with close consultation from her, but it also gives
insight into my research journey, as discussed here in the introduction.
I refer to this transformative methodology as interwoven oral history,
which documents claims, recovers, analyzes, illustrates, and amplifies
voices that have been marginalized under the false pretense of neutrality,
and centers their narratives to expand the historical canon with theory
and empathy. Interwoven oral history is a framework that encompasses
multiple interview sessions that intricately intertwine the "personal,
political, and professional" aspects, borrowing the terminology coined
by Taylor in her 2008 essay.[54] Our relationship is personal because,
for me, it is impossible to do this work and tell these stories without
self-investment. My fondest memory of Ericka is when she called me
when my father passed away in 2020. Although my father was a predominantly absent figure, I experienced complex feelings and emotions
about his untimely death. Still, Ericka called me with words of comfort.
She routinely showed me that she cared about my personal well-being. I
first met Ericka in 2010 while I was pursuing my doctorate; independent
scholar Angela D. LeBlanc-Ernest had introduced us and I arranged for
a phone interview with her. Since then, Ericka and I have had many
conversations, sat on panels together in person at the Schomburg Center for Research in Black Culture and the University of Chicago, and

discussed the making of this book from our different perspectives at Queens University Belfast. We have also served as guest speakers virtually in a graduate course at the CUNY Graduate Center. We have broken bread together at restaurants during these times as well. In our professional relationship, I am keenly aware of our relationship's boundaries, which is a delicate ongoing negotiation.

Sometimes I asked her questions that she did not want to answer. I knew when she was being evasive or vague. It took time for both of us to open up and share more of our lives. Ericka shared not only her life, but also contacts with many people in her network. She connected me with other academics doing scholarly work on the BPP and other political activists to interview about her life. Through my research work I also connected her with people from her past whom she had not talked to since her imprisonment. It takes more than interviewing a subject to gain an understanding of their life. I turned to others, including Ericka's friends, colleagues, lawyers, and fellow BPP members, published oral interviews, BPP autobiographies, and archives, to provide more context and color to challenging times in her life.

My interwoven oral history with Ericka was unlike interviewing a family member, a politician, or an artist. She is a Black Panther Party veteran and former political prisoner; given this fact, there were political consequences to our continued conversations. The limited oral histories and collections on radical Black women on the fringes of society who survived incarceration required me to develop a close relationship with Ericka. I found myself confronted with what Taylor describes as "the problem posed by finding 'less'" in the archives.[55] As I write this, there is no singular archival collection exclusively about Ericka. Pieces of her life lay scattered in numerous archives I explored, such as the Catherine Roraback Collection of Ericka Huggins Papers at Yale University, the Dr. Huey P. Newton Foundation Collection at Stanford University, Black Panther Billy X's archives of the *Black Panther* newspaper, the State Archives at the Connecticut State Library, and published oral histories through the Bancroft Library's Regional Oral History Office at the University of California, Berkeley, the Southern Oral History Program with the Smithsonian Institution's National Museum of African American History and Culture and the Library of Congress, and published interviews in journal articles.[56] While these archives contained important information on her life as a Black Panther, her trial, prison conditions, family background, and stories of her youth, I needed a fuller portrait of her familial life and coming-of-age years, life lessons, and her response to a prison conduct log that corrections officers recorded on her behavior during her incarceration.

These archival gaps, coupled with the fact that Ericka was a radical political prisoner, made distance and objectivity between Ericka and me impossible and thus required me to turn to my living source for details that only she knew. In the words of historian Françoise N. Hamlin, "Objectivity is a farce; we make choices all the time about what to study, how to collect and treat data—our questions, our methods, our motivations all consciously or unconsciously shape our scholarship."[57] Objectivity is obscured. Although not new, my closeness with a living person while writing this book is a valid methodological practice unique to Black women. My methodological approach shifts the narrative from the top down to the bottom up. Taylor wrote that "it is usually under the most challenging archival conditions, however, that one must call most creatively and rigorously upon historical methods and theoretical ideas."[58] The absence of so much of Ericka's life from the archives compelled me to approach this book in a nontraditional way as conventional methods were pushed to their limits to accommodate new possibilities of history. Therefore, it would be misguided to label my book biased. Utilizing these archival collections and conducting oral histories with Ericka to fill in the gaps allowed me to approach not just biography but the landscape of Black women's biography differently.

The oral histories and conversations at the heart of this book are the result of the decade-long relationship developed with Ericka. With our enduring relationship, she trusted me enough to give me permission to write this book. I have had exclusive access to her and have close to a thousand hours of interviews with her and people who knew her. Using information I gathered from my conversations with Ericka, I was able to find some of the women in the Sister Love Collective and their families. Ericka's friends and comrades shared their personal papers and inner lives with me. These Black women's personal writings and reflections were critical in gaining a better understanding of ideas of gender, feminism, history, and motherhood during the Black Power era. I conducted rare interviews with social activists such as Angela Y. Davis; Lennox

Hinds, renowned attorney for Davis, Assata Shakur, and Nelson Mandela; and famed Connecticut-based Black Panther Party attorney John Williams. I have also interviewed those who perpetrated violence against Ericka, such as the correctional officer who assaulted her and her former cellmates, and the warden, Janet S. York, who presided over Niantic while Ericka was imprisoned. York was ninety-six at the time of our interview; she is now deceased.

Ericka's stories as a living Black Panther Party member exemplify her agency. My interpretation of these stories allows for a new kind of history that invokes passion and feelings. This project shifts how historians think about and interpret what happened as a kind of storytelling deeply engaged in the process of collecting the narrative. Oral history interviews play a critical role in reconstructing Black women's lives, and they capture the importance of passion and emotion in history making. People often think of history as dry facts. But Ericka's story reveals the importance of our inner world of emotion. Oral history interviews offer a way to unpack emotions and provide intimate details of the experiences of BPP members.

Ericka agreed to talk with me under the condition that my research be accessible beyond the ivory tower. I have attempted to do this in my narrative writing style throughout this book. In essence, Ericka wanted to ensure that BPP veterans and other revolutionaries could find themselves in this story. In paying attention to emotion and the spiritual, inner life of activists, I do just that: move beyond dry facts to capture the passion that fueled a movement and produced new theories of how to live in the world. It is a radical intervention that captures an important subjective point of view and functions as a feminist methodological praxis that privileges personal experience.

This book uses biographic material as a case study of radical women's spiritual wellness practices and the emerging carceral state. The book is as much a history as it is an oral memoir. What emanated from the vast oral history archive I have created via interviews and primary source materials is both a deep and wide portrait of BPP leadership and practice. The coupling of archival collections with oral histories readily embodied not only an interdisciplinary approach to historical research as it relates to biography but also shed light on the distinctiveness of Black women's biography. The writings and letters of Ericka and peers, court and prison records, newspaper articles, photographs, unpublished material, and BPP internal memos on the Black Panthers' Oakland Community School (OCS) only began to scratch the surface of Ericka's life. I was privy to rare documents, including an archive of never published letters she penned in prison and a conduct log kept by correctional officers on her activities and movement in prison. These materials, coupled with my long-term research engagement with Ericka, allow me to tell a deeper story on the inner workings of her life and the profound impact of her feminist organizing in the BPP and in prisons. So, although this book starts with oral history and memories, these elements are always in conversation with archival documents from the past. I use historical scholarship to substantiate Ericka's memories. This approach is ultimately a dialogue between past and present, memory and meaning making, what is known and what is forgotten.

Ericka's desire to feel included as part of this storytelling and oral history repositions women from historical objects to historical subjects. In our ongoing conversations, she emphasized the importance of primary sources in conveying the experiences of BPP members. She wanted to ensure that I had read—really read—what BPP members wrote about their lives: "I just want you to understand how it feels to be written about while we are still alive."[59] Ericka recognized the power dynamic within the research process. Inasmuch as she recognized the power I held as a historian of Black women, she also owned and exerted her agency as a Black Panther veteran and social activist. Her words demand attention to feelings in the past, feelings that come up in our conversations, and feelings about being a part of history by making them a precondition to the interview. In our first phone interview, she expressed her commitment to affective relations; she stressed, "I care about your work."[60] Empathy, for Ericka, is crucial to human connection and political action. For me, it is important to both activism and the process of making history.

Ericka's personal account serves as political and historical intervention. This BPP intervention included the development of an alternative analysis in understanding intellectual work that departs from Eurocentric models of scholarship. It insists that scholarship promote intercommunal solidarity to legitimize the power of the community. Ericka does not make distinctions about who can be a scholar based on their level of formal education. The ideas of BPP co-founders Huey P. Newton, Bobby Seale, and former chairperson Elaine Brown form a powerful narrative, but what is that narrative? Ericka forces us to wrestle with such questions as, Who controls the narrative? Who has voice, volume, and value? Whose words have power and meaning? My framing of Ericka's theories is centered in conversation with historian Ashley D. Farmer's study on the significance of Black women's intellectual production in challenging and changing how Black Power operates and how we understand it through the lens of gender.[61] Ericka's ideas, perspectives, analysis, and leadership in and out of prison represent her intellectualism. Ericka's theory on the role of the scholar builds on Antonio Gramsci's concept of the "organic intellectual," which is about the working class challenging hegemonic structures and norms created by the capitalist class by articulating and validating their lived experiences and perspectives and putting other ideas forward. Her analysis also aligns with Walter Rodney's project of the "guerilla intellectual" as one who engages in the battle to transform knowledge within learning institutions by "taking the best that it has to offer which is, in a sense, expropriating bourgeois knowledge" to make it serve the people.[62] She critiqued the rigid definition of the term "scholar" as exclusively defined through formal education, the only kind of access to the "inside" of complex thinking. While a person participating in an alternative economy might remain on the "outside" of the mainstream, Ericka's feminist perspective informs her belief that life experiences are comparable to traditional qualifications such as formal education or paid positions. She takes Black people from a marginal status, "outside," and places them on the "inside," at the center of knowledge production. Similarly, the affect in her personal narrative is repositioned as critical to the inside of history.[63]

My conversations with Ericka revealed that our approaches to history aim to address and rectify the kinds of exclusions that would otherwise marginalize Black people. This view redefines the notion of legitimate sources, the utility of oral history, and the official historical record. Ericka explained, "The prostitutes and the former gang members that were in the Los Angeles chapter that I first joined were scholars. They could tell you how the United States infrastructure oppressed us. They didn't read it in a book, they didn't learn it in a class."[64] Through her bold defiance of the status quo, Ericka's point of view challenges the social hierarchy by elevating the underground world to the fore-front, effectively subverting the traditional notion of what is considered mainstream. She acknowledged the marginal as critical in articulating a complex understanding of social power structures. Like Ericka, the BPP defined scholars very differently. BPP leaders mandated no formal educational training for members, meaning that academic degrees were not required for scholarly recognition in the BPP. Still, they did require that members read the works of thinkers, intellectuals, and global leaders in political education classes.[65] In their political practice, the Black Panthers considered lived experiences as knowledge, a practice that intersects the BPP and the Black feminist movement. Consequently, the Black community already consisted of individuals whose members possessed and maintained critical insight into the political discourses of the structural inequalities that affected them.

Ericka's oral history represents a Black woman's subjectivity as the counternarrative to the institutional modes of knowledge and power that would render her silent. As Spencer-Antoine explained, "Black women have remained on the outskirts of Black Power: their marginality central to the movement's definition, but their agency and empowerment within the movement effectively obscured."[66] To date, there are few book-length manuscripts and an even smaller number of oral histories on women in the Black Power era and the BPP.[67] Ericka's recollections also attest to the inefficiencies of mainstream historiography and its attendant role in ranking social value. Interviews allow women to serve as the "representations of their own reality."[68] This analysis resonates in discussions about the value of oral history as a form of scholarship. The interviewer and interviewee engage in a crucially important relationship of trust and negotiation in the oral collaboration process. Intimacy with the source privileges a new "inside," in which the personal narrative gives voice to the humanity of the marginal. Nwando Achebe adds that this allows for "a true exchange of ideas and experiences based on mutual respect, support, and accountability."[69] This returns us to Ericka's need for mutual understanding—"I just want you to understand how it feels"—and the importance of feelings in transgressive history. Oral history restores power to the subject as the narrator of her own story to recreate moments and shed light on knowledge we may not otherwise know. It honors the fundamental principles of grassroots politics.

The intimate nature of oral history fosters a personal exchange that effectively captures and preserves the emotions and experiences often lost in other kinds of history. Particularly, oral history insists on personal sensibilities—emotion and affect—as central to social relations. Sara Ahmed recognizes that "emotions do things, and they align individuals with communities—or bodily space with social space—through the very intensity of their attachments."[70] Their powerful effect allows for human connection, encouraging empathy to create political urgency, which mobilizes and aligns communities. Here, feeling inspires political action. BPP identity as a political group depends on the shared outrage of its members and their mutual commitments to justice, producing a conscious awareness. In the BPP context, these kinds of intense attachments not only organize the community, but also inform the personal feelings that characterized Ericka's exemplary voice in 1970s Black women's political history. Moreover, this energy mobilized communities and served a vital role in challenging the lens of a traditional history that marginalized the political and social experience of Black people.

The BPP's personification of Blackness as a political statement establishes a connection between shared emotions and a collective consciousness of a broader struggle. Just as Ericka's story highlights how political conflict has personal effects, personal feelings can also have political consequences. The 1978 Combahee River Collective's "Black Feminist Statement" announced the crucial importance of feelings relative to radical feminism: "There is also undeniably a personal genesis for Black feminism, that is, the political realization that comes from the seemingly personal experience of individual Black women's lives."[71] For this working group of Black feminists, "personal genesis" reiterated the fact that political practice begins with feeling. They insisted on personal experience as crucially bound to radical community politics. They argued for the political in the personal. This thinking defined second-wave feminist organizing as well as BPP politics. The Combahee River Collective asserted that Black feminist politics are intersectional and that their theories combat structural inequalities affecting the individual and collective lives of Black women. Ericka's historical intervention stands at the crossroads of racism and sexism, building on the intersectional analysis detailed in the Combahee River Collective's manifesto.

Lessons and Ethical Challenges

As I researched this project about Ericka's life and its intersections with Black Power, the Black Panthers, African American women's history, Black feminism, and the emerging carceral state, our mutual interest in this project created invaluable personal lessons for me. I have learned from Ericka to be calm. While writing this book, Ericka introduced me to meditation and yoga. I came to meditation first and integrated it into my lifestyle. Yoga came later, followed by other mindful practices, such as mindful eating and deep breathing. I wanted to put theory into practice and experience firsthand the endless possibilities these practices could have on my mind and body. I learned the value of patience and presence. My work with mindful practices speaks to Black feminist care work in Ericka's present. Our closeness does not invalidate my historical account of her life. In writing this book, I combine a sensitivity to the passion and emotion that Ericka has foregrounded with the historical facts that I have uncovered in the archive. I do not see tension between these two stances, as each tells one part of a fuller story. Furthermore, I present Ericka's full humanity with respect, love, and compassion. Ericka's story is powerful—and it is a story for everyone, in and outside the academy.

Throughout this process, Ericka and I gained a deep respect for one another. My relationship with Ericka as a writer and biographer is one of complex camaraderie. By this I mean that we have a relationship complete with high and low moments. There were moments of care, joy, and laughter and sometimes friction and discomfort. Writing a monograph on a living person deeply invested in this project was not without methodological and ethical challenges. Our biggest challenges included moments of conflict in how she envisioned her life and my interpretation of the sources on her life through my critical eye as a professional historian and scholarly standards.[72] Hamlin writes, "Every scholar must grapple with the ethics of the profession, and as a scholar invested on the ethics of care," I had to make important and difficult decisions regarding what parts of Ericka's story to include in the book.[73] In navigating these aspects, I constantly negotiated respect for her privacy and her resistance to letting the world see her unguarded, scissoring out some stories and parts of her life per her request. While Ericka and I established trust over a decade ago, she often protected herself from me as a writer. Perhaps she might have feared my power to write her into history according to my historical interpretation, not hers. Ericka illustrated this by protecting her loved ones and their need for privacy. At times, her revolutionary activities continue to bring harm and sadness to others. The past continues to be present in the lives of people who experienced it. Thus, our oral history sessions evidence what her experience with movement work could produce. Ericka's personal accounts helped me understand that it is difficult to accept oneself fully and, and even more so, to tackle one's deep-seated internalizations from sexist, heterosexist, and patriarchal practices within community. Because of our phone conversations and email exchanges over the course of writing this book, it is highly likely that I know more about Ericka than most academics do; however, I also know that there are stories she will never tell me.

Chapter Organization

Black Panther Woman is composed of this introduction, followed by six chapters and an epilogue. The book begins with Ericka's earliest spiritual teachings and lessons as a child, then charts her spiritual wellness pathways to social justice through her teenage and college years. Finally, the book recounts her joining the BPP and surviving incarceration as a Black woman political prisoner. In chapter 1, "A Spiritual Childhood," I explore Ericka's formative years with spirituality and wellness, her earliest memories as an activist, and her beginnings in the BPP. I recount how Ericka came of age in Washington, DC, during the Jim Crow era. Her youthful experiences, family stories, and lessons offered her a spiritual foundation and impacted her political maturity as a Black Power era activist.

Chapter 2, "Becoming a Black Panther," turns to Ericka's blossoming political activism during her teenage and college years, attending the March on Washington at fifteen and joining student organizations, including the Black Student Congress, and immersing herself in the Black conscious community while at Lincoln University. I frame Ericka's youth activism as part of the zeitgeist and part of a broader movement of children and teenagers across the nation protesting injustice during the civil rights and Black Power movements. Her youth activism influenced her to join the BPP. I contextualize her past in relation to her violent confrontation with the state hours after learning of the murder of her husband, John Huggins, and friend Bunchy Carter. This confrontation, coupled with her travels to Connecticut and her efforts to establish a BPP chapter in New Haven, helps explain her subsequent incarceration at Niantic.

Chapter 3, "Gendered Prison Violence," examines Ericka's less familiar prison narrative in solitary confinement and the nature of her spiritual activism. I document Ericka's conditions, prison surveillance, and the violence she and the other New Haven Black Panther women suffered by correctional officers at the Connecticut Correctional Institution for Women in Niantic, presently known as the Janet S. York Correctional Institution. This chapter offers a window into the prison system and how it affected Black women political prisoners as they endured strip searches, no rights to motherhood and breastfeeding, mail censorship, inadequate prenatal care, and violent beatings and childbirths. Prison served as a turning point in Ericka's life, which forced her to engage in multiple resistance efforts such as self-help and community care to survive the horrors of prison.

In chapter 4, "Surviving Solitary," I describe Ericka's spiritual wellness practices, including yoga and meditation, to protect herself, her mind, and her soul. Ericka developed a critical praxis of spiritual maturity that allowed her to resist submitting to harmful forms of institutional power. I focus on Ericka's engagement in hunger strikes and her letters challenging the violence and mistreatment of her pregnant comrades, and how the Black Panther women used their physical bodies to fight back against beatings they received by correctional officers.

Chapter 5, "The Sister Love Collective," analyzes the work of a multiracial group developed by Ericka to support the medical, emotional, social, and political needs of newly admitted imprisoned women. In a carceral space designed to oppress women's bodies, they engaged in poetry, homosocial bonding, and romantic love, as well as modes of cultural production such as beauty, hair, and fashion to restore their womanhood and assert their sense of agency. The work of Sister Love offers a lens into the kinds of inventive political tactics utilized by Black women activists of the 1960s and the 1970s. Their practices could be instructive today in prisons nationwide to help women restore themselves.

In chapter 6, "Joy on Trial," I examine friendships Ericka forged with correctional officers that helped to humanize her experience as she confronted the state during her trial. I offer an analysis of Ericka's handwritten letters composed for Jan Von Flatern, a young white political writer who chronicled her trial. Ericka's letters reveal a powerful narrative of love and solidarity with incarcerated women. She writes passionately to reconnect women with their families and secure basic resources and legal support for women, including pregnant women at Niantic. Through her letters to Jan, Ericka builds a collective inside Sister Love that involves cross-racial affection and feminist resistance to carceral power. I also detail Ericka's use of hair and self-fashioning to navigate identity politics during her trial. Finally, in the epilogue, I focus on her work writing and editing for the BPP newspaper, leading the BPP's school, and serving on the Alameda County Board of Education, as well as her spiritual experiences and her educational and restorative justice practice following her departure from the BPP.

Throughout the book, I refrain from using the word "inmate," as the term dehumanizes and situates individuals as "other" and less deserving of compassion. Additionally, I refer to most of the people in this book by their first names as part of my feminist practice. First names are more humanizing to the women whose stories I tell. My use of "Ericka" reflects the sisterhood cultivated between us in the making of *Black Panther Woman*.

Black Panther Woman is an intersectional examination of Ericka's survival story as a political activist in the movement for Black Power. Black Power activism was not just about community control and cultural agency. For some, it also involved spiritual enlightenment and self-discovery both inside and outside the prison walls. This book offers a new model for understanding the BPP and Black Power through care work and healing. Without documenting Ericka's contributions, the history of the BPP remains incomplete. *Black Panther Woman* is an invitation to engage in the work of Black women activists and the world they shaped. My hope is that historians will continue to explore Ericka's life and the women of the BPP.

1

A Spiritual Childhood

Coming to terms with spirit means bringing yourself into harmony with the world within and around you. One finds one's way to spirit through woundings, through nature, through reading, through actions, through discovering new approaches to problems.
—Gloria E. Anzaldúa

"Who lives in me?" Ericka said aloud to herself at the tender age of nine as she looked in the mirror while diligently brushing her teeth. The morning sun beamed through the bathroom window. Her younger siblings, Kyra and Gervaze Jr., were still sleeping. Ericka was an early riser. The smell of her mother's homemade biscuits, sunny side eggs, bacon, and grits wafted from the kitchen. She could also hear music from the small AM radio in the kitchen that played on until the end of each day. As she gazed at herself in the mirror, Ericka fell into her own eyes. It did not feel scary or creepy. Instead, she was curious. She felt that she was more than the tween looking back at her. There was more to her. Ericka needed answers. She dropped her toothbrush in the sink and ran downstairs to the kitchen, toothpaste still all over her mouth.

"Momma, momma, who lives inside my eyes?"
"Oh, Ericka, you having one of your questions again? I don't know, Suga. Maybe it's God."
"Okay, Momma."

When recalling this moment in her young life, Ericka released a full belly laugh. Ericka always asked lots of questions. Her mother often taught her that God lived in heaven and was not a figure that you could literally hold; God was infinitely complex and multitudinal. Even young Ericka knew that her mother was telling her in the best way she knew how, "God lives inside you."[1] While her mother did not fully answer the question, Ericka remembers how the query satisfied her curiosity that day and left a lasting mark. Her mother always had something helpful and healing to say. Even so, for years, Ericka continued to ponder the question.

When she was twelve years old, Ericka woke up in the bedroom she shared with her younger sister, Kyra. A deep question weighed on her mind: "Who am I?" She wrote the question everywhere—on a poster in large capital letters, on a poster that she and her sister used to draw on and decorate in their bedroom, and on the bathroom mirror. Then, she turned to Kyra.

> "Don't you already know? You're Ericka," replied Kyra, who was now nine years old.
>
> "But, Kyra, there's so much more to me and there's so much more to you. Who am I?"
>
> "You're Ericka. Son of Gervaze and Cozette. You live on Fifty-Fifth Street in Southeast Washington, DC. You're a Black girl and you're tall."[2]

Kyra innocently and matter-of-factly pointed out the obvious, external aspects, but Ericka's questions hinted at something deeper, something not so easily named or described. At twelve years old, Ericka's soul was stirring, longing to identify her life's purpose.

These youthful moments marked the beginnings of Ericka's journey toward spiritual discovery. She came to understand the presence of a timeless, ageless, infinite power inside every human being, and that this power lived within her. In the pages that follow, I explore Ericka's early familial life. I address Ericka's years coming of age in the Jim Crow era of Washington, DC, her search for self as a young child, her relationship with her parents and siblings, lessons from her parents, spiritual teachings from her mother, her church experiences, and the impact of her parents on her care practices, including writing poetry and listening to music. These times trace Ericka's inquisitiveness and her search for spiritual knowing and ethics that would serve as a foundation for her political desires, the desire to struggle for the people, and, later, her practice of self-care and collective concern for the humanity of others.

Mr. and Mrs. Jenkins

Gervaze Joseph Jenkins, Ericka's father, was born in Washington, DC, in 1910. His incomplete high school education, coupled with racism, restricted the kind of work he could secure.[3] As a young adult, he primarily worked as a chauffeur while residing with his parents, Joseph D. Jenkins and Sadie B. Jenkins.[4] Following the attack on Pearl Harbor, he was drafted into the army on July 6, 1942, in Fort Meyer, Virginia.[5] He was then placed on furlough for two weeks, during which he was instructed to report to his assigned military camp on July 20, 1942.[6] His World War II enlistment record listed his occupation as a general office clerk.[7]

Cozette (Davis) Jenkins, Ericka's mother, migrated from the small rural town of Enfield, North Carolina, in the Raleigh-Durham area, to Washington, DC. She grew up in Enfield, in a home that sat on a small piece of farmland surrounded by cotton, corn, tomato, and watermelon fields.[8] She was one of eleven children, six sisters and five brothers in total. Large families were typical in agricultural economies as they tended to the farmland. Born in 1918, the year of the Spanish flu outbreak, Mrs. Jenkins was the oldest girl, which meant that her caretaking responsibilities began at eight years old. This included cooking dinner for the family and caring for her mother, Lula Davis, who was often sick. Grandma Lula (to Ericka) endured a life of constant medical discrimination in the context of her battle with uterine cancer during the last fifteen years of her life. Hospitals were far away, and physicians would not travel to rural Enfield to treat Grandma Lula.

According to Ericka, Grandma Lula was the granddaughter of a French admiral (also a Louisiana slaveholder) and a domestic woman. Mrs. Jenkins's father, Ossie Davis (known as Grandpa Ossie to Ericka), was a descendant of a freedman and worked as a tobacco farmer.[9] Enfield was known for its bustling tobacco market.[10] While also tending to the farm, Grandpa Ossie also shared the childcare responsibilities. He frequently managed to send the children to school when the agricultural schedule permitted. The demands of the tobacco farming season dictated their attendance, with the boys often staying home and the six girls going to school. However, the girls' schooling was intermittent, as they sometimes could only attend seasonally. Mrs. Jenkins and her sisters walked a mile to a modest, segregated one-room schoolhouse that served Black students of all ages, from elementary through high school.[11]

Due to the constraints she faced, upon reaching adulthood, Mrs. Jenkins moved to Washington, DC, to establish her autonomy, secure better work opportunities, and finish high school.[12] As a Black southern migrant, she participated in what historians Chris Myers Asch and George Derek Musgrove refer to as "the greatest internal migration in American history." Like many other migrants, she was "pushed by agricultural woes and racial violence and pulled by the promise of economic opportunity."[13] She considered Washington, DC, a desirable place for social advancement and upward mobility, adhering to Paula C. Austin's assessment that "the appeal of [Washington] DC was a product of both perceived and actual employment possibilities and the possibilities for social and political equality."[14] Upon her arrival, she soon confronted what most migrants were experiencing: a historical record of systemic injustices, including segregation, inadequate education, overcrowded schools, challenges in accessing suitable housing, and limited work prospects.[15]

In 1941 federal safeguards against discriminatory practices were established in both military sectors, as stipulated by Executive Order 8802, and the workplace, as enforced by the Fair Employment Practices Committee. These developments were largely influenced by the activism of A. Philip Randolph, who served as the president of the Brotherhood of Sleeping Car Porters, the inaugural labor union dedicated solely to the representation of Black workers.[16] Nevertheless, as noted by Asch and Musgrove, Black workers continued to be limited to occupations with the lowest wages.[17] Black women, specifically, were limited by the oppressive structures of racism and sexism. Notwithstanding these obstacles, there existed narrow pathways for employment within the government sector. Mrs. Jenkins seized these opportunities as she completed the requirements to obtain her high school diploma and secured employment as a clerk typist for the State Department.

Not long after her arrival in Washington, DC, she met Mr. Jenkins at a party.[18] Their friendship resulted in their matrimonial union in 1944.[19] While serving in the military at the time, Mr. Jenkins returned home for his nuptials. He rose to the rank of sergeant, but as historian Thomas A. Guglielmo noted, service in a racially segregated military resulted in "black officers seldom enjoying the full range of advantages to which their rank entitled them."[20] He was later discharged from the service in 1945 and found work within the government as a file clerk in the Pentagon's Adjutant General Office, a job similar to that of Mrs. Jenkins.[21]

Mr. and Mrs. Jenkins were both hard workers who labored as state clerks.[22] Like many young couples, they found themselves in need of familial support. Living with family afforded them the chance to amass financial resources for the purchase of a home while confronting housing difficulties resulting from swift migration, high population densities, exorbitant rental costs, racist lending practices, government-led demolition initiatives in Black neighborhoods, and opposition to racial integration.[23] Ericka was born in 1948, the year President Harry S. Truman positioned civil rights as a priority in his platform for reelection. His Committee on Civil Rights put forth recommendations that included the desegregation of the armed forces, federal anti-lynching laws, and the abolishment of voter suppression. These policy changes to integrate the military harkened back to the racism experienced by Mr. Jenkins in the army. Black soldiers suffered dehumanizing and degrading treatment as they were subjected to segregated trainings, dangerous job assignments, and insufficient provision of equipment.[24] After experiencing such violence and injustice overseas, he returned home to Washington, DC, to face the same oppression. Nevertheless, around 1950 Mr. and Mrs. Jenkins successfully moved into their new home, when Ericka was nearly two.[25] In 1951 Kyra, their second child, was born; their only son, Gervaze Jr., was born the following year.

Mrs. Jenkins worked day shifts; some years she also worked the swing shifts, also known as evening shifts. On the days she worked swing shifts, she would call Ericka, once she was old enough, to have her begin preparing dinner for the family. "Take the chicken out of the freezer. When I get home, I'll make it, and you should peel the potatoes," she would say, depending on the dinner options.[26] Sometimes, on the evenings when her mother worked late, Ericka cooked dinner with her father. As a preteen, she was taught to be responsible and to care for her family, instilling a disciplined work ethic and a spirit of resourcefulness.

Through her parents' teachings, Ericka learned about racial and class politics and segregation in the rural South. Like her mother, Lula, Mrs. Jenkins had a lighter skin tone, allowing her to escape some racial discrimination that many of her siblings could not because of their brown skin tone.[27] "She taught me to regard every human being individually. And so did my father," Ericka remembered of both her parents.[28] Her parents' experience with colorism inspired their teachings. As school-aged children, Ericka, Kyra, and Gervaze Jr. heard stories from Mrs. Jenkins about living in poverty and walking a mile to school in response to their complaints about taking the bus to school. These stories were designed to teach them responsibility and gratitude.

Mr. Jenkins came from a much smaller family than Mrs. Jenkins. In 1865, after the abolishment of slavery, Mr. Jenkins's family acquired property, which allowed him to come of age in a middle-class setting.[29] In an interview with Fiona Thompson, Ericka clarified that her use of the term "middle-class" pertained to the Jenkinses' status as property owners only. "I don't mean that they had fantastic jobs and huge savings," she added.[30] Ericka's father had only one sibling, Thelma. Both had inherited the gentleness of their mother and the fire of their father.[31] Ericka remembered Aunt Thelma's sense of style, which she believed influenced Kyra's flair for fashion. As young women, Ericka and her sister looked up to their aunt, who instilled in them a feeling of self-assurance. "Black women must walk proudly throughout the world," Aunt Thelma would say.[32] She consoled Ericka when her grade school peers teased her because she was the tallest in her class, explaining to her that her height made her regal. Aunt Thelma advised Ericka, Never round your shoulders or make yourself look smaller. Always carry yourself as a queen.

Ericka described her mother, Mrs. Jenkins, as keenly intuitive, fully present, and a kind and patient person who embodied a southern spirit. She was the kind of mother the kids in the neighborhood desired. When young kids visited Ericka, Kyra, and Gervaze Jr., Mrs. Jenkins ensured that they were comfortable and well fed. No furniture or rooms were off-limits to visitors in the Jenkins family home on East Capital Street, a predominantly Black area in Southeast Washington, DC. Ericka loved her mother for her consistent, unwavering hospitality and open heart. "She welcomed all guests, even those she did not like," said Ericka, chuckling. "Even if she did not like you, she still fed you."[33] Mrs. Jenkins taught her children by example, always helping those in the community and respecting everyone, including her elders. Mrs. Jenkins's love and care also had a fierce side—one that revealed a commitment to responsibility, hard work, and collective care. That fierceness, that conviction of no compromise, often emerged on Saturday mornings when she needed to wake Ericka, Kyra, and Gervaze Jr. to do chores they did not want to do.

Ericka turned to her mother to help her understand the world around her. She remembered the class stratification and gentrification of Washington, DC, in those early years. She saw this most vividly when the Jenkinses attended public holiday festivities in front of the White House. She recalled the affluent white neighborhoods surrounding the White House and the stark contrast on their return home. Concerned for people who lived in poverty in a city of tremendous wealth, Ericka asked her mother about the class divisions. "There were people who have a lot and don't want to share it, and there are people who have nothing and don't know how to get it. And there was a history behind that," her mother explained.[34] Living in a racially segregated neighborhood, she had limited interactions with white people, only with those who lived in poverty on the Maryland border.

Ericka's interactions with white people were fraught with racism; to this day, these memories of prejudice linger. Racial segregation did not protect Ericka from the daily psychological wounds inflicted by whites. White children spat on Ericka and dehumanized her through their use of the n-word.[35] Ericka grew up in the shadow of the *Brown v. Board of Education* decision, amidst the push for desegregation of schools and buses in Montgomery, Alabama, and against a backdrop of media representations of racial tensions. The 1950s television images of state-sanctioned violence by white supremacists against Black people, coupled with local reports on protests and legal battles against segregation at John Philip Sousa Junior High School in Southeast Washington, DC—where eleven well-dressed Black children were denied entry—shaped the era. Despite this, Ericka maintained a conviction that her peers would not continue the cycle of racial violence.[36] In confusion, shock, and anger, she turned to her mother. In response to her emotional turmoil, Ericka's mother shared her own experiences of racial violence in the South. She told Ericka that the white children learned racism from their parents and other adults. In that conversation, Mrs. Jenkins began to arm her children with the knowledge they needed to navigate a violent, racist, and patriarchal world.[37]

The Use of Storytelling

Storytelling was a cornerstone of Mrs. Jenkins's spiritual bond with Ericka, serving as an educational instrument to impart life lessons that emphasized virtues like patience, hope, care, focus, and empathy. Often she conveyed these narratives through proverbs, or what Ericka referred to as "country sayings."[38] "Don't worry about the mule being blind, just put him in the road and hold to the line," was a memorable saying Mrs. Jenkins shared with her children.[39] Mrs. Jenkins wanted to stress to her children, Do not let hardships paralyze you. Be resilient. Keep moving forward. These were lessons Ericka drew upon to focus her attention on what was important—her passions and goals. To emphasize these points, Mrs. Jenkins shared a story from her childhood when she and her younger sister Altomae were out too late walking one of the cows. They were supposed to be back home by dinner time as the meal still needed to be cooked. But they got lost with the cow. As young girls, they became worried.

> "What do we do?" Cozette sobbed to Altomae.
>
> "It's going to be okay. Don't cry. The cow knows the way home. Let's just hold on to the cow's rope and say something to let him know that we're going home now and not just out walking," Altomae instructed.[40]

The cow then led them home. In telling this story, she aimed to impart multiple lessons to Ericka and Kyra: to pay attention, trust their instincts, care for each other, remain faithful, respect animals and their intelligence, and depend on nature—all lessons that later manifested in Ericka's political values.

Another memory Mrs. Jenkins shared with her daughters involved a lesson of trust and the importance of having genuine familial connections. She told the story of her close bond with her brother Reginald and their fun times as young children. They often went looking for one another if they didn't see each other around the farm. One day, when she could not find him, her instincts told her that he was in the woods "doing something." She called his name once she arrived in the woods.

"Reginald! Reginald! Where are you?"

"I'm over here, Cozette." She headed over to him.

"I'm out here making hooch. You know what that is, Cozette?"

"Yeah, I know. You making some liquor."

"And if you tell Mama or Papa I'm out here making hooch, I will kill you," he grinned.[41]

Mrs. Jenkins remembered that she and Reginald laughed. She kept her word and never told. It was important to her that her children trust each other with their secrets, just like she could with her brother.

Ericka and Kyra were a rapt audience. The kitchen was the setting of their mother's storytelling, whether about the overt racism of the Jim Crow South or Ku Klux Klan violence, or farm life in Enfield. Ericka recalled a memorable story of white people's dehumanization of Black people. And her Grandpa Ossie from North Carolina stood at the center of the tale.

"White people referred to your Granddad as 'boy,'" Mrs. Jenkins explained.

"Mama, that's awful. He wasn't a boy," Ericka said.

"I know, sugar, but that's how it was."

"What? Did anybody stop him, mom?" Ericka retorted imagining some white man disrespecting her grandfather.

"Stop them? This is what they called everybody. You were not a human. And if they deemed to call him anything, they called him Davis."

"Mama, nooo!" Kyra added, outraged.

"Mama, they would have killed me. If I would have grown up during your time. I would have got into trouble."

"No, Ericka. They wouldn't have because you would not have allowed yourself to get killed. You would have thought about all the people who love you."

Mrs. Jenkins wanted Ericka and Kyra to understand the level of cruelty Grandpa Ossie experienced and the danger he risked had he responded. She also instructed Ericka and Kyra on how to deal with their anger more productively. Mrs. Jenkins taught Ericka and Kyra about regulating their emotions amidst discrimination, channeling their anger into productivity. This reflects the signature trait of an emotionally mature caregiver, someone who exemplifies and teaches emotional regulation, particularly in perilous situations. The stories from her mother correlate with Ericka's subsequent adoption of mindfulness in prison, where she mastered the art of observing her emotions without instantaneously responding to them.

Ericka and Kyra continued with their line of questioning, asking their mother how she handled racism. They needed to know how she approached situations similar to Grandpa Ossie's.

> "Mama, how'd you respond when whites called you out of your name?"
>
> "I would correct them, especially if they were white. When someone speaks to me, that I do not know, they must call me Mrs. Jenkins. They don't get to call me Cozette or Jenkins."
>
> "Oh my God, you correct them?" Ericka asked.
>
> "I am Mrs. Jenkins," she declared.[42]

Mrs. Jenkins's proactive approach, compared to Grandpa Ossie's passivity, was a sign of the changing times. She was guiding Ericka and Kyra to establish limits in response to white supremacy's blatant disregard for boundaries and disrespect of Black individuals. Defiance or a calm, poised disarming response still involved a measure of danger. By sharing her story of how she confronted white supremacy, she taught Ericka and Kyra to advocate for themselves and demand their humanity. Ericka loved her mother's defiant spirit.

Their mother's lessons continued as they traveled each summer to what they called "the country," the family homestead down South in North Carolina. Mrs. Jenkins wanted her children to value animals, nature, and agriculture. Ericka had many fond memories of these times. As young kids, they had the freedom to run, play, explore, and spend time with extended family. She recollected that she always smiled when she saw her mother's brother, Uncle Reginald, because he was hilarious. He had the capacity to make her laugh no matter the circumstances in her childhood. He shared Grandma Lula's sweet nature. Once Ericka was older, the family shared stories of how loving Grandma Lula and Grandpa Ossie were to her. As a newborn, they held Ericka and talked to her while sitting on the front porch of the family homestead. Ericka's connections with her mother were mirrored in her interactions with other family members, from whom she learned about inequality and privilege. Her visits to relatives in the countryside, especially Aunt Altomae and her cousins, enriched her understanding of class disparities. "I didn't have a sense of poverty until I visited Aunt Altomae's trailer," Ericka remembered.[43] Aunt Altomae, her husband, and her nine children lived in a trailer, not a house. Ericka learned the inner strength of her mother's sisters as Aunt Altomae maintained a cohesive family unit in tight quarters.

All these lessons culminated in Ericka's first but certainly not last confrontation with the carceral state. It was her parents' lessons about racism, family bonds, and faith that gave Ericka and Kyra the courage to confront the police in 1961. Ericka would have been about thirteen, and Kyra around ten years old. Ericka was close to the same age as fourteen-year-old Chicago native Emmett Till when white supremacists lynched him in Mississippi in 1955. Ericka and Kyra were very aware of Emmett Till's lynching and the racial violence and discrimination that plagued Black America. They also knew about the ongoing Black protests to desegregate public spaces. In their neighborhood, they often saw the police harassing Black people for no apparent reason. One day, they were walking to the corner store when they saw two police officers jump out of their car and attack an elderly Black man. The girls yelled at the police, "Stop harming that man. Stop it right now. He hasn't done a thing."[44] Their actions drew a crowd. Once a crowd formed, the police stopped attacking the innocent man, got into their car, and screeched off. The man was grateful. The girls' loving hearts gave them courage to confront the police, but it was not until later that they realized that their actions could have gotten them killed.

The Church and the Spirit

While Ericka was gaining knowledge from her relatives, she was also beginning to display an independent streak that would shape her spiritual life. This stood in contrast to Mrs. Jenkins, who was a devout Christian and encouraged Ericka to be one, too. She raised her children in the local Baptist missionary church, within walking distance of their home. She took her children to Sunday school and church services every week and went alone other nights of the week. On occasion, Ericka, Kyra, and Gervaze Jr. tried to feign sickness to get out of going to church. "I have a headache," one would say. "My tummy hurts," another would follow, but Mrs. Jenkins always called their bluff and took them to church. From the pulpit, the pastor taught his congregation that all people were sinners who must repent for their sins. His sermons stressed that all people would die sinning; thus, they needed to turn their lives over to God and consistently repent. Mrs. Jenkins resonated with these religious views, yet they were incomprehensible to Ericka. The concept of being a sinner was beyond eight-year-old Ericka's grasp, and the God described in the pastor's sermons was a source of fear. "Oh, Ericka, he doesn't mean it like that," her mother told her. "You're born that way." A young Ericka wondered how her mother could know that, insisted that she was not a sinner, and turned to her Sunday school teacher for more answers. In response, the teacher threw her out of Sunday school for asking such skeptical questions. Perhaps she assumed that Ericka was being disrespectful.[45]

The pastor's message about a wrathful God made going to church challenging as Ericka questioned his ideology, but gospel music became her haven because it was so heartfelt. She loved the songs, the hymns, and the music, but the rest of church life, she recalled, "I could have thrown out the window."[46] Ericka's parents influenced her love of music. Her mother made music central to their lives, constantly playing music in the home. Ericka grew up listening to Black music: blues, gospel, jazz, folk, Motown, and other rhythm and blues. Although they did not have much money, their mother ensured that her children took piano lessons, which Ericka claimed they hated; however, their father's love for music, particularly jazz, resonated with Ericka and Gervaze Jr. As a gifted musician, Gervaze Jr. liked jazz and all types of music and played the saxophone and the drums, both loaner instruments from his public high school. The three siblings briefly sang in the church choir, but eventually quit. They could never tolerate mean-spirited people, and to them, the choir director was relentless and demanding in his approach.

Reverence for the spirit was not automatic for Ericka, maybe because the message and, sometimes, the messengers seemed insincere or lacked grace for others. Ericka remembered gazing at some of the congregants' bodies full of spirit and laughing at them with Kyra in church. As young girls, Ericka and Kyra did not understand what was happening inside these individuals, moving, jerking, and dancing with holy passion. However, they learned fast to respect the sanctity of the Black church and the people it housed: their mother would quickly cut her eyes at them and slightly lean forward in the church pew with *that* look to let them know that when they crossed the line, a whipping would be waiting for them when they got home. It was not until Ericka was an older child that she understood that the Holy Spirit was moving through the women and men in the church. In her words, they were being "infused with God's love."[47] She eventually experienced it for herself when the choir sang hymns. Hymns soothed her mind and body and allowed her to surrender to what she described as a "place that was so serene and untouched by anything external."[48] She recognized this bodily experience as God being inside her. Ericka considered this feeling to be the same spirit that moved through the church congregants. Everything about Ericka's childhood resurfaced in her adult life. Maturity brought her clarity and appreciation of what her mother endeavored to instill in her.

The church and the inauthenticity of some congregants taught Ericka unintended lessons. Among them were to actively listen and consistently practice kindness with others. While Ericka would run errands with her mother, she was struck at how some people they knew from church would barely speak to them, and yet they acted friendly and sweet in church. She noticed that her mother, however, was the same person at church as she was at home. Her mother's unwavering example taught her the importance of consistency—of being the same person in every space, every day, not just on Sundays.

As adults, Ericka and Gervaze Jr. chose nontraditional spiritual paths, influenced by their father. Ericka adopted parts of Christianity and rejected others that did not serve her in her quest for surviving in a difficult world. Presently, Kyra practices Christianity and is also spiritual. While Mrs. Jenkins frequented church, Mr. Jenkins was not religious and never attended church with the family. Hypocritical church members pushed him away. He also shared this perspective with Ericka, which became clear when she noticed that the pastor was a hypocrite too.

Mrs. Jenkins's parents raised her in a Pentecostal church during her childhood, but she converted to Baptist teachings. Because Mrs. Jenkins was so religious, in that she adhered to stern rules and order, while also

spiritual in her path to discover her soul, she was Ericka's most significant spiritual influence. She gave Ericka insight on the deeper parts of
herself. As a naturally inquisitive child, Ericka had a multitude of questions about religion and spirituality. Her mother sometimes found the
barrage of queries taxing. In their dialogues, after addressing many of
Ericka's questions, Mrs. Jenkins would gently indicate her need to attend
to other responsibilities and suggest that they continue the discussion
the following day. Thus, Mrs. Jenkins honored Ericka's relentless curiosity without disparaging it, even if it meant taking periodic pauses from
their conversations.

More broadly speaking, Ericka's father was not nearly as patient. In
fact, he could be abusive. At times, her home environment was fraught
with tension because of her father's dominating nature. He was reserved,
but ran the house with order and discipline, a by-product of his military
background. These traits did not set well with Mrs. Jenkins, Ericka, Kyra,
or Gervaze Jr., which meant that he did not always get his way at home.
To make matters worse, he was a functional alcoholic who drank each
day after work. The traumas and stressors of serving in a racially segregated military during World War II, which, as described by Guglielmo
"had more to do with leaders' own sentiments about black people's supposed inferiority as soldiers and as officers and their deep investments
in white domination and black subordination," deeply impacted Mr.
Jenkins.[49] He turned to alcohol to manage his feelings and took the oppression he experienced abroad and unleashed his pain on his wife. He
physically abused Mrs. Jenkins and was emotionally absent. Any hint of
disrespect, and Mr. Jenkins responded with a slap, backhand, or wallop.
He also hit Ericka, Kyra, and Gervaze Jr., but not with the same kind of
rage that he unleashed on Mrs. Jenkins.

Familial Abuse

Ericka learned to practice resilience early on by confronting patriarchal abuse at home. As the oldest, Ericka tried to protect her mother
and her siblings, but she was still just a child herself. Most of the time
she communicated her feelings through her facial expressions. "I
just looked at him like, 'Leave my mother alone. Leave my sister and
brother alone. Leave me alone.'"[50] On one occasion, she intervened

when her father was violent with her mother. She was afraid for her mother. "Why do you beat our mother?" she loudly belted out as she put her body between them as a force against the harmful blows.[51] Her dad beat her for asking. "I just wanted my father to stop beating my mother. But I tried as best I could to not upset him, which didn't work because I always did."[52] She wanted an end to the strife in the family stemming from her father's abuse.

Mr. Jenkins was fastidious. One day, he became angry about old food left in the refrigerator. He called Ericka, Kyra, and Gervaze Jr. into their small kitchen and told them to clean out the refrigerator. They listened, did as they were told, and did not talk back. As they cleaned, their mother walked in and said, "Gervaze, leave the children alone. I'll clean the refrigerator."[53] He combusted with fury. He pushed past his children and began beating his wife. While protecting herself from the blows, Mrs. Jenkins immediately instructed Ericka to take her siblings to the other room. But Ericka did not want to leave. Her mother repeated her instructions, and reluctantly, Ericka took Kyra and Gervaze Jr. upstairs. There, they could hear less noise, and Ericka held her brother and sister close to her body. Mrs. Jenkins tried to argue quietly and calm her husband down. But he raged on. Even when Mrs. Jenkins often fought back, there was no winning, no reprieve, no halt to the violent blows and words. The army had changed the man she once knew, and he brought the war home to his wife and children.

Ericka rushed into adulthood in the face of her father's abuse. "I became the other mother," she recalled. "That's what happened. I was a child taking care of my mother in a way."[54] As historian Stanlie M. James writes, "Othermothers can be defined as those who assist blood mothers in the responsibilities of child care for short- to long-term periods, in informal or formal arrangements."[55] Ericka harbored no resentment for assuming the secondary maternal role, despite her own youth. She believed that it was her responsibility to protect her younger siblings and to aid her mother as effectively as possible. In doing so, she was inadvertently emulating her mother's path—Mrs. Jenkins had similarly adopted a caretaking role in her family as the eldest daughter to her siblings and her own mother, Grandma Lula. However, Ericka's circumstances were shadowed by the specter of Mr. Jenkins's alcohol-induced violence, a stark contrast to the illness that had beset Grandma Lula.

Ericka felt as if she were living in the middle of an "unknown war."[56] She believed that if she were bigger and older, she could stop her father. His alcoholism and physical abuse broke their family. She was often afraid, sad, confused, and on edge. These are intense emotions to handle for an adult, let alone a child. She did not understand why her father was drinking so much and why he was violent to their mother. "I know your father is mean and I know sometimes he feels hateful, but it's that alcohol," Mrs. Jenkins rationalized to her children. Ericka, however, was not buying it. She needed more than an explanation for her father's abuse, she wanted to know why her mother stayed.[57] One day, when there was no friction in the house, Ericka decided to speak to her mother quietly and privately in her bedroom about his abuse. She needed answers. Honest answers. She saw her mother alone in her bedroom and quietly closed the door after she entered.

"Mama, why do you stay?"
"Because of you children," she explained.
"Mama, I think we'd be just fine if you left," Ericka responded.

In a few words, Ericka let her mother know that they would feel better if she left their father, but her mother did not want to break up the family. As Ericka saw it, her mom did not realize that their family was already broken. The persistent abuse was taking its toll.

Mr. Jenkins's violent episodes traumatized Kyra and Gervaze Jr. Kyra was often vocal about her feelings and would sometimes run into the street and scream, "Help, help. My daddy's beating my mom." No one in the family stopped her from yelling for help, although she never fully expressed the emotional weight of her father's abuse. It was unclear whether anyone in the streets heard her plea for help. Kyra was the only child who could get her father to listen because Mr. Jenkins had a soft spot for her. Kyra told him what she did not like about his behavior. She would say, "This is how I think about it, Daddy."[58] Mr. Jenkins rarely, if ever, got upset with Kyra. Sometimes, Kyra's words made an impact. Ericka believed that this was because of how much their father loved Kyra. She understood his way of being. Kyra and her father had a special relationship. He sometimes asked Kyra to sit next to him. Ericka was grateful for their relationship because Kyra made attempts to compel his compassion with thoughtfulness and care. Unlike Kyra, Gervaze Jr. locked his feelings inside. He was observant but quiet and withdrawn. He was a "pair of eyes," but he took all that trauma in.[59] At times, he confronted his father with sobering and honest statements, but was ignored. At other times, Gervaze Jr. conveyed his unspoken thoughts to Ericka. They spoke through their eyes.

"This is awful," he would express, looking at her.
"But we'll be okay," Ericka communicated back.

He nodded his head in agreement. Gervaze Jr. and Ericka had an unspoken connection. Their attachment as siblings involved protecting and caring for each other. This was an early form of spirituality at work: Gervaze Jr. and Ericka's resistance against attempts to break their spirits. Amid crisis and violence, Ericka and Gervaze Jr. sought to console one another. They needed peace.

Mr. Jenkins did not have a connection with his only son because of his inability to understand Gervaze Jr. An inquisitive and thoughtful boy, Gervaze Jr. became known as "the little preacher." Indeed, he would go to the back of the house, stand on a wooden table, and preach, not about God or religion, but on "what it meant to be living on the earth" from his perspective as a young child.[60] As children, they listened and laughed at him, but as Ericka reflected back on her childhood, she realized that "there was something deeper going on."[61] He was on a spiritual path.

Ericka was the peacemaker among her siblings, embodying tranquility, distinctiveness, and contemplation, often heeding her inner voice. Kyra admired Ericka's knack for creating harmony. Kyra herself brought levity and laughter, often through song, which became a potent means of nurturing their bond. Their playful teasing acted as a balm, and together they harnessed humor and affection as their prime tools for coping with adversity. The siblings' solidarity and their refusal to be stripped of their humanity in abusive situations were testaments to their spiritual resilience.

In addition to her mother and siblings, Ericka's maternal Aunt Irene served as a spiritual influence in her life. She was the glue that kept the Davis family together, so Ericka knew that she could turn to her for support and counsel. Aunt Irene helped Ericka sort out life's challenges. She could speak to her about deep topics that she could not mention to her mother, such as her father's abuse and, later as an adult, her own sexuality. When Ericka discovered that she was attracted not only to men but also to women, she turned to her aunt. As a young girl, Ericka always knew she was "somewhere on the spectrum in sexuality"; however, in response to homophobia and what historian Darlene Clark Hine described as a "culture of dissemblance" ("issues that black women believed better left unknown, unwritten, unspoken except in whispered tones") surrounding queerness in her church and neighborhood community, she refrained from expressing her same-sex desires.[62] "This was not the time to be showing how much I like girls," she recalled.[63] She needed someone she could trust, someone who was able to listen actively, validate her feelings, and offer profound insight and advice.

Aunt Irene offered an emotional outlet and a place to find solace in the face of violence. But Ericka also created peace for herself through poetry and music. This enabled her to heal from and resist her father's violence. She did what she called "talking to paper" with her poetry writing.[64] Poetry became a form of self-expression and ultimately a spiritual practice, one that allowed her to soothe her pain and suffering and search her soul. She would go to the bathroom for privacy. It was the only door she could lock in the house and then be alone. There, in safety, she wrote down her feelings without interruption or unsolicited critique. This time was sacred. She could turn inward and speak honestly and openly without having to explain herself to others.

While Ericka used poetry as a source of protection from her father's violence, it is quite possible that she obtained her talents from her father. Mr. Jenkins was also talented and a poet. His abuse and his love of beauty in art existed side by side. When all the children were adults, Gervaze Jr. found his father's poems in 1985, the year he died.[65] While living, their father never shared that part of himself. One wonders why he kept his poetry hidden away. Maybe it was his investment in hypermasculinity. Perhaps as a father and husband, he did not want to share his vulnerability with his children or his wife. But they weren't completely in the dark about his artistic skills and talents. In the fifth or sixth grade, Ericka needed help drawing a picture, so she asked her father for help. That's when she learned that he could draw, really draw! She was in awe. It marked the first time that she saw a person complete a picture without looking at a photograph.

Ericka remembers that Mr. Jenkins wasn't always mean and abusive. When he was sober, he taught his children valuable lessons. For instance, Ericka recalled a conversation with her father about shoes. She wanted a particular style, the same kind her teenage peers wore in school. She went to her mother first, but her mother sent her to her father. Her father explained that they did not have that kind of money. She frowned and began to walk away, feeling disappointed. But her father stopped her and said, "Don't just follow what other people do; be your own person. Step out in your own way. Do you understand me?"[66] A quest for shoes led to a lesson on how to walk her own path. She loved her father immensely and took his words to heart.

Ericka was in her early teens in the 1960s when the drinking took a toll on the family as well as her father's physical and mental well-being. Ericka wanted her father to get the help he needed. He checked himself in to a hospital; the alcoholism was damaging his liver. Boils were erupting all over his body, which were symptoms of the toxicity of his organs within. Upon his release, he was quieter at home as he recovered from his medical treatment in the hospital, but eventually he started drinking again. Then he was diagnosed with cancer. He was so sick at the end of his life, he could not hold the alcohol down.

Mr. Jenkins died in 1985 at the age of seventy-five.[67] Before he passed away, he asked Ericka for her forgiveness. Ericka explained that she never blamed her father for his violent behavior. She understood him well enough to know that he did not intend the harm he caused. Instead, she considered her father to have the disease of addiction and blamed the alcohol. Later in her life, spirituality allowed Ericka to have compassion for him as she tried to understand what his life might have been like as a Black man coming of age under segregation in the early twentieth century. She believed that if he had had more options in his life, he would not have turned to alcohol to escape his unbearable pain. Systemic racism and patriarchy would not allow him to be his full self, so he drank. Not only that, but he also likely suffered from post-traumatic stress disorder from serving in the military.

Mrs. Jenkins lived on for another twenty-one years. Toward the end of her life, she developed scoliosis and vascular dementia, which contributed to memory loss. She was also legally blind.[68] In 2006, when Mrs. Jenkins was eighty-eight years old, Ericka moved her from Washington, DC, to Oakland, California, to live with her at the start of her cognitive decline, but the financial costs of her mother's health care needs were too much for Ericka to handle on her own. As a widow of a wartime veteran, Mrs. Jenkins qualified for Veterans Administration survivor's benefits, which enabled Ericka to place her in assisted living. Ericka visited her mother frequently. As Mrs. Jenkins neared death, she requested that her family bring her body back to the East Coast to bury her next to her husband. "I just want to be buried next to Gervaze," Ericka recalled her saying.[69] Her mother did not remember any of his abuse at the end of her life. They respected her wishes. She was almost ninety-six years old when she transitioned peacefully in 2014. Uncle Reginald could not bear the loss of Mrs. Jenkins, his closest sister. He was grief-stricken. He loved her deeply and their bond was immeasurable. Everyone processed their relationships and communicated their love and trauma with each other differently, but in the end, they imprinted on one another their resilience and ability to navigate the world with endurance.

During her childhood and adolescence, poetry, art, and music became integral parts of Ericka's internal world and manifested as spiritual practices. These spiritual practices were aided by the powerful and loving figures in her life, her mother and aunt. This was the first example of Ericka turning to other women to find strength when resisting patriarchal violence. The bitter trauma she experienced in her childhood home by her abusive father pushed her toward care. When some people experience trauma, they replicate it. Ericka, however, ran toward love and care practices. She drew on her parents' wisdom—from both the nurturing and harsh experiences that influenced her upbringing. The teachings she received imbued her with a resilience that she drew upon during her incarceration as a young adult. It was in her essence to seek out the positive and reclaim her strength from within.

When Ericka asked herself as a young child, Who lives in me?, the answer was everyone. Mrs. Jenkins, Mr. Jenkins, Kyra, Gervaze Jr., Grandma Lula, Grandpa Ossie, Grandma Sadie, Grandpa Joseph, Aunt Irene, Aunt Thelma, Aunt Altomae, and Uncle Reginald live in her. They all embedded in her the best parts of them, as best as they could. They all gave her tools to equip her for the trials that would come. In hard times, she would need her mother's kindness, courage, and community-oriented nature; her father's joy in music; her sister's laughter and creative abilities; her brother's profound insight; Grandma Lula's endurance; Grandpa Ossie's fortitude; Grandma Sadie's gentleness; Grandpa Joseph's forthrightness; Aunt Thelma's wisdom; Aunt Altomae's inner strength; Aunt Irene's empathetic nature; and Uncle Reginald's sweet sense of play. Who is Ericka? She is her ancestors' hopes and faith made flesh. She was forging her own path, simultaneously learning from others' experiences to inform her journey. Her childhood steps along that path would shape her identity as she came of age in high school and college. In her familial artistic and cultural community, she developed skills that enabled her to express herself in multiple ways and helped seed "the spiritual" in what blossomed into her well-honed, conscious understanding and praxis of spiritual wellness—a realization that was still over a decade in the future.

2

Becoming a Black Panther

I left the university. There were no questions asked. I was
unapologetic. I told my family. They thought I had lost my
mind. I explained, "I'm going to fight for our people because
we're going to die if we don't fight."
—Cheryl Dawson, Black Panther Party veteran

In the autumn of 1962 Ericka entered McKinley Tech, a predominantly
Black high school in Washington, DC. Her unwavering sense of self was
shaped by her mother's stories of transcending race and class, instilling
in her a deep-rooted passion for activism. It was more than a mere interest; it was a calling, a destiny she couldn't escape. In August 1963, when
the March on Washington for Jobs and Freedom was announced on television, Ericka felt called to attend. She was only fifteen years old, not the
legal age of official adulthood. Like many other young people, she knew
she must witness the event with her own eyes and was determined to get
there no matter what her parents might say.[1]

"I'm going!" she declared.

"You know, that's no place for a fifteen-year-old," her mother promptly
responded.

"Why not?"

"The police will be there. It's unsafe for you," Mrs. Jenkins explained.

"But mama, you don't want me to go, you're afraid for me, but you
taught me to love Black people."

"I know I did."

"And you taught me to stand up for Black people," Ericka insisted.

"I know I did, but I didn't mean you. I didn't mean I want you to
do it."

"Well, I am, and I'm going.[2] You can punish me when I return,"
Ericka insisted, even as her mother tried to dissuade her.[3] Mrs. Jenkins

instructed her to tell her father, who was sober at the time, what she was about to do. He was shocked and quiet.[4]

Ericka remained resolute as she sensed the impending life-altering impact of the March on Washington. Amidst the racial unrest of the 1960s, participating in the March on Washington posed great danger, including the ominous presence and deployment of law enforcement and the fear of potential uprisings. The haunting memories of children peacefully protesting in the spring of 1963 in Birmingham, Alabama, assaulted by water hoses and attacked by police canines were indelibly etched in her mind. These harrowing images, captured on film and broadcast all over the world, sent a chilling message that no one, not even youth, was safe from the perils of mob and police violence. What if Ericka got arrested? What if she got hurt? Ericka's parents worried about their daughter's personal safety, but ultimately, they did not stop her. Ericka, in turn, stepped into her independence and asserted her identity as an individual able to make her own decisions. Deep within, she knew that the large crowd of people would act as a shield against any potential harm.[5]

Ericka traveled roughly forty-five minutes alone on the bus, which included a transfer from her home on Fifty-Fifth and East Capital Street Southeast to the March on Washington in Northwest DC. Years later, she recalled, "It was my singular destiny at that point in time in my life. I was supposed to do it alone."[6] Ericka's memory reveals her determined intent to ward off any outside influence, to be true to herself; looking back, she saw that this was a crucial turning point in her life.

Once fifteen-year-old Ericka arrived at the march, she stood on top of a heap of dirt so she could "see over the sea of people" and take in the experience from the highest vantage point possible.[7] The march, organized by A. Philip Randolph and Bayard Rustin, assembled nearly all the key civil rights figures of the time. Over 250,000 people gathered on the National Mall to hear Dr. Martin Luther King's most famous speech. Ericka was among approximately 10 percent of native DC residents in attendance.[8] The sheer number of Black, Brown, and white people amazed her. She remembered that each speech propelled her to ask herself, "Who am I in relationship to all of this? What part do I want to play?"[9] Ericka then had a realization. She could blend compassionate care with justice, dedicating herself to the service of others. The March on Washington was a watershed event in her teenage years. A moment of political maturity, the march served as a catalyst, fueling her determination and preparing her for a lifelong journey of activism in the Black freedom struggle.

In this chapter, I attend to Ericka's youth activism and the pivotal moments in high school and college that shaped her political subjectivity. These experiences informed her earliest memories in the Black Panther Party and were foundational precursors to her spiritual development. I also show how and why Ericka joined the BPP and explain the BPP community care politics, the murders of John Huggins and Alprentice "Bunchy" Carter, and her arrests. Her political activities as a BPP member helped her transition into a spiritual space during her imprisonment. Ericka became a mother, a widow, and a political prisoner in less than two years after joining the BPP. She demonstrated her political commitment, losses, and sacrifices against insurmountable odds. Many Black Panthers faced formidable challenges and made tremendous sacrifices, combatting oppressive violence in the ways they knew how. But Ericka and a select few of her comrades relied on spiritual practices. Her youth experiences significantly shaped her worldview, leading her to prioritize well-being and care as fundamental pillars in navigating the trials of her life.

The March on Washington was another beginning. Like her childhood learnings and teachings, Ericka began to "see" more as she experienced more. What may have been seemingly inconsequential or "just the way it was" became rays of light, insight, and awareness of care. As a teenager, she did teenage things like dating, volunteering, and participating in student organizations in college. She remembers her first boyfriend, Demetrius Granville Jackson III, also known as Jack. Jack and Ericka engaged in fun and mundane acts like talking on the phone, going to movies, and attending blue-light basement parties. He also would take Ericka with him on the weekends to visit his twelve-year-old disabled younger brother, Theophilis, whom everyone called T. These visits proved remarkable ones for Ericka on her journey to spiritual awakening. T lived at a state facility for children with disabilities in Maryland.[10] T's parents would have had to quit working to care for him as a disabled person. Instead, they chose to place him in a state home, believing that the care would be better.

Each time Jack and Ericka visited T, they witnessed how labor short-ages at the large facility led to neglect. More than anything else, they noticed how the understaffed workers failed to bathe T; he also lacked properly fitting clothes.[11] During the day, T was also cloistered in a dor-mitory with other children who did not share his particular needs. This made his learning experience incredibly challenging.[12]

Ericka described the state facility as nothing more than a "jail for disabled kids." Jack and Ericka would often leave in tears because of the negligent treatment T experienced.[13] Eventually, his mother and father took him out of the state's care, brought him home, and cared for him for his remaining years. He died young due to his disorder. After visiting T, Ericka was so distraught and devastated that she made the decision to pursue education with the intention of one day opening a school, as she informed Jack, "to help kids like your brother."[14] However, she also understood that she could have an impact beyond the classroom. Indeed, serving children became part of the vow she made to herself at the March on Washington.[15] She remained faithful in her aspiration to work with children as she did at her first volunteer opportunity at a recreation center.[16]

She carried her dedication to working with children in conjunction with her passion for the arts into college. In 1965 she graduated from McKinley Tech and enrolled at Cheyney State Teachers College, now Cheyney University of Pennsylvania, the first historically Black college in the nation. She completed her general requirements and cultivated her love of the arts by taking a Survey of Music and an Elementary Art course in her spring semester.[17] Frustrated with Cheyney's party atmo-sphere, she transferred to Lincoln University, another HBCU, after com-pleting her first year.

Lincoln University

At Lincoln University, Ericka's political consciousness grew. In her first year, she took general requirements, her first education course, Intro-duction to Education, and arts courses such as Principles of Acting, Studio Art, and Advanced Studio Art.[18] In the neighborhoods of rural Pennsylvania, she noticed the same devastating poverty and under-resourced schools that she saw back home in Washington, DC. This raised her awareness of how racism and classism determined people's quality of life. During this time, her volunteer work as a tutor until the age of nineteen exposed her to the educational inequalities in Pennsylvania, further fueling her desire to be an educator. She personally witnessed racial violence—the Ku Klux Klan burnt crosses on the lawn across from campus.[19] Driven by her witnessing of this racist act, she learned of the Deacons for Defense and Justice, founded in 1964 in Jonesboro, Louisiana, to protect Black people against the intimidation and harassment of the Ku Klux Klan.[20] They had chapters in Louisiana, Alabama, and Mississippi, and Ericka resolved to study and comprehend this group, recognizing them as an important subject. This marked the beginning of her activist path through political education.

The same year, Kwame Ture (Stokely Carmichael) proclaimed Black Power as the new Black freedom mantra during his speech at a March Against Fear rally to support Black voter registration in the aftermath of James Meredith's 220-mile solo march from Memphis, Tennessee, to Jackson, Mississippi. On the second day of the march, Meredith—the University of Mississippi's inaugural Black student enrollee—was shot by a white supremacist and hospitalized. Prominent civil rights activists including Dr. Martin Luther King Jr. finished the march. It turned into Mississippi's biggest-ever civil rights march.[21]

Ericka attended listening sessions with Ture and Charles V. Hamilton, reading excerpts of their co-authored manuscript *Black Power: The Politics of Liberation*, written at Lincoln University while Ericka was a student.[22] Ture and Hamilton were part of a long line of activists, writers, poets, and other professionals associated with Lincoln University, including the Pulitzer Prize-winning poet Gwendolyn Brooks, prominent civil rights attorney and the first Black American justice on the Supreme Court Thurgood Marshall, founder and first prime minister and president of Ghana Kwame Nkrumuh, and award-winning poet, novelist, and playwright Langston Hughes.[23] Ericka believed that an educator must raise the consciousness of her students: "I wanted to be a teacher who could tell the truth to her students, or encourage them to tell the truth about their own lives, or both."[24] She knew that to achieve this, she needed to immerse herself in reading and learning about Black history and culture.

The slogan "Black Power" gained national popularity when Ture and Hamilton published *Black Power* in 1967. Their book offered a framework for understanding Black Power as expressions of self-determination, collective agency, and economic independence. According to Ture and Hamilton, Black Power "is a call for black people to begin to define their own goals, to lead their organizations, and to support those organizations. It is a call to reject the racist institutions and values of this society."[25] Yet, despite Ture's declaration of Black Power as an affirmation of Black humanity, the media weaponized Black Power, constructing it as threatening rhetoric against the white power structure.[26] Quickly understanding how the media misrepresented the term Black Power as "power over" a group of people, Ericka intentionally looked for a more expansive term that still mirrored Ture's analysis. "Black liberation" conveyed an "expansive, freeing feeling."[27] It exuded self-determination and, in turn, loving care for one's self and the community.

Ericka moved from the theory of Black liberation to the practice of it. She joined the Black Student Congress (BSC), a small Black nationalist student organization at Lincoln University that subscribed to the tenets of Black Power.[28] Mentored by Hamilton, the BSC consisted of a broad range of committees that addressed culture, speaker visits, fundraising initiatives, education, communications, special projects, and anti-draft activism. These committees organized a plethora of activities, including meetings and programs that featured prominent speakers, a Black Power conference, and protests, for example, against KKK campus violence and apartheid in South Africa.[29] The BSC student activists' protests also included meetings with university administrators to address many concerns, including the hiring of white faculty, among other topics.[30] As a member of the organization, Ericka recognized the intersections of race and gender. She fought against sexism to gain membership into the BSC, which had a primarily male membership. She remembered that the predominantly male leadership "didn't appreciate women joining the Black Student Congress, as it was called then," but they did let her join."[31] The BSC was also resistant to her because it claimed that her "hair didn't have enough curls."[32] Ericka's experience in this organization not only speaks to the political moment but to cultural developments as well. As the comment about her hair indicates, her body was read as both "inside" and "outside" Blackness. This cross-fertilization between Black empowerment and notions of Black beauty positioned Ericka as both an insider and an outsider. Her inside status was her Black womanhood, while her so-called outsider status was linked to hair texture as a superficial representation of non-Blackness. During this time, cultural Black nationalism and its imagined understanding and performance of Black femininity kept many Black women on the periphery of this struggle. However, Ericka overcame the sexism, colorism, and hair discrimination of the organization and continued to cultivate her political education despite these difficulties.

Ericka's growing political consciousness was shared by her future husband, John Huggins, whom she met on the campus of Lincoln University.[33] John stood five feet nine. He was small-framed but physically strong, with light brown skin, soft dark brown eyes, and a full Afro. A native of Connecticut, John hailed from a middle-class household but earned a partial scholarship to the all-male, elite private Hopkins Grammar School; the scarcity of Black students there only added to his sense of alienation.[34] "He was treated extremely badly by students, teachers, and the headmaster, in that when crisis arose there was no one at the school who could understand him or come to his aid."[35] In search of solace and a means of articulating his ideas, he sought refuge in the debate club, but as time went on, he experienced increasing levels of racism and discrimination from his white peers. Consequently, he transferred to James Hillhouse High School, a New Haven public school with a well-integrated student body across various socioeconomic backgrounds.[36] After graduating at the age of seventeen, he joined the navy, where his job was to assist pilots in dropping bombs.[37] Reflecting on the racism he faced from fellow white soldiers during the war in Vietnam, he remembered that "in the Philippines they call them 'monkeys' because they're darker and a little shorter. . . . I just wondered what they called me behind my back."[38] He began to critically examine the rationale for the Vietnam War and left the navy in the wake of the Sixteenth Street Baptist Church bombing in Birmingham, Alabama, which killed four girls—Addie Mae Collins, Cynthia Wesley, Carole Robertson, and Carol Denise McNair.[39] He then enrolled at Lincoln.

Through their conversations, Ericka quickly discovered that John was politically conscious. As she got to know him, she considered him "a nice person, just a little bit arrogant."[40] He was kind, honest, outspoken, and generous of heart. Ericka appreciated that he was his authentic self: he did not try to hide who he was or perform a masculinity that was not natural to him. She shared, "He was the only man I'd ever met who took a [bubble] bath." Sometimes during his bath time, he would invite her in to talk about freedom.[41] John let his vulnerabilities show. He was also confident and strong enough to be himself and do what made him feel good. His feminine side radiated, and he appreciated Ericka's androgynous nature. When Ericka told him that she desired both men and women, he accepted her for all that she was. He was loveable and eclectic. Ericka recalled that he frequently dressed in thrift shop clothes, a "suit jacket and a shirt" that he regularly washed. Ericka appreciated him but was not ready for a relationship; she believed that they would evolve into best friends, and with time, they did.[42] School was her focus, and she completed the spring semester of 1967 with a 3.0 grade point average.[43]

As her interest in political activism increased, Ericka underwent a significant shift, diverting her attention from school to joining the Black Panther Party with John. The Black Panther Party, founded by Huey P. Newton and Bobby Seale at Merritt College, aimed to effect social change in Black and poor oppressed communities by integrating nationalist frameworks with Malcolm X's teachings and creating parallel community institutions, as outlined in the Ten-Point Platform and Program.[44] At its peak, the organization expanded to encompass offices in almost seventy cities across the nation, including an international chapter in Algeria.[45] Ericka came across *Ramparts*, an underground political left-leaning magazine, in the student union and became aware of social movements worldwide. She also gained greater insight into US racial unrest. One of the stories in the magazine discussed charges against Huey for the murder of an Oakland police officer. The story included a photograph of Huey, without a shirt, strapped to a hospital gurney, with a bullet wound in his stomach (figure 2.1).[46]

Huey's inhumane treatment devastated her. Inspired by the image and the story, Ericka decided that she wanted to join the Black Panther Party.[47] "I felt called," she remembered, as she had with the March on Washington.[48] She wanted John to join her. In her Swahili class, she handed John a sheet of paper that read, "John, I am going to California, you comin'?" "Yes," he replied.[49] Ericka then dropped her fall semester courses, withdrawing from Lincoln on November 15, 1967, and drove out west to California with her new lover, John.[50]

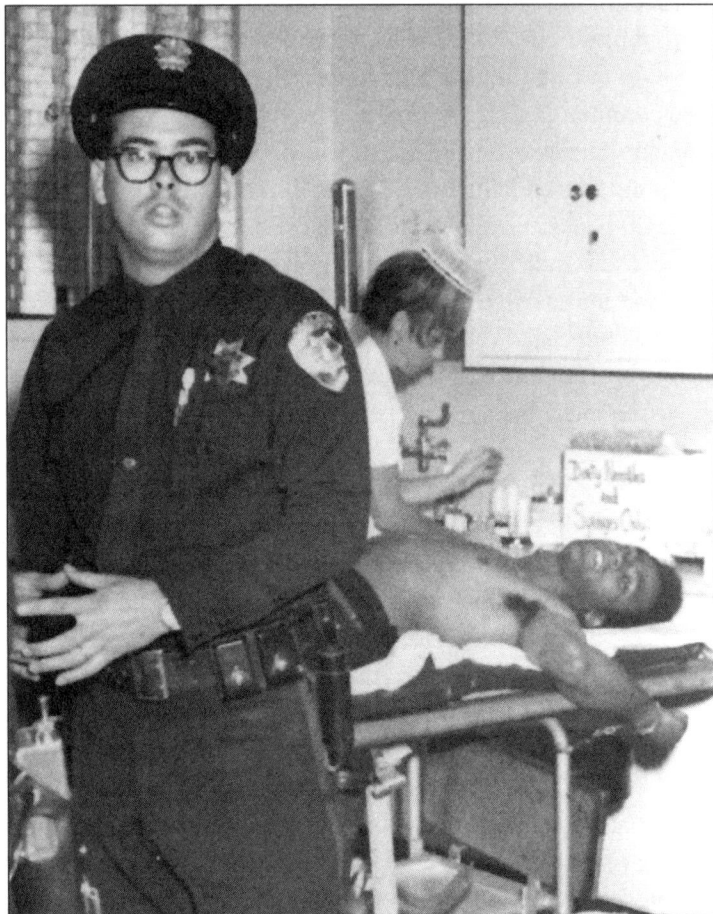

Figure 2.1. Huey P. Newton at Kaiser Emergency in Oakland, California, following the October 28, 1967, incident with the police. AP Images, "Wounded in Battle," October 28, 1967.

The Black Panther Party

Ericka would miss her family, but she was excited about the journey ahead. She knew she needed to tell her mother her plans but dreaded the conversation. On the way to Los Angeles, they stopped in New York for a few days to attend John's sister's wedding.[51] It was in New York that Ericka decided to call her mother.[52] During the phone call, silence on the other end conveyed her mother's discontent with her decision, but as with the March on Washington, she did not stop her.[53] "If that's what you feel you have to do, that's what you should do," Ericka remembered her mother saying to her.[54] Her decision hurt her mother, and her siblings resented her, feeling abandoned because she was no longer present to offer loving comfort, particularly in times of peril when their father was violent.[55] Although Ericka could not protect her siblings while she was in college, perhaps her family resented something about the permanence of being a BPP member and the literal and figurative distance it may have created from them. Like Ericka, they also longed for refuge from their father's violence.[56]

Ericka and John arrived in Los Angeles around Thanksgiving 1967. They secured employment at an automobile factory in rural Los Angeles and moved into an inexpensive studio apartment in Venice Beach.[57] Shortly after they arrived and before they joined the BPP, they learned of a "Free Huey" rally in the Shrine Auditorium organized by the BPP communications secretary, Kathleen Cleaver. The rally was part of a mass movement to free Huey, who was caged at the Alameda County jail on felony indictments for murder, assault, and kidnapping. Although they had not yet joined the BPP, Ericka considered the "Free Huey" rally their entry point into the organization. Attending the rally again brought back the same emotions she had as a teenager at the March on Washington. She vividly recalled that Huey's mother took the rally stage. Her words, full of love and care for her son, assured Ericka that she was on the right path, following her calling.[58]

In their effort to find the BPP headquarters, Ericka and John drew upon their memories of a brief trip to New York, where they saw members selling the *Black Panther*, the organization's newspaper. Because of this, they knew they would eventually find Black Panther members doing the same in Los Angeles. They soon came across a male BPP member selling the newspaper, which they purchased; then they asked him the location of the BPP headquarters. "They are in a building called the Black Congress in South Central Los Angeles," he replied. They quit their factory job and settled in Los Angeles to work full-time for the Southern California BPP chapter, founded by Alprentice "Bunchy" Carter.[59] A week later, they arrived at the Black Congress Building and a member quickly put them to work selling the BPP newspaper, cleaning the BPP office, answering the phones, typing material, attending political education classes, and watching over the office because of police surveillance.[60] The BPP recognized operational tasks, manual labor, and administrative tasks as valuable activist work.

John was adamant about justice and equity. Bunchy asked John to help him lead the Southern California BPP chapter in Los Angeles. They became close comrades, and as co-leaders of the LA chapter, they embraced a leadership style undefined by gender. BPP members requested the same tasks from men and women in the Los Angeles chapter. Eventually, Ericka even served as a spokesperson for the chapter, just like her male counterparts.

Ericka and John struggled to financially survive while working for political change. Within the following year, Ericka became pregnant with her and John's child, Mai. As BPP members, Ericka and John lived communally in a two-level apartment on West Century Boulevard in Los Angeles with other comrades, including fellow BPP member Elaine Brown.[61] Spencer-Antoine explains that this intertwined living and activist environment served as a "collective structure" that enabled "the total commitment of its membership."[62] In doing this, she writes, "they attempted to meet the needs of its cadre for food, clothing, and shelter."[63] They regularly shared clothes. They made money where they could, for example, selling BPP newspapers, but for Ericka, John, and others in their communal household, it was still not enough. Their unwavering dedication to the people took a heavy toll on their personal needs, necessitating more funds and resources. The harsh reality was that the state did not allow those without much money to survive and support their families, prompting a need to increase their food supply. Ericka applied for Aid to Families with Dependent Children (welfare), which enabled her to purchase groceries. Her welfare check became the primary source of income for the household, but it was still not enough to feed everyone.

In Point 10 of the BPP's Platform and Program, the Black Panthers demanded the right to "land, bread, housing, education, justice, and peace."[64] These core values did not align with those of a capitalist society; for that reason, John and Ericka needed to adopt innovative methods to survive. John believed in the BPP's political ideology of the human right to quality food. Ericka and John often frequented Safeway, the local grocery store, sometimes with others. John did not want Ericka and their baby to be without food. He wanted to protect and provide for them, so he would graze and steal food as he and Ericka walked down the grocery aisles with growling stomachs. "Nobody should have to pay for food. Nobody should go hungry. Eat this. Safeway's not going to struggle if you eat this food," Ericka remembered he said to her. "So that's what we'd do." He taught Ericka to be fearless in the expansion of her political consciousness.[65]

For the BPP, community support was another critical aspect of survival. While in Safeway, Ericka and John came across a friendly Black woman cashier who knew them from their regular visits. They would attempt to purchase $150 worth of groceries for their communal household with Ericka's welfare check. Since they did not have enough food stamps, the clerk rang their groceries up at a lower price of only five dollars as she softly made eye contact with them and smiled to communicate compassion and understanding. "All of us ate off of my welfare check, not including the food that John stole," Ericka remembered.[66] John eventually stopped stealing once the clerk offered them assistance. Support from the community helped BPP members sustain themselves and the people they served each and every day.

Communal living involved shared responsibilities and total commitment to BPP tasks. A typical day of communal living included heading to the BPP office after breakfast to "do whatever work it took."[67] This included advocating for the release of BPP members from jail and cultivating relationships with people in cafés, local stores, and barbershops, and on the streets of Los Angeles. In 1968 Ericka served as a BPP spokesperson with others, attending high-profile celebrity events to seek support from Hollywood progressives and fundraise in the evening. Because of their presence, community engagement, and service to the people, the community embraced the BPP. The BPP developed friendships with many people, from the mothers, fathers, and grandparents who often kept Ericka and other pregnant BPP women well-fed, to teachers, grocery owners, state workers, teenagers, and high-profile entertainers in Hollywood. Ericka recalled a Hollywood actress and friend giving her a crib that overflowed with baby clothes.[68]

Ericka and John agreed to raise their daughter, Mai, born in December 1968, as a married couple, although they never lawfully married.

At the same time, communal party relations seeped into their partnership. Like many BPP members, they engaged in nontraditional sexual relationships. Against the backdrop of the "free love" movement, the BPP experimented with sexuality and shared relationships. For Ericka, sexuality was a way for her to imagine a fuller life. Her simultaneous relationships with both men and women reflected the cultural moment. She recalled that some men were unable to release hypermasculine ideas about sexuality, which prevented them from being open about their male lovers. On the other hand, Ericka recalls women being more forthcoming about their intimacies. Her experiences support social and cultural studies scholar of education Ronald K. Porter's analysis that "the excavation of homosexuality in the context of the Black Panther Party reveals a whole host of characters and actions adding both breadth and depth to the black and LGBTQ experience in America."[69] Historian Tracye A. Matthews's scholarship echoes this sentiment about sexuality and employing alternative relationship structures.[70]

These sexual pleasures and freedoms were sometimes fraught. "The fact that they viewed themselves as revolutionaries engaged in a war against injustice complicated matters of sexuality and gender relations," Matthews argues. For some, their everyday battles with political repression and fear of death intensified their need to find pleasure and explore eroticism.[71] At times, their approach to sexual freedom led to arguments, infighting, sexual exploitation, or even sexual abuse. BPP member Elaine Brown recalled that John gave her a hatchet to protect herself against unwanted sexual advances by BPP men.[72] In arming Elaine to fight her assailant, John advocated against male chauvinism. He was progressive about gender politics and empowered women to protect themselves against male violence. He believed that women should have their own agency.

Ericka was fully committed to the BPP and worked around the clock even while pregnant. She recalled, "I was nine months pregnant and couldn't get around as easily. Pregnancy did not slow down the work of BPP women. There wasn't anything I wasn't being asked to do."[73] By this time, she was surrounded by an increasing number of other women who had joined the BPP.

She soon met Angela Y. Davis, a graduate student at the University of California, San Diego, who became a dear friend and comrade in the struggle. Angela was initially a member of the Black Panther Political Party, a group whose "role was to develop theoretical analyses of the Black Liberation Movement, as well as to build structures."[74] The Black Panther Political Party was a separate organization from the BPP founded by Huey P. Newton and Bobby Seale and was part of a consortium called the Black Congress, which contained many groups, including the BPP, Maulana Karenga's US organization, the National Welfare Rights Organization, and the Community Alert Patrol, among others.[75] The Black Panther Political Party reshaped itself into the Los Angeles Student Nonviolent Coordinating Committee (LA SNCC), which would function to support the student-driven civil rights organization.[76] Despite having SNCC's name attached to it, it was independent of the national organization.[77] Once LA SNCC dissolved, Angela joined the Communist Party USA (CP USA) and the Che-Lumumba Club, a Black cadre within the Communist Party.[78] She also joined the BPP, where she met Ericka and John in 1968.[79] Initially, she felt a closer comradeship with John than with Ericka because of the day-to-day organizing that Angela and John conducted out of the same office. John persuaded Angela to run the political education program and the liberation school. Angela helped develop the curriculum with John and taught young people in the neighborhood. The curriculum included studying texts such as Vladimir Lenin's *State and Revolution*, which explored the relationship between the state and the proletariat revolution. In the text Lenin explained,

> Only the proletariat—by virtue of the economic role it plays in large-scale production—is capable of being the leader of all the working and exploited people, whom the bourgeoisie exploit, oppress, crush, often not less but more than they do the proletarians, but who are incapable of waging an independent struggle for emancipation.[80]

As an educational text, Lenin's ideas represented how the BPP thought about the state and the power of the proletariat and workers in the revolution. In recalling these experiences, Angela reminisced about the steadfastness of an illiterate Black male teenager who had an intense desire to read Lenin. With his persistence and Angela's guidance, he learned how to read. The heartening experience let her know that the "joy of learning is something that has to be awakened in people" and is not always found in formal education.[81]

Upon meeting Ericka, Angela instantly connected with her and was impressed by her undeniable passion for political activism. Angela remembered thinking that Ericka possessed a remarkable amount of inner strength. She admired Ericka's natural qualities, such as her good-natured spirit and love for people. Their friendship endured even after the BPP told those with membership in other parties to choose between the organizations. Angela decided to leave the BPP and remain in the CP USA; however, she remained active in the defense of the BPP.[82]

By 1968, the BPP membership consisted predominantly of women. According to BPP scholar Angela D. LeBlanc-Ernest, by this time women "represented approximately 60% of the Party's membership."[83] Greater participation by women in the BPP prompted discussions on male chauvinism and sexism, and women's vocal protests advanced the BPP's position concerning gender. According to Ericka, the work was not divided by gender in Los Angeles; however, there was significant gender inequity in some other chapters. Ericka described an incident at a meeting while visiting the Oakland national headquarters with other BPP members from northern and southern California during her pregnancy. Women were in the kitchen cooking. After preparing the food, a woman announced, "Brothers, you can eat now." Ericka did not understand what the woman meant, so she asked the person next to her for clarification when the announcer stated, "Sisters, brothers eat first." Ericka was famished and pregnant. "Oh no, please excuse me while I go in the kitchen and fix my plate," she declared.[84] Ericka's interruption was necessary because she refused to delay taking care of her body and her child's needs. The other woman's request demonstrated internalized sexist and misogynistic ideals that placed women and children beneath men. It took stamina and courage for Ericka to openly defy the cultural norms in the room and assert her humanity and that of her unborn child. Ongoing debates on the reproduction of gender norms within the BPP broadened the organization's reach. LeBlanc-Ernest noted that "as the Black Panther Party expanded in 1968, so did women's participation in Party activities."[85] The BPP shifted its tactical analysis to one that prioritized community programs and de-emphasized armed self-defense during this period. "The Panthers had boldly and legally picked up the gun—and had been forced to lay it back down," argues Spencer-Antoine.[86] The BPP expanded its community programs, including free programs that served the social, economic, political, educational, health care, and medical needs of Black and poor people in the United States.[87]

In response to the shortcomings of Lyndon Johnson's War on Poverty, these initiatives provided Black communities with crucial access to essential services and resources. Johnson's legislation "established the vision for the subsequent research and analysis of minority poverty."[88] The War on Poverty, according to sociologist William Julius Wilson, failed because "the emphasis was mainly on environments of the poor. . . . This vision did not consider poverty as a problem of American economic organization."[89] The federal government's management of economic difficulties and the institutionalized forms of oppression against people of color were fundamental problems inherent in 1970s racial politics that the War on Poverty did not address.

Impassioned by the 1960s assassinations of nonviolent civil rights leaders, the BPP saw its radical display of community service as another form of self-defense to challenge institutional violence and police terror within Black communities. Its message was one of community empowerment and community protection. Its revolutionary spirit coupled with its community programs made the BPP a target of ongoing government assault and violence from programs such as COINTELPRO.[90]

External forces, notably the FBI, played a significant role in shaping the gender dynamics within the BPP. In 1969 political repression had a profound and devastating impact on the BPP; ethnic studies scholar Ward Churchill emphasized that the "Black Panther Party was literally sledgehammered [by the FBI's COINTELPRO program]. Of the 295 counterintelligence operations the bureau has admitted conducting against black activists and organizations during the period, a staggering 233, the majority of them in 1969, were aimed at the Panthers."[91] The police and other government forces gained information on the BPP to destroy, distort, and misrepresent the BPP to the public.[92] Because of sexist and racist ideas, FBI agents often targeted male BPP members. Amidst the intense governmental repression of that era, the BPP adopted a strategy of closing ranks and implemented quality control measures, resulting in the expulsion of numerous members. Notably, women were placed in more leadership positions. As LeBlanc-Ernest noted, "Expansion of female participation became critical for the organization to function effectively."[93] Women became central to the BPP programming.[94]

The BPP and the US Organization

Political repression soon hit close to home for Ericka as the FBI claimed the lives of both John and Bunchy on the campus of UCLA. Leading up to the tragedy, members of the UCLA Black Student Union (BSU) requested support from John and Bunchy to assist them in a highly charged meeting concerning the directorship of the High Potential Program, an equal opportunity program.[95] John served as the captain and later deputy chairman of the LA chapter, and Bunchy was the deputy minister of defense and a UCLA student.[96] The BPP revered Bunchy. He educated himself during his time in prison, politicized and organized the Slauson gang, and recruited many of them into the BPP. The BSU with John and Bunchy were in discussions with another group, Maulana Karenga's US organization.[97] Ericka remembered Bunchy as always well-dressed, projecting a regal nature and strong sense of integrity. He was a grassroots intellectual who taught political education, emphasizing a pedagogy of community love. Ericka, who was highly attuned to care politics, was particularly moved by his teachings, which emphasized that care work did not reproduce gender norms within the organization.[98]

John and Bunchy were fearless BPP leaders who considered women equal partners in the struggle. On January 17, 1969, tension reached its zenith at a meeting in Campbell Hall when John and Bunchy were shot.[99] Ericka contended that the FBI infiltrated the BPP, the US organization, and the UCLA campus, and murdered John and Bunchy.[100] The FBI strategically leveraged the differences between the BPP and US into a major conflict. The scholarship of Ward Churchill and Jim Vander Wall on COINTELPRO illustrates the kind of FBI memos, cartoons, and letters fabricated to prompt tension between the BPP and the US organization. They shed light on a 1968 FBI internal memo by J. Edgar Hoover that directs offices "to fully capitalize upon the BPP and US differences as well as to exploit all avenues of creating further dissension."[101] In doing this, offices were then instructed to produce a biweekly letter on the "imaginative and hard-hitting counterintelligence measures aimed at crippling the BPP."[102] COINTELPRO's efforts to violently dismantle the BPP were illegal, intricately planned, and ghastly.[103]

Ericka recalled that two weeks before the FBI killed John, she had a dream in which the state had taken him away. Dreams are described by Chicana feminist writer and scholar of cultural and queer theory Gloria E. Anzaldúa as a "form of experience, a dimension in which life and mind seem to be embedded."[104] In the event that Ericka's dream "experience" foretold what was to come, she immediately told John about her dream as soon as he walked in the door. "They took you away," she said as she embraced him tightly. He "peeled my arms off of him and held me and looked me in the eye and said, 'I'm here now. Where's the baby?'" His poignant reply, "I'm here now," conveyed the profound realization that they had to embrace the present moment, acutely aware that death was looming. "It was in the air all around him," explained Ericka.

She directed him to the room Mai was sleeping in; he closed the door so he could be alone and held Mai for hours, as if pronouncing his final goodbye. They never mentioned the dream to one another again. They deeply sensed "a knowing" about what was to come.[105] Ericka always listened to her intuition, which she learned from her mother. John felt called to attend the meeting on UCLA's campus that day. His intuition warned him of the potential life-threatening consequences. Nevertheless, it was a sacrifice he was willing to make for the cause. Ericka was at home with her three-week-old daughter when she learned of the shooting. Soon thereafter, other traumatized BPP members gathered at her house. "Ericka Huggins left the world then, it seemed," according to Elaine. "I watched her stand at the kitchen sink, her long, thin body surrendered, her eyes glazed."[106] Ericka did not even have time to grieve the loss of her husband because within a matter of hours, the police arrived at her house to arrest her and the other BPP members.[107] As police were preparing to arrest Ericka and the BPP members, other comrades, including Angela Y. Davis, had begun arriving at the house to offer support and solidarity.[108] Walter Bremond, the head of the Black Congress consortium, who was also with the group of comrades, took Mai into his care.[109] Walter was the only person Ericka could think of at the time to call to take Mai overnight, although she was unsure how long she would be gone. She trusted him and his wife to care for her baby. Ericka recalled of the police, "They booked us on something ridiculous. . . . They wanted us off the streets. They treated us like members of a gang."[110]

In concert with the FBI's COINTELPRO, the local police used whatever tactics they could, including anti-gang tactics, to disband the organization. Although women were less likely to be targeted by the FBI, both men and women remained under surveillance. Their gender did not preclude women, such as Ericka, from experiencing COINTELPRO repression. As a target of the state, Ericka encountered intimidation, violence, and harassment. In this instance, police ordered her and the other BPP members out of the house. One officer even pointed a gun at baby Mai while she was in her mother's arms, as recalled in the introduction of this book.[111] Once Ericka was able to calm the officer down and get him to lower his weapon, the two male officers put her in the backseat of a police car with a white officer. The police transported all the other BPP women in one vehicle to the Sybil Brand Institute for Women. The men traveled in another car. Ericka assumed that they were taking her to the police station, but they stopped at the morgue first to taunt her and did not even allow her to identify John's body. "We're gonna make sure your husband's really dead. Okay, Huggins?" one of the male officers said.[112] Then they verbally abused her by racially insulting her daughter. She remembered that the woman police officer never said a word or tried to stop her colleagues from being violent toward her. Experiencing the weight of individual and institutional cruelties, the now widowed Ericka was confined in jail in the Sybil Brand Institute for Women. For the first time, she allowed herself to weep.[113]

Ericka described the FBI infiltration she saw while detained at the police station. She watched agents who had posed as members of the US organization interact casually with the Los Angeles police department.

> We were sitting at the Seventy-Seventh Street Police Station in Los Angeles at that time. Two men in African print shirts who Party members knew to be members of the US organization came into the police station, not in handcuffs like all of us, not escorted in for questioning like us, but freely walking. . . . [They] stopped to answer the police.[114]

Ericka was now certain that the FBI wanted to destroy the BPP. In the midst of tragedy, glimpses of policing agencies' orchestrated acts against the BPP emerged. Hours later, a group of comrades and family members, including Angela, Ericka's brother-in-law Evan, and the husband of one of John's sisters, bailed her out.

As her comrades offered aid, support, and their deepest sympathies, Ericka looked at their long faces and asked, "Why is everyone so sad?" She reminded them that they "needed to find the courage to stand up and fight because there would be a great deal of struggle ahead."[115] Unbelievably, Ericka's spirits were high. At that moment, Angela considered Ericka "the strongest Black woman in America."[116]

We know this sentiment because it is captured in Angela's personal, published letter, which was designed to interrupt the official script and official archive. In her 1971 letter to Ericka, she described what it was like to see Ericka unbroken and ready to take on the world:

> You had been immediately arrested on a manifestly fabricated charge—conspiracy to retaliate, or something equally ridiculous. We were hurting with your pain. While we watched your approach—you were now walking through the jail's iron gates—our silence was throbbing with inexpressible pain. And as we were desperately searching for words to convey our unyielding solidarity, it was your strong, undaunted voice that broke the silence. . . . Your unflinching determination as you clenched your fist and said, "All Power to the People," prompted me to think to myself, this must be the strongest, most courageous Black woman in America.[117]

Personal testimony offered an alternative history to political struggles. Angela began by indicting the US justice system for what she believed was a "manifestly fabricated charge" against Ericka in its attempt to silence her political activities. Instead, she inserted a direct reference to pain, humanizing Ericka. Angela expressed collective empathy and sorrow: "We were hurting with your pain." Her transition from "we" to "you" showcases her individual feeling and political connection with Ericka and the community activists who shared her sentiment. Angela's letter is a public document, one that politicized the personal. She recognized Ericka's absence as the authorities purged her from the record when she wrote, "Our silence was throbbing with inexpressible pain," and she reflected on the collective inability to challenge institutional power when she compared powerlessness to speechlessness. Her letter identified Ericka's example as more than speech but also defiance against institutional injustice. In Huey's words, "'All Power to the People' sums up our goals for Black people, as well as our deep love and commitment to them. All power comes from the people, and all power must be ultimately vested in them."[118] Ericka's "clenched fist" thus represented a declaration of emotional intensity and deep love. As she chanted "All Power to the People," she underscored the values of the BPP: community practice of love, action, authority, and change, all rooted in the collective strength of the community.

Constant infiltration and trumped-up criminal charges plagued the BPP. Under siege, the BPP struggled to reclaim its identity as a community advocate in the public imagination. The BPP consistently challenged the FBI's violent onslaught, and its self-determination and resistance linked it to the long history of Black protest. Ericka highlighted the parallels between Black women's activism in the BPP, the resistance efforts of formerly enslaved women, and Black women's organizing during the civil rights movement, emphasizing that "all of them had the same goals in mind."[119] Their shared goals included the liberation of Black and poor communities. In doing this, they encountered obstacles, including racism, sexism, and classism. Likewise, Angela Y. Davis wrote, "The status of black women within the community of slaves was definitely a barometer indicating the overall potential for resistance. This process did not end with the formal dissolution of slavery."[120] Both Ericka and Angela recognized those women as the forerunners of 1970s Black liberation.

Black Panther Party New Haven Chapter

Ericka left Los Angeles with Evan to give John a proper homegoing and begin her new life in his hometown of New Haven, Connecticut. She took the train with Mai to New Haven to bury his body.[121] Soon after that, at the request of community members, including students from Yale University, she opened the New Haven BPP chapter. Ericka remembered that the New Haven chapter sold newspapers and started a breakfast program and a health clinic.[122] Political repression soon followed as she was targeted in another orchestrated plot organized through the nefarious COINTELPRO. Three months after her arrival in New Haven, the police arrested her along with Bobby Seale and other BPP members for the murder of New Haven BPP member Alex Rackley.

In the New Haven chapter, infiltration contributed to Alex's interrogation, torture, and brutal murder by fellow Black Panthers Warren Kimbro and Lonnie McLucas, under the direction of George Sams. At the time, the BPP members were misled by George to believe that Alex was an informant, which cost him his life. As a result of paranoia, sexism, and patriarchy within the New Haven chapter, Ericka was forced to record Alex's interrogation, which the state used to charge her and the rest of the BPP members with his murder.[123] This interrogation and Alex's ultimate murder demonstrate the complicated way violence, intimidation, paranoia, and desperation became a poisonous combination that impacted the larger political goals of the BPP. The BPP strategy of self-protection from infiltration unfortunately mirrored the hegemonic culture's use of domination and violence to secure its vision of freedom. At the same time, as in all efforts to figure out how to subvert racism and anti-Blackness, not all BPP members agreed to use the master's tools.[124] In fact, many members like Ericka tried to push back against the culture, but dominant forces made it impossible to shift the current patriarchal ideas of freedom.

Ericka's intuition informed her that the FBI had once again orchestrated the series of troubling events that culminated in the killing of Alex Rackley. Much later, she learned that she was right. After Alex's murder, Ericka knew that the police would soon arrive at the townhouse apartment shared by the BPP members. She looked out of the window at the darkness of the night, holding Mai as she slept, thinking that this might be her last night free of a jail cell. "How would I protect my daughter?" she thought. Everyone else in the house was sleeping. Just as she was having those thoughts, the police arrived in a large group with two members of the FBI dressed in dark suits and broke into the house, knocking down all the doors. Some came in through the open windows. Their loud and violent arrival startled those in the house, including New Haven BPP chapter members Maude Francis, Jeannie Wilson, Margaret "Peggy" Hudgins, and Rose Smith, who was pregnant. Many of the men who were usually there were gone. The police yelled to evoke fear in the women. Babies started crying. Notably, Mai was now awake but not crying. It was complete chaos. They ransacked the house, poured out sugar, salt, and flour, and dumped bottles looking for drugs. As they were destroying everything in the house, the BPP women waited quietly, attempting to keep the children calm.

During the storm induced by the state, a Black police officer discreetly approached Ericka to express his sympathy. "I'm so sorry for what happened to your husband. I am so sorry for what's happening to you. I know the Huggins family. They're a good family. I'm so sorry." Ericka nodded, took his hand, and thanked him with a few words. He then went back with his colleagues. She held on to that precious moment but still feared the worst. She knew that the police intended to make it look like she murdered Alex. An FBI member called her to come upstairs. She then asked one of the other women in the house to hold Mai. She did not want to hear or feel the energy of the FBI agent but did as she was ordered and walked to the top of the stairs, calmly standing in the hallway between the bedrooms. She knew he was about to say something hateful to invoke fear intentionally. "Well, Huggins, you've done it now. We'll see you burn in the chair. Huggins, this isn't just for smokin' a little bit of weed. So you may as well tell me what you did. Because we're gonna see you burn in the chair." She looked at him and waited. Assuming she might speak, he paused.

"Are you finished?" she replied.
"Well, unless you gonna . . . you know," he said blustering. "No, I'm done."
"I'm gonna go back downstairs to my daughter."[125]

He just stood there, shocked at her response, as if to say, "Wait, what?" She walked deliberately, at her own pace, back downstairs to be with Mai. She worried that the officer would carry out his threat. They eventually arrested everyone and took them to the New Haven jail, where they were booked and allowed a phone call. Peggy's sister, BPP member Frances Carter, who was also pregnant, was later arrested at her place of employment.[126] The BPP women called family members to pick up their children. Ericka called John's mother, Mrs. Elizabeth Huggins, who came to get Mai.

As BPP members committed to social justice and community engagement, they found themselves subjected to the violence of COINTELPRO operations. Peers looked to Ericka's leadership and response to state violence. The impact of COINTELPRO on women's lives was profound, as Spencer-Antoine reminds us that "the fact that women became the majority of the organization's membership by 1969 shaped how repression and gender intersected."[127] In addition, many of these women were mothers and faced the challenges of raising their children while incarcerated. At age twenty-one, Ericka quickly became the poster child for Black Panther leadership as a political prisoner, all the while facing a potential life sentence.

Officers transported the BPP women to the Connecticut Correctional Institution for Women in Niantic, commonly referred to as Niantic. Ericka was in an altered state of mind as she was still grieving John's death. The drive to the prison gave her some time to reflect on herself, her state, and the future. She wondered what life would be like for her daughter. Mai was already fatherless; now she was also motherless. Ericka knew that John's mother would take good care of Mai and raise her like her own daughter, but she worried about her being without her parents or feeling abandoned. Mai was heavy on her mind. She was a nursing mother but felt too sad to try to release the milk that filled her breasts. She remembered, "I could not feel. I didn't feel like I deserved to be alive" because Alex Rackley and John were not alive.[128] She was experiencing survivor's remorse. Although Ericka did not murder Alex, she felt heavy remorse and an aching heart for being separated from Mai. She knew she needed to summon her inner strength and consciously build and cultivate care practices to survive and endure Niantic.

3

Gendered Prison Violence

The aim was civil death: the mortification of the self, everything a young woman had been and might be ended at the gates.
—Saidiya Hartman

Six BPP women—Ericka, Rose, Frances, Peggy, Maude, and Jeannie—entered Niantic on Thursday, May 22, 1969. They were each accused of murder, kidnapping, binding, and conspiracy charges and detained without any sentencing.[1] They were not offered the option of a legal bond. Ericka was a widowed, breastfeeding mother, and Rose and Frances were both pregnant. None of that mattered. Niantic officers purposefully ignored their numerous requests for medical attention as pregnant and postpartum women. Peggy, Maude, and Jeannie had their own difficulties. Peggy dealt with extreme flare-ups of her rheumatoid arthritis, which worsened during her incarceration. Maude and Jeannie were only teenagers, and would soon be separated from their comrades and transferred to a juvenile home.[2]

Forced out of the New Haven community by the state, all six were traumatized, exhausted, grief-stricken, overwrought with sadness, and deeply worried for their loved ones' safety as well as their own. The police intimidation, violence, and verbal abuse they endured during their arrest had left them humiliated. With the transfer of the teenagers, the remaining unsentenced women were all twenty-one years old, except for Frances, who was a year younger. They only had one another for support, even as Maude and Jeannie lost a measure of that. Even so, they forged a new activist practice based on love and care, a thread that weaves through Ericka's life story as her time at Niantic hinged on her collectivist and mutually supportive relationships with her BPP compatriots.

The women's purposeful cultivation of intimacy and care offers a window into the prison system and its disastrous impact on young

Black women. To know their story of collectivism and care while imprisoned is to know how incarceration is intended to corrode Black women's communality and self-worth and how Black women successfully countered this intentional violence with care for others and themselves. Indeed, their stories and the experiences of Black womanhood deepen our understanding of women, gender, and mass incarceration. Their stories illustrate the many ways state authorities sought and failed to break their spirits. Black women squashed these efforts by protecting, caring for, and uplifting one another when faced with brutality, and the torture of solitary confinement in particular. I focus here on how they collectively endured separation from their children and families, poor medical care, disgusting and insufficient food, physical and mental abuse, and isolation. By sharing resources and support, which entailed striking and securing legal aid and childcare, they conjured an indomitable will and resilience; together, they forged what I call spiritual wellness. I define spiritual wellness as everyday acts of resistance to oppression that cultivate a feeling of connection and community and transcend white supremacist institutional abuses that aim to isolate and punish dissidents. In recounting Ericka's story communally, cognizant of the women who shaped her and whom she shaped, I utilize this chapter to anchor her story of incarceration in the profound display of spiritual wellness among the BPP women incarcerated at Niantic. This is exemplified by Frances, a woman who resisted having her spirit broken, owing her survival to her BBP connection and community.

Upon the women's arrival at Niantic, correctional officers escorted Ericka, Rose, Frances, Peggy, Maude, and Jeannie to Davis Hall to begin the solitary and humiliating intake process. Officers brought the six women through the building's back door and placed them in a holding room equipped with phones under the officers' control.[3] Harsh fluorescent lights filled the space. Officers then separated the women, taking them one by one to take a "mug shot" (identification photograph) and complete the paperwork to register each one as a prisoner.

Strip searches upon intake were standard, serving to normalize state control and state-sanctioned sexual assault. Matrons ordered each woman to strip so that they could search their body cavities for drugs and other illegal contraband. Ericka remembered having her vagina and anus probed: "We didn't have any drugs on us. That wasn't what we were about."[4] Whatever humiliation Ericka and the others felt during the invasive search was irrelevant to the officers. In her autobiography, New York BPP chapter member Assata Shakur recalls a conversation with Joan Bird and Afeni Shakur, two New York BPP chapter colleagues, about their experience of a prison strip search. Joan and Afeni were sent to Rikers Island with nineteen others on primarily conspiracy charges, fifty days before Ericka's incarceration. Joan and Afeni characterized their strip search as "getting finger-fucked."[5] Assata's account of her experience echoes the horrific nature of the procedure.

> The "internal search" was as humiliating and disgusting as it sounded. You sit on the edge of this table and the nurse holds your legs open and sticks a finger in your vagina and moves it around. She has a plastic glove on. Some of them try to put one finger in your vagina and another one up your rectum at the same time. . . . I wanted to punch that nurse clear to oblivion.[6]

Assata's vivid description offers insight into the state-sanctioned gendered violence inherent in a strip search, and the rage Ericka and others felt during and after the sexual violation.

Feminine gender norms in Niantic in this era dictated that women wear dresses in every conceivable setting, no matter how uncomfortable. After the strip search, matrons sprayed a foul-smelling delousing solution on the six women. Matrons then handed each woman a white bra, underpants, a bathrobe, and a prison uniform. The uniform included a thin cotton shirtdress with dreary flowers and pockets on each side, with buttons down the front sewn by women imprisoned at Niantic.[7] The thin fabric offered no protection against the cold Connecticut winter. Women with the means were able to obtain sweaters or jackets to wear over the flimsy dresses. Most had to suffer the frigid temperatures.

After handing out clothing, matrons transferred the women to medical segregation, a type of solitary confinement reserved for evaluations, sometimes with a counselor, to ensure that those imprisoned would not harm themselves or others.[8] They were placed in separate cells, each with a metal-framed bed and a dresser, and left there until their placement in administrative segregation—yet more solitary confinement.

Gender played a significant role in shaping the methods used by the carceral state to punish Black women. In the late 1960s, Niantic officials used outdated language for their times to describe life in prison, which suggests that the prison also used dated techniques.[9] For example, the prison employed the term "matron" to represent correctional officers who identified as women. While matrons were professionals charged with safeguarding imprisoned women from sexual violence and serving as moral compasses, they fulfilled neither role throughout Ericka's and the other BPP women's stay. Nicole Hahn Rafter, a feminist scholar of criminal justice, and historian Estelle B. Freedman explained that as early as the mid-nineteenth century, prisons employed matrons to regulate and surveil imprisoned women.[10] Early penologists, according to Rafter, believed that "matrons were necessary because female prisoners by nature needed special treatment that only other women could provide."[11] In theory, the "early matrons" were meant to serve as exemplars who reinforced "positive change in their charges" rather than filling "a custodial function."[12] In practice, this ideal often fell short, as matrons "had no authority with which to realize such an ambition."[13] Rafter underscored the "subordinate" position of women in prison management in relation to their male counterparts.[14] She also noted that matrons were subject to termination by wardens, often men, if they deviated "too far from prison tradition."[15]

In 1918 Niantic was named the Connecticut State Farm for Women, a product of the women's prison reform movement in the mid-nineteenth century.[16] Reformers reinforced domesticity as a rehabilitation method for white women who transgressed the cult of true womanhood, described by Barber Welter as "four cardinal virtues—piety, purity, submissiveness, and domesticity."[17] Black women, however, were considered the antithesis of these virtues and therefore outside the purview of rehabilitation. Nevertheless, the state still imprisoned Black women, and maternalism still shaped Black women's experiences, relegating them to subservient maternal roles. Given the reformers' focus on teaching "proper" gender roles, imprisoned Black women became trained as domestics as their population increased.[18] In a 1929 article, Helen Worthington Rogers argued that women's reform placed an "emphasis on educational rather than punitive methods of reform and on the family or cottage system."[19] Niantic's approach to reform was motivated by patriarchal ideals of the cult of true womanhood: it trained all women for domestic work and homemaking. Prison labor included housekeeping duties such as sewing clothes, cleaning the facilities, and maintaining the laundry; additionally, imprisoned women worked on the farm on Niantic's grounds.

Over the past century, some things have changed, and some have not. Niantic continues to operate a sewing industry, with imprisoned women still making uniforms and bed linens for the State of Connecticut's prison population. However, as of 2020, imprisoned women are paid only seventy-five cents per day for their labor. In contrast, Niantic hired imprisoned women outside the facilities for custodial work such as groundskeeping, carpentry, cleaning highways, and painting houses, paying them a higher wage of $4.50 a day.[20]

As a pretrial detainee, Ericka was granted immunity from incarcerated women's normal work demands. However, she refused to recuse herself from such work. The prison staff placed a sewing machine in the BPP wing so that the women could sew clothes in-house. Ericka utilized the skills her mother had taught her as a young girl in creating and mending the clothing other women wore. When she was transferred from solitary confinement to the general population, Ericka signed a work waiver, provided by the prison, indicating that she did not want to work less than full-time. Niantic's work waiver indicated that prison officials believed that full-time work would increase prisoners' mental calm and wellness. Ericka substituted her own understanding of the situation onto the form before signing (figure 3.1).

On the form, Ericka wrote "untrue" next to the statement, "for my own piece [peace] of mind and well-being, I request to be assigned full time duties."[21] In doing this, she rejected Niantic's claim that prison work contributed to her wellness, thereby resisting the language of the state. On the back of the form, she further indicated that her participation in work had to do with community engagement as critical to her survival, stressing that imprisoned women were treated like children rather than as adults:

> I do not believe that it will benefit me at all to sign this waiver however because I *enjoy* doing things with people, I put my name to it. If I'm told to do something that is degrading I will not do it, however. This waiver shd be revised to accommodate women rather than children.[22]

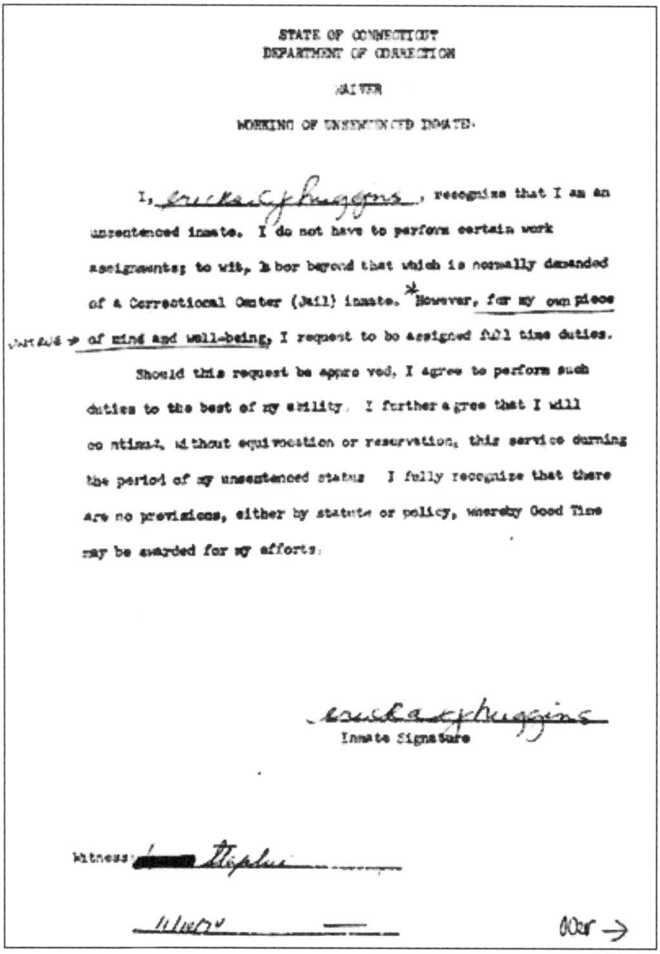

Figure 3.1. Connecticut Department of Correction waiver for Ericka Huggins, November 10, 1970.

By asserting her humanity and advocating for the collective agency of others with her written declaration and critique of the state, she insisted that Niantic treat women with dignity and respect.

Perhaps she was also responding to the part of the form that stated, "I fully recognize that there are no provisions, either by statute or policy, whereby Good Time may be awarded for my efforts," thereby making clear that work would not result in additional recreational time or a reduced prison sentence.[23] The prohibition of work rewards was a form of punishment inflicted by Niantic on pretrial detainees. Sewing clothes, in particular, did not bother Ericka, but housekeeping work annoyed her. "Everybody hated it," she remembered.[24] Still, most women tolerated it as it served as a respite from the long days of boredom.

Niantic officials designed the grounds to reproduce dormitory-style buildings. Today, the prison is known as Janet S. York Correctional Institution and spans 425 acres. When it underwent renovation in 1994 to include a maximum-security prison, it was named in honor of former deputy commissioner and warden Janet S. York. The State of Connecticut recognizes York as its only state prison for women.[25] I use the term "Niantic" because Ericka used it to refer to the prison when she was detained. Niantic, with its beautiful surroundings, including lakes and parks, enforced domestic work in its "cottage plan," described by Rafter as "holding groups of twenty or so inmates in small buildings where they could live with a motherly matron in a familial setting."[26] Yet the BPP women seldom saw the natural settings. The violent structure of Niantic overshadowed the public narrative of kindness and support. The façade of beauty could not erase prison officials' abuse and control of the BPP women. As Ericka put it, "I don't care what it looked like; I didn't have the keys."[27] Correctional officers restricted and monitored the BPP women's movement; ultimately, the exterior veneer did not change the suppression Niantic tried to enforce.

When the BPP women were first imprisoned, Niantic's population was 49.2 percent Black, 49.2 percent white, and 1.6 percent Puerto Rican.[28] Within a year, the percentage of Black imprisoned women rose to 56.8, while the percentage of white imprisoned women decreased to 35.1, and the percentage of Puerto Rican imprisoned women rose to 2.7.[29]

Niantic perpetuated state violence against pregnant women and their children. Eventually it built a nursery for mothers and their babies. The idea was to assist imprisoned mothers until their children reached the age of two.[30] The prison nursery was short-lived, however. The cost of caring for the increasing number of children became the state's excuse for closing the nursery, after only two years in existence.[31] Niantic had also contained a maternity ward and a maternity hospital for mothers, but both were long gone by the time of Ericka, Rose, Frances, Peggy, Maude, and Jeannie's imprisonment.[32] Niantic officials claimed to provide care for babies and postpartum mothers; however, in reality, they facilitated infant mortality. They did not have enough labor to manage the high number of infants served.[33] Two miles from Niantic lay the tiny bodies of babies of poor mothers imprisoned in Niantic from 1919 to 1967. The infants were buried in Angel Memorial, a special area in Union Cemetery to commemorate their precious lives ended because of state-sanctioned death.[34] Medical neglect, such as the lack of quality health care and vaccinations, resulted in preventable childhood diseases and cut their lives short.[35]

Lactating in Prison

Prison officers and officials denied mothers at Niantic all the rights of motherhood. For Ericka, the embodied experience of breastfeeding while imprisoned added to the already unspeakable stress of incarceration. As her breasts were engorged with milk and hardened, Ericka manually expressed milk, squeezing the breast to release the milk to ease the growing physical discomfort before Mai's first visit. The inability to expel her milk as her ducts filled would have placed her at great risk for a painful and dangerous breast infection. Manual expression of milk helped to prevent the worst symptoms of engorgement, but the fact that this was her only mechanism was an emotionally horrifying experience. Her previously fully breastfed daughter was permitted to visit only once a week.

The separation represented by the wasted breast milk was physically and emotionally painful. John's mother and Mai's paternal grandmother, Mrs. Huggins, took care of Mai during Ericka's incarceration. She made the forty-five-minute trip to Niantic each Saturday so that Ericka could maintain her mother/daughter bond. Ericka fiercely dedicated herself to maintaining a family and community outside the prison walls. Her family members and loved ones on the outside made significant sacrifices to emotionally care for the imprisoned and keep those bonds intact. Knowing that her daughter was safe also eased Ericka's mind.

Two days after Ericka's imprisonment, Mrs. Huggins brought Mai to visit. She placed Mai in Ericka's arms for her to nurse. As Ericka held Mai, a nurse swiftly approached the visitation area. She handed Ericka tiny dark red pills containing hormones to stop her milk production.[36]

"Take the pills," the nurse commanded, not for the first time. Ericka told the prison staff once again that she would not take the pills. She wanted to continue breastfeeding her baby.

Ericka was distraught. Her husband had been assassinated by the government only four months and seven days earlier. She lost precious years in her daughter's life and now, the state was also trying to take away the one sacred aspect of motherhood she could control—the ability to breastfeed her daughter. The state had already robbed her of so much of her life. It would not take that, too. "I was done with them," Ericka asserted, and then thought to herself, "What else do you want to suck out of me?"[37] While Ericka knew that she was unlikely to continue to produce adequate milk without the presence of her child, she did not want to be forced to relinquish her right to breastfeed.

Mrs. Huggins stared at the nurse in disbelief. Ericka remembered looking into her hand at the little red pills. "Should I throw them away and wait until next Saturday?" she wondered.[38] She hoped that refusing to take the pills would allow one more opportunity to breastfeed Mai. Ericka remembered her choices vividly: "I knew my body was not meant to take the pills. I didn't want to be sick. I wanted to be living and well for my daughter."[39] The following Saturday, the prison staff reported in a log that Ericka "did not come for 4 p.m. meds."[40] Ericka refused to take the medicine, in hopes that she would again be able to nurse Mai. Mrs. Huggins, irate, immediately questioned the lack of lactation services for Ericka.

"Can't we pump the milk?" she asked the authorities.
"No, we don't allow for that," they responded.[41]

Accommodating an imprisoned mother's desire to breastfeed was considered outlandish at the time. Their rebuff is only one example of the long history of state violence perpetrated on Black women's bodies. "They were doing this ostensibly to take care of me, that's how they put it. But that didn't take care of me," Ericka recalled.[42]

Ericka put off taking the pills as long as she could. "I kept trying to be brave about my breasts hurting," but it was evident that her breasts were painfully engorged. She was roughly one month shy of hitting the six-month mark of imprisonment before she was unable to endure the pain of engorgement any longer. She finally took the pills. "I knew at that moment, something about my connection with my daughter would be lost. And I was right."[43] She lost the emotional connection that comes from the warm hugs and snuggles she felt as she cradled Mai to breast-feed. Ericka mourned the loss, and it served as a driving force in her determination to care for other people.

With her other children, born after her release from prison, she breastfed for far longer. She nursed her oldest son, Rasa, for almost one year and her youngest son, Yadav, for three years. Breastfeeding has a dose/response relationship—the longer babies are breastfed, and the longer mothers breastfeed, the more likely both are protected from long- and short-term illnesses and other medical conditions. Thus, Ericka and Mai were deprived of more than the immediate benefits of breastfeeding—the state thus inserted itself into the budding relationship between Ericka and Mai.[44]

The shift from breastfeeding to bottle-feeding babies some form of animal milk began in the last quarter of the nineteenth century, as the United States urbanized and industrialized. By the late nineteenth century, rather than breastfeed for the customary two years, many women had begun to breastfeed for only months, often introducing cow's milk or adult foods to their infants as early as three to four months. According to historian Jacqueline Wolf, proprietary infant food companies originally appeared "to save orphaned and abandoned infants dying of diarrhea in foundling homes due to ingestion of spoiled and adulterated cow's milk."[45] The wares of these companies soon attracted the mothers who had begun to truncate breastfeeding. Physicians' sexist beliefs about women's bodies' ability to successfully breastfeed, coupled with the pasteurization of cow's milk by the 1920s and 1930s, contributed further to the increase in rates of women bottle-feeding.[46] By 1970, only 25 percent of American women initiated breastfeeding, defined as breastfeeding once before hospital discharge; two years later, breastfeeding reached an even lower point.[47] Bottle-feeding also tracks with women's employment outside the home, especially in jobs with no personal agency. This concern bears some structural resemblances to Ericka's experience in Niantic.

In the 1960s, public accommodations for any breastfeeding women did not exist, let alone accommodations for women who wanted to breastfeed in prison. Ericka's choice to breastfeed was heroic given that her decision was well outside the norm for the time. Breastfeeding was "intuitive" for Ericka and indicated that Mai easily latched and breastfed successfully; Ericka was especially pleased that human milk was free. She also knew that breastfeeding provided nutritional, immunological, social, and emotional benefits for the baby, and positive health outcomes for mothers, in addition to the economic ones.[48] In the present day, the American Academy of Pediatrics recommends that mothers exclusively breastfeed their babies for the first six months of life and then continue to breastfeed for a minimum of a year while also introducing other foods.[49]

As a women's prison, Niantic failed to accommodate lactating mothers and instead treated motherhood as a privilege, not a human right. Given that Niantic was a women's prison, Ericka insists to this day that prison officials could, and should, have dealt with breastfeeding differently. Ericka remembers once asking a woman officer who came to serve her food, "Why is it that they treat a mother this way? . . . Why isn't there a better option?" The officer leaned forward, responding sympathetically, "It's cruel," shaking her head in disappointment.[50] Ericka remembered that another woman officer offered to give her keys to the entry and exit doors so that she could walk out of prison in outrage at the unfair treatment she and the other BPP women were experiencing in Niantic. "I told her no, thank you, and she just started crying," Ericka remembered.[51] Some officers disliked the dehumanizing nature of prison and were remorseful about the treatment of the young BPP women.

Biases and assumptions about sexuality, immorality, and class also were embedded in Connecticut state laws from World War I through the 1960s. Young women from poor backgrounds and unwed pregnant women were locked up for violating "sexual norms." Outrageously, their "offenses" included being raped, sexually assaulted, or abused, engaging in consensual sexual activity, and the mere act of getting pregnant without being married.[52] The latter offenses conform to what Freedman identifies as "public order offenses . . . crimes against chastity or decency, applied almost exclusively to women," which date to the nineteenth century.[53] These gender norms shaped Niantic's history of Ericka's treatment during her incarceration as Black mothers were treated with particular contempt.

Ericka's ordeal with breastfeeding likely served as the reason for her excessive, sixty-hour stay in medical segregation.[54] Alongside Ericka, the other five women were also held in medical segregation longer than sixty hours. In 1970 Frances called comrades at the Black Panther newspaper. "We were supposed to get out of that 60 hour isolation, and they kept us there and they told us that we weren't going to get out," she explained.[55] The harrowing conditions experienced by the Black Panthers elicited a strategically planned protest by some imprisoned women. Frances explained that fellow imprisoned women staged a strike to display solidarity with the women. "They refused to do the linen," she explained.[56] Their prison strike illustrates care-based activism, a foundational aspect of the Black Panthers. Care work is communal and intended to engender new conditions for existence, which fostered spiritual wellness. Spiritual wellness involves mutual reciprocity. Those involved in the strike understood that their lives within the carceral state were intertwined with the fate of the Black Panther women.

On building an ethic of care, feminist historian Tiya Miles explains, "Our only options in this predicament, this state of political and planetary emergency, are to act as first responders."[57] In striking, the women served as "first responders" to the penal threat against the Black Panther women, whom they hardly knew. They were fighting not just for the survival of the Black Panther women but for their own survival.

While it is unknown how long the women were on strike, we do know that the extraction of prison labor prompted an angry response by Stewart H. Jones, the US attorney for Connecticut. "Keep them in there," he stated, referring to keeping them in medical isolation.[58] Jones's words reflect the inhumanity of the carceral state. Rather than letting them go, Niantic officials punished the Black Panther women for the prison strike, keeping the women in medical isolation indefinitely and prohibiting items associated with the Black Panther Party in the cells. Correctional officers subjected the BPP prisoners to constant bright lighting to intentionally impair their vision, time recognition, and mental health. "We had constant vamps [loud buzzing mercury-vapor lights] on our corridor; they took down our posters and everything because they say they don't want any political propaganda up on the walls. They said that Black Panther papers were contraband," Frances explained.[59] The contraband included reading materials and spirit-boosting items such as

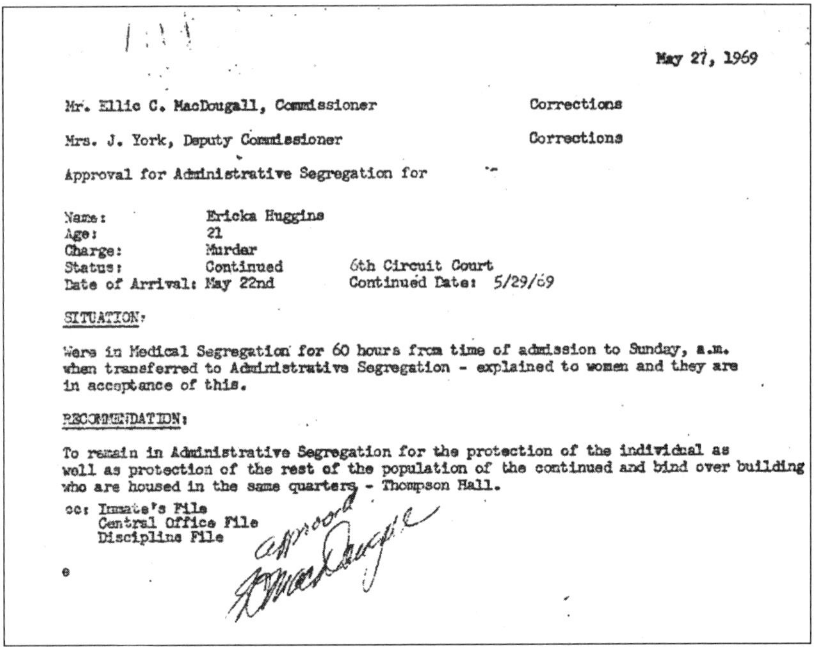

May 27, 1969

Mr. Ellie C. MacDougall, Commissioner — Corrections

Mrs. J. York, Deputy Commissioner — Corrections

Approval for Administrative Segregation for

Name:	Ericka Huggins		
Age:	21		
Charge:	Murder		
Status:	Continued	6th Circuit Court	
Date of Arrival:	May 22nd	Continued Date:	5/29/69

SITUATION:

Were in Medical Segregation for 60 hours from time of admission to Sunday, a.m. when transferred to Administrative Segregation - explained to women and they are in acceptance of this.

RECOMMENDATION:

To remain in Administrative Segregation for the protection of the individual as well as protection of the rest of the population of the continued and bind over building who are housed in the same quarters - Thompson Hall.

cc: Inmate's File
Central Office File
Discipline File

approved
E. MacDougall

Figure 3.2. Approval for administrative segregation for Ericka Huggins, May 27, 1969. Reprinted with permission from the Connecticut State Library, Hartford.

heartfelt letters from loved ones and supporters.[60] This action was another mechanism employed to break their psyche. Inevitably, they lost their sense of time and had difficulties keeping track of calendar days. Ericka and the others felt stuck in a kind of hell. They questioned prison officials' basic humanity.

Ericka's medical segregation ended roughly on May 25, 1969, but this was immediately followed by an administrative segregation, a kind of segregation in which she was isolated in a ward with the other BPP women.[61] The reason for her transfer from medical segregation remains unclear. Was it retaliation or a response to demands? A memo states that an explanation was provided to the women; however, explanatory details are excluded (figure 3.2). The state's language implies that the women agreed to seclusion. Niantic staff drafted the memo to appear as if they were ethical in their decisions, promoting the falsehood that the women had freely chosen their confinement.

In truth, the women had no control over their fate in Niantic and, according to Frances, they were locked in medical segregation for longer than sixty hours.[62] They were moved around several times without consent or information. They were the first political prisoners in Niantic's history, and the staff did not know what to do with them. The memo was intentionally edited to prevent culpability and protect the state. Prison officials and correctional officers believed in a myth of "Black vengeance" and feared the BPP women, claiming that they would stoke the emotions of others imprisoned, incite rebellion, and cause danger. It is unclear whether these fears were truly believed, or whether they were only an excuse for cruelty. Recall that some of these women the state deemed "dangerous" were pregnant. In any case, Niantic assigned a separate officer to police each woman; this officer abused and harmed the BPP women.

Administrative Segregation

Ericka hardly registered the day when she was awakened to the sound of footsteps and keys as officers entered her cell to transfer her downstairs to administrative segregation.[63] As they walked her down the hall, she asked where they were taking her. Her question was answered with stern silence. Rose, Frances, and Peggy joined Ericka in administrative segregation. Two days into their incarceration, officers transported Maude to a juvenile detention home in Hartford, Connecticut. On May 26, 1969, Jeannie was also discharged to juvenile detention.[64] Three days later, Niantic admitted Loretta Luckes on the same murder and kidnapping charges as the other women.[65] Like Frances and Rose, Loretta arrived pregnant.[66] Ericka and Frances claim that Loretta was not imprisoned with them but likely as a political prisoner, she was also placed in administrative segregation and experienced similar treatment as the others.[67]

Confinement in administrative segregation meant that they were kept in a double-locked ward in a large, dimly lit wing in Thompson Hall, Niantic's high-security building at the time, for almost twenty-four hours a day. Historian Akinyele Umoja explains that political prisoners are treated more inhumanely than others imprisoned. They are given maximum sentences and isolated from human contact in conditions that could damage their physical and intellectual capabilities. These state abuses are meant to punish activists, expunge them from their communities permanently, and, if possible, terrorize them into abandoning their political affiliations.[68] This treatment is traumatic because it is meant to disconnect people from love. The state terrorizes political prisoners and then cuts them off from the people who are supposed to help them cope with the terror. As political prisoners, the young women endured violence at every turn. Their sleep was interrupted by "excessive offensive and unnecessary noise from clanging cell bars, malfunctioning walkie-talkies, and lights at night."[69] They were beaten and refused adequate health care. Prison staff redacted their mail. According to Frances, because of this, it took "sometimes 15 days for [mail] to get from one place to another."[70] The mail delay and redaction of important materials were deliberate acts of abuse, inflicting severe emotional trauma. Frances's account described the daily experiences with isolation and high surveillance, familiar tactics of military interrogations and imprisonment. Sustenance was especially medieval. The food was uncommonly gross, characterized by the young women as gray and expired. Often those imprisoned were unable to identify the food served to them. Compounding the bleakness of the food was the prison's concrete décor.

The highly restricted light beige-colored wing that housed the young women consisted of cells on each side of a hallway. One side of the hallway included three cells, and the other side of the hallway contained two cells and a small kitchen area with chairs and a borrowed black-and-white television. The cold, damp wing contained a small bathroom, and a rickety AM radio lay on the floor plugged into the wall in the hallway.[71] Inside the cell, the floors were painted a dreadful dark beige color with light tan walls in a yellow tint. Each cell consisted of a single bed and a sink, all made of steel, a barred window, and a heavy locked door made of wood.[72] Each morning at 7:00 a.m., a matron unlocked the young women's cells for showers and breakfast, and only then were they allowed to move around the ward under supervision until lights out at 9:00 p.m. At that time, a matron double-locked them in their cells.[73]

It was in administrative segregation that the young women were able to reconnect since laying eyes on one another their first day in Niantic. They felt dehumanized but relieved to see and touch one another. Ericka was grateful to see them. "We just sort of embraced and cried and sort of rejoiced at the same time that we were all very much alive," Frances explained.[74] Frances and her sister, Peggy, worried deeply about each other. It had been twenty-four hours since they reunited in administrative segregation. The mental stress took a physical toll on Frances, disabling her in a way that caused her to develop a severe migraine, throat irritation, heavy sweating, and constant nosebleeds. After she made several requests for medical attention, an officer gave her medicine for her migraine.[75] Frances and Peggy held tight to each other. Their sisterhood was unbreakable. Ericka's recollection of her first day in administrative segregation contrasted slightly with Frances's. She noted that she did not cry, but Rose and Frances wept often. Peggy was the most stoic of the group, possibly resulting from her arthritis, which placed her in constant pain. Ericka believed that the agony she experienced might have prevented her from shedding any tears.

The BPP women were on alert. They watched the correctional officers and listened to their movements intently. Ericka's paranoia increased as Frances and Peggy began to compare their brutal experiences under police custody. She knew that they were under the watchful eye of the FBI's COINTELPRO program. "Look, just don't talk because this whole place is bugged," Ericka demanded. If she had any hope of seeing her infant daughter again, she needed to be cautious and encourage the others to do the same. "*You* don't talk!" Frances retorted. Peggy agreed with her sister. Ericka glared at them. "It was like if you didn't, your whole head would split wide open," Frances explained in reference to Ericka's matter-of-fact tone.[76] Or was it something else? In reading Frances's interview, I could see that she was trying to make sense of her trauma and incoherence. Ericka's desire for silence and Frances and Peggy's inability to give her silence reflect the paranoia, fear, and anxiety that they all felt. They had no sense of safety. Ericka felt safe in silence; however, Frances and Peggy felt safer processing with one another. Ericka's emphasis on silence was a response to the real threat of prison surveillance, a state apparatus akin to the racist campaign of COINTELPRO. As radical Black women activists, they were still seen as dangerous.

It was under these circumstances that Ericka began her physical spiritual practices, including meditation and yoga. Both helped her cope with being separated from her five-month-old daughter. She thought of Mai a lot, and often pulled out her photo, which she kept hidden in her cell. It was forbidden to put pictures or art on the walls in administrative isolation. When Ericka looked at it, she thought about how Mai was new and sweet and delicate. She was the spitting image of John, her love, who was no longer with them. Mai was hitting milestones that she was missing. She could smile, coo, roll over, and was likely learning to sit up on her own. Ericka grieved the time lost with her child, especially given that the first year of an infant's life includes the fastest and most intense growth. Ericka missed Mai's smell, her squishy thighs, her soft tufts of hair; she missed nourishing her with her body.

Frances and Peggy

Frances and Peggy would huddle and continue to share and converse. How did they end up here, in prison? they asked themselves. They tried to put the pieces together, to make sense of it. They reflected on "every entire little thing" in their BPP experiences since they joined as teenagers. They went back and forth and replayed moments. "We were pointing out different things where we should have been," Frances explained.[77] They wished they would have asked more questions as BPP members. Even so, Frances acknowledged that she felt empty without the BPP. She missed the organization she had come to love.

Prior to her imprisonment, the culture in the New Haven chapter had begun to shift from a pleasurable atmosphere to one of uncertainty. With these changes, Frances had a premonition that darkness would descend upon the New Haven chapter. She no longer recognized the organization. Before she knew it, there was "this whole nightmare that broke out" involving Alex Rackley's torture and murder. Expressing deep sorrow about the internal culture of the BPP that bent toward violence out of fear and infiltration, Frances stated, "we should have felt more."[78] What Frances meant was twofold. First, they should have known better; they should have paid more attention to the deep state violence against Black activism. She might have ignored this as a youth. Perhaps the draw to the BPP caused her to feel empowered and invincible, as youth tend to feel. I read this moment as an indication of spiritual wellness. "We should have felt more" is a response to liberation that was dependent upon the body and soul. This means trusting inner feelings and intuitions. Frances was compelled to join the BPP because of its tenets, which defined revolutionary activism as care work. Black people needed to feel the fullness of humanity from their partnerships to their children and to their love of self. The infiltration and internal violence crushed a love and care ethic from within. The treatment of the BPP women in prison was intended to strip them of their humanity, mentally, physically, and socially. In prison, these young women were fighting to feel human, and to protect their identities as women and mothers.

After rehashing their BPP experiences, Frances and Peggy were still confused as to what landed them in prison. They hoped that the police would "realize they made a mistake" and release them.[79] As time progressed, they soon understood the seriousness of the matter. They learned that BPP member Alex Rackley was brutally murdered, and they were being falsely accused of the crime. In her interview, Frances laughed as she imagined her parents coming to Niantic. "We told you so," she believed her father would say.[80] The day Frances and Peggy informed their parents that they joined the BPP before their imprisonment, their parents received the news with disapproval and shock. In defense of their actions, Frances replied, "You don't understand. See, these folks say they're gonna effect some change. We're gonna have a revolution." Mr. Carter was outraged. "BULLSHIT!!! What do you MEAN?" he rebuked. Frances knew that her father "moved into the white community to be accepted, and we're talking about tearing that down."[81] This was a measure of Frances's disagreement with what she believed to be the naivete of her own parents.

Mr. and Mrs. Carter were trying to raise proper suburbanite children, not activists. They moved to the white suburbs in hopes of giving their children a better life, but upward mobility can come with anti-Blackness you must fight against. While the white suburbs were not safe havens, they provided access to class betterment; however, for Black people, white suburban life involved isolation, which potentially helped to radicalize Frances and Peggy. The Carters were law-abiding entrepreneurs. They owned a barber shop on Stratford Avenue, an inner-city neighborhood in Bridgeport, but they lived in the fancy white suburb of Trumbull.

Mr. Carter knew that his young Black suburban daughters were unaware of the depths of racial injustices they were about to endure as Black Panthers. He instructed his wife to call a psychiatrist. Clearly, there were some heated conversations, resulting in harsh, emotional ramifications that ultimately tore the family apart. "He wanted us to go lay on a couch somewhere," Frances recalled. "These girls have gone crazy. What's wrong with them, Helen?" he asked his wife. Frances was puzzled because her father instructed them not to hang out on Stratford Avenue. "You didn't want us down there on Stratford Avenue no more, hanging out. So, we decided to change that [by joining the Black Panthers]," she remembered telling her father. "Take a bath for two or three days, at least?" he instructed them. "You're brainwashed. You need some deprogramming," their parents continued. In the end, their father gave them an ultimatum, forcing them to choose between living with them or serving in the BPP. "You know, I wish you didn't say that," Peggy replied to her father.[82] Mr. and Mrs. Carter's ultimatum was a persuasive strategy to keep Frances and Peggy out of the BPP. They hoped that they would not want to lose the comforts of home. They chose the BPP. While their parents were invested in their middle-class status, Frances and Peggy knew that that status was temporary.

Frances and Peggy believed in the Black Panther practice of determining your own destiny. At the time, they felt, "We're just learning how to believe in something else—in different values and different things—and especially things that affected us. We had such a quest to learn, so we're willing to give up and make a lot of sacrifices. . . . It hurt a lot, and it hurt them. . . . We just asked them to please understand."[83] They yearned to be independent thinkers and embark on their own journey. It hurt to go against their parents' wishes, but for Frances and Peggy, revolution meant being a part of an organization that nourished, fed, protected, and established a sense of community, one expanded beyond the narrowness of the white supremacist idea of the nuclear family. In their decision to forsake their parents, Frances and Peggy wanted to join a broader family within the BPP. I consider their choice to become part of the BPP family political and a form of care work. They understood that the BPP was trying to recreate the blood-tie intimacy that they already had as sisters. They listened to their hearts.

As Black Panthers, Frances and Peggy were able to engage in acts of care with their community work. They learned how to love passionately in a way that affirmed the humanity of Black people. As their case became local headline news, they thought to themselves, "Oh, Mom and Dad can't find out. (Maybe they won't see it?)"[84] They were apprehensive about the potential media portrayal of them and their case, fearing that their parents would come across the coverage and be negatively affected emotionally. Their primary concern was their parents' well-being. Frances leaned on her big sister to survive prison and took her lead. "I was the type that always primarily followed. If Peggy would start something, I would just automatically join," she recollected. "I don't think I would have probably left home, if it weren't us leaving together," she added. Without Peggy, Frances believed, her days in Niantic would have been relentless. "I was a little more serious than Peggy," she said. Peggy was lighthearted, "bubbly, and had so much life."[85] Peggy kept Frances's spirits lifted and drew on her strength. After being separated from Peggy during their arrest, Frances wanted to always have her big sister by her side.

> I never wanted to be separated from her anymore. . . . I don't care what it was. We were going together, and we made a pact that that would never happen to us again. So, the best thing in the world was that we were together during the whole ordeal. Which tended to be very hard on my parents, but the best thing in the world for each of us. They didn't understand that. But then I had faith.[86]

They depended on each other, instinctively looking out for and caring for each other. Their pact symbolized their loyalty to each other as sisters. Frances was grateful to be in prison with her sister and maintained faith that they would one day get their freedom. However, their incarceration weighed heavily on their parents, as it pained them to have either of their children in prison.

Resisting Carceral Violence through Care Work

Ericka, Frances, Peggy, Rose, and Loretta endured state interrogation multiple times without their lawyers' permission. Each woman was taken separately by correctional officers for FBI interrogation. They employed a "divide and conquer" technique through intimidation and fear in search of a confession.[87] Two FBI officers interrogated Ericka about Bobby Seale and Alex Rackley, among others. Ericka composed herself during the interviews, made eye contact with the officers, and maintained her silence, stating only her name. To get her to speak, they offered her a deal. "We'll get you a boyfriend, and you can leave for a day, Huggins," one of the agents said. Ericka resisted the urge to laugh aloud. The two officers looked at one another as if to say, What are we going to do now?

"Are you both done?" Ericka asked.
"You're uncooperative," fumed one of the officers.

A matron escorted Ericka back to her cell, and she burst into laughter. Ericka's account illustrated the absurd tactics of the FBI and the assumption that the BPP women were ignorant and easily swayed.[88] It is also likely that they were interrogated multiple times even as Ericka scoffed at the idea of ever revealing anything.

Around dawn each day, the young women heard footsteps approaching. Officer Walsh, a short, heavyset white man, keyed into their wing carrying something resembling breakfast on a Styrofoam tray and coffee without much sugar or milk to put in it. If a matron was unavailable, he brought the food. At times, he would let other officers know that he was bringing food to the BPP women. "I'm in the wing feeding the Panthers," he would announce over his walkie-talkie. Ericka, Rose, Frances, and Peggy responded in laughter. "Are we in a zoo?" Ericka replied aloud.[89] They used humor in a subversive way to throw the ridicule back at the state. Officer Walsh placed the tray on the kitchenette table and proceeded to unlock each of the young women's cells. Despite the food items listed on the breakfast, lunch, and dinner menu, it was nearly impossible for Ericka to describe them because they were indiscernible. The women considered the meals disgusting and referred to meat products as "mystery meat."[90] While the menu reproduced in figure 3.3 is more contemporary and very different from the actual meals during the incarceration of the Black Panthers, it still represents unexplainable foods that are highly processed and high in sugar and salt. It is laden with redundancy, and none of the food groups contributed to a balanced or nutritious diet.

In prison, food was its own form of punishment. Much of the time, the food was rotten or expired. Ericka described the food as disgusting and the same color: gray, adding that any gravy, bread, rice, and potatoes served were routinely white. Even cooked vegetables were gray.

CYCLE: 1   York CI   CONNECTICUT D.O.C. MENU

Day	BREAKFAST	LUNCH	SUPPER
SUNDAY	Applesauce (4 oz) Oatmeal (8 oz) Cottage Cheese (4 oz) White Milk 1% (8 oz) Coffee (8 oz) Sugar (4 tsp) 4 packets	Roast Beef Stew (8 oz) C.F. Fish (1 ea) C.F. Tartar Sauce (1 oz) Gravy (3 oz) Mashed Potatoes (1 cup) Green beans (1/2 cup) White Milk 1% (8 oz) 100% Whole Wheat Bread (2 slices)	Chicken Cacciatore (8 oz) C/F Meatless Cacciatore (8 oz) Pasta Elbows (1 cup) Mixed Vegetables (1/2 cup) Ice Cream (1 ea) Beverage (8 oz)
MONDAY	Fresh Fruit (1 ea) Boiled Eggs (2 ea) Grits (8 oz) 100% Whole Wheat Bread (2 slices) White Milk 1% (8 oz) Coffee (8 oz) Sugar (4 tsp) 4 packets	Chicken and Gravy (8 oz) C.F. Meatless Chicken & Gravy (8 oz) Rice (1 cup) Carrots (1/2 cup) White Milk 1% (8 oz)	Chicken Sausage Pattie (1 ea) Cheese (1 slice) C.F. Sausage Veg. Pattie (3 oz) Mashed Potatoes (1 cup) 100% Whole Wheat Roll (1 ea) Cabbage (1/2 cup) Jello (4 oz) Beverage (8 oz)
TUESDAY	5 Citrus Juice (4 oz) Farina (8 oz) Yogurt (4 oz) Bran Muffin Square (1/48) White Milk 1% (8 oz) Coffee (8 oz) Sugar (4 tsp) 4 packets	Hot Dogs (2 ea) C.F. Veggie Patty (1 ea) Vegetarian Baked Beans (1 cup) Sauerkraut (1/2 cup) Bread (white-2 slices) Mustard (1 oz) White Milk 1% (8 oz)	Chicken Ala King (8 oz) C.F. Meatless Ala King (8 oz) Brown Rice (1 cup) Peas (1/2 cup) Sugar Cookies (2 each) Beverage (8 oz)
WEDNESDAY	Grapefruit Juice (4 oz) French Toast (2 ea) Syrup (3 oz) Corn Flakes (1 pkg) White Milk 1% (8 oz) Coffee (8 oz) Sugar (4 tsp) 4 packets	Tossed Salad (1 cup) Chicken (3 oz) Garbanzo Beans (1/2 cup) Italian Dressing (2 oz) C.F. Boiled Eggs (2 ea) Peaches (1/2 cup) 100% Whole Wheat Bread (2 slices) White Milk 1% (8 oz)	Popcorn Chicken (8 oz) C.F. Fish Patty (1 ea) Rice (1 cup) General T's Sauce (2 oz) Carrots (1/2 cup) Fresh Fruit (1 ea) Beverage (8 oz)
THURSDAY	Apple Juice (4 oz) Oatmeal (8 oz) Bran Muffin Square (1/48) White Milk 1% (8 oz) Coffee (8 oz) Sugar (4 tsp) 4 packets Peanut Butter (1 oz)	Chicken Patty (1 ea) Chickenless Patty (Vegetarian) (1 ea) C.F. Mayo (1 oz) Rice (1 cup) Mayonaise (1 oz) California Blend Veg. (1/2 cup) Bread (2 slices) White Milk 1% (8 oz)	Meat Loaf (1 ea) C.F. Veggie Patty (1 ea) Mashed Potatoes (1 cup) Gravy (3 oz) Green Peas (1/2 cup) Fresh Fruit (1 ea) Beverage (8 oz) 100% Whole Wheat Bread (2 slices)
FRIDAY	Grapefruit Juice (4 oz) High Fiber Hot Cereal (8 oz) Corn Square (1/48) White Milk 1% (8 oz) Coffee (8 oz) Sugar (4 tsp) 4 packets	Peanut Butter & Jelly (3 oz ea) C.F. Same Whole Wheat Pasta Salad (1 cup) Cole Slaw (3/4 cup) Fresh Fruit (1 ea) Bread (white - 2 slices) White Milk 1% (8 oz)	Fish Patty (1 ea) C.F. Same Tartar Sauce (1 oz) Rice (1 cup) Collard Greens (1/2 cup) 100% Whole Wheat Bread (2 slices) Applesauce (1/2 cup) Beverage (8 oz)
SATURDAY	Cranberry Juice (4 oz) Boiled Eggs (2 ea) Grits (8 oz) 100% Whole Wheat Bread (2 slices) White Milk 1% (8 oz) Coffee (8 oz) Sugar (4 tsp) 4 packets	Beef Patty (1 ea) C.F. Veggie Patty (3 oz) Cheese (1 slice) Mashed Potatoes (1 cup) Corn (1/2 cup) Roll (1 ea) Ketchup (1 oz) White Milk 1% (8 oz)	Sloppy Joe (8 oz) C.F. Meatless Sloppy Joe (8 oz) Rice (1 cup) Gr. Beans (1/2 cup) Pudding (1/2 cup) Beverage (8 oz)

MENU SUBJECT TO CHANGE, ANY CHANGE MUST BE APPROVED PRIOR.   WP-GHTS = COOKED PRODUCT
C/A WI. YORK   ROBERT J. DeVeau, RD., CD-N I-53637

REVISED 5-4-16 @ 11:00 a.m.

Figure 3.3. Food menu, York Correctional Institution, May 4, 2016. "C/F" means common fare for those with vegetarian or plant-based dietary restrictions.

Processed food was normal fare. Fish and fruits were rare and, when provided, they were always canned. There were no vitamins and supplements. Malnourishment was common. But some imprisoned women cultivated solidarity if they could. Those who worked in the kitchen would discreetly add extra food to the trays of the BPP women, accompanied with a concealed caring note so that the correctional officers remained unaware.

The BPP women treated one another with tenderness and compassion as they took care of one another. This included caring for those in the group who were medically ill and pregnant. They would give Frances and Rose the better parts of their food. "If there ever were vegetables or fruit, we would give almost everything to them," Ericka added.[91] But it was hard for them to eat what they were offered. The food made Frances sick. The smell made her queasy and nauseated. She was unable to consume the food and sometimes cried when the hunger pangs were unbearable.

Later, when the BPP women started going to court, the items given to them by friends and supporters offered them comfort and respite from their ill-treatment in solitary. Frances recalled how Peggy was the "the most beautiful person" in her "big and wide" Afro. She would take what people gave her in court at her hearings, such as cigarettes and marijuana, and "stick them in her hair," sharing them with the BPP women upon her return. Marijuana likely curbed any nausea the BPP women were experiencing. Frances laughingly described how Peggy would come from court, take the items out of her hair, "stretch a little bit," and "light a cigarette."[92] Peggy's subversive measures in solitary brought her joy and solace. This story also points to the significance of hair as an aspect of the spiritual wellness practices that would inspire Ericka's collective activism after she was transferred out of solitary and into the mainstream population.

As the days came and went, the BPP women fell into a wellness rhythm to protect themselves against neglect and violence in solitary. They collaboratively used their commissary (money from work, families, and friends) to supply themselves with toiletries, feminine products, and other essentials.[93] Ericka could not remember whether they had ever requested essentials from the BPP's Free Commissary for Prisoners Program, which operated through sponsorships that facilitated purchasing and distributing items to prisoners in need.[94] If they did, they would have shared those resources. They worked together on tasks, including keeping their wing clean. Whenever they engaged in tasks together, they turned on the radio and sang along to the music. They pulsed to the tunes of artists like the Young Rascals, Stevie Wonder, Sly and the Family Stone, Diana Ross and the Supremes, the Temptations, Peter, Paul and Mary, Tammy Wynette, Neil Diamond, and the Beatles. Music gave them pleasure and served as a temporary respite from confinement.

All the young women also worked collaboratively to keep Peggy safe and as comfortable as possible. She had crippling rheumatoid arthritis that worsened during her imprisonment due to the frigid cement floors and cold temperatures in prison, especially during the winter months. Because Niantic intentionally denied Peggy the care she needed, she often experienced excruciating pain and stiffness in her joints, making it difficult for her to move. In the mornings, when she awakened, her pain was so severe, she could not pull back her bed cover or get out of the bed. She felt the coldness penetrating her body. With her inflamed joints locked in place, she needed help. It became common practice for Ericka, Rose, and Frances to assist Peggy out of the bed and throughout the wing, as needed. Even in their fragile state, Frances and Rose lifted Peggy to move her around. As a form of spiritual wellness, they offered communal care and protection in the face of Niantic's cruel treatment.

The Violence Frances Suffered While Giving Birth in Prison

One of the most difficult situations the women would face involved Frances's labor and subsequent isolation. Months into her imprisonment, Frances gave birth under torturous conditions.[95] Although the medical professionals were aware that Frances required a cesarean section, they opted to prolong her labor for a duration of twenty-three hours. It was only when her baby boy began to emerge—in distress with a deformed head—that they finally gave her a cesarean section.[96] Then they gave her medication that she made a deliberate effort to remember. She wanted to be able to "tell Katy [Catherine Roraback] or John [Williams, her lawyers] or somebody when they came, exactly what I was ingesting."[97] Like the rest of the BPP women, she did not trust the doctors and considered them "rejects from their profession."[98] She wanted to avoid prison doctors at all costs, but Niantic refused to grant her permission to use her own doctor to deliver her baby.[99] As if all this were not enough, many FBI agents, police, and matrons were in the labor room. She vividly recalled their laughter. "They were . . . laughing and making light of the fact that they were just letting me lay there and suffer. . . . It was bad."[100] The state officials took pleasure in her misery as medical professionals denied her timely care when it was needed most. There is a question as to whether Frances was shackled during the process of childbirth. While Frances does not explicitly address the issue of being restrained during childbirth in her interview with Lewis Cole, it is justifiable to contemplate this possibility, given the inhumaneness of her labor experience as a political detainee, and given that it was not until 2018 that Connecticut passed anti-shackling legislation for pregnant women.[101] After her delivery, the police persisted in their cruelty by using her baby as leverage to interrogate her again. Frances recalled the police officer saying,

> "Well, you got a choice. You just had this little baby, and I know you want to be home with him and what are you gonna do. . . . Tell us about this one, tell us about that one."
> "Tell you what?!! I don't know what to tell you!!!!"
> "Ohhhhh, yeeees, you do, yeeees, you do," he replied.[102]

In the face of state taunting, Frances maintained her silence. Their refusal to allow her mother-infant bonding time placed her baby at risk of experiencing skin hunger due to the absence of human touch. She only saw her baby boy, Osceola, "maybe twice throughout the whole time."[103] Her mother and one of her siblings came to get Osceola.[104] As indicated in Frances's story as well as Ericka's, intergenerational family care, particularly by grandmothers, was pivotal in keeping children out of foster care and connected to their biological mothers.

While we don't have an account of Rose's or Loretta's delivery, we know that they had their babies in prison and most likely endured similar brutal treatment as Frances. According to Frances, Rose's baby went into the care of a white couple.[105] Given that Loretta was taken to Lawrence + Memorial Hospital on January 21, 1970, as indicated on her prisoner index card, it is likely that she gave birth on that day.[106] It is unknown whether Rose or Loretta were placed in the medical wing after their delivery, as Frances was.

In the medical wing, Frances did not receive any postnatal care. She was sick, frail, hungry, dehydrated, under the influence of multiple prescription drugs, and now weighed ninety pounds, roughly forty pounds lighter than on the first day of her imprisonment.[107] They did a poor job of suturing her after her delivery. The wounds were now open and seeping. She described it as "the nastiest thing anyone would ever want to see."[108] She urgently needed medical attention, but they never washed her body or changed her bandages. As a result, she developed gangrene. "I was stinking. . . . I was full of crabs. . . . I was just like rotting away," she recalled.[109] She needed support and help and attempted to advocate for herself. Niantic punished her for doing that by placing her in solitary confinement for roughly a month.[110]

In solitary, she was still denied care. Food was brought to her and placed underneath what she called a "small thing in the door," but rats often got to it first.[111] Her grievances about her medical conditions were met with scorn. Correctional officers would open the door to let her out of the dark solitary room and lead her to another small area for ten minutes, during which she continued her plea for water and a bath.

"Any water, or something? I could wash. . . . This thing is getting worse."
"Oh, fuck you. We don't care if you die," the matrons raged.[112]

The matrons were trying to kill Frances. In the interview, she pointed out how they did not open her door to give her food, but did so after her request for water and for the medication they forced on her while also throwing water at her. She refused the medication.[113] The violence Frances endured speaks to the brutal lengths Niantic went to immobilize women. Her experience with forced medication paralleled that of others. Many imprisoned women believed that the drug saltpeter was laced in their food to keep them subdued and complacent.[114] Many were confident that Niantic wanted to keep women sluggish, not only with the saltpeter but also with a high-carbohydrate diet.

Frances was in such poor health that she was not able to go back and forth to court. She believed that prison officials did not want those in the courtroom to see how sick she was and that they were worried she would tell others what she was experiencing in solitary. She was incensed by their tortuous treatment. "You can kill the revolutionary, but you can't kill the revolution," she bellowed to the matrons, using a phrase from Fred Hampton's 1969 speech.[115] "They will tear this whole place apart," she continued to rage. "There will be bombs all over the place! The skies will light up."[116] She was driven to speak aloud despite the threat of violence because of her understanding of herself as just one part of a larger liberation project. Frances's language is powerful but also recognizably hyperbolic, inspired by the torture of her incarceration. In other words, she lashed out, but it was clear that her threats couldn't be enacted as such. The threat of bombs on the prison was directly aimed at the state and its property; it is also metaphoric in the ultimate quest to dismantle white supremacy. In the interview, she explained, "I was still trying to get to [the matrons]," to buttress herself against further psychological harm.[117] She resisted the process of the psychological onslaught of solitary confinement by disrupting their comfort with the logic and violence of the state. With the help of an unknown person, perhaps a fellow prisoner, who brought her food through her cell door, she sent Peggy a message to give to Katy Roraback, her lawyer at the time. "Please get to Peggy. Tell Peggy to call Katy right away."[118] That same unknown person also offered Frances the care she needed in order to stay alive. By colluding with a BPP member, they risked punishment by association, yet recognized the extent of white supremacy. Akiba Solomon and Kenrya Rankin argue that white supremacist violence relies on the notion that "it makes civilized sense that one group of people gets to annihilate, enslave, incarcerate, brainwash, torture, sterilize, breed, and terrorize other people."[119] Frances's experience reflected the grotesque approach the state took toward Black women, pregnant bodies, and their future. The person who brought her food resisted this logic through an understanding of Frances's humanity and her right to seek liberation. In that way, it was a deed of spiritual wellness.

For days, Frances heard footsteps sprinting above. She assumed it was Ericka, Peggy, and Rose running from the correctional officers, as they sometimes did while on walks. Officers Hoffman, Cohen, and Douglas were gasping for air as they chased them.[120] Frances hollered in despair for help. To her delight, they answered. They were thrilled to hear from her as they were uncertain where she was. She shared the horrific details of her labor and treatment in solitary, and they immediately informed Katy Roraback, who filed a habeas corpus claim for her release from her punitive confinement.[121] It was Ericka, Peggy, and Rose's care work that got Frances released from solitary, although it is important to note that Frances and Ericka have competing memories of these events. For example, Ericka does not recall running from correctional officers, which begs the question of how Frances let her friends know that she needed legal help from Katy Roraback.

Frances was soon released on bail from Niantic due to insufficient evidence, but only for a brief time before the prosecution summoned her to testify in court.[122] She chose "to reject the 'bribe,'" which placed her in contempt of court and bond revocation, a decision that cost her more time away from Osceola. She was not willing to "sell out" her fellow BPP comrades. As she explained in the BPP newspaper the *Black Panther*, Frances "knew that justice could only be had for a price, and in this case, the price was too high to pay."[123]

If the prison's greatest weapon was neglect, the ultimate tools of resistance were care and compassion. Defiance and activism were pivotal. Solitary confinement was used to break the spirit, but the spirit of these women proved unyielding. By cultivating bonds and inspiring care, they managed to survive despite institutional neglect. Shortly thereafter, the incarcerated women resorted to hunger strikes to protest the lack of prenatal and postnatal care for pregnant women, as well as the substandard nutrition and horrific prison conditions. Ericka soon initiated her wellness practices of meditation and yoga.

4

Surviving Solitary

Inner peace is a journey. Self-care strategies (like meditation, music, prayer, yoga, and exercise) are vehicles on this journey. Stressors are events that inhibit smooth travel on our journey, and chronic stress may stop our movement on the journey to inner peace altogether. The struggle for inner peace is real, but manageable.
—Stephanie Y. Evans

How does self-care relate to political activism? If Ericka's life story is instructive at all, it highlights the significance of wellness—both personal, within the BPP, and in the larger Black community—as an integral aspect of the history of political prisoners in the United States. The history of the BPP women is a testament to the critical importance of wellness of self and others to our understanding of the history of political prisoners and also their radical survival practices. In the previous chapter, I revealed how Ericka's story shines a light on the communal effort put forth by BPP women to love and affirm themselves and others when imprisoned. In this chapter, I center on Ericka's attention to self and demonstrate how this attention is equally vital to the care-based communal activism that saved the lives of so many imprisoned BPP women. Ericka was grappling with multiple forms of mourning and grief when incarcerated, reeling from the loss of John and her separation from her newborn, Mai. She wanted to be alive and well during Mai's weekly Saturday visits, recognizing the need for inner strength to meet her goal, especially given the challenges of her imprisonment. Ericka turned to yoga and meditation, practices that had transformative effects on her mind, body, and spirit. These tools were rooted in a rich history of Black women's wellness practices in social justice circles, a subject thoroughly explored by historian Stephanie Y. Evans, which I will turn to momentarily.

Drawing from this historical context, I examine how Ericka's use of these tools aligned with the self-care practices of other BPP women. Together, their practices reveal the array of protest methods BPP women had at their disposal, including hunger strikes, self-defense against physical assault by correctional officers, and the use of humor. I emphasize the importance of their self-care, and Ericka's in particular, and encourage scholars and enthusiasts of the BPP and social justice movements to recognize how individual self-care is central to community building and serves as an effective means of counteracting violence in prison.

Yoga and Meditation

Unsure of how to proceed with improving her wellness, Ericka turned to Charles Garry, Bobby's lawyer, whose yoga practice involved daily headstand postures.[1] When Ericka asked Charles Garry for a book on yoga, he gave her Jess Stearn's *Yoga, Youth, and Reincarnation* (1965). Stearn recounts his spiritual journey through yoga while living in Massachusetts. Yoga involves both the mind and body through meditation and the practice of physical postures. In his book, Stearn explains that hatha yoga "developed the physical side" while other types of yoga styles engaged "the meditative, apparently enhanced by the mind control developed through the physical exercises."[2] The postures and breathwork align to balance the mind and body, forming a union. Stearn's interpretation of hatha yoga enabled Ericka to transform her time behind prison walls, and the practice became her salve. With her yoga practice, Ericka repurposed the solitary nature of prison, finding moments to connect with her mind and body.

Ericka practiced yoga in the late 1960s and 1970s, when yoga was reaching a larger audience because of the "Eastern" and/or non-Western ways of knowing embraced by leftists and hippies.[3] According to historian Stephanie Y. Evans, Black radicals of the 1960s and 1970s such as Angela Y. Davis also practiced yoga as a form of wellness and care. In fact, as early as 1965, Rosa Parks, in her early fifties at the time, was practicing and teaching yoga classes.[4] Rosa, Ericka, and Angela are part of a legacy that Evans calls "Africana yoga, [which,] simply put, is Black women's tradition of inner peace practice."[5] Today, yoga is often primarily packaged and advertised to thin, wealthy, white women. Evans reminds us of the long history of Black women's engagement in East Asian and Indian practices and argues that "a Black women's tradition exists alongside holistic health practices around the world." She adds that these "unique (sometimes overlapping) pathways to holistic health and personal power" illustrate the creative capacity of Black women to attend to their wellness and care for their mind, body, and soul.[6] This is the practice I call spiritual wellness. Spiritual wellness is about connecting to oneself and the larger community. Through yoga, Ericka prepared herself to work for her community—her child, her friends, and those in the struggle for Black liberation.

Given that time can be considered elusive, and those imprisoned are not in control of it, Ericka's yoga and meditation practice did not begin as a practice that she started at the same time daily. Niantic dictated the daily schedule for those imprisoned, so Ericka squeezed in yoga when she could—after breakfast in the mornings, in the afternoons, or the evening before being locked in her cell. Most days, she would only have thirty minutes to practice self-care; more time was a luxury that she was not afforded. State evidence corroborates that Ericka and the other BPP women were allotted only thirty minutes for exercise. In Ericka's prison conduct log, it is briefly noted that the young women "went to exercise for ½ hour."[7]

For Ericka, exercise primarily consisted of yoga and meditation, although it could have varied for other BPP women, who may have exercised in different ways. Ericka did not recall her compatriots doing yoga. In the small hallway in the solitary wing, Ericka practiced hatha yoga, making do with the confined space available for her to stretch her tall, thin body and practice the postures. She taught herself yoga by mimicking the black-and-white photos of poses in the training pages of the book. She positioned her body in downward facing dog and forward bends, among other poses, and followed Stearn's instructions to sit quietly and follow your breath. Ericka gained great mental and physical strength from yoga. Yoga stopped the arthritis joint stiffness she had experienced since her teenage years. Yoga afforded her mind respite, allowing Ericka to mentally escape from imprisonment, albeit momentarily. Yoga facilitated her meditation practice; sitting still and taking notice of her breath cultivated her own sense of freedom, sustaining her in a system that held her in solitary confinement for nearly twenty-four hours a day.

Yoga provided her with the tools to be fully in the moment and to cultivate a sense of calm and fortitude despite the challenges of imprisonment. Ericka's desire not to forfeit her connection to Mai motivated her yoga practice. She wanted to develop a sense of gratitude: "I went into prison teaching myself to meditate, not wanting to take my life for granted, not wanting to take my baby for granted, not wanting to take my friends and family for granted." She added that yoga "helped me to love Mai at a distance and to remain attuned to her for that one hour each Saturday that I was able to visit with her."[8] After a visit, Ericka remembered, "I would go back in my cell and cry, but while I was with her, I was fully present."[9] Yoga became increasingly critical as Mai began to walk and talk. Ericka felt that it "was really important that she did not see me as a wilted flower and that she saw me being happy to see her."[10] Given that Mai was only an infant, Ericka was unsure whether Mai understood that she was her mother and why she was not with her, but, with the support of Mrs. Huggins, she continued to bond with Mai. Meditation engendered in her the propensity for patience, which helped her sustain the hope that she would be released and reunited with Mai one day. Meditation enabled her to remain present with her mother during her bimonthly visits from Washington, DC, and it informed the way she wrote letters to her siblings, Kyra and Gervaze Jr., so that her emotions wouldn't burden them.

Essentially, yoga acted as a coping mechanism to aid Ericka to withstand the trials of imprisonment, enabling her to build both mindfulness and resilience. With continuous practice, Ericka worked through the long process of developing control over her thoughts and emotions to keep herself sane and balanced while also not suppressing her emotions. In *Yoga, Youth, and Reincarnation*, Marcia Moore, Stearn's yoga teacher, insists that "with control comes detachment, and we detach ourselves not from life, but from the fears that make living difficult and becloud our purpose."[11] These words likely resonated with Ericka. Meditation allowed her to focus inward to develop internal space for insight. It "impacts the center of your being and makes you very awake, alert, and clear," Ericka shared.[12] Moore states,

> We come to know ourselves acutely through the exercises and the meditation, and then, knowing, become gradually aware of unsuspected forces

within. A regeneration takes place, as the separate forces begin to merge in a meaningful manner, because we have achieved control.[13]

That regeneration is the work of spiritual wellness, practices to sustain the mind, body, and soul, which prevented her from internalizing the trauma of imprisonment. "I was able to quiet my mind and my emotions. They didn't go away. . . . I was training my mind to be less invasive. [I was] training myself so that my thoughts did not invade my experience in every moment," she explained.[14] She noticed her emotions, and while she wanted to shed tears during visits with Mrs. Huggins, Mai, or Mrs. Jenkins, she did not act on those emotions during the hour she was with these visitors. She was sensitive to Mrs. Huggins's already profound suffering, having lost her only son. She was fully cognizant of her own mother's pain and distress over her incarceration. She also did not want to spread her own sadness to her daughter. At that moment, Ericka may not have grasped that she was training her mind to be more resilient. This not only aided her in coping with anxiety but also improved her alignment of breath. She vividly recalled how deep breathing would redirect her attention back to the present moment, particularly during instances of overwhelming emotions that triggered a surge of hormones and other chemicals in her body.

Ericka leaned into her trauma as a means of healing through yoga.[15] Black studies scholar Maryam K. Aziz identifies embodied practices such as yoga as "movement arts," which are "meditative, healing arts that allow the body to physically release and move through trauma, violence, and cultural and spiritual colonization."[16] Through movement arts, Ericka was able to quiet her mind, safeguarding herself from the harmful psychological symptoms of imprisonment. She might have become worried and agitated, possibly even combative, without meditation. The violence of imprisonment is all-consuming. Movement arts allowed her to take care of her mind, body, and soul. Ericka lived feminist poet and writer Audre Lorde's words, "*Caring for myself is not self-indulgent, it is self-preservation, and that is an act of political warfare.*"[17] Movement arts became critical to her survival in prison.

She became more grounded in her sense of self, which enabled her to engage in her prison activist work with more clarity. Ericka teaches us that self-care is intimately connected to community care. Thus, spiritual centeredness is revolutionary to Black freedom organizing. Ericka had the wisdom to teach herself hatha yoga. She stumbled through horrific adversity and meditated on who she was and the world around her as a route to self-improvement, personal power, and growth. "The experience of being in prison was good in the sense that it taught me a lot about myself. I could focus on my inner work, so I'm grateful to prison for that."[18] In this way, prison served as a turning point in her life. In captivity, she materialized her self-making process through the wellness practices of yoga and meditation for soul, mind, and body care.

Ericka's embrace of spiritual wellness provided her with a means to combat certain stressors. On December 4, 1969, roughly six months into Ericka's imprisonment, she, Frances, Peggy, and Rose gazed at the television in their wing, devastated as they learned of the Chicago police's brutal murder of Fred Hampton, the bright and charismatic deputy chair of the Illinois chapter, and Mark Clark, defense captain of the Peoria chapter, widely known as a peacemaker with a bold, charismatic personality.[19] Ericka, Frances, Peggy, and Rose wept in helplessness, aware of the devastating effects of these deaths on the BPP. Ericka drew on meditation and yoga to cope with the mental health realities of being an activist, such as isolation, cruelty, and grief. She constructed her own spiritual sanctuary, her private space for restoration from the highs and the lows of activist life.

Ericka transformed herself through spiritual practice in a white supremacist world, ultimately arriving at a new sense of bliss, manifesting as an evolved consciousness between the physical and metaphysical. Ericka defined this state as one of spiritual maturity, a form of feminism that challenges white patriarchy and limited gendered identifications through consciousness-raising and introspection. As she explained, it means "reaching to the depth of your heart. Your own spirit . . . [and] the most powerful, unchanging timeless part of you" through the culmination of profound centeredness.[20] The process of spiritual maturity can manifest at any age with practice. For Ericka, it was sitting still in prison as a young adult and meditating daily. "I had to look for the goodness in my heart and for the work I had to do to improve my relationships in the world. I did. And it was hard work," she explained.[21] She had to learn how to accept herself and value the goodness within. Meditating allowed her to emotionally care for herself and manage external challenges outside her control. Ericka further explained that being spiritually mature means "looking for the best in others while holding humanity in its highest regard and telling the truth about what we need to work on."[22] Her theory and practice of spiritual maturity illustrate the significance and power of Black radical women's attentiveness to a deeper awareness of themselves as necessary for liberation.

The Power of Hunger Strikes

The power of Ericka's meditation is evident in her ability to suppress her hunger pangs in the many fasting periods she endured out of necessity. These fasts were in response to the lack of adequate prenatal care and nutrition that Frances, Rose, and other pregnant women imprisoned in Niantic were forced to contend with. She also went on a fast to protest Niantic's refusal to treat Peggy's arthritis. The BPP shaped Ericka, Rose, Frances, and Peggy's understanding of nutrition. Food carried political implications as the BPP considered access to quality food a human right. Food served as fuel to thrive. The BPP regarded hunger as a top priority; its free food program, breakfast program, and grocery distribution directly addressed food insecurity in Black and poor communities nationwide.[23] Along with Ericka, Rose engaged in hunger strikes as a form of resistance to poor nutrition and health care. In the letter reproduced in figure 4.1, Ericka wrote the following to her lawyer, Katy Roraback:

> Venceremos! 28 july 1970—The year of the people. hi, i just wanted to tell you that along with our support on the streets rose and i are refusing to eat except for liquids and fruit until peggy has adequate medical care and they begin to treat us like humans (maybe they don't know how) it has been terrible these last few days peggy seems to be catching the worst of it all (will explain later)—our spirits are high though. rose and i refuse to eat because there just isn't enough for the 3 of us and when there is—it is so nasty or dirty till we can't deal with it. were not complaining tho, some of the people eat worse! we made it thru yester-day on coffee and tea will make it until peggy gets better (she ate real good last night). we have lots of things to tell you when you come up. if this letter doesn't go out—that'll be another strike against the enemy. hope to see you soon. love, power, strength, ericka. Don't work too hard! Rose sends her love.

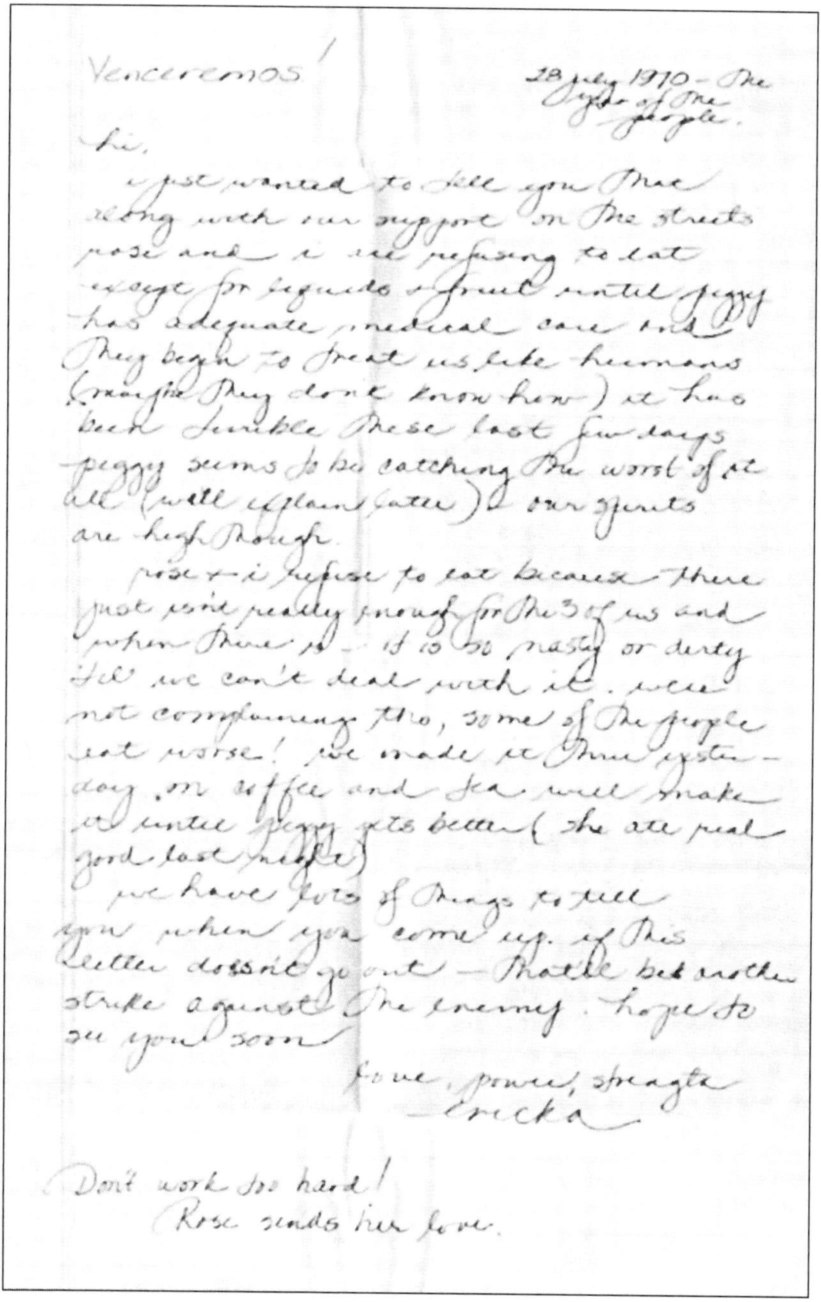

Venceremos!   28 July 1970 – The
                                      light of the
                                          people.

Hi,

i just wanted to tell you that
along with our support on the streets
rose and i are refusing to eat
except for segundo + fruit until peggy
has adequate medical care and
they begin to treat us like humans
(maybe they don't know how) it has
been terrible these last few days
peggy seems to be catching the worst of it
all (will explain later) our spirits
are high though.

rose + i refuse to eat because there
just isn't really enough for the 3 of us and
when there is – it is so nasty or dirty
til we can't deal with it. were
not complaining tho, some of the people
eat worse! we made it thru yesterday on coffee and tea will make
it until peggy gets better (she ate real
good last night)

we have lots of things to tell
you when you come up. if this
letter doesn't go out – that'll be another
strike against the enemy. hope to
see you soon

          love, power, strength
              –Ericka

Don't work too hard!
   Rose sends her love.

Figure 4.1. Letter from Ericka to Catherine (Katy) Roraback, July 28, 1970. Catherine Roraback Collection of Ericka Huggins Papers.

Ericka opens the letter with the proclamation "Venceremos," meaning, "we will overcome," alluding to the 1969 Venceremos Brigade, an organization composed of activists, including BPP members, who supported the Cuban Revolution and sought to unite with Cuban workers. Ericka emphasized that out of all of them, Peggy was in the worst condition, given that her arthritis had worsened. Rose and Ericka went on a hunger strike to protest Peggy's poor conditions. Likely, the others joined them.

Ericka engaged in a strict fast. She drank water, tea, and what she called "mysterious coffee" in the morning, consuming food only occasionally.[24] It was not until nearly seven months into Ericka's imprisonment that her hunger strike was first recorded in her prison conduct log; however, she was on strike during her entire incarceration.[25] On December 20, 1969, the log documents that "E. Huggins had only tea for breakfast."[26] The following line in the entry illustrated Ericka's attention to cleanliness as she prepared for a Saturday visit from Mrs. Huggins and Mai. "E. Huggins cleaned courtroom mirror and bathroom door and tried to wash off writing on courtroom wall while waiting to go to visit."[27] Ericka believed it was essential that one of the few spaces where women could meet, see themselves, and get bathroom privacy was respectful and clean.

Ericka's fasting served as a method of resistance against Niantic's attempt to control prisoners. By refusing to eat, she enacted mastery over her body in one of the only ways available to those who are imprisoned. It was a form of spiritual wellness in that it affirmed her autonomy and connected her to a greater purpose—better conditions for human bodies under state control. On Christmas Day, five days after the previously discussed entry, a Niantic official typed the following in her prison conduct log: "All [BPP women] ate their dinner except E. Huggins who ate bread and butter, drank her tea, nibbled a little of dinner but no dessert."[28] Ericka refused the food, finding it unappetizing and devoid of any festive appeal. "Most women just ate it, but I decided I was not doing that. I'm not going to eat everything they put in front of me. I don't even know what this meat is . . . so I decided: always drink tea," Ericka explained.[29] As previously mentioned, the meat served was often a dismal gray color. Occasionally, Ericka could distinguish chicken because it did not share the same gray hue, but other types of meat remained indiscernible. She was confined, battling for her innocence, and the idea of celebrating

Christmas seemed utterly absurd to her. Through her fast, she resisted Niantic's efforts to exert control over the prisoners. In doing so, she embodied spiritual wellness and asserted her autonomy.

There were moments when Ericka was battling personal challenges, and her fasts were indicators of her sorrow rather than of political protest. She was often melancholy after Mai's visits, as seen in the entry recorded days after Mai's first birthday. Not being able to be with Mai to celebrate her birthday depressed and consumed her, taking away her appetite. The staff noted, "E. Huggins ate no supper."[30] In a later entry written after Mai's visit on January 17, 1970, prison officials reported that she was depressed and refused lunch.[31] This day posed particular challenges, as it marked the one-year anniversary of the deaths of John and Bunchy, plunging her into deep sorrow.

At other times in her incarceration, she fasted to challenge Niantic's brutal rules, even those that impacted the general population, from whom she was separated. Niantic punished women imprisoned for petty offenses. Officials would confiscate property or withhold food for acts of disobedience. In one instance, Officer Russo took cigarettes from Diane, an imprisoned woman, for not standing in front of her cell door at the time of the morning roll call.[32] The prison conduct log draws attention to the ways Ericka, while in solitary, supported other women with her hunger strike. The words of Ericka and her compatriots were regarded as contraband.[33] Accordingly, to maintain docile bodies, prison officials deliberately separated the BPP women from those in the general population. Correctional officers went to extreme measures to keep them segregated from others imprisoned. They worked to ensure that others imprisoned were not in close vicinity when they took the women on walks. Ericka remembered that in some cases, "they would [even] shut everybody else down" by making them report to their cells during their walks.[34] Despite their various and many attempts to segregate the women, officers were not able to prevent those in the general population from communicating with the BPP women. Women in the general population found innovative ways to connect, such as speaking to them through the door. Sometimes they would put notes on food trays or indicate their solidarity through waves or loving gestures or even solidarity strikes, if necessary.[35] These care-based acts were practices of spiritual wellness.

Of course, this solidarity carried with it a potential cost—punishment. On New Year's Eve, Ericka fasted when she learned that officers were punishing Elizabeth Marie, an imprisoned woman, for communicating with her and the rest of the BPP women. "E. Huggins says she wants only tea or coffee, no meals, until —— is out of discipline," a prison staff member noted in her prison conduct log.[36] Ignoring Ericka's grievance, officers tried to change her mind by informing her that Elizabeth Marie was eating; we don't know whether Elizabeth Marie had been on a fast or had been denied food as punishment. Ericka remained steadfast in her convictions, firmly responding, "this makes no difference."[37] She wanted Elizabeth Marie out of discipline altogether, not just fed while still being punished. Several other women were also put in solitary for communicating with the BPP women. This is evidenced both by Ericka's recollections and by the prison conduct log. For example, a prison staff member locked up Anne, another imprisoned woman, "for visiting at [the] Panther's door."[38] Ericka found out about it while she and one of the other BPP members awaited visitors; as Ericka sat in Officer Douglas's vehicle waiting to be transported to administration to begin her visit, she saw Tammy, yet another imprisoned woman, running toward her. Tammy needed to share some distressing news.

"I'm locked for talking to you."[39]
Ericka sighed; her face became blank.

Mrs. Frederickson, a matron, recorded the scene in Ericka's prison conduct log. Officers locked Tammy in solitary for five days for her defiant act.[40] During Tammy's stay in isolation, Ericka remained on her fast. Ericka considered all the women visiting her friends and was unwavering in her solidarity with them.

Roughly three months earlier, when Ericka defied Niantic rules and gave "loud speeches," a matron warned other imprisoned women of the dangers they faced for conversing with the BPP women.[41] But what Ericka and the other BPP women had to say captured the attention of many of the women trapped in Niantic. In these speeches, Ericka talked about self-determination and interdependence, but in Niantic's prison record, it was not presented this way. Instead, they depicted her as an agitator intent on brainwashing the women. One time, on a daily supervised

walk, according to the prison conduct log, Ericka spoke aloud for thirty
minutes to ensure that all in earshot could hear:

> We are revolutionaries. We are for you. There is a clear line of demarca-
> tion. Which side are you on? Ours, or the —— matrons and that ——
> MacDougal? No one will ever be locked for talking to us again. We will
> take it to a higher authority. Now, we are out of cigs [cigarettes]. What are
> you going to do about it?[42]

She confirmed that the state's account sounded like the remarks she
gave, but she denied the state's interpretation of those words. To the
state, Ericka's speech was incendiary with the goal to incite a prison
rebellion. For Ericka, however, these words were a way to engage in the
BPP practice of political education despite her solitary confinement. Her
use of "we" conveyed the power they held to abolish the system within
Niantic. With this, Ericka disrupted the master narrative that situated
the BPP as a hate group by declaring them revolutionaries. She made
clear that the matrons and MacDougal, the Connecticut Department of
Corrections commissioner, were oppressive forces of state power and,
therefore, enemies of the people. Her question "Which side are you on?"
implied that the state inherently counters agency and personal freedom.
She alluded to Niantic's threat of violence through solitary, and with
conviction, she illustrated the magnitude of her inner power; her soul
was at work rendering her fearless in challenging the state. She appealed
to those bearing witness to make a sacrifice despite the consequences
imposed by the state, and many of the women responded in kind, risk-
ing violence to support the BPP women. Ericka understood that she had
allies and emphasized the state's withholding of cigarettes from them as
a form of punishment; she knew that someone in the community they
built would supply them.

In response to Ericka's speech, a prison staff member not only reported her to Mrs. Ralston, likely a superior, but also refused to acknowledge her presence. "I said nothing to Erica but smiled at the other
girls and said quietly 'she's wrong, you will be locked' [for talking to
her]."[43] The officer's smile indicates that they took pleasure in the power
they held to inflict misery on the women, whom they commonly referred to as "girls" to oppress them. The quiet tone was a strategy to

promote fear and compliance. Mr. Davis, a male officer who arrived on the scene to remove the women from Ericka's proximity, furthered the carceral terror. The log reports that his taking Ericka away made them calm down.[44] By threatening violence, the officers reinscribed the fear that Ericka was trying to abolish.

The state invested in depicting Ericka as an agitator in her prison conduct log. Officials construed her communist views as negative. They wrote, "E. Huggins never stops her Communistic brainwashing, and she is concerned that the corridor may be 'bugged.'"[45] Such observations were a strategy to portray Ericka as an enemy of the state and a threat to US democratic principles. This was connected to larger COINTEL-PRO strategies to paint the BPP as terrorists. Ericka had valid reasons for her suspicion that the state wiretapped the wing where she and her compatriots stayed in Niantic. While there, they were subjected to the same kinds of governmental state repression they experienced and witnessed on the outside. They experienced heavy surveillance, and prison officials would inquire about their affairs. "We'd be having conversations, and somebody would walk in and ask what we were doing."[46] Their queries suggested that Niantic tape-recorded them. For example, two days after Ericka was labeled a communist, an officer indicated that Ericka communicated with other imprisoned women traveling from a meeting and work responsibilities from 4:15 to 5:00 p.m. "Erica Huggins called to all of them—'Power to the people.'" The officer closed the entry with a cautionary warning indicating that it was a "bad time" for the "W. Corridor girls" to travel back to Davis Hall because "Erica takes advantage of every opportunity to agitate if there is anyone within shouting distance."[47] The officer suggested that the "girls" be brought back inside Davis Hall before 4:00 p.m. or 6:30 p.m. to prevent interaction with Ericka.

Ericka reclaimed the humanity of those imprisoned with her, which the matrons and officers sought to strip from them through various methods of punishment, including the use of demeaning language. On several occasions, Ericka challenged the prison staff, including Janet S. York, the warden, for routinely calling them "girls." "We are women," she declared. "Please don't call us girls."[48] In this moment, she also drew on a salient tool necessary for her spiritual wellness: writing poetry about her experience.[49]

Fighting Back, Black on Blue

Ericka protested with a hunger strike when officers inflicted vicious beatings on the BPP women. The *Black Panther* newspaper detailed an incident involving an officer beating Rose. The article, entitled, "Report from New Haven: Rose Smith Beaten by Pigs in Jail 2/16/70: The Report Was Given by Someone That Happened to Be at the Scene," reported that Ericka, Peggy, and Rose learned that prison officials punished Frances by placing her in the "dungeon," a type of solitary confinement. The BPP women were determined to communicate with Frances. As an act of solidarity, Rose bellowed, "All Power to the People" to Frances. A correctional officer reprimanded Rose by ordering her not to speak to Frances, but she persisted. He then forcefully grabbed her to take her back to her cell. Five officers arrived when she resisted the officer's repeated orders to enter her cell room. Four of them proceeded to assault her physically. The *Black Panther* reported that "one of them twisted her arm behind her back, one of them hit her in the face."[50] Another officer threw her on the bed.

The officer's attacks accelerated her heart rate. In addition, she was famished because she had not eaten since noon the day before, but this did not stop Rose from defending herself. As one of the officers left her cell, Rose grabbed an object from her dresser and threw it at him, hitting him in the back. In response, he "threw her against the dresser" and "down on the floor." She was left "unconscious for sometime."[51] In response, her compatriots fought the officers. One officer held Peggy by the neck while another threw Ericka to the ground. After the officers' attacks, the BPP women likely did not receive any medical attention. This incident prompted Ellis McCable, the corrections commissioner, to visit the BPP women. Commissioner McCable asked Rose to give a statement about the incident and informed her that the state could charge her with "assaulting an officer," a crime with a possible sentence of six to seven years of imprisonment.[52] The article reported that Rose refused to make a statement and that her attorney, likely Katy Roraback, visited her the next day.

In an interview with me, Officer Walsh admitted to physically attacking the BPP women when they refused to go into their cell rooms.[53] Prison authorities called him in for what they considered "problems" with prisoners. He remembered that he "physically took hold of [one of the BPP women] and put her in a room."[54] Ericka also recalled another instance of physical abuse involving Officer Walsh and his objections to the frequency of the BPP women's cigarette smoking.[55] Prisoners were only allowed to smoke a certain number of cigarettes per day; Officer Walsh believed that the BPP women exceeded that amount and harassed the women about it. "That's not any of your business. You can leave now," Ericka responded. "No, I'm not going to leave," he replied.[56] Ericka warned him that if he did not leave, she would flush the cigarette carton down the toilet. "You can stop the toilet," he yelled.[57] Ericka then jammed the carton of cigarettes down the toilet. "You can't control me with cigarettes or anything else," she declared to him as she walked into her cell.[58] He flushed red in anger and grabbed her, but she was able to pull away. He called for backup and three correctional officers arrived. The correctional officers pushed, shoved, and threw the BPP women around the wing. "Stop beating us, you're not gonna push my body,"[59] Ericka recalled the women declaring as they fought the officers back. Ericka remembered that Officer Walsh let her go after she "kneed him in the balls."[60] Matrons who arrived at the scene stopped the male officers from continuing to attack the BPP women; "leave them alone," they told the male officers.[61] Before the male officers left, the BPP women told them they would be informing their lawyers of their harassment. Since they were unsentenced women, they were exempt from disciplinary measures that could have involved extended prison sentences for fighting the officers. After the incident, Ericka quit smoking cigarettes. She refused to allow the correctional officers to use cigarettes to control her. Likely Ericka's meditation and yoga practice helped her curb her cravings to smoke.

The young women always protected themselves and each other from verbal and physical attacks by correctional officers and often used laughter to mock the prison officers. In the prison conduct log, a correctional officer wrote, "After everyone left the corridor, the girls laughed hilariously. Rose was bragging about biting one of the guards."[62] It is unclear whether the officer was referring to the previous incident involving Ericka and her cigarettes, as that story was not recorded in the prison conduct log. Laughter, however, was common practice among the BPP women. Rose likely used laughter to show her surprise that she escaped punishment for biting one of the correctional officers. As an aspect of spiritual wellness, laughter was a way to build community, a source of healing, and a way to subvert power and authority nonviolently. Frances recalled, "We had the worst of times, we had the best of times."[63] They used laughter to make light of heavy situations and to keep their morale up even in terrible circumstances.

These types of scenarios and various forms of punishment meted out to the BPP women by correctional officers repeated themselves until the release of all the BPP women except for Ericka. On June 12, 1970, Frances was released.[64] Loretta's release followed almost three months later.[65] Roughly three weeks after that, Peggy and Rose were released on October 2, 1970.[66] They left Ericka behind. Ericka was happy for her comrades but sad to see them go. Now alone, she had to dig deeper into her reserve to stay sane.

Shortly after the departure of the BPP women, Ericka was told by Officer Walsh that another Black Panther was coming to her wing. Her name was Ruth.[67] Upon her arrival, Ericka went to meet Ruth, but correctional officers would not allow Ruth to come out of her cell, which struck Ericka as odd because the young BPP women could walk around the wing during the day. When they finally conversed, Ruth told Ericka, "I am leaving and want you to go with me. We need to get out of here."[68] Ericka declined her invitation to escape with her. She did not believe that Ruth was who she said she was. She had not seen her in the BPP before. She believed she was dangerous and trying to kill her. It is unclear why Ericka believed this. Perhaps it was Ruth's reserved nature, emphasis on escaping prison, lack of recognition, and/or her short stay as her roommate, but Ericka knew that she needed to stay away from her. Ericka later learned from other prisoners that Ruth had escaped and was returned to prison. She planned to escape prison again, but this time with Ericka. These prisoners informed Ericka that Ruth was now placed in another isolation room and that they were relieved that she did not attempt to escape with Ruth. Ericka drew on her spiritual wellness principles to resist Ruth's advances and remain at peace. Soon thereafter, correctional officers moved Ericka to a smaller solitary cell room with no roommates, where I estimate she stayed for roughly thirty days.[69]

The Release of Ericka and Bobby from Solitary

Like Ericka, since his arrest Bobby Seale was held in administrative seg-regation and solitary confinement at the Montville Correctional Center in Montville, Connecticut, and engaged in a hunger strike to protest his prison conditions.[70] Legal recourse was needed to get Ericka and Bobby out of solitary confinement. Their lawyers filed a Complaint for Declaratory Judgement, Injunction, and Other Appropriate Relief with the US district court in New Haven, based on cruel and unusual punish-ment. In the complaint for declaratory and injunctive relief, the lawyers described Ericka and Bobby's state as "unconstitutional and oppressive conditions of pretrial confinement, which infringe basic liberties."[71] They argued that the "unwarranted and illegal conditions of pretrial detention threaten to preclude a fair trial."[72] The conditions included lack of communication, lack of visitation, denial of effective represen-tation, violation of privacy and human dignity, denial of medical care, imposition of punishment without trial, treatment as convicted persons, and denial of equal protection of the laws.[73]

The complaint for declaratory and injunctive relief also asserted that Montville prison denied Bobby visits with his minor child, Malik, and that Montville correctional officers placed him in administrative seg-regation for refusing to shave his beard. Ericka and Bobby's lawyers documented the invasion of their privacy, including but not limited to "electronic eavesdropping and secret observations of consultations." They believed that records of their client consultations were made ac-cessible to the prosecution. Access to the doctors and medical care of Ericka and Bobby's own choosing were refused (and although not listed in the complaint for declaratory and injunctive relief, the other BPP women were also denied medical care). The complaint asserts that Er-icka was informed that unless her attire complied with the "petty and arbitrary standards" set by Niantic, she would not be allowed to attend court. It is also noted that after Ericka repeatedly requested Niantic staff for the rules and standards, they were not produced, published, or oth-erwise made accessible to the public.[74] As stated in the Memorandum of Decision, most of the concerns were resolved with agreements and stipulations.[75]

This complaint for declaratory and injunctive relief allowed Ericka to soon transfer to the general population.[76] While alone in isolation awaiting transfer, according to the prison conduct log, Ericka often refused recreation and meals. Likely, her refusal was an emotional response to being without the other BPP women. It perhaps was also informed by the correctional officers forcing her to stay in her cell room. A correctional officer noted in an entry in the prison conduct log, "Ericka Huggins refusing all meals until someone see her and tell her why she has to stay in her room all the time."[77] As in the case with the cigarettes, Ericka disciplined her body to resist the control of the correctional officers.

The complaint for declaratory and injunctive relief was successful. Ericka was scheduled to soon be moved to the general population, but without the items she had in her possession in solitary. Correctional officers denied her request to "take the sewing machine, TV, radio, and record player with her when she was moved" to the general population and described her as "annoyed about not receiving [additional items such as] her clothing, books, and her radio."[78] She enjoyed sewing, and the radio kept her attuned to the rest of the world.[79]

Even with the departure of the other BPP women, Ericka consistently received support from women in the general population, as many continued to risk punishment to communicate with her. As typed in the prison conduct log, less than a week before Ericka's transfer to the general population, an incarcerated woman was punished for "5 nights for conversing with E. Huggins outside of Ericka's door."[80] The communication, love, and solidarity she received from other imprisoned women created opportunities for the spiritual wellness practices she later cultivated during her time in the general population through the work of the Sister Love Collective.

Ericka, Frances, Peggy, and Rose translated their shared convictions, deeply rooted in BPP principles, into concrete actions to endure solitary confinement, deplorable conditions, and imprisonment. In their dire circumstances, the BPP women found solace in one another, offering mutual support through the sharing of food and caregiving responsibilities. The prison had stripped them of their ability to care for their own children, and in response, they stepped in for each other, fostering a bond that ultimately led them all to walk out of the gates of Niantic. However, Ericka's release from prison would not occur for approximately another eight months, during which she continued to rely on her BPP principles and personal wellness practices to help her endure the time without her sisters.[81]

5

The Sister Love Collective

To love is to turn away from the prioritization of the ego or even one's particular party or tribe, to give of oneself for another, to transfigure the narrow "I" into the expansive "you" or "we." This four-letter word asks of us, then, one of the most difficult tasks in life: decentering the self for the good of another.
—Tiya Miles

After 536 consecutive days of administrative segregation, the Department of Corrections finally released Ericka to the general population on November 9, 1970.[1] Ericka immediately returned to the BPP care practice that is integral to the BPP's approach to building Black communities for Black people. This practice focuses on creating spaces where Black people can develop self-knowledge and self-love as a means of propelling Black liberation and envisioning a Black future. This practice is a revolutionary act in its affirmation of Black humanity within an anti-Black society.

Ericka actualized this revolutionary care practice through the implementation of the Sister Love Collective, a loosely structured feminist, multiracial, collective space. This collective welcomed and enabled women from a spectrum of ethnic backgrounds and sexual identities, empowering them to forge ingenious gendered strategies of resistance. It did not matter how women racially or sexually identified; the Sister Love Collective provided anyone who wanted it with mental wellness as well as medical and emotional support to help them survive imprisonment. By creating a multiracial informal collective of women, Ericka redefined BPP care as one that centered cross-racial coalition work for women inside prison walls in the pursuit of Black liberation.

At its core, the Sister Love Collective cultivated meaningful (and sometimes intimate) relations among women prisoners and advanced

a politics of solidarity, fundamentally contesting white heteropatriar-
chal power and violence. These relations fostered self-transformation
and spiritual well-being. In the spirit of cross-racial solidarity, Ericka
co-founded the Sister Love Collective with another prisoner, a Puerto
Rican teenager named Millie Rivera. It was important for the Sister
Love Collective to be an inclusive collective because Ericka cared about
herself and created a context in which she could live a full life, but not
only for herself. As a BPP member, she recognized that freedom was
collective, and she needed comrades who were invested in a more eq-
uitable existence. The Sister Love Collective enabled that collectivity.
Being placed in the general population inspired Ericka to resist the inhumanity of her incarceration by embracing the beauty of everyone's
humanity within the prison walls. In her new space, a panoply of emotions enveloped her: fear, disenchantment, anxiety, joy, and vulnerability, the same feelings she experienced before being moved to the
general population.[2] She understood that she was in an entirely new
world, and to survive, she needed to cultivate new relationships. By
founding a hair salon, the Sister Love Collective cleverly masked its
political objective to actively resist incarceration from the watchful eyes
of the correctional officers. It harnessed the power of beauty, intimacy,
self-confidence, care, and communal health as potent tools to under-
mine the oppressive forces of white supremacist state violence.

   I contend that communal care and emotional labor were pivotal
components of spiritual wellness within the Sister Love Collective. Ericka has shared that at the time, the women of the Sister Love Collective did not explicitly categorize their actions as either political or
spiritual. Yet I position their activities as both political in nature and
emblematic of spiritual wellness practices. The Sister Love Collective
served as a crucial space in which Ericka and her fellow participants
clearly delineated the significance of spiritual wellness. Their engagement in spiritual wellness harmoniously integrated self-betterment and
profound introspection, bridging the mind, body, and soul in a united
front against the oppressive forces of white supremacy. This synergistic
alliance of the mind, body, and spirit forms the essential groundwork
that paves the path to true freedom. Spiritual wellness was instrumental
in fostering a sense of freedom, as it empowered the women to up-
hold their mental autonomy in the face of physical incarceration. The

practices and beliefs cultivated within the Sister Love Collective served as a beacon of hope and resistance, guiding these women toward a future where their minds remained unchained, despite the confines of their physical surroundings.

While the Sister Love Collective was specific to the women's prison, spiritual wellness work can be employed by anyone in or outside the confines of prison. Sister Love was a gendered collective due to the sex segregation of mass incarceration, but spiritual wellness is not. In the following chapter, I recount the multiple ways the women of Niantic mobilized the Sister Love Collective under the auspices of spiritual wellness. First, Ericka and Millie developed a prison hair salon, which served as the informal Sister Love Collective headquarters. They appropriated space to enable women to feel good, feel safe, and share their personal stories.[3] Second, Ericka skillfully applied makeup on herself and others, ingeniously using body paint and markers, to double as lipstick, blush, or eyeliner. The act of "getting dolled up" transformed the meaning of "pretty" into a powerful political statement. Third, women in the prison began to refashion their uniforms. Bringing originality to the everyday banality of drab clothing was a form of resistance and another attempt to claim beauty for themselves. Fourth, Ericka and others placed value on health and their inner beings. The Sister Love Collective was used to support women in recovery from drug use and help them obtain proper medical care. Fifth and finally, Ericka and Millie created a women's bail fund. By combining their limited finances and calling on BPP lawyers, including Katy Roraback and John Williams, women were able to funnel their support to those who needed to survive state, personal, or domestic violence.

Women-centered informal networks are part of a long tradition of subversive resistance tactics to challenge various forms of oppression. These networks function to facilitate a gender-based community firmly grounded in principles of camaraderie and sisterhood. On the margins of a nation entrenched in "white supremacist capitalist patriarchy," informal clandestine networks insist on women's collaboration for survival.[4] Women-centered networks yield a safe and brave space to cope with the realities of oppression and serve as a defense against the second-class status of women in the United States. As members of these informal networks, women care for and protect one another.

Interdependency and the ability to remain veiled from outsiders is vital to the staying power of an informal, covert system. The roots of the Sister Love Collective echo what historian Deborah Gray White describes as a network of survival.[5] In the same way, community care was essential to the imprisoned women of the Sister Love Collective. Their positive deeds cultivated a channel for pleasure, laughter, dialogue, and political education to withstand the hardships of prison. Ultimately, the Sister Love Collective sharpens our understanding of women's resistance in the 1960s and 1970s.

Interdependency and covertness are especially significant in the carceral space. Historian Dan Berger argues that "prison is a fluid and fluctuating institution."[6] Its fluidity required Ericka to be inventive, resourceful, and imaginative in how she developed gendered strategies of resistance. She contested state power through the creation of the Sister Love Collective as a secret, self-sufficient political group designed to support the medical, social, emotional, and political needs of Black, Latina, and white imprisoned women from lower- and working-class backgrounds. Within the confines of prison, Sister Love grew organically. As the architect of the Sister Love Collective, Ericka maintained a steady presence and became a vital force in maintaining its daily activities. Because of the transitory nature of prison, it is unknown how many women were in Sister Love. Some of the women who came through Sister Love saw Ericka only once, but even minor encounters could have been enough to spark the seeds of spiritual wellness.

The Hair Salon

The Sister Love Collective began with hair. Combing, brushing, curling, twisting, and braiding were the time-consuming practices that fostered community and intimacy among imprisoned women. Interestingly, "doing hair" allowed Ericka and others to camouflage their resistance, that is, to conceal the critical conversations they had about the prison and the larger world under the guise of reproducing femininity.[7] Haircare sessions in Niantic had a history of being ignored, considered trivial and unimportant to jailers, which enabled women to escape attention and censure. The prison officials at Niantic were unaware that imprisoned women formed an informal group that catered to their desires and that fostered criticism of their arrests and mistreatment. The Sister Love Collective's concealed activities align with Robin D. G. Kelley's definition of "a 'hidden transcript,' a dissident political culture that manifests itself in daily conversations, folklore, jokes, songs, and other cultural practices."[8] Accordingly, the Sister Love Collective was a "hidden transcript," and haircare was a guise for political activity. Ericka articulated this phenomenon in her emphatic response, "Of course the prison didn't know—we didn't want them to! To them, it looked as if we were just 'doing hair.'"[9] The Sister Love Collective also embodied what scholar Lora Bex Lempert describes as "guerilla cunning of the oppressed," or the "decisions about how to creatively and selectively engage with other women and with their keepers."[10] They used the skills within their means, such as "doing hair," to elude correctional officers. "Doing hair" in the open failed to draw scrutiny from those in power. This is notable in that state correctional institutions typically strip prisoners of the ability to engage in public displays of intimacy. The assumption that the women were "harmless" allowed the Sister Love Collective's organizing talk to go unnoticed by the state even under heavy surveillance.

While the politics of haircare was invisible at Niantic, hair in the broader society can articulate a hyper-visible statement, often of resistance, rebellion, and survival. The Sister Love Collective wielded hair as a marker of resistance in the same way some people in the broader community use hair to navigate society. As historian Tiffany M. Gill argues, "Beautification provided a fruitful and important base for black women to launch some of their most significant agitations for social and political change."[11] The Sister Love Collective transformed a space at Niantic in the early 1970s into a beauty shop that functioned as an autonomous, protected, and fearless space for political discourse and action. Journalist Silja J. A. Talvi explains that women cope with isolation in prison differently than men did. She cites lawyer Ellen Barry, founder and former director of Legal Services for Prisoners with Children, who claims that their response

> takes on an even more significant dimension because of the way that gender differences play out in society. Women turn to each other for support and basic survival in ways that men don't as often. So the isolation takes on an even deeper [meaning] for women.[12]

The Sister Love Collective's investment in hair broke the bounds of fear and monotony. Through collective care, women engaged in a process of beautification to survive isolation and the mundaneness of prison.

While grooming hair, they planned swift and clandestine actions, blending theory and practice.[13] They transformed the lives of the women in Niantic. Ericka believes that "one of the reasons why Sister Love worked is because . . . people were watching my trial and thought that I was something special."[14] Perhaps those imprisoned learned about Ericka's BPP affiliation and her charges regarding Alex Rackley's killing from television and newspaper headlines. The public media often portrayed the Black Panthers as a criminal hate group. While it is fair to assume that this characterization could have caused those imprisoned to act reserved or even frightened in the presence of Ericka, she suggested that it had the opposite effect. Moreover, her calming disposition could have potentially forestalled any adverse perceptions from fellow imprisoned women. She assumed that the high-profile nature of her case on the local and national level and her status as a Black Panther worked to legitimize her call to action among those on the inside.[15] But Ericka downplayed the importance of her BPP status because she believed that everyone could be an agent for liberation: "I assured them that I wasn't anything special, that we were all special and that we were all capable of making change."[16] Ultimately, the Sister Love Collective manifested from Ericka's core values of community building, creating connections, and loving affirmation.

The salon sustained itself through haircare and conversation and in turn, granted women the ability to hide in plain sight. As evident in their name, Sister Love, they boldly announced a politics of love based on kinship. Audre Lorde wrote that most often human beings "do not develop tools for using human difference as a springboard for creative change within our lives."[17] Sister Love, however, achieved just that: by serving and employing women from various races, ethnicities, and sexual orientations, Ericka and Millie utilized a diverse range of aesthetics and politics to assist those imprisoned in transforming their daily lives at Niantic.

Self-actualizing pleasure offers a window into the distinct kinds of resistance imprisoned women utilized to restore their femininity, assert respectability, and convey personal ideas about self-preservation. The

Sister Love Collective used beauty, makeup, fashion, and style to take care of one another and as a defense against human cruelty. Their efforts resemble those described in historian Tanisha C. Ford's account of Black women in both domestic and international contexts, including those in organizations such as Brixton's Black Panther Movement Youth League in London, which used "soul style [that is, attire, hairstyles, and accessories indicative of Black Pride] as a symbolic baptism in freedom's waters through which they could be reborn, liberated from the cultural and social bondage of their slave or colonial pasts."[18] The Sister Love Collective captured "soul style" as a pathway to inner freedom and new beginnings. Ford adds that "style [served] both as a response to social and physical violence and as a source of pleasure."[19] Her explanation captures the Sister Love Collective's use of femininity. Given that prisons dehumanize and often strip women of their femininity, Black women can reclaim their femininity as a form of progressive body politics. In this way, style becomes a means of asserting the importance and value of their bodies within institutional spaces that are structured to neglect, punish, or even harm them.

Some prisons deny access to grooming supplies such as makeup and haircare products, particularly for Black women who need natural hair combs, brushes, and hair oils. Prohibiting beauty options punishes women, denies their existence, and strips them of their self-respect and dignity. Women must create opportunities to overcome gendered barriers.[20] Specifically, hair carries cultural and social significance. Under bondage, hair styling serves as an intimate expression of love. Ericka believed that women entrapped in prison deserved to take care of themselves and feel fully cared for. Particularly for Black women, femininity was not always accessible. Given that femininity was traditionally the property of middle-class white women, adopting a feminine identity can be liberating. The roots of her beliefs came from the teachings of her mother, who instilled in her the notion that dressing up is intricately tied to mental wellness. Often, our mothers are the first people in our lives to introduce us to the practice of dress and adornment. They dress us as children, and children often like to watch their mothers get dressed. Children will mimic their mothers putting on lipstick or high-heeled shoes. Accordingly, grooming practices are also born in partnership and outside solitude.[21]

Figure 5.1. Millie Rivera making art at age sixteen, North Haven, Connecticut, 1970. Photo courtesy of Millie's childhood friend Nancy Shia.

Through meditation practice, Ericka conceptualized the idea of a hair salon to benefit imprisoned women. Then she shared her vision of the salon with Millie, an imprisoned visual artist and poet.[22] Millie grew up in poverty in Astoria, Queens, and lower Manhattan. Abuse in Millie's family pushed her to the streets. At the age of nine or earlier, she ran away from home with her brother Ivan. Both homeless, they often slept on park benches.

During a confrontation, Millie stabbed someone in self-defense, which landed her at Long Lane School for Girls in Middletown, Connecticut, a notorious prison for teenage girls.[23] She entered Niantic at the age of sixteen on charges of aggravated assault and theft.[24] Unlike the Black Panthers Maude and Jeannie, whose status as minors and political prisoners placed them in juvenile, Millie was kept at Niantic even though she was also a minor. Prison officials likely did not send Millie to juvenile because she was not a political prisoner.

Although she was only four feet eleven, her tough nature and her big hair in "spiral tight curls" made a statement, as did the tattoos that adorned her petite body.[25] "Love" was tattooed on her hand, and a small heart was tattooed on her ankle. Despite her record, she exuded kindness and compassion for others, traits that she wore proudly.[26] Her fiery personality and tender heart reminded Ericka of the Black women she grew up with in Washington, DC. Nonjudgmental, energetic, and armed with a heart of gold, she bonded with Ericka through laughter. "What I loved most about her is that I could laugh with her. She was so lighthearted, and she got my wacky sense of humor," Ericka recalled.[27] While Ericka's idea of opening a salon failed to resonate immediately with other women, Millie understood its significance and considered it a way to connect with others. Ericka recalled a conversation with Millie about a name for the salon.

"We can't call it the salon?" Millie asked.

"Yeah, we can for the purpose of the guards, but really it's the love between us women 'cause we're all like sisters."

They looked at each other. "Let's call it Sister Love," Ericka suggested.[28]

As co-founders of Sister Love, they worked together to appropriate open space in the dining area of Thompson Hall through the assemblage of chairs, towels, and hair supplies such as combs and brushes. To build the salon, Sister Love collectively used their individual commissary to share an assortment of items such as bobby pins, plastic combs, candy, snacks, and cigarettes with one another.[29] By word of mouth, they disseminated the news of its launch.

In a large room, women expressed intimacy as they combed, brushed, braided, curled, crimped, and straightened one another's hair. Some women sat in stackable chairs as their hairdressers stood over their heads to work on commonly requested styles such as pin curls, braids, cornrows, and straight or curly locks. The salon smelled fruity from the mist of hair spray. Dana laid her head on Ana Maria's knee as she reached for more hair grease and gently finished her cornrow braids. Yolanda rested her arms between Wendy's thighs as she softly brushed her hair. Jennifer felt a tingle down the spine of her back as Michelle massaged her scalp with hair oil.[30] Karen used a blow dryer to straighten Sandra's curly hair. Care-based virtues of compassion and kindness shaped the Sister Love Collective as a space of comfort and support, thus deepening the women's sense of self-worth individually and collectively.

The physical environment of the hair salon evoked the concept of a "rival geography," used by historian Stephanie M. H. Camp to refer to formerly enslaved persons gaining "mobility in the face of constraint."[31] Camp explained that "the rival geography was characterized by motion: the movement of bodies, objects, and information within and around plantation space."[32] She further noted that it "provide[d] space for private and public creative expression, rest and recreation, alternative communication, and importantly, resistance to planters' domination of slaves' every move."[33] Her explanation of "rival geography" can be applied to the lives of incarcerated women and the significance of the Sister Love Collective's hair salon, a place of leisure and resistance, a spirit-affirming setting where the sensibility of intimate care and honest conversation blossomed. This care was rooted in restorative practices that tended to the women's inner and outer selves. Their beauty pursuits upended the procedural practices of isolation and seclusion.

In community, women were able to look at the state of the world by virtue of their personal encounters and observations. For some, the Sister Love Collective marked the first time they shared their personal experiences aloud. They felt comfortable disclosing confidential information about themselves on various topics such as confrontations with the state, intimate partner abuse, poverty, elected political officials, and the sadness of being separated from their children. In their conversations, they identified those with children the state threatened to take away, those in need of legal support, and those feeling depressed or suicidal.[34]

In the group, telling stories to one another had a healing effect. Women were able to take the necessary steps to free themselves from past stories and old ways. The Sister Love Collective created a setting that equipped all the participants with the language to name and speak out against the state-sanctioned violence that typified their lives. In this respect, the women's spirits were actively affirmed as they were afforded a political education, creating the conditions for spiritual wellness that shaped much of Ericka's time with the Black Panthers in her post-prison years. Because of the spirit-affirming beauty practices that Ericka and Millie established, the salon was a time and place where women could come to find spiritual rest.

Historically, storytelling played an important role in struggles for social justice. Historian Premilla Nadasen documents how storytelling shaped a political movement for domestic workers in the post-1945 era. She explains, "Storytelling was a form of activism, a strategic way to make sense of the past as well as the present."[35] In the Sister Love Collective, women shared personal stories in a protected space. Ericka remembered, "We braided and curled each other's hair and over the hair-doing we had all kinds of conversations about how we wanted the world to unfold. It looked so harmless to the prison guards, but it was revolutionary."[36] Through the personal act of haircare, they validated one another as thinkers and conveyed their hopes for a different world. The close bonds that emerged from same-sex intimacy through haircare and conversation became essential for building a sisterhood. Likely they openly discussed their sexualities and homoerotic desires.

Cross-Racial Sisterly Bonds

It was in prison that Ericka first fell in love with a woman. Joanne was a Black woman whom Ericka met in the general population.[37] Their cell rooms were directly next to one another, and the beds were placed near the walls. Ericka and Joanne developed a heartfelt and spiritual attachment. Ericka often put her hands on the wall, and Joanne did the same. Even though a prison wall separated them, Ericka remembered that she could feel Joanne's energy through the plaster when her hand was on the wall. The first time it happened, Ericka asked Joanne whether her hands were on the wall simultaneously. "Well, of course," Joanne responded. "She was always on my mind. I was always on her mind," Ericka remembered.[38] They were so connected that they would finish each other's sentences when they could talk. When they were able to come together, their hands sometimes touched, but they were never sexual or physical with one another; yet their relationship was intimate and deeply spiritual. They supported one another as they were able. They read spiritual books together, including Hermann Hesse's novel *Narcissus and Goldmund*, a love story beyond the physical.

After reading the book to express her love, Joanne wrote a song for Ericka. "When they lock us in tonight, and the windows are open, I will sing the song to you," she told Ericka. As the evening approached, Ericka opened her barred window. She heard women communicating with one another across the open barred windows. Once Joanne started singing, everyone became silent to listen to her melodic voice. At breakfast the following day, the imprisoned women asked about it:

> "Who was singing last night?" Carolyn asked.
>
> "It was so beautiful; I fell asleep to the night music. Who was being sung to?" followed Lois.
>
> "Joanne was singing to me," Ericka gushed.[39]

At that moment, Ericka announced her love for Joanne. She manifested her queer desire for Joanne using the spirit. Ericka refrained from assigning a label to their connection, understanding that queer desire is not constrained by identity categories. The women within the Sister Love Collective crafted infrastructures that fostered queer intimacies, defying the spatial restrictions imposed upon them. After Joanne received her sentence from the State of Connecticut, she was relocated to a different floor by correctional officers, disrupting the spiritual bond she shared with Ericka. Ericka suspected that the correctional officers intentionally separated them, aware of their profound connection and aiming to keep them apart. The Sister Love Collective epitomized cultural scholar José Esteban Muñoz's concept of futurity in its world-making, embodying a queer approach to envisioning and investing in the future. Its adoption of a queer understanding of care expanded to encompass the needs of all women within its fold. Consequently, the Sister Love Collective emerged as a diverse, multiracial queer space, empowering women from a multitude of ethnic backgrounds to develop innovative, gender-specific methods of resistance.

The Sister Love Collective emboldened women of all racial backgrounds beset by state violence to engage in loving care practices. Connie Civita, a slim sixteen-year-old white Italian teenager with medium-length brown hair from the Bronx, New York, was locked inside Niantic for shoplifting. Like Millie, she was not moved to juvenile despite her age, presumably because she was also not considered a political prisoner.[40] She played a pivotal role styling hair in the collective. In contrast to her outspoken nature, her soft face and brown eyes conveyed a quiet presence. She used her cosmetology skills to create all kinds of hairstyles in the salon. As a rebellious youth, Connie ran away from Long Lane School for Girls with another young girl. They stopped at a store, and her traveling partner stole a record album. The Hartford police arrested them and sent them to Niantic. "This chick steals an album, and they scoop us both up like we're terrorists," she remembered years later.[41] While the parents of the other young girl came to get her, Connie's parents refused to bail her out, hoping to teach her a lesson. Styling hair allowed Connie to find a source of happiness in prison and indulge in her passion. Connie developed an intense attachment to Ericka that started with haircare. Their friendship transcended racial boundaries, with their shared experiences and discussions about their hair acting as a catalyst for a deep emotional and intellectual bond. "She inspired me. I was in awe of her from the moment I met her," remembered Connie. She adored Ericka and described the two of them as "kindred spirits." While critical figures including Ericka, Millie, and Connie took center stage in the Sister Love Collective, many other women found refuge in the group. Connie explained, "We would all sit and talk, and have our tea and coffee and just do what women do when they are around each other."[42] The Sister Love Collective provided Connie with a vital sanctuary where the simplicity of being women—engaging in gossip, sharing laughter, and confiding their pain to each other—was celebrated and embraced.

According to Ericka, race shaped hair politics. Black and white women fancied each other's hair textures: "The white women wanted their hair to be curly or wavy, so we would braid it wet and then take the braids out, and they'd have crimpy hair. It was popular then. And the Black women wanted their hair to be straight or braided."[43] They also snipped off the ends with scissors slipped to them by a correctional officer if women wanted a trim. External standards of beauty and popular hair fashion trends influenced their style preferences. The women who took part in the Sister Love Collective relied on hairdressers in the group to fulfill their desires for a new look, which granted them a possibility to reinvent themselves.

For Black women, styles such as braids celebrated their African cultural roots and protected their hair from damage due to wear and tear. Connie used to pin curl Ericka's hair. Styling pin curls involved taking pieces of Ericka's hair and wrapping them around circular rubber molds.

The pins set the hair for a wide curl. Once Connie removed the pins, Ericka's hair would bounce into perfectly coiffed layers of curls. The final product was both soft and feminine, even classy. Pin curling involves a delicate process. Its installation is a loving act that requires time, attentiveness, care, and consideration. Perhaps Connie taught herself how to style Black hair, or she learned through her girlhood experiences or relationships in prison.

Ericka left a profound impression on Connie and shared similar sentiments for her in a poem, "for connie, a rollingstone," which she wrote on a napkin while Connie pin curled her hair:

> if there is cosmic beauty
> then your face holds it
> if there is human understanding
> then your soul is capable of it
> if a mind ever thought of freedom
> yours has flown to where freedom
> lives and has drifted back
> here to tell your body about it
> and you long for it
>
>   i can see it in your eyes
>   aquarius sister-love
>   i can see it . . . you
>   must know that one
>   day we will all
>   be
>   FREE[44]

In the above poem, Ericka's use of "human understanding" transcends their racial differences. The name "aquarius sister-love" references Connie's birth month, her affiliation with the Sister Love Collective, and their solidarity. Ericka stressed the utility of connecting the mind, body, and soul with notions of freedom in bondage. She closed the poem by drawing attention to Connie's "eyes" and reassures her that freedom is in sight. In the essay "Poetry Is Not a Luxury," Audre Lorde writes that poetry for women forms the "hopes and dreams toward survival and change, first made into language, then into idea, then into more tangible action."[45] Poetry became an outlet for Ericka to express what was happening around her and a way to heal. She embodies Lorde's theory by intertwining poetry with her communal care practices, demonstrating the interconnectedness of artistic expression and collective support.

Connie and Ericka's friendship and cross-racial political alliance speak to the way the Sister Love Collective served as a multiracial feminist space where women reconstructed ideas and practices of femininity, beauty, and womanhood. Almost fifty years later, Connie only faintly recalled much of her experiences at Niantic, but she remembered that she cherished her times with Ericka. By exploring different hair textures, Connie enhanced her social awareness and understanding. "We talked about political things, women things," she added.[46] In prison, Connie gained knowledge through relationships inaccessible to her in the free world. Ericka added, "We talked candidly about the current issues affecting us and sometimes that led us to history, sometimes it didn't, it almost didn't matter. That women could feel whole and complete and beautiful was the point."[47] Ericka underscored the significance of feeling beautiful as a vital component of self-empowerment. Her message serves as both a critique of the penal system, which denies women this essential right, and an expression of solidarity with the "Black Is Beautiful" movement. Aesthetics provide tangible representations of beauty that can be immediately perceived visually. In contrast, the beauty inherent in love, attraction, and the soul often eludes expression in words due to its profound and intangible nature.

Historically, Eurocentric values deny Black beauty and associate Blackness with unattractiveness and deviance. The Black Is Beautiful movement of the 1960s and 1970s countered derogatory societal attitudes about Blackness. This movement encouraged freedom of self-expression and pride in Black aesthetics, history, and culture.[48] Hair politics in the Sister Love Collective celebrated the Black Is Beautiful movement and what would become third-wave feminism.[49] Members manipulated their hair in a way that made them feel good. "Getting pretty" functioned as a statement of self-definition, and conversing while serving one another's personal needs evoked happiness. "I really enjoyed being with, talking to, and engaging in social and political and other kinds of conversations with the women. We talked about everything," Ericka confirmed.[50] Their conversations politicized Connie and pushed her to think in more complex ways about the power of Eurocentrism: "We would just be women in this common situation, but we rose above it because we were so idealistic. We were political. We refused to participate in Thanksgiving or Christmas. We fasted. We didn't want to eat anything tied to their shit[ty], Santa Claus they brought [to us]."[51] Imprisoned during the height of the Black Is Beautiful movement, the Sister Love Collective rejected European societal norms.

At such a young age, Connie's self-development was fueled by reading revolutionary literature and first-person accounts of disenfranchised voices. As she recollected, the "things that we read and talked about, for me to be sixteen, blows my mind till this day."[52] With attention to spirituality and mental health, the Sister Love Collective developed a culture of resistance for personal protection: "You have my physical body, but you do not have my mind or my spirit. We were not locked up in that way at all," Connie pronounced.[53] This language helped the members separate their physical imprisonment from their mental and spiritual well-being. Although their bodies were confined within the prison walls, they realized that they could liberate their minds and spirits, thereby fortifying their resilience and enhancing their capacity for survival. This idea connects with Ericka's poem "for connie, a rollingstone" as she explains through poetry the need for the alignment of the body with the mind and spirit/soul. In effect, they mentally liberated themselves from state surveillance.

Pin Curls and Cosmetics as Protest

While correctional officers largely disregarded the hair salon, certain hairstyles caught their attention. For instance, pin curls carried a political import in Niantic that placed a prisoner at risk for punishment. In preparing for a court appearance, a correctional officer admonished Ericka for wearing pin curls, as documented in the prison conduct log. Her inner strength protected her during an episode of conflict with correctional officers over her pin curls. On December 17, 1970, Niantic authorities reported that Ericka broke the rule on pin curls. They wrote, "E. Huggins appeared in the dining room [the day before] during the supper meal with her hair in pin curls."[54] Mrs. Monk, a matron, reminded Ericka of the ban on pin curls. In response to her verbal reprimand, Ericka declared that "according to the rules this is allowed."[55] The record keeper called attention to "the letter 'D' of rule #4 under clothing which states: Curlers may be worn in the dining room area only in the evening after supper and only if a woman is going to court the next day."[56] The correctional officer responded in a gut-wrenching and aggressive manner to a delicate feminine curl. Ericka was scheduled for a court appearance the following day. In an act of resistance, she opted for silence in response to the correctional officer's reprimands. Defiantly keeping her pin curls in place, Ericka made a powerful statement about her individuality, rejecting the New England expectation that one should be "dressed" for dinner in Niantic.

Pin curl coifs symbolize femininity, a gender performance directly in conflict with the institutional order of Niantic. At Niantic, the prohibition against pin curls represents the ways femininity was stripped from women as a form of punishment.[57] To allow women time to prepare their hair for a court appearance comes with a specific set of rules. The implications of an unfinished curl could have devastating consequences. Moreover, the complicated nature of these rules placed one at risk of punishment for violations. Hence, to wear pin curls, a style most policed by the correctional officers, put Ericka in a position fraught with danger. Blank space in the prison conduct log on Ericka could suggest events that occurred the next day; however, the log skips two days before the next dated entry. Next to the blank space, it notes Ericka's rage upon returning from court because of a bracelet seized from her, which was likely retaliation by authorities for her wearing pin curls. Her late husband, John, had given her the bracelet. The prison conduct log omits identifiable information on the keeper who seized the bracelet or its whereabouts to absolve themselves from any wrongdoing.[58]

As a tactic to protect the state, these glaring omissions erase the liability of the keepers for their harsh treatment of imprisoned women and the ways institutions police historical memory. The log continues with details on Ericka's food intake: "Tray was served. Ate nothing. Had a ½ cup tea, 1 glass milk. At 9 p.m. when checking Ericka for court she did say when she gets angry she can't eat. Gave her 2 glasses of milk."[59] Ericka's lack of appetite was likely a response to the traumatic loss of her property, a tangible connection to her late husband, John, exacerbated by her ongoing hunger strike. This was not just any property; it was

Figure 5.2. Connie Civita and her six-month-old daughter Lisa at a family home in Hartford, Connecticut, circa 1973. Photo courtesy of Lisa Cowell, Connie Civita's daughter.

jewelry, which often holds deep sentimental value. John gifted Ericka the jewelry as a symbol of his love and affection. The state's intervention in their relationship, culminating in the seizure of her bracelet, forced Ericka to relive the pain of losing John all over again. This act was more than just theft; it was a blatant violation of the emotional bond she shared with her late husband. The jewelry symbolized more than femininity; it was a physical reminder of John's love and a declaration of her worth. Just thirteen days after this incident, the Sister Love Collective experienced another loss when Connie's leadership came to an end, as the State of Connecticut dismissed her case and granted her release.[60] Connie made a profound impact in the Sister Love Collective despite being imprisoned in Niantic for roughly one month.

While Niantic placed restrictions on pin curls, it considered makeup contraband. To overcome this restriction, the Sister Love Collective mysteriously accessed beauty essentials. "We found makeup and markers, and somewhere we got body paint," Ericka explained. With these products, "everybody painted their faces kind of like kids do in whatever beautiful, flowery, butterflyish fashion they could come up with." Makeup made them feel some autonomy and control over their bodies. They wore makeup not for the male gaze, but for their own pleasure. They staged a silent protest spearheaded by Ericka to communicate their disdain for the makeup ban. Ericka gave the following instructions on the protest plan: "When we go to dinner today, we can wear whatever we're wearing and just be silent." Fearing a planned uprising, the correctional officers were alarmed by their silent outcry and summoned backup. "They thought we were planning something," recalled Ericka. Their subversion provoked confusion and aimless movement among the keepers. Members of the Sister Love Collective reveled in their amusement as they watched the keepers in chaos. "It was a great joke for us because, no makeup, well we can think out of the box." Survival rested on the ability to think innovatively. Ericka remembered, "It was fun and, on some level, that small activity was so empowering."[61] Playing with makeup allowed them to express their personality and resist alienation and exploitation.

Fashioning the Prison Uniform

In addition, the Sister Love Collective used carceral sartorial practices to challenge antiquated prison uniforms. The design of the state dress lacked shape and allowed for imprisoned women to slip in and out of it. Ericka compared wearing her uniform to "wearing a bag."[62] As a symbol of state power, prison wear preserves uniformity and renders selfhood invisible in such a way that bodies become a product of exploitation. Fashioning the prison uniform became a way for the women to adorn their bodies in ways that pleased them and served to counter the dehumanizing effects of imprisonment. Their alterations, which included hemming, tailoring, and stitching, repairing holes, rips, and torn areas as well as adding embellishments to create a new prison uniform, mimicked elements of material patchwork practiced by those formerly enslaved.[63] Women applied their craft to alter the uniform to their liking to shape their bodies. In this manner, they encouraged body positivity and self-confidence. Their creativity varied; some added seams to tuck the uniform in at the waist or make it shorter or tighter to show their legs, thighs, and beautiful bodies. Others created belts to wrap around the dress or bedecked themselves in hand-crafted leather or cloth headbands. They made the headbands the width of a belt and placed small holes in them for a string to tie in the back of their head. Ericka noted that "Black, Brown, white women, and all kinds of women wore headbands during this time. It was something that just floated through the culture."[64] Headbands became a trendy fashion statement of the 1960s and 1970s.

The use of style pushed back against objectification and transformed the uniform from a symbol of prison labor to a garment that invoked individual expression, distinguishing the individual from the nameless mass of incarcerated people. The uniform's new meaning represented a defiant affirmation of self and a rebellious love of self. Prison-bound "dressed bodies" evoked autonomy and dovetailed with the Black Is Beautiful movement, which validated varied body shapes of women of color rejected by Eurocentric beauty standards.[65] Ericka stressed, "It was mostly Black and Latina women, and we were not going to wear a sack."[66] Women risked punishment to remake their prison uniforms and affirm their sense of self. This suggested that as part of its rehabilitation efforts, Niantic implemented a dress code aimed at promoting modesty.[67] Dresses that were too tight or short caught the correctional officers' attention and were confiscated. Camp pointed out that women's enslaved bodies represented "a fiercely contested terrain between owner and owned."[68] Women's bodies evoke the same positionality in prison.[69] Across generations, women used dress as a political tool. Reshaping their prison uniforms functioned as overt resistance in the same way captive Black women in the post–Civil War era set fire to their manly looking prison uniforms to signal their personal freedom, as described by historian Talitha L. LeFlouria. She wrote, "The burning of clothes became a way in which some African American women reclaimed their bodily integrity and attempted to burn away their convict identity."[70]

The idea of stripping away a "convict identity" also rang true for Niantic women—Black, white, and Brown—as they redesigned their prison uniform to claim their dignity, showcasing, in the Sister Love Collective, bodily integrity, self-making, identity, and belonging as critical components of spirit-affirming women's prison organizing. The women of the Sister Love Collective used beauty and style to counter what LeFlouria identifies as "social rape" to characterize the "physical and psychological oppression experienced by African American women who were forcibly defeminized and masculinized . . . and stripped of their choice and *right* to be socially recognized as women."[71] The instances of "social rape" at Niantic were pronounced, with women from various racial backgrounds subjected to deplorable treatment. In response to these violations and the authoritarian control, the women united, leveraging their collective strength to resist "social rape" and assert their womanhood.

The inventive beauty routines employed by the women served as an oasis from the grim realities of prison life. They cunningly circumvented the correctional officers to meet their beauty needs, simultaneously resisting the dehumanizing treatment meted out by the correctional officers and the state. By choosing to adorn themselves in ways that uplifted their spirits, they also inspired other women in Niantic to practice self-care as a means of spiritual affirmation. The Sister Love Collective embodied a radical politics of care and spiritual affirmation that was indecipherable to the correctional officers. The restorative, care-based strategies pioneered by Ericka and Millie significantly shifted the culture within Niantic at that time. In aligning spiritual wellness practices of beautification and adornment with the Black Panther movement's principles of self-love and community care, Ericka and Millie effectively imported Black Panther politics into the prison environment. Their actions served as a powerful vehicle for empowering and uplifting women, demonstrating how they could reclaim their agency and self-worth.

Reducing Withdrawal Discomfort

In addition to practicing political activism through the spiritual activist practices tied to beauty culture, that is, haircare and adornment, Millie and Ericka used the Sister Love Collective to create restorative care-based tactics to preserve and sustain women's physical health. Millie pointed out to Ericka the deadly consequences of drug detoxification at Niantic, where prison officials frequently neglected to provide addicted women with necessary medical attention. Drawing from her own experiences and previous knowledge, Ericka was already well aware of this grim reality.

Drug detoxification consisted of prison officials placing women "in an isolation room to kick [detox from drugs, especially heroin] without any medical intervention."[72] Ericka was alarmed one night by the blood-curdling screams of Linda, an imprisoned woman who was enduring this dangerous detox practice. It was obvious to Ericka that Linda was suffering physically and emotionally from anguishing muscle and stomach pain. Though Ericka yelled from her cell for help, she was unsuccessful in her attempts to get assistance for Linda. "I couldn't sleep at all that night because of this [and] I knew she was dying. I just sat for meditation as best as I could in the hope that her pain would subside."[73] After the screams stopped, Ericka heard a loud silence. The next morning, before dawn, authorities finally arrived in an ambulance with lights flashing and the siren muted. They removed Linda's lifeless body.[74] Ericka and other imprisoned women knew that Linda had died in her cell that night. That morning at breakfast, Ericka and others asked a cordial matron about Linda. "Oh, she had a bad withdrawal. We took her to the hospital," the matron responded. "Come on, she died," Ericka and the women persisted.[75] With their own detective work, they learned that peritonitis inflammation in the abdominal wall, commonly due to infection, served as the primary cause of Linda's death.[76] They complained to the prison administration, but were disregarded, so they took action without formal authorization. They cared about Linda, and her death motivated them to add physical health, detox, and inner healing to their agenda.

Millie and Ericka quickly organized the Sister Love Collective to assist newly admitted imprisoned women dependent on heavy drugs.[77] They used their commissary as well as other women's items and commissary to engage in illicit activity as they distributed candy and cigarettes to women in the detox isolation cells.

Ericka had come up with the idea to "smuggle cigarettes and candy, if the women smoked, but definitely candy or anything sweet to ease the muscle pain and the agony of it all."[78] Ericka and Millie believed that candy and cigarettes could ease the pain of withdrawal.[79] Christine offered candy and cigarettes to detoxing women passed to her by her boyfriend while they sat hand in hand during his visit. Likewise, Alice gave detoxing women the candy and cigarettes she received from her family and friends. After Christine's visitation, prison officers did not find any outside items on her during her strip search because of how she hid them on her person, as did Alice.[80] Some in the Sister Love Collective might have also made a deal with correctional officers to get supplies to those in detoxification. Moreover, to maintain a line of communication with those undergoing detoxification, the Sister Love Collective participants lay on the floor to talk to women in the isolation cell through the heating vents between the floors. "Talking to them kept women alive," Ericka remembered.[81] They saved lives; without it, women could die. Upon leaving the isolation room, women expressed gratitude for the Sister Love Collective's gestures of care, which had touched their souls. The group sought to restore the body to physical health even if it meant engaging in illegal activities.

Ericka informed Katy Roraback and Charles Garry, two members of her legal team, about Niantic's drug detoxification procedures. They arranged for one of their legal colleagues to speak with the Connecticut Department of Corrections. Following their involvement, Ericka claimed, Niantic offered medical treatment to women withdrawing from drugs.[82] However, Ericka noted that Niantic failed to offer women psychological counseling services at the time.[83] When women could not gain professional help, they turned to each other for support. Mentorship was often a surrogate for therapy.

Many women in the Sister Love Collective understood the necessity of mentorship, particularly in the drug recovery process. Maria, an older woman who suffered from an addictive disorder, often acted as a mentor for young women. Ericka recalled Maria in dialogue with Kimberly, a passionate teenager. In an attempt to "wake up" Kimberly, Maria explicated the dangers of drug misuse.[84] "Who the fuck you think you talking to?" Kimberly angrily responded.[85] Maria called attention to the reality that she could lose years of her life because of her risky drug behavior. This moment marked the first time another person took the time and energy to talk with Kimberly. Since Kimberly wanted to continue to use drugs, she found Maria's words triggering and sobering. Maria then began to use her body as a learning tool. "You think I wear long sleeves because I'm cold?" she said. She lifted her sleeves to reveal some of the keloid scars on her skin from IV drug use. The ghastly sight made Kimberly, Ericka, and others recoil in shock. "Her arms were like she'd been tortured but she'd done that to herself, so she could find a new vein to put the needle in," Ericka remembered. Maria's cautionary tale of self-inflicted abuse brought Kimberly to tears. "How do I do this?" Kimberly asked Maria as she surrendered to her fear.[86] In the outside world, everyone is taught to value individual grit, but prison could not be combated in this way. In fact, individual isolation quickens one's demise. Healing required collectivism. Recovery was found in solidarity. Maria showed Kimberly how to do this by first reminding her that she was not alone.

On another occasion, Maria talked with a group of women, including Sandra, a white teenager, who stated during the conversation, "I wasn't raised right."[87] Sandra's observation spoke to the personal trauma she experienced during her formative years. Maria stressed the importance of being addiction-free and surrounding yourself with people who will keep you out of prison. She removed her shoes and socks to illustrate the damaging effects of drugs from IV administration between her toes. She also wanted to display the limited veins that were still intact. Listeners were deeply affected by seeing the extreme effects of her drug use. Ericka often walked women over to the place where Maria sat, to hear her powerful testimony. Over time, Maria talked to dozens of women on a one-on-one basis and in group settings. Time and time again, she revealed the scars on her belly, arms, legs, feet, and chest from injecting drugs. Ericka described mentorship-in-action as "a beautiful experience."[88] Mentorship was an emotional investment in the care of others. It meant that women could help each other slay the demons that preyed upon them all their lives, to get and stay in remission.

Women's Bail Fund

The Sister Love Collective established a bail fund specifically designed to assist women whose bail costs were $150 or less. In deciding to create this fund, they took into account the economic status of the imprisoned women, their inability to post bail, the deplorable conditions within the prison system, and the importance of maintaining familial bonds. For women who were cash-strapped and lacked access to financial resources, this modest fund became a crucial lifeline. Jan Von Flatern, a white twenty-one-year-old political journalist, played a significant role in maintaining the fund. Katy Roraback likely helped many of the imprisoned Sister Love Collective participants, including those newly released. They raised money informally through public donations.[89] Jan remembered once requesting donations at a party at her house. As soon as Ericka learned that a woman needed to post bail, she contacted Katy Roraback for legal help. With the bail fund, they collected enough money to post bail for a few women before their trial date.

While Jan worked to keep the fund afloat, within the prison walls, Ericka's community-minded spirit moved her to continue to help women with quotidian struggles. She regularly gifted women poetry she wrote, headbands and neckbands she stitched, and care boxes and books obtained from others, including her legal team, Katy Roraback, Charles Garry, and David Rosen.[90] She shared these items with women at Niantic for good wishes and special occasions such as birthdays and prison releases. Literature fed the revolutionary spirit for Ericka. She read all kinds of books in prison. She remarked on the profoundness of Kwame Nkrumah's *Dark Days in Ghana*, which charts the rise and fall of Nkrumah's leadership in Ghana. She also mentioned Ethel and Julius Rosenberg's prison letters to their sons as they neared their execution for an espionage conspiracy charge. She read the poetry of Gwendolyn Brooks. Brooks became the first Black poet that Ericka connected with because of her deep analysis on the Black experience. Once she acquired books from Charles Garry, she circulated them through the many hands of imprisoned women, until the books fell apart; however, matrons often seized their books.[91] Her mother once brought her new underwear that she gave to another imprisoned woman in need.

At the helm of the Sister Love Collective, Ericka drew on the Black Panthers' community programs. She contested horrific prison conditions and worked to relieve the emotional strain of confinement. The collective's experience in carceral life was transformed by its covert protests.[92] Together, through spiritual wellness, the Sister Love Collective changed prison conditions, not with the help of the state, but despite the state. These women refused and rebuffed death. Their collective political acts reclaimed their womanhood and humanity. From then on, Ericka might have been separated from her family, but she was not alone, and she was not without love. And equally important, neither were the women with her.

Most women imprisoned with Ericka lacked access to legal aid. Aware of her access to a legal team, she tirelessly labored to help imprisoned women obtain lawyers. Her efforts echo the BPP's Legal Aid for Prisoners Program, which functioned as a "referral service" for legal support and representation.[93] The Sister Love Collective's women's bail fund is deeply rooted in the Black traditions of mutual aid, benevolent societies, and women's clubs, representing an early precursor to the prison support activities undertaken by contemporary community groups such as the National Bail Out collective. Started in 2017, the National Bail Out collective ties its work to the history of self-emancipation "where our enslaved Black ancestors used their collective resources to purchase each other's freedom."[94] Shaped by Black resistance, their political work on bail reform aims to "free black mamas and caregivers" from local jails on Mother's Day each year.[95] Since its inception, it has posted bail for hundreds of Black mothers through its Black Mamas Bail Out initiative. The group's leadership represents a myriad of social identities across gender, sexuality, class, and age. They provide a wealth of resources, including jobs, housing, food, medical care, treatment for unhealthy substance use, and emergency transportation services.[96] They produced a toolkit for the public to combat the injustices of the pretrial legal system and mobilize with activists and organizations across the country on their reform efforts. This is the fruit of Ericka, Millie, and the Sister Love Collective's labor, a legacy that continues to invest in the lives of imprisoned women battling the carceral violence of the state and federal government.

The impact of the Sister Love Collective reached the courtroom as the trial of Ericka and Bobby approached. Once the jury selection started, the collective expanded its efforts. In letters passed to Jan in the courtroom, Ericka requested resources for pregnant women and support in connecting mothers with their children and families. She was able to see herself in the lives of each and every woman imprisoned. She knew what it meant to suffer, to lose a loved one, and to be a mother separated from one's child. Her letters offered insight into her endless labor as an avid advocate for imprisoned women.

6

Joy on Trial

Freedom. I couldn't believe that it had really happened, that
the nightmare was over, that finally the dream had come
true. I was elated. Ecstatic. But i was completely disoriented.
Everything was the same, yet everything was different.
—Assata Shakur

On November 17, 1970, Ericka woke up early.[1] She knew that this was
the day she would find a brief reprieve from the walls of her prison cell.
This trip and each subsequent trip to the courthouse started with the
same mechanized routine. "Good morning, officers," Ericka stated as
Officers Smith and O'Conner escorted her outside Niantic to the caravan prepared to transport her to the New Haven County Courthouse.
Smith never spoke back to Ericka; however, O'Conner unfailingly
responded politely. "Morning, Huggins," he uttered as he lightly handcuffed her and gently bent her head to prevent her from hitting the
door frame while getting in the backseat. He strapped Ericka into her
seatbelt and sat in the front passenger's seat while Smith silently drove
on Interstate 95 to the courthouse "as if a robot was driving the car,"
Ericka thought to herself.[2] Invariably, Smith stayed stiff and kept his
head forward. These same correctional officers took her back and forth
to the courthouse daily.

This chapter chronicles how Ericka defended her personhood by employing survival tactics that I interpret as acts of care related to spiritual
wellness. These include forming friendships with the Niantic staff like
Officer O'Conner and reporters such as Jan Von Flatern. While Ericka
was on trial, her spiritual wellness practice shifted from acts of self-care
to providing assistance for incarcerated women as a whole. Ericka demonstrated her commitment to advocacy through her continued work
with the Sister Love Collective, notably by exchanging letters with Jan
and building an enduring friendship. Her collaboration with Jan was

instrumental in connecting prisoners with legal assistance, securing bond money, and organizing travel for those nearing release as well as providing support for expectant mothers.

The significance of Ericka and Bobby's trial transcended their individual cases, symbolizing the broader struggle against systemic oppression. The trial galvanized student activists and community members from all racial and socioeconomic backgrounds, uniting them in their support for Ericka and Bobby, seen as emblematic figures in the fight against ongoing attacks on the movement. The widespread protests, marches, and demonstrations advocating for Ericka and Bobby's freedom were not just about their lives as political prisoners, but were also about safeguarding the lives of future generations. Their release from prison after over six months was evidence of the people's tenacity in supporting political prisoners and Black Power organizers.

The Power of a Smile

One day, while Ericka was traveling to the courthouse, she noticed that her wrists were small enough to unshackle herself.[3] As often as she could, she slipped her wrists in and out of her handcuffs.[4] To amuse herself, she turned this activity into her private game. Focused and reflective, she thought about the freedom she felt during meditation. This led her to the idea of removing her handcuffs as if symbolically liberating herself. She wondered whether others thought of shedding their chains, embracing the mindset of being free. "After I began to meditate, I realized they couldn't hold me, that I was free no matter what constraints they put on me. I laughed about how this inner freedom was something they couldn't touch or take," she declared.[5] Inner freedom helped her realize that the state could not contain her. It gave her a way to recognize her power. On chilly days, she took off her handcuffs and used her coat to cover her bare wrists. The handcuffs were big and clunky, forcing her to move carefully so as not to alert the officers. Danger lurked when the handcuffs got lost in the folds of her coat, and she had to dig around to find them without drawing the attention of the correctional officers.

As they neared the courthouse, she put the handcuffs on. Being uncuffed would bring trouble not only on herself, but also on the officers responsible for her. Upon their arrival, O'Conner assisted Ericka out of the vehicle. Ericka immediately looked up at the sun. It was shining bright on this warm, lovely spring day. She cherished this moment. As a captive at Niantic, she rarely saw the sun. "Wow, O'Conner, the sun is so bright. Isn't it beautiful?" O'Conner, a slim white man with kind brown eyes and a friendly face, stood slightly shorter than Ericka, who was five feet eleven. Dressed in his state patrol uniform—a pressed shirt, dark slacks, and a campaign hat—with his firearm tucked away in his holster, he seemed conscientious about his presentation. He wore a special jacket in the winter months. Niantic trained O'Conner how to behave around those imprisoned. "She is a monster," cautioned fellow officers, so he contemplated his next step. He slowly raised his head. "Yeah, Huggins, it is beautiful." They smiled at one another as he escorted her into the courtroom.[6]

At the end of the court day, they headed back to Niantic. Ericka paused her private game. "Hey, Officer O'Conner, you have a beautiful smile." He turned his body from the front seat to have a conversation with Ericka. As he began to talk, Smith's neck flushed red. His shoulders were tense. He stiffened. He was visibly uncomfortable; however, O'Conner was intrigued by Ericka's words and a bit flattered.

"Really?" he asked.
"Yeah, you should smile more often."[7]

Her message registered: smiling felt good. Smith cast a sharp glance at O'Conner. He frowned when O'Conner communicated with Ericka. The next day, the everyday ritual proceeded, and a caravan of cars arrived at Niantic to take Ericka to court. This time, she took in the beautiful Connecticut countryside during the drive. After some time, O'Conner turned around and seriously looked at Ericka.

"Hey, Huggins, I told my wife what you said."
"You did. What did she say?" She eagerly anticipated his response.
"She said, you are right. I should smile more."[8]

They laughed. Smith pursed his lips and tightened his face. He seemed to seethe with anger. Ericka imagined that Smith assumed she was having a love affair with O'Conner. Their interactions represented a human connection between an imprisoned woman and a state patrol officer and served as a reminder of the presence of kindness in her otherwise hostile carceral life. Ericka explained that because of O'Conner's kindness, she made an intentional effort to be friendly with him. Ericka wondered whether there were officers "who didn't settle or go along" with anti-Black violent practices.[9] O'Conner, who failed to exhibit racist behavior, made her feel safe enough to ask him about the six police cars that traveled with them to the courthouse.

> "What do they think is going to happen? Why a caravan?" she inquired.
>
> He fumbled over his words. "Well, I don't know, Huggins. We fear some people with guns will come in a helicopter or cars, park discreetly on both sides of the road and break you out of prison."[10]

She refrained from laughing but thought that the idea was ridiculous. Ericka was not interested in living in exile or running for the rest of her life. She was determined to stand trial. O'Conner was kind as he helped Ericka, handcuffed, into the vehicle with care each day. This simple consideration during their transports back and forth to court propelled Ericka to have a conversation with him. His kindness challenged Ericka's long-held perception of the police, shaped by her upbringing in Washington, DC, where the police were dangerous and unpredictable. She began to entertain the possibility that not all officers were devoid of humanity. Sensing O'Conner's authenticity, she considered her small talk as a way to pursue a friendship with him, hoping that it might alter his perception of her in a positive way. It seemed to work, evidenced by the fact that he told his wife about their friendly conversation. She saw him as courageous for talking to her in front of his partner, and by virtue of his kindness and their conversations, felt that they shared an "unsaid friendship."[11]

The personal relationships Ericka forged with white male correctional officers served as a strategic attempt to maintain and assert her humanity. She illustrates that a little kindness goes a long way. Ericka's smiles, charm, and laughter not only reflected her authenticity but also helped her gain sympathy and human recognition to disarm O'Conner and the other officer. In the context of meditative practice, a smile is a moment of human recognition. The dynamic between Ericka and O'Conner enabled him to feel validated and allowed her to be recognized as a person.

"It helped me a lot," she remembered.[12] Through smiles and relationship building, she challenged their vision of her as a criminal. Ericka's experiences shed light on the act of smiling as a potent tool of resistance.

Ericka took days to reflect on the possibility of being locked in a cage for the rest of her life. She resolved that she would withstand it and live as fully as she could. Regarding the trial, she believed that "whatever was supposed to happen would happen."[13] Ericka's realization was tempered by the poignant fact that it would cause her to miss significant moments in her daughter's life. However, the presence of Mai at the trial, brought by John's mother, Mrs. Huggins, offered some solace, as it allowed Ericka to see her daughter regularly.[14] The charges against Ericka meant that she faced either life imprisonment or the death penalty. Despite the unknown possibilities, she felt protected by the love and kindness she received from family, friends, supporters, and the news reporters who befriended her. Some supporters even brought their children to the trial.[15] The courtroom, chilly and densely crowded, often turned away latecomers due to its limited capacity. Ericka drew strength from the overwhelming support of the attendees. Aiming to project an air of composure and resilience during the trial, she consciously chose to smile, signaling to the jury her ability to remain steadfast despite the challenging circumstances.

Inside the courtroom, body language was both critical and political. Ericka's meditation, yoga practice, and gratitude for life gave her reasons to smile. She made sure to smile as much as she could; a pleasant demeanor could help set people at ease or, at the very least, affirm her humanity. Inside and outside the courthouse, she smiled at everyone. She appreciated her lawyers' hard work, the Sister Love Collective, the notes and letters from friends, including Jan, sent to her through Katy Roraback. Those who attended the trial often displayed their solidarity by raising their fists and smiling at her. Smiling became contagious, and she acknowledged this by addressing them in the same manner. Crucially, smiling evolved into a source of empowerment for her, serving as a confirmation of her visibility and presence.[16]

Ericka also smiled to support BPP chairman Bobby Seale. She felt a sibling bond with him as they stood trial together. According to her, Bobby tended to look stern in court, so that onlookers were unable to discern what he was thinking or feeling. During recess, he relaxed with Ericka as they discussed the events of the day. They laughed at comments by prospective jurors. "They would bring in prospective jurors with wacky understandings of what it meant to be innocent until proven guilty. I'm not so sure they understood who Black people are," Ericka explained.[17] Most prospective jurors were reluctant to serve, came to court with prior knowledge of the case, and/or expressed their thoughts on the Black Panthers' guilt or innocence.[18] The defense challenged jurors with negative opinions about Black people in general and the Black Panthers specifically.

Jury Selection

The defense team, Katy Roraback, Charles Garry, and David Rosen, insisted on jury representation that included Black men and women as well as white women. It was a demanding and time-consuming process to locate appropriate residents of New Haven County. According to Donald Freed, former humanities professor and friend of the Black Panthers who attended the trial, "The defense charged a statistical 'sampling error' or distorted jury profile in violation of the Constitutional rights of Bobby Seale and Ericka Huggins."[19] As a result of discrimination based on race, gender, and class, the jury pool reeked of male bias, made up primarily of white men.[20] The New Haven County population included roughly 50 percent men, and the jury pool was over 60 percent male.[21] During the months-long jury selection process, Katy Roraback and Charles Garry were given every opportunity to question jurors by Harold M. Mulvey, whom Ericka remembered as a fair judge who never muttered about the Black Panthers or grumbled about the length of time taken to seat the jury. David Rosen noted that Katy Roraback "never let any of the men, including the defense, forget" that the jury pool process institutionalized rampant sexism.[22] The trial transcript indicated that "some 1,500 names were drawn and about 1,100 persons examined before a jury could be selected."[23] During jury selection, the atmosphere was tense. One day, Mr. Johnson, a prospective juror who was a white middle-class racist, reached the front of the line to be questioned. Recess had ended, and people were still exhausted. Garry began his line of questioning.

"Mr. Johnson, do you have any Black friends?"
"Yes I do, sir. I have a friend who is a Negro."

"Well, good, Mr. Johnson. Tell me about your friend."

"He does my gardening."[24]

The courtroom erupted in laughter; people even stomped their feet at the hilarity of Mr. Johnson's comments. Members of the press started writing vigorously. Judge Mulvey, struggling to conceal his own smile, banged his gavel to gain control of the courtroom. "Thank God for this recess," Ericka recalled, grateful for a much-needed break.[25]

This incident shed light on the white, racist, and conservative politics of New England in the 1970s. Ericka believed that Judge Mulvey's witnessing of racist occurrences firsthand by potential jurors shifted his view toward her and Bobby, prompting him to confront and address his bias toward them. She added that during the trial, he looked at her and Bobby with compassion in his eyes. The defense ended up with a twelve-member majority-women panel, with five Black women and three white women.[26] In David Rosen's interview with historian Amy Kesselman, Rosen claimed that the case included the largest number of Black jurors in Connecticut history at that time.[27] By the time the state completed its four-month-long selection process, it made history as the state's longest.[28]

Relationship Building with Jan Von Flatern

Ericka formed relationships with fellow prisoners, correctional officers, and reporters during court proceedings. Jan Von Flatern, a white, slim, petite woman with dark brown eyes and long brown hair pulled back in a ponytail, stood out among the many journalists who covered the trial each day in the New Haven County Courthouse. They were only a year apart, both in their early twenties, but Ericka seemed much older with her life experience. Jan had a quiet, peaceful disposition and a pleasant demeanor. A journalist, Jan was covering the trial for the Liberation News Service (LNS), a left-leaning underground wire service. Activists Raymond Mungo and Marshall Bloom started LNS in 1967 as a central hub for underground news.[29] For updates on the case, Jan's assignment included attending the trial each day and writing articles for LNS. The demands of the job forced her to take a year off her studies at Albertus Magnus College, a small private liberal arts Catholic college located in Prospect Hill, a suburban neighborhood in New Haven. Since Jan was a writer for a countercultural news organization, Mulvey kindly assigned her a seat in the press box. "He was bending over backward to show that he was open to the underground press," Jan recalled in an oral history with me.[30] Because of her designation as press, Jan had a seat in the front row, which allowed her to meet Katy Roraback, who soon became her communication link to Ericka.

Jan engaged in a note-taking process at the trial. During jury selection, she kept a detailed written record of the number of men and women potential jurors each day as they were questioned, along with their racial backgrounds. Humorous or racist comments by prospective jurors and the prosecution caught her attention. She recalls, "I would do quotable quotes or things that they would say that were either funny or struck me as stupid or racist."[31] The days were long, so absurd remarks in the courtroom entertained her and diverted her attention from the monotony of the trial. One day, as Jan pushed through the monotony, she looked at the clock as she awaited recess. She felt confined and needed a break for the day. "I need to leave to write and get some wine," she thought.[32] While Jan felt confined to the courtroom, she remembered that Ericka's time in court served as her outings, which she used as a creative outlet. To resist the way others defined her, Ericka wrote an autobiographical poem:

> tall
> skinny
> plain i am
> ericka,
> fuzzy hair
> droopy eyes
> long feet
>   i love people
>   love nature
>   love love
> i am a revolutionary
> nothing special
>   one soul
>   one life   willing
>   to give it
>   ready to die. . . .
>   Ericka[33]

In this poem, Ericka described her physical features, her interests, and her revolutionary politics to reclaim her humanity. She declared her ethic of love as central to her being.

Jan's link to Ericka and the community she formed with other reporters deepened, fueling her sustained interest in the trial. Each day following dismissal, Jan typed up what was called the *Panther Trial News*.[34] Then, she took three to five days of the *Panther Trial News* and abridged the information into an article for LNS. Jan made sure not to obsess over every detail, but instead drafted a careful and coherent article for a general audience that focused on the courtroom's highlights. Occasionally, she dictated her articles over the phone. LNS lightly edited her work, kept her byline, and sent it to its subscribers. On the twelfth day of the jury selection process, Jan wrote,

> The *voir dire* (jury selection) continues in the trial of Ericka Huggins and Bobby Seale. Thus far 300 candidates have been considered—a third of whom have been excused without appearing because of medical or financial hardship. Of the 200 or so others, approximately 10 have been black. Nearly all of the white people questioned have been excused because of their exposure to negative pre-trial publicity and their prejudice against the defendants or the Black Panther Party in general.[35]

In the passage above, Jan sheds light on institutional racism, negative coverage of the trial, and preconceived ideas against the BPP and its impact on the jury pool.

LNS regularly compiled and distributed packets of content from its correspondence to its newspaper subscribers. While the *Panther Trial News* circulated throughout New Haven, Jan hand-delivered the newsletter each day to the Black Panther headquarters on Sylvan Avenue in the Hill neighborhood, a distressed area in New Haven, not far from where she lived. She vividly described her visits, remembering that she felt like "this little white girl tripping up these stone steps to the house." The Black Panthers tightly secured the big heavy front door of their row house with "seventeen locks." Jan heard "clang, cling, clang, boom, bang" as two big men unlocked the door for her to give them the *Panther Trial News*. "I tripped in there like it was no big deal. I had a lot of innocence that I am glad I had at the time," she recalled.[36] She added, "There was cross-racial warmth. I never felt threatened. I always felt welcomed." Jan's feelings reflected the Black Panthers' approach to coalition politics, showcasing their willingness to collaborate with a wide range of progressive people.

Ericka's relationship with Jan began when she gave Katy Roraback a note thanking Jan for coming to her trial. Jan replied, and their relationship evolved through a steady stream of letters and notes privately exchanged in the courtroom through Katy Roraback until Ericka's release.[37] Sometimes, Katy Roraback would give Jan an envelope with six letters in them at a time. Ericka's letters to Jan served as a political and social survival strategy. Occasionally, Ericka referred to Jan as "January" or opened her letters with "sister-love," "sisterloves," "sisterlovefriend," "jan, my sister," "jansisterlovefriend," "jan, sisterlove," or "my sisters."[38] The letters discussed Ericka's internal world, her emotions, her desires, her love for others, her prison conditions, her advocacy for other imprisoned women, and her resistance efforts.

Jan became enamored and impressed with Ericka as she learned more about her through their letter exchange. "We never talked, Jan and I. She would sit there writing her notes for the Liberation News Service. I would sit there in my defendant's seat. Our relationship was based on letters and looking at one another," Ericka explained.[39] Their relationship began as a convenience, especially for Ericka, and developed into a loving friendship. "I ended up being a friendly face in the courtroom when she very much needed one," Jan recalled.[40] This connection with Jan alleviated Ericka's anxiety as they communicated in the courtroom, not just through letters but also via facial expressions. They developed a friendship where they could "speak" with their eyes, providing mutual comfort. Ericka's ability to see the inherent value in people enabled them to be their authentic selves, sometimes even sparking romantic and sensual feelings. Ericka and Jan enjoyed a romantic friendship, described by feminist philosophers Sukaina Hriji and Meena Krishnamurthy as an "intense desire to know and be known." They both wanted "to be seen."[41] In this respect, Ericka's strategies of care were platonic and sensual, encouraging bonds between women that some would argue were queer in nature. The queer dynamics speak to the ways Ericka embraced a survival strategy that transgressed heteronormativity through friendship, self-discovery, and love.

They developed a strong sisterly bond that transcended race based on their identity as women. Ericka felt familiar to Jan, "like a good friend feels when you meet someone or a romantic partner too." Jan declared, "I recognized Ericka, and she appeared to feel the same way."[42] Ericka made it clear that she always searched for "something deeper inside every human."[43] Perhaps this search appealed to Jan as she described their friendship as profoundly intense, personal, and peculiar. Their relationship gave Jan insight into her humanity. It satisfied their individual needs at the time. It provided Ericka with an outlet and a lifeline to the outside world, and it helped Jan to write knowledgeably about Ericka as a news reporter. This helped Jan to refute false depictions and narratives concerning Ericka. Jan stated, "I had this enormous interest in and affection for this woman that they were accusing of murder, and it was not the woman that I was getting to know."[44] She learned that Ericka was introspective, caring, and generous. For Jan, political journalism fostered sincere affection. Although she was deeply invested in the trial's outcome from its start, she became anxious and afraid for Ericka. She thought of how scared Ericka must have been and considered it her obligation to attend the trial every day. Ericka remembered Jan saying in a letter, "Today, in court, I almost walked out. I couldn't bear how sad you were. I couldn't look at you and understand why you were incarcerated."[45] Jan expressed her genuine concern for Ericka in her letters.

Ericka and Jan shared similar intellectual interests and ideas regarding sexuality. "I'm gay," Jan wanted to make clear in an oral history with me.[46] She assumed that Ericka knew she was gay as they began their friendship, because Jan saw herself as "very out at the time."[47] Jan did not recall any discussions they had about their personal sexual identities, but believed that Ericka was not "out" during this period of her life.[48] Their bond was further solidified by their shared beliefs and love that Ericka expressed in her letters. Under the intensity of the trial, Jan eventually fell in love with Ericka. In return, Ericka loved her, but was not sure that she was *in love* with her.[49] However, Ericka and Jan forged a deep and enduring relationship that defied definition.

Through her meditation practice, Ericka was embracing self-love and extending that love to others. In response to the isolation she experienced at Niantic, she greeted outreach from others with warmth and affection. Jan highlighted the cultural connections they shared, deepening their bond. "Other than the fact that she's Black and I'm white, she thought about the same kinds of things, and she read the same books," Jan remembered.[50] The prison letter exchanges between Ericka and Jan are examples of spiritual wellness and also exemplify what historian Sarah Haley describes as "freedom transcripts," in that they "illuminate both the mobilization of ferocious state violence and the vigorous efforts to reject the world that such violence sought to create."[51] The love and care expressed in their letters became a political force against racial state violence.[52]

Through letters, Ericka and Jan were able to bare their souls to one another and reach a deep spiritual connection through literature. They were both readers of spiritually edifying books, especially Hermann Hesse's. In a letter to Jan (figure 6.1), Ericka shared her observations on Hesse's novel *Steppenwolf*, which explores a personal journey toward spiritual transformation:

> I just finished Steppenwolf. It is all so close to what I was saying about people/love/friendship-the body-mind-spirit. . . . I love you even more after finishing that love people more do you understand? yes, I think you do—it is trying to be quiet in here now. The turn-keys are checking doors. making sure we can't get out—I wonder if all the women are wishing for freedom like I am right now. freedom for all of us and the
>
> whole
> universe.
> 13 January 1970
> 8:40 p.m.

Steppenwolf helped Ericka express her love for Jan and people more powerfully. The storyline's interest in the reciprocal nexus of "people/love/friendship" and "the body-mind-spirit" helped her articulate the idea that people desire sincere, loving friendships free of judgment. Her reference to correctional officers whose jobs were to secure cell rooms to prevent escape—"turn-keys are checking doors"—underscores how the intense alertness of incarceration encouraged her reflection concerning the other imprisoned women who were simultaneously yearning for "freedom for all."

Art offered Ericka a creative outlet to organize her thoughts. She noted that she used the novel to focus away from the "circus [in the

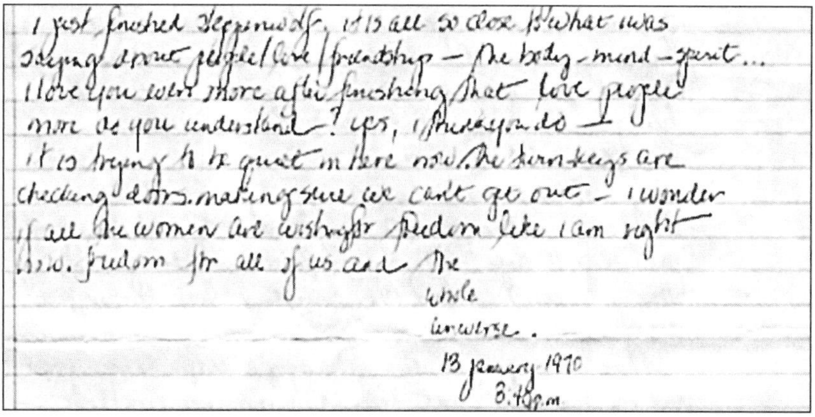

Figure 6.1. Letter from Ericka to Jan, January 13, 1970. Ericka wrote this letter at Niantic. From Jan Von Flatern's personal letters.

courtroom] and be with myself."[53] In a letter to Jan, she drew a portrait of herself crying (figure 6.2). Her eyes are boldly represented, signifying for Ericka the invitation she extended to Jan into her soul. "Many people, even old folks, say that the eyes are the mirror to the soul, and that was our connection."[54] She placed a star in the middle of a teardrop with the word "Steppenwolf" in all caps underneath the lower eyelid on the left eye. She identified with *Steppenwolf*'s trope of dislocation, given her prison confinement, and related to the main character, Harry Haller, and his attempt at self-discovery. The teardrop conveyed her inner pain and suffering. As Ericka's primary contact to the outside world, Jan symbolized the physical manifestation of the star in the teardrop. She invoked her like a beam of light for happiness as she called on her to "make me smile sisterlove" amidst the literal and figurative darkness of prison life and the courtroom.

The other side of the self-portrait illustrates Ericka's originality (figure 6.3). Surrounding the image are sentences presented in a nonlinear manner. The nonlinearity of the sentences breaks from the structural boundaries often seen in letter writing, making it challenging to locate a beginning, middle, and end to Ericka's thoughts. Starting with the sentences that closely frame the image and then circling clockwise, the letter reads as follows:

Figure 6.2. Ericka's self-portrait sketch accompanying an undated letter to Jan. From Jan Von Flatern's personal letters, 1970–1971.

SOMEONE STARTED TO DO A THOT [sic]-DRAWING/GUESS THEY GOT BORED OR STOPPED IN THE PROCESS. THAT'S HOW I FEEL TODAY BORED and STOPPED IN THE PROCESS[.] I DON'T EVEN FEEL CAPABLE OF THINKING TODAY OR BEING—ALL MY SISTERS ARE SO FAR AWAY IT SEEMS AND THE WORD NOISES THESE TURN-KEYS MAKE HURTS way down in my soul. love is why we feel pain. love is why. love is. I want to scream women do not know how to be sisters men do not know how to be brothers humankind has lost all sense of peoplelove. (this is not a message or a poem this is a long sigh). In green ink butterfly who is the one who started this sigh) wrote freedom—see it? and she deserved it and we deserve it the world deserves . . . butterfly-youngsisterlove who *is* joy and happiness just like her name and her soul[.] 10AM COURTROOM BLUES AGAIN. NO MORE TO SAY. I LOVE YOU JANUARY.

The doodle art includes geometric shapes carefully placed in the middle of the page. The word "freedom" is bold and artfully written in all caps. It outshines the other words on the document, making it a central theme of the piece. To ensure that Jan did not overlook this, she directed her attention to the words "wrote freedom—see it?" The capitalized sentences throughout the letter add emphasis to her emotions. The action of drawing geometric shapes and images inspired by nature calmed Ericka, and the designs of the geometric shapes, the "butterfly," the eye, the flower, and the circling of the words represent "freedom." She begins in the third person as she describes herself, SOMEONE STARTED TO DO A THOT-DRAWING," to indicate that the piece reflects her inner thoughts. By the second line, she owns her feelings, declaring, "THAT'S HOW I FEEL TODAY BORED AND STOPPED IN THE PROCESS."

This art project served as a way to keep her busy in the courtroom. The moments of interruption in the piece are evident in the parts of the "THOT-DRAWING" left blank. She announced her exhaustion and expressed loneliness and fear in her words, "ALL MY SISTERS ARE SO FAR AWAY IT SEEMS AND THE WORD NOISES THESE TURN-KEYS MAKE HURTS way down in my soul." Again, she returned to the "turn-keys" as they remain a present reminder of surveillance. Articulating her rage, she wrote, "I want to scream women do not know how to be sisters men do not know how to be brothers humankind has lost all sense of peoplelove." Her critique of the societal conditions that allow for incarceration resonated in the absence of "peoplelove" in prison. In parentheses, she proclaimed, "this is not a message or a poem this is a long sigh," one that is melancholic as she recorded that her "COURTROOM BLUES" started at "10AM" and lasted throughout the day. Ericka referred to Jan as "butterfly-youngsisterlove" as she epitomized "joy" and "happiness." Her last words, "I love you January," not only express her adoration for Jan but also represent another form of connection between them. The word "January" carried a double meaning within their relationship, signifying Jan's first name and Ericka's birth month. The letter and the images Ericka created to convey her love for Jan, her emotional frustration concerning the trial as well as her imprisonment, and her deep sadness concerning the loveless-ness of US society accentuate the extent to which Ericka leaned deep into her personhood to face as well as manage the matrix of emotions the trial and imprisonment brought forth within her. More than that, this exchange with Jan served as an indication of

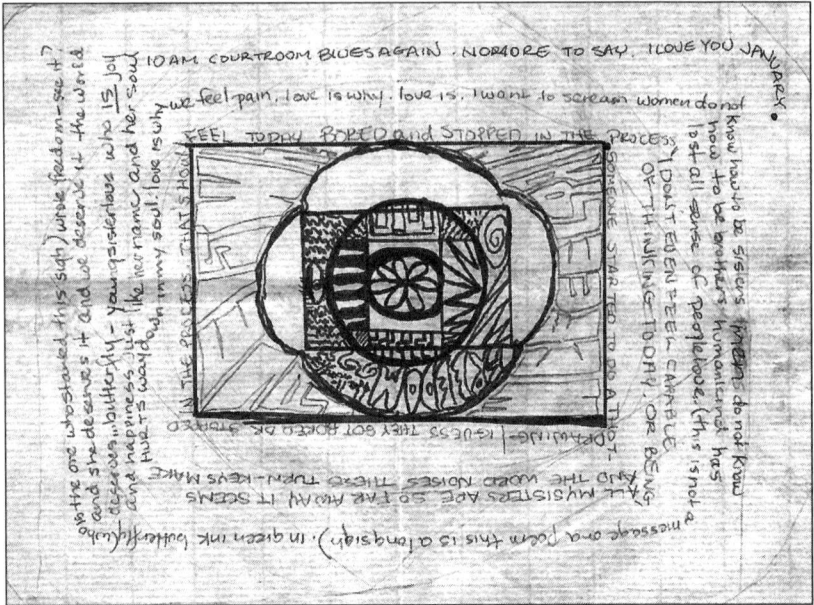

Figure 6.3. Undated letter from Ericka to Jan, on the reverse side of the self-portrait. From Jan Von Flatern's personal letters, 1970–1971.

the care strategies of self-love and person-to-person love, which were key to the spiritual wellness that Ericka would pursue when imprisoned.

Ericka lacked access to writing equipment in prison. It was in the courtroom that Katy Roraback and the rest of her legal team supplied her with paper and pens that she used for letter writing and "art-making." She also used cards given to her by supporters that she used for drafting letters and notes. In her definition of "art-making," cultural history scholar Nicole R. Fleetwood includes factors that influence the creation of the creative work, such as supplies obtained, location, choices, and the conditions of imprisonment.[55] Ericka's art project is a manifestation of her self-connection and a mechanism that strengthened her social bonds.

While incarcerated, Ericka continued to invest in the well-being of others, living a life that extended beyond her own immediate concerns—a remarkably challenging feat under the constraints of captivity. Her letters to Jan often included requests for her to support other women at Niantic. Ericka's letters became another form of activism in the Sister Love Collective. As a result of Ericka's relationship with Jan, she brought her into the collective's community as she referenced the word "sisterlove" in many of her letters.[56] She trusted her with sensitive information as she briefed her on the legal cases of those imprisoned. Historian Dan Berger notes that "prisoners had different tools for challenging authority than did those who were not incarcerated."[57] In prison, Ericka's tools for challenging authority were based on a support system. Prison culture thrived on isolation, but women who had advocates could gain resources essential to their survival in prison. Ericka called on Jan to locate legal support, secure bail money for the impecunious, support pregnant women, reconnect families, carry out wellness checks, and supply transportation for those preparing to leave Niantic.

Jan's labor in this capacity explains her role as a bridge for the Sister Love Collective to the outside world. For example, in a letter to Jan, Ericka wrote, "I'm giving you a list of people who need bond money and 3 who need lawyers."[58] In another letter, she wrote about Isabel, a Puerto Rican woman who spoke little English and was in desperate need of a lawyer due to her public defender's unfair treatment. Her bond was set at $2,500 for the sale of heroin.[59] Ericka solicited Jan for legal aid for other imprisoned women, including Margaret, who was charged with manslaughter and needed a lawyer.[60] The Hartford Superior Court set her bond at $10,000. Ericka wrote, "(seems to me like an accident in this situation)—very important that she gets a better defense than a p.d and a deal."[61] Ericka insisted that a public defense lawyer and a plea deal would fall short of justice for Margaret, especially as she indicated that her crime was due to an accident.

Ericka went on to ask Jan to inquire whether John Williams could meet with Millie at her next court appearance. John Williams legally represented Ericka's co-defendants, Frances and Peggy.[62] Millie liked John Williams's compassionate disposition and "human attitude towards her."[63] He didn't treat her like a lawbreaker. Ericka then requested an update on family visitations for other imprisoned women; "how are the phone calls for visits going," she wrote."[64] She continued with an inquiry on the status of lawyers for other imprisoned women.[65] She closed the letter by asking Jan to give copies of a poem leaflet to Millie's mother and several others. Ericka shared Millie's relief with Jan when she found her a lawyer. She wrote, "she was happy to hear about a lawyer. . . . I'll have a new list of people who need bonds/trans./lawyers—no one expects miracles tho!"[66]

Ericka supplied Jan with a continual list of imprisoned women in need of bond money, lawyers, and transportation upon their prison release.[67] Her efforts paralleled the BPP's bussing to prisons program, which provided free transportation for families to visit their loved ones in prisons and jails. According to the *CoEvolution Quarterly*, the Southern California BPP chapter in 1970 established the first bussing to prisons program, offering weekly transportation arrangements to preserve "the bond between prisoners and their families."[68] Other chapters and branches such as Washington State and Illinois launched a bussing to prisons programs.[69] Aware of these BPP community programs across the country, Ericka replicated similar efforts behind prison walls for those imprisoned with her and their families. In an undated letter, Ericka requested an update from Jan on transportation arrangements for women preparing for release from prison and urged her to reach out to Millie's family to visit her. "How is the transportation going? Let me know by a nod of the head if you don't have the time to write or [send] a message thru Katy, ok? Millie wants to see her people too," she wrote.[70] To express her gratitude, she added in a letter, "you don't know how much hope people get from just hearing that you're for them."[71] As Millie demonstrated, knowing that Jan was urgently working to find lawyers gave women at Niantic peace of mind. Moreover, she mentioned a mother who expressed happiness "to know that people care."[72] Ericka pleaded with Jan to make sure someone was present when Barbara, another imprisoned woman, was released from prison. She noted that if the state failed to drop her charges, Barbara would like to repay the fund for posting her bail at five hundred dollars. Women were grateful and willing to return the favor that was bestowed upon them.

Ericka also sought to keep children bonded with their imprisoned mothers and reached out to families to visit their loved ones. She supplied contact information for the family members of Helen and Doris, two imprisoned women, in hopes that Jan could get their loved ones to bring their children to visit them.[73] On the back of the note, she wrote that Tammy "was really happy to see her mama and little sister."[74] Ericka went as far as to suggest possible days for visitations to unite families. "Maybe this Saturday would be a good day for her to see her mama," Ericka wrote about a daughter arranging to see her mother in prison. As a mother in bondage separated from Mai, Ericka understood the toll of the carceral system in breaking up families. She worked to serve the needs of imprisoned women, including those carrying a child.

Jan fulfilled Ericka's requests as much as she could by working with local legal clinics and Yale Law School. She tracked down family members to find out the whereabouts of children with imprisoned mothers at Niantic. Mothers were often looking for their children because in some cases, protective services took children away from family in the middle of the night and placed them in emergency shelters. Once Jan found the children's physical location, she communicated that information to Ericka.

At one point, Ericka reached out to Jan because the state removed two-year-old Richard from his grandparents' home due to accusations of alcohol abuse. His mother, Dorothy, searched frantically for her son. Ericka wrote to Jan, "[Dorothy] needs someone/we need someone/to do us a great favor."[75] Ericka implored Jan to make other arrangements for Richard. "The boy-child wd [sic] be better off with people that loved him rather than the state," she claimed.[76] She pointed out that the state taking over his guardianship failed to serve his best interests; instead, the women believed he needed to live with a loving family, especially since Richard was a toddler with a heart murmur. "If you can just make him comfortable somewhere so that he will not fall into state hands. [Dorothy] is so worried you know (and she may[be] sitting at Niantic for a while)," Ericka explained.[77] She stressed that many of Dorothy's relatives had large families living in cramped spaces. "We really appreciate anything you cd [sic] do Jan. . . . [Dorothy] wd [sic] go crazy if anything happened to him. I don't need to explain what it is to be poor and Black in Amerika," Ericka added.[78] To help Richard escape the realities of Black poverty, Ericka went as far as to recommend possible sleeping arrangements.[79] In other situations, Jan learned that a family member, friend, or supporter whom she referenced as a "woman sister" wanted to know how her loved one was doing in prison but was uncomfortable communicating directly with the person, so she wrote to Ericka for a wellness check.[80]

As part of her work within the Sister Love Collective, Ericka also served the needs of pregnant women. In a letter whose recipient is unknown, Ericka explained the need for care and support for Millie, whose pregnancy will be discussed in the section that follows, and Bonnie, another pregnant and imprisoned woman at Niantic:

> 18 january 1971
> almost 10:00
>
> millie goes to court tomorrow. hope somebody will be there to support her—she's one of the most freedom-loving sisters I've met in a long time. she reminds me of jan—a whole lot!
>
> tomorrow, I shall see you again. I wonder what mood I'll be in—and you.
>
> today they pretended they didn't know that [Bonnie] is pregnant. They asked her if she was "having trouble with her menstrual cycle!" . . . bitches!!! They felt her stomach and said oh—"you look pregnant, but will have to take tests" . . . I hope somebody comes to see her *soon!* The poem says some of it. a day at the camp—it's almost time to begin another one. for tomorrow I wish you joy and happiness. everyday—I wish freedom for the people of the world—tell all the sisters. I love them.
>
> love to you—and
> strength.
> ech.
>
> 19 january 1971
> 10:00
>
> make sure someone gets to see millie—she's in this building today. make her smile/love
>
> ericka.[81]

Ericka pointed out how Millie's energy mirrored Jan's, as they were both "freedom-loving sisters." Ericka's contemplation of emotions, as seen in her musings like "I wonder what mood I'll be in—and you," accentuated not only her own humanity but also that of her correspondent, especially in an environment where imprisonment often leads to harsh treatment. Her anger toward the nurses' indifferent attitude regarding Bonnie's pregnancy was palpable. Ericka aimed to highlight the apathetic response of the nurses, underscoring the dehumanization and increased prenatal risks that mothers like Bonnie endured in such settings.

When Ericka wrote, "it's almost time to begin another one," she was indicating that it was time to start another poem. Ericka used poetry as a source of healing from Niantic's prison camp. Through poetry and letters to those outside prison, Ericka provided women with caring words and resources, a reminder that they mattered. She closed the letter with wishes of "joy and happiness" and freedom not only to the reader but "for the people of the world." With words like "tell all the sisters," she instructed the reader to empathize with the gender oppression experienced by women. "Love" and "strength" served as operative words Ericka used to soothe others, disarm negativity, and conquer hard times. Accordingly, she ended the letter with a request that someone visit Millie while she was in the building to "make her smile."[82]

In addition to Jan, she collaborated with her legal team to procure lawyers and funds for commissary expenses for those incarcerated, as well as arrange transportation for those being discharged from prison. David Rosen was exceptionally benevolent. She regarded him as the most adept at promptly addressing her requests. "David was the best. He was young like me at the time. He would say, 'Okay, I'll get on it.'"[83] This is apparent in a letter to Von Flatern dated January 16, 1971, where Ericka recounted a visit from David Rosen. She penned, "david rosen just came to see me. he's so gentle . . . it's as if every word he says were meant to be part of a very meaningful thing."[84] He was thoughtful and kind. Ericka believed that because they were close in age, he would always be the legal representative to visit her in prison and share updates on her case. During their visits, they engaged in stimulating discussions about his legal education and his observations in the courtroom regarding racism and injustice.[85] He aspired to actively engage in and meaningfully contribute to the preservation of justice. However, he noticed that justice was not being upheld in the courtroom. According to Ericka, it was "breaking his heart."[86] He was a newly graduated law school student, who exhibited a deep curiosity and ethical principles. He utilized his visits with Ericka as an opportunity to acquire knowledge about the Black Panther Party and social movements.

Millie's Escape and Capture

On Sunday, July 19, 1970, Millie remarkably managed to escape prison with four women.[87] At sixteen, she was the youngest in the group. According to the *Hartford Courant*, the women "used a wedge and a coat hanger to remove a screen from a window."[88] The lack of physical security measures such as fences or barbed wire at Niantic allowed women to walk off the prison grounds.[89] Millie and the other women in her group put each other's lives on the line for their freedom, which deepened their bond and trust for one another.

For these women, breaking out of prison during the summer spared them from the potentially lethal cold weather. In what was likely a sweaty endeavor, they were careful not to get tracked down and captured as they ran into the woods. It is unknown what their life on the run looked like. We don't know whether they parted ways immediately after their escape or traveled together for some of the time. As an escapee, Millie reconnected with family, paying her brother Ivan a visit in New Haven.[90] Her act mirrored those of formerly enslaved people in 1865 upon learning of their freedom and their efforts to reconnect with loved ones. Millie's life on the run was short-lived, as she was captured on a cold December day almost five months later.[91] One of the other escapees died in Boston.[92] It is unknown whether the rest of the escapees survived their fugitive status. Demoralized that she was back in prison and now newly pregnant, Millie especially needed encouragement from the Sister Love Collective.[93] Millie and the women she left Niantic with were part of a long history of attempted escapes at Niantic.[94] The Niantic quarterly meeting of the board of directors discussed the issue of escapees and proposed addressing what they referred to as the "runaway problem" by hiring more personnel and constructing a high-security facility.[95]

In a letter to Jan dated February 2, 1971, Ericka turned her attention to a nurse's unscrupulous treatment of Millie. In all caps, she explained,

NURSE TELLING MILLIE THAT IF SHE COULDN'T TELL HER HOW MANY MONTHS PREGNANT SHE IS THEN[,] SHE "COULDN'T HELP HER[.]" MILLIE TRIED HARD TO RESIST THE URGE TO STRIKE BACK/CRY/CUSS/ THE NURSE KEPT PLUCKING AT HER

AS IF SHE WERE KEEPING SOMETHING FROM HER (BUT WHAT?)
MILLIE SAID WHAT SHE FELT FOR THE WOMAN'S DEHUMAN-
IZING ATTITUDE AND THE NURSE SAID "I HOPE YOU DROP IT"
(THE BABY, THAT IS) I CRIED WITH HER BUT THE HURT WAS
NOT WASHED AWAY WITH THE TEARS.

I wrote that so slowly. It took real control to even put it on paper. . . .
"I hope you drop it"—the nerve/the genocidal/degrading/racist, etc etc
(ad nauseam) female. we have so much work to do/so much to change,
destroy[,] rebuild.

. . . she is

strong

small

fiery.[96]

Millie was unfamiliar with prenatal care and was likely confused by the
nurse's questions, prompting the nurse's anger by her aloof answers.
The nurse was also likely dismissive because she saw her as an unfit
mother. Any young girl who was imprisoned was seen as deviant
regardless of her actions. Millie dared to escape, returned pregnant,
and did not know how far along she was in the pregnancy. No one
viewed her as the child she was. In the eyes of the nurse and the greater
public, Millie was nothing more than a defective mother unworthy
of her child. Perhaps the nurse assumed that Millie was intentionally
hiding the stage of her pregnancy. Consequently, she became violent
with her. Saying "I hope you drop it" deeply hurt Millie. Compassion
was nonexistent in prison because motherhood and incarceration were
incompatible.

As a mother herself, Ericka understood her pain. She, too, was seen
as a deviant, hypersexualized mother. Though Ericka was partnered at
the time she had her child, she was aware of the stigma associated with
Black motherhood, which was portrayed as deficient. The trauma cut so
deep that their tears could not wash away the pain. Ericka recognized
her feelings of dehumanization when pointing out that the nurse perpetuated racist ideas that depicted Black and Puerto Rican mothers as
inadequate and neglectful of their children and their overall health. She
credited Millie for being strong and fiery despite the nurse's treatment
of her.

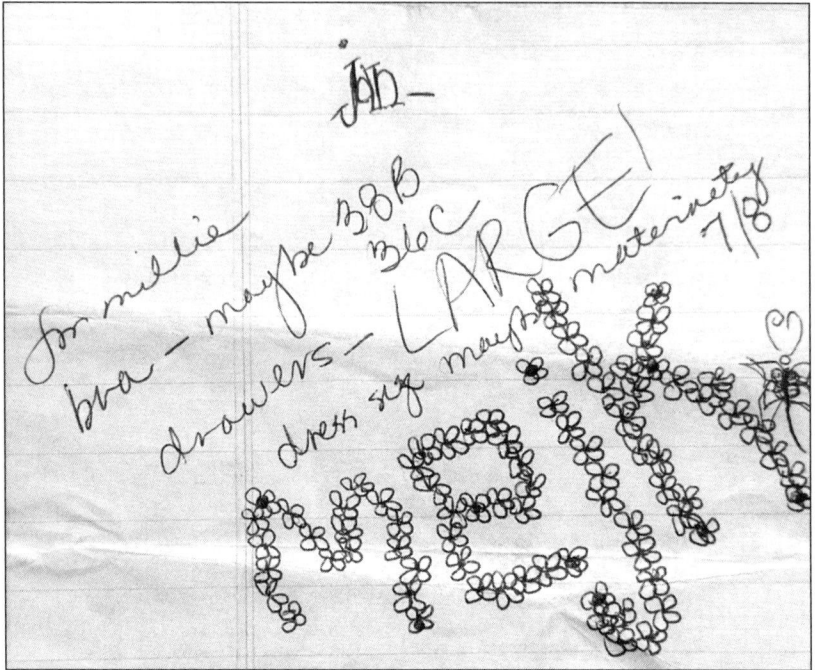

Figure 6.4. Undated note from Ericka to Jan. Von Flatern's personal letters, 1970–1971.

To help Millie through her pregnancy, Ericka appealed to Jan to acquire maternity clothes for Millie using her social networks. She requested essential items including undergarments such as a bra and underwear: "do this for me. . . . (millie is very down) would you please see if someone could get millie some support underwear like a really good bra—breasts are very sensitive when you're pregnant—also some drawers that won't cramp her stomach."[97] In a separate brief note, Ericka included Millie's maternity clothing sizes (figure 6.4).[98] Under the sizes, in flower-like shapes, Ericka wrote "mejk" with a heart-shaped rose adjacent to the image. The word "mejk" was Ericka's way of representing her circle of friendship with Jan and Connie and her love for them. "Me" indicated herself; *j* stood for Jan, and *k* for Kani/Connie. Ericka understood their collective companionship as magical; her play on letters speaks to her creative poetics.

Millie's pregnancy failed to protect her from harsh treatment at Niantic as prison officials did not even provide her with proper undergarments. Correctional officers compounded her misery by taking away Millie's valuable property during her pregnancy. "before I left this morning[,] they were fuckin with her too. [trying to take her ring . . . ?]," Ericka wrote.[99] To help her recover from sickness and loneliness, Ericka asked Jan to tell Millie's mother how they were treating her. She believed knowing that her mother knew about her condition would lift her spirits. She added, "if you cd [sic] have seen her yesterday—she cd [sic] hardly make it to her cell room, holding her stomach . . . she was so sad, jan."[100] In her letter, Ericka underscored that Niantic matrons were "still giving her vaginal exams (for dope)."[101] Millie was forced to undergo the humiliating and invasive process of vaginal searches.

Infuriated, Ericka expressed how she wanted the Niantic matrons to let her be: "why don't they leave her alone? It hurts."[102] She explained that the medical staff sent Millie for blood tests that morning. As a result, they finally acknowledged her pregnancy and gave her vitamins. Bonnie and Millie both struggled to survive pregnancy at Niantic. Ericka worked relentlessly to offer tangible support to Bonnie, Millie, and other women, employing caring words, poetry, and resources as a testament to their significance and value. In March, three months before her delivery date, Millie was transferred to Lawrence + Memorial Hospital for roughly a week for reasons unknown.[103] Given her cruel treatment by nurses, it is fair to assume that her hospital stay was related to poor prenatal care.

Courtroom Self-Fashioning

During her court case, Ericka carefully navigated her identity as a Black woman revolutionary using hair and fashion. In a 1971 picture taken by the Associated Press, Ericka smiles with her handcuffs up as she greets supporters and the press with the Black Power salute before an officer (likely O'Conner) helps her into the car to take her back to Niantic after a long day in court (figure 6.5). As a sign of solidarity, people often greeted one another with a Black Power salute. It served as an expression of racial pride and self-determination and represented the idea that social change lies in the hands of those oppressed.[104] In the photograph, Ericka is dressed in a fitted long-sleeve shirt someone sent her, a shawl she made in prison, dark pants, and a small shoulder bag packed with a hair comb. Her mother had taught her to dress up when she did not feel good, so she was thoughtful about what she wore to court.[105]

She remembered the excruciating pain in her throat as a young child sick with tonsillitis. Her mother put braids and a big yellow bow in her hair despite her fever and body aches. Although apathetic about bows, Ericka let her mother dress her up. She did this every day until Ericka's illness abated. It helped her feel better, at least mentally. This value passed down from her mother empowered her to face the courthouse by piecing together clothing items sent to her by her mother and younger sister, Kyra, as well as her friends.

Jobless at the time, Kyra mailed Ericka clothes she no longer wore. Ericka also wore items she made for herself, such as shawls or sweaters she crocheted.[106] Dress offered relief from the bleakness of prison and the courthouse. The fashion of the time included eclectic looks and wild colors. "Everything was out the box," Ericka recalled.[107] Styles ranged from headbands to bell-bottoms. Adornment remained a powerful tool. What Ericka wore not only impacted her outlook but also influenced how people perceived her ability to care for herself.

Hair was another aspect of her presentation. Ericka chose to wear her hair parted down the middle and let her long natural hair flow on both sides. In prison, she was unable to get a decent haircut, so she let it grow. When she was a young girl, her grandfather told her that they had Native American ancestry. Her hairstyle served as a way to honor her heritage. Freed remembers Ericka regularly changing her hairdo for court. He wrote, "Ericka entered smiling. Each day her hair looks different. Today she wears a pretty Indian band."[108] Although his reflections contrasted with Ericka's, his reference to her "pretty Indian band" aligned with the honor she displayed to her Native American lineage through her fashion in the courtroom. His reference to her smiling also speaks to the positive energy she projected. Moreover, Ericka suggested that musician and folk singer Buffy Sainte-Marie was the inspiration for her hairstyle. She adored Sainte-Marie's voice and songs, finding resonance in her music, which explored the intersections of class, race, and gender. The rawness of her lyrics captured the plight of being poor, Native, and a woman.

The day the Associated Press captured the photo of Ericka, jurors were on their third day of deliberations for her case.[109] Ericka recalled what she had later learned about the deliberations. One of the women

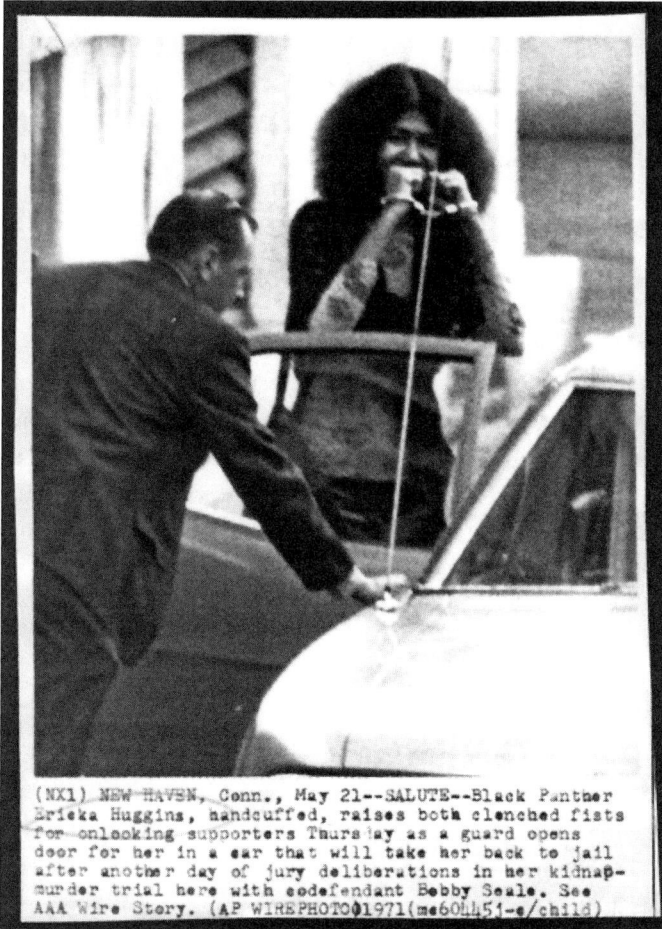

(NX1) NEW HAVEN, Conn., May 21--SALUTE--Black Panther
Ericka Huggins, handcuffed, raises both clenched fists
for onlooking supporters Thursday as a guard opens
door for her in a car that will take her back to jail
after another day of jury deliberations in her kidnap-
murder trial here with codefendant Bobby Seale. See
AAA Wire Story. (AP WIREPHOTO)1971(me60hh51-e/child)

Figure 6.5. Ericka greeting supporters with the Black Power salute. AP
photo, May 21, 1971.

jurors, reacting to a male juror who was unwilling to come to a decision,
had picked up a chair and threatened, "Let these defendants go. You
know you don't have any evidence. If you want to confine them to prison
for the rest of their lives, go on and try it, but I swear I will kill you
to death."[110] In recalling this moment leading up to her release, Ericka
described how the juror's remarks had a "no-nonsense, don't cross me"
tone, making note of the juror's gender as a woman, her whiteness, and
her occupation as a nurse. She learned about this critical information

at the completion of the trial, admitting, "Thank God with everything in me, because when it came to declaring a verdict, the women were the ones that said, 'You know there's no evidence. Why are we trying these people?'"[111] Ericka's account illustrates the key role she believed women played in granting her freedom. She also claimed that one white male juror held out to the very end. After the jury deliberated twice without a verdict, Judge Mulvey declared mistrials and dismissed Ericka and Bobby's case.[112] Ericka stated, "The judge said, 'Let them go, we cost the taxpayers of Connecticut too much money. The defendants are free to go.'"[113] Evoking her feelings of triumph, she continued, "So Bobby and I walked out that day."[114] Her phrase "walked out" represents a feeling of liberation from the burden of injustice. Ericka walked out of the courtroom in a long-sleeved white dress with a black shawl she made in prison draped over her shoulders, accessorized with a choker and a purse containing a comb and likely $30.99 issued to her from her commissary upon her release (figure 6.6).[115] She paused, lifted her head to take in the sunshine and fresh air, and smiled. While Ericka relished her newfound freedom, Bobby, on the other hand, was immediately re-handcuffed and extradited to Chicago for inciting riots during the 1968 Democratic National Convention. There, for seeking the right to self-defense when his attorney, Charles Garry, was ill, he found himself bound, gagged, and shackled to his chair. Freedom did not come to him until 1972.[116]

Ericka and Bobby's victory represented the tireless labor of their supporters, as seen by the regular demonstrations, most notably the May Day protests that gathered approximately fifteen thousand demonstrators to downtown New Haven on May 1, 1970.[117] Ericka was now a prominent name, and loving friends wanted to celebrate her with a party. The night sky was clear as Ericka arrived at the house party. She reunited with her legal team, BPP comrades, family members, and friends. She was content but could not ignore the fact that two years of her life had been erased. She was now quieter and less playful. Reuniting with others was comforting, but crowds felt stifling. After taking in all the social pleasures, Ericka left the party with Jan to wander around New Haven. Prison life normalized isolation, and Ericka wanted to escape from the crowd. As a returning citizen, Ericka needed to rest her mind from the fast pace of life outside prison. Jan vividly remembered walking down the middle of Whalley Avenue. "It was kind of a magical thing for me," she gushed.[118]

Figure 6.6. Ericka with Katy Roraback and Elbert "Big Man" Howard on the day of her release. AP Images, May 25, 1971. Photograph by Dave Pickoff.

She still felt a strong bond with Ericka. As they strolled, Ericka gazed at Pegnataro's, a major grocery store, and car dealerships. She cultivated her sense of gratitude through the practice of meditation in prison and took nothing for granted.

Ericka's Love for Angela

News of Ericka and Bobby's release on May 25, 1971, reached her close friend Angela Y. Davis, who was ecstatic to learn that Ericka was out of prison.[119] While Angela was incarcerated, Ericka visited her multiple times on the West Coast. Angela was detained on suspicion of conspiracy, kidnapping, and murder during Jonathan Jackson's armed takeover of the 1970 Marin County Courthouse with guns allegedly belonging to her. Jonathan Jackson was the brother of George Jackson, a Black Panther and member of the Soledad Brothers. The Soledad Brothers were accused of killing a correctional officer at Soledad Prison in 1970.[120] Jonathan's seizure was intended to free the Soledad Brothers from prison. Before her trial began, Angela's lawyers arranged for Ericka to visit her in solitary confinement and to bring scissors to give her a haircut. It brought her joy to know that her sister comrade would be the person who would "do" her hair. They shared an intimate moment as Ericka used an Afro pick comb to "pick" her hair out, cut, and then shaped it in an Afro. She felt the lightness in her hair afterward, and she emphasized that Ericka was attentive and showed love. It was in that moment of care that she felt good. Knowing that the groomed look came from a place of love made her feel even better. Angela affirmed that the moment was one of the highlights of her imprisonment.

Angela's Afro was often the most talked-about aspect of her appearance.[121] She laughed as she recalled, "People always talked about how big my Afro was. Well, that was because they would not let me get my hair cut when I was in jail in Palo Alto at the time."[122] Ericka returned to the care politics of the Sister Love Collective and spiritual wellness when she shared in Angela's intimacy of beautification. Ericka styled Angela's hair in a manner reminiscent of how Connie had prepared her before her own court appearance, aiming to convey dignity. This gesture of Ericka doing Angela's hair served as an act of resistance against the defeminization of women in carceral settings. Ericka maintained her support of Angela by attending her trial. During the chaos of her trial, Angela remembered peaceful moments with Ericka. She regarded Ericka as a pillar of strength, capable of enduring the most horrific experiences while remaining focused on her interior self. Ericka brought much-needed tranquil energy to Angela. "She understood long before most of us how important it is to attend to the spirit and to cultivate a way of being with oneself."[123] Ericka politicized spiritual practices by focusing on developing a connection to heal the mind, body, and soul as a layer of protection from white supremacy.

Angela recollected that it took her a while to realize what Ericka learned in prison, that spiritual practice must be at the center of political awareness. As we have seen, Ericka developed practices of introspection during her time in prison, including yoga and meditation. These practices allowed her to delve into her inner self during adversity. In contrast, it was not insight that brought Angela to yoga while imprisoned; her physician suggested she practice yoga to treat her tension and headaches.[124] She also engaged in other types of physical activities despite prison restrictions. In her autobiography, she wrote, "They [jailers] could do nothing to prevent me from doing calisthenics, katas, or head-stands when I felt like it in the work cell."[125] Much like the feeling of immersing herself in her work, yoga and other forms of physical movement were "a fundamental condition of survival and sanity" and helped sustain her during her imprisonment.[126] "If we are trying to change the world, if we try to imagine a new way of being in the world," she remarked, it encompasses "healing from past traumas and the capacity to relate to other human beings on various levels including on that spiritual level."[127] She admired Ericka and considered her a pioneer in bridging political and spiritual awareness.

She vividly remembered Ericka's portrayal of imprisonment as a gift, shared at a restorative justice conference years earlier, which resonated with her. It was hearing Ericka speak about imprisonment in this way that inspired her to reflect on what she had learned. Angela's reflection on how Ericka shaped her spiritual consciousness supports Evans's assertion that "meditation and yoga enabled her to heal herself, claim herself, and resist (at least in part) her jailors' capacity to dehumanize her."[128] Ericka's loving and timely visit to see her comrade following her own imprisonment is evidence of the state's inability to claim the mind, body, and soul of these Black revolutionaries and shake their enduring commitment to community care politics. Angela won her trial in 1972 and was found not guilty of any of the allegations. Angela's trial, like Ericka's, showed the ability of the people to organize in support of political prisoners.[129]

Millie's Labor Experience and Release

Roughly a month after Ericka's release from prison, Millie, still in prison, went into labor. Family support from her brother Ivan was a source of comfort for Millie during the birth of her son at Lawrence + Memorial Hospital in New London, Connecticut. Upon reflection, Ivan doubted that Millie gave birth in shackles. The specifics involving Millie's postpartum care remain unclear, including whether she received the necessary care for recovering after giving birth. It is also unknown whether nurses allowed Millie to have skin-to-skin contact with her new baby or breastfeed. Just three days after the delivery of her son, Millie was returned to prison and her son went into foster care.[130] The trauma that Millie must have endured upon losing contact with her newborn son is unimaginable. In Niantic, motherhood was especially punished, and women were often labeled unfit mothers and undeserving of their children. Nurses in Niantic viewed Millie as a lascivious criminal. Correctional officers likely gave her pills to dry up her breast milk, as they did with Ericka. This routine practice stripped mothers of the opportunity to nurse their newborns.

On July 23, 1971, fifty-nine days after Ericka got out of Niantic, Millie was released. Her brother Ivan was perplexed as to how she was able to get released from prison after a failed escape. "How in the hell did you ever beat the charge?" he asked. "Well, I told the judge that I did it because I wanted my freedom," she responded.[131] Simply put, she insisted that the judge see her humanity. Ivan admired his sister's bravery and fierce nature. In boldly advocating for her freedom and that of others, as illustrated in her leadership in the Sister Love Collective, she modeled spiritual wellness practices. "I came home and got my baby" is how she put it, as recalled by Millie's second child, Delinah, on her mother's reflections about getting out of prison.[132] Upon her release, she reunited with her son, who was almost five weeks old (figure 6.7). Words could not describe Millie's feelings on being able to hold, touch, and love on her baby boy. She was overflowing with joy and happiness. Though he was still an infant, she knew that she had lost precious time bonding, perhaps breastfeeding, and doting on him as any new mother would.

As a returning citizen, with the help of Ivan, their village of friends, including Millie's childhood mate Nancy Shia, and other good people, Millie was able to start her new life. Millie took on odd jobs and enrolled in school. Her friends tutored her in various subjects as needed and helped her secure an apartment. They encouraged her to maintain a positive outlook as she rebuilt her life.[133] Yet, after her release, Ericka and Millie lost contact with one another, perhaps intentionally. They both needed to start over as free women and mothers. Because of the transiency of prison, sustaining the Sister Love Collective after Ericka and Millie's release proved impractical. Nevertheless, the collective would have a place both inside and outside the prison walls.

Inspired by haircare in the collective, Millie earned a cosmetology license and worked as a mobile hairdresser, primarily serving housebound

Figure 6.7. Millie Rivera holding her infant son in New Haven, Connecticut, 1971. Photo courtesy of Millie's childhood friend Nancy Shia.

senior citizens. She also worked with preschool children as a teacher's aide.[134] Millie's former preschool teaching supervisor, Alicia Caraballo, described her as "vivacious, personable, full of energy, and streetwise." She "fit right in. I remember her being an amazing educator in the classroom. She was exceptional."[135] Millie later left early childhood education and turned to politics; however, it is unknown what that path looked like for her. Ivan could not recall all her accolades and contributions. But he knew that she was highly respected in the community and her

Figure 6.8. Jan Von Flatern, Washington DC, 1973. Photo
courtesy of Jan Von Flatern.

efforts earned her a prestigious award.[136] At the age of fifty-seven, Millie
suffered a fatal heart attack.[137] Her life was hard, but she took what she
learned and tried to improve the lives of others, striving to prevent more
young people from entering the system.

As she had with Millie, Ericka eventually lost contact with Jan. After
the trial, Jan finished her bachelor's degree and pursued a law degree.
Jan was deeply inspired by Katy Roraback's defense of Ericka in the
courtroom. Recommended to Ericka by the Huggins family for her
reputation as an eminent, forward-thinking lawyer, Katy Roraback was
known for representing marginalized communities and believed that
no detail about a case was beneath her. Observing Katy Roraback in

motion, Jan developed a resolute commitment to labor tirelessly.[138] Katy exhibited kindness, but in the courtroom, one would be wise to avoid provoking her.[139] She was determined, nonjudgmental, fully committed to her clients, and an ally for the Black freedom struggle. Her law practice engaged a round-the-clock, detail-oriented work ethic that included "always defending the underdog."[140] She did not rely on legal assistants, volunteers, or law students to do the primary work on her cases. Instead, she read every document regarding a case herself and listened to and learned from her clients. "I found that to be a better way to practice law and certainly a better way to be a trial lawyer," Jan recalled.[141] This model served Jan well as she practiced aviation law for thirty years. For the first time in almost fifty years, Ericka and Jan reconnected during the making of this book.[142]

Motherhood for Ericka after Prison

Once the State of Connecticut released Ericka, she initially stayed in New Haven with John's mother and father, Mrs. and Mr. Huggins. She later left for California to search for an apartment for her and Mai. Once Mai could speak, she referred to Ericka as "Mommy Ericka" to distinguish between her mother and grandmother. Mrs. Huggins had formed a strong bond with Mai as she assumed the role of an "other mother," a common occurrence in situations where the biological mother is incarcerated and someone else within the family or community steps in to mother the child.[143] Though Ericka lived without Mai for two years, she was keenly aware of how strong the bond was between Mai and her grandparents and knew how difficult it would be for them to live without the one connection to their son. It broke Ericka's heart to separate them, but having been robbed of precious time, she wanted to reclaim her life with her daughter. She had missed most of Mai's major developmental milestones: her first steps and her first words. She could not bear to miss anything more. Her deepest desire was to be present with the child who was both part of John and part of herself. Her biggest challenge was how to be a good mother to Mai. Looking back, Mai described what it was like to move between so many parental figures at such a young age: "It was more like yet again replacing a parental figure for this little girl, [taking her from having] two parents [John and Ericka], to only one parent [Ericka], then to two new parents [Mr. and Mrs. Huggins], to one new parent [Ericka]. So much change for someone who had only lived 2 ½ years."[144]

In prison, Ericka lost the feeling of being a capable mother. She doubted that she could be the mother Mrs. Huggins had been for Mai. Thankfully, in Oakland, she was delighted to be with comrades who helped her transition into a new life. This lessened her feelings of inadequacy. Living collectively, she shared space, essential family resources, and parenting with other BPP comrades. Though Mai had a sense of family in the BPP, removing Mai from her grandparents' home in New Haven to resume work with the BPP in Oakland took her far away from the only person Mai knew as her mother. Ericka could not afford to fly back and forth from Oakland to New Haven so that Mai could spend time with her grandparents. Ultimately, things worked out with John's family. Due to the generosity of Mai's grandparents, she was able to visit them during the holidays and spent every summer of her young life with her extended Huggins family.

Mai recounted how being with her family in Connecticut gave her the stability she lacked in California and helped her feel grounded. "My grandparents lived in the same house, which is still in the family, for more than forty years and their household and neighborhood were always very stable. I knew what to expect when I was there," she remembered.[145] Her grandparents' two-parent household, the family history of their home, and the large number of relatives who would visit her in an effort to remember John, their brother, cousin, or friend, offered Mai a foundation that her mother was incapable of providing as a BPP member.

As a child of high-profile BPP members, Mai experienced constant, unrelenting state violence that no child should see and feel.[146] She learned to expect the unexpected in California. Mai admitted, "Being in New Haven, which is a pretty small city, helped me feel grounded, and it offered a real connection to my father." Although many of her BPP peers were also fatherless due to absence or loss, she noted that unlike her own situation, "there was often no place for them to foster a connection, even if their fathers were alive." In response to the tragic loss of her father, Mai's paternal side lavished her with unconditional love and, in her words, "stepped up and over-compensated." Mr. John Huggins Sr.

was not only her grandfather; she described him as "the closest I ever came to having a father figure."[147] As she came of age, she considered her mother, grandmother, and her father's sisters, Carolyn and Joan, all mothers to her.[148] Each of them carefully protected her. "I remember a time when I'd have to check in with each and every one of them, all the time, and about every, single thing!" She was aware that they recognized her father in her. "They always wanted the best for me. They wanted me to do well."[149] Ericka wanted the same for Mai.

Ericka was grateful for the extended family that embraced and surrounded Mai. She desperately wanted her daughter to feel safe and stable, but after her release, she fumbled and punted major moments in her daughter's life. The paradox lay in Ericka's ability to lead and care for her community, forging strong bonds of sisterhood, while finding motherhood particularly challenging. The circumstances Ericka faced were extraordinary and traumatic: she became a mother, lost her husband to murder shortly afterwards, and then faced incarceration by the State of Connecticut. Post-prison life often saw her torn between caring for her own child and attending to the needs of children in the community. Mai was Ericka's only child until her brother Rasa was born in 1974 to Ericka and Saturu Ned (James Mott), a member of the BPP funk band the Lumpen.[150] With the birth of Rasa, Ericka continued to live collectively but moved to a house with fewer adults. She raised Mai and Rasa as though they had countless siblings. They had a village, but often, children want their parents' undivided attention more than anything else.

Although Ericka was able to spend more time with her children, her BPP political obligations—including her work for the Black Panther newspaper, pursuing her lifelong passion for education as the director of the BPP's Oakland Community School, an elementary institution, and beginning her political career as "the first woman and the first Black person" to serve on the Alameda County Board of Education—often took her away from Mai and Rasa, even though they were both enrolled OCS students.[151] Ericka survived and even thrived as a leader, but parenting as a single mother was complicated. The expectation for Black women to juggle multiple roles and responsibilities, prevalent in the 1970s, persists even today. During that era, men were not typically expected to be heavily involved in child-rearing. As for whether Ericka gave her best to Mai and Rasa, I believe she did. Whether her best was sufficient, however, is a question only Mai and Rasa can answer.

Ericka's life is both a marathon and a relay with no finish line. She wants the best for everyone. She did not always get it right, but she modeled grace toward herself and others, embodying the essence of being beautifully human. Unapologetically embracing her Blackness, Ericka stands as an exemplar of spirituality as a form of political resistance. A staunch champion for the oppressed and marginalized, she intertwines social justice and wellness. Her life invites us to rethink and expand our understanding of the radical principles of the BPP to encompass society's most vulnerable: mothers, children, prisoners, and the poor. In her vision, we all deserve wellness, community, freedom, protection, and love, united in a shared bond of sisterhood and brotherhood.

Epilogue

meditation? check. tea and oatmeal? check. writing exercise?
check. mantra in the name of the mothers? check. stretch-
ing? check. slightly scenic walking? check. being love. being
flight. being all of it. being light. being free. being loved for
it. being table. being tree. being generational degree. being
water. being dirt. being sun daughter. all three?
—Alexis Pauline Gumbs

In this intimate biographical portrait of Ericka's life, I underscore Black
women's strategies for Black liberation, through the lens and language of
spiritual wellness. Spiritual wellness—Ericka's blend of self-disciplined
love and healing practices of resistance through her creative expressions,
poetry, mind-body exercises, and communal care experiences—serves
as my theoretical intervention. Through this framework, I argue that
spirituality, love, and sisterhood are inherently political. Ericka's life
exemplifies how spirituality, when fused with politics, married liberation and ethics. It addressed both the macro and the micro, the external
and internal, the causes and conditions, systems and ideals, local and
global dynamics, and individual and collective care—all underpinned
by an emphasis on wellness-driven social change.

Ericka's struggles provide a clear lens into the world she navigated
and the inner strength she derived from her community. The founda-
tions of her spiritual wellness trace back to her childhood, family influ-
ences, school experiences, collegiate political activism, and Black Panther
Party leadership. Ericka's disciplined daily practices propelled her to a
level of profound spiritual maturity—a veritable baptism by fire. Her
post-incarceration life was shaped by the spiritual work she cultivated in
prison. In Ericka's new phase, she drew from a divine ethical practice in
institutionalizing and formalizing spiritual practices, with young people
especially, in her continued role as a political activist in the BPP. In this

epilogue, I delve into the generative moments when Ericka embodied the spiritual practices and global ethics she had learned and honed while incarcerated into her work for the BPP newspaper, in electoral politics, and as a leader for the BPP's Oakland Community School. She emphasized spiritual practices, including meditation, yoga, and body movement, introducing restorative practices to the youth at the OCS. Even in her post-BPP life, she remained a dedicated educator, fervently working to transform the lives of women and children. I spotlight her restorative justice work and the wisdom of her political activist life.

The Black Panther Party Newspaper Cadre

Ericka's personal and professional transitions were seamless. In 1971, after her release from prison, Huey suggested her first assignment, to work for the BPP newspaper. The Black Panther Intercommunal News Service had been in operation for four years by the time she joined the newspaper cadre. Christian A. Davenport wrote that the BPP newspaper "performed multiple functions for the BPP that included establishing and maintaining organizational identity, recruiting members, providing information about political events, generating revenue, and most importantly, conveying the message of the organization."[1] The publication represented the BPP's ideas, attitudes, and beliefs as "alternative news" to the mass media.[2]

From its inception, women were integral to the BPP newspaper.[3] Ericka was a member of the editorial team with Elaine Brown and Joan Kelley. Davenport explained that those in "the newspaper cadre investigated stories, wrote text, took photographs, drew pictures, and designed the layout of the paper before it went to press on Thursday nights."[4] They added context to stories that they received from all over the world. For instance, occasionally they would utilize a letter or news clipping they had received from someone to weave a broader and more detailed story for newspaper publication. Ericka felt compassion for people who sent in stories of suffering and trauma, which I attribute to her spiritual work. She engaged in a meditative approach to being in the world while working for the BPP newspaper.

The newspaper cadre encouraged collective living, an asset for Ericka as a single mother. There were times when others took care of Mai for three days a week while Ericka worked day and night. She, Elaine, and Joan would stay in the BPP office until they finished writing each article and decided on the newspaper's layout. The layout team included artist Gayle "Asali" Dickson and minister of culture Emory Douglas. Many times, finishing the paper meant staying up half the night. "It was like a marathon every week," Ericka recalled. They lived in the BPP office during that period, sleeping on pallets on the floor with blankets and pillows. "We washed our faces and brushed our teeth, but we were not ready for the outside world."[5] Although the hours were long, they filled the time with moments of laughter and joy as they worked toward the weekly deadlines. Once they finished all the tasks, they turned the paper over to Emory, Malik Edwards, and John Seale for physical printing and final layout adjustments while they went home to their children. For the newspaper release, this process was a weekly affair.[6] Ericka cherished her time with Mai, especially since her political commitments as a Black Panther consumed much of her time. After her lengthy prison sentence, she sought to reclaim all the time she could with Mai.

While Ericka contributed to the newspaper cadre, Huey decided to collaborate and co-author a book of poetry with her.[7] He advised her to leave Oakland for a monthlong retreat at the San Francisco home of his friend Dr. Phillip Shapiro, a psychiatrist and member of the Medical Committee for Human Rights. This would allow Ericka a quiet place to rest and review the poems she wrote while incarcerated and provide the necessary space to compose new poetry.[8] "I couldn't fathom resting," she remembered.[9] As a team player, she initially didn't consider it fair for her to be absent from the newspaper cadre. The production of the newspaper required the assistance of all hands. "This is the only way the book is gonna get written," Huey remarked as he observed Ericka contemplating.[10] Creating the book offered Ericka her first chance at respite. It allowed her to return to her spiritual wellness practice of writing poetry uninterrupted. This practice of poetry writing aided her healing from the oppressive confines of her captivity. Her new living arrangement included a private bedroom and bathroom and prepared meals. Since she was accustomed to sleeping in a jail bed as a former prisoner and a dormitory and communal bed as a BPP member, Ericka considered this a luxurious space. Once she settled in that first evening, she could not keep her eyes open and missed dinner. In addition to the physical niceties, Ericka's stay was made more comfortable by Dr. Shapiro and his wife's kindness, generosity, and understanding of her BPP lifestyle, which necessitated late nights and early mornings. After her first full night's sleep in many months, Ericka began the work of cleaning up old poems, writing new ones, and sketching art for the book.

Ericka and Huey settled on the book title, *Insights and Poems*, to describe Huey's thoughts and Ericka's poetry. Huey's insights spanned topics including "revolutionary suicide," love and the search for self, prison and rebirth, health as liberation, and religion and spirituality.[11] Ericka's feminist poetry, addressing such subjects as childbirth, racial injustice, jail hardship, gender oppression, life in Oakland, and pieces dedicated to Huey and fallen comrades John and Bunchy, comprised more than half of the collection. Each section was prefaced with illustrations drawn by Ericka. The back of the book featured photos of Huey and Ericka (Ericka was pregnant in her second trimester with her son Rasa in her photo). One of the poems in Ericka's section was "A Reflection on Niantic," written during a brief time outside her cell:

> brown
> fall the leaves of
> golden yellow on
> cold ground
> brown the feet
> of the dispossessed
> brown around
> the asphalt
> that darkens the
> road
> there is no end
> no opening
> the winter comes
> brown is covered
> with snow
> and heavy prison coats
> my sisters linger in the night air
> hover by the door
> handcuffed or not
> the jail holds their bodies—brown;
> holds their minds—blue.[12]

In the poem, Ericka reflects on how race operates within the carceral system. As the seasons—spring, summer, fall, and winter—come and go, Niantic expands to accommodate the cyclical influx of women of color. Because of structural racial inequities, Niantic holds not only Black and Brown bodies physically but also the minds of many who are in thrall to white supremacy, which is symbolized by the color blue.[13]

In 1972, as *Insights and Poems* went into production, the BPP leadership asked Ericka to join the Berkeley Community Development Council, an antipoverty council, while also administering the OCS. Her aim was to address poverty through electoral politics. The council, including Ericka and three other BPP members—Audrea Jones, Herman Smith, and William Roberts—drew on federal funds to provide services to the poor, including young people and senior citizens, and encouraged participation in elections.[14] Their work supported Elaine's and Bobby's campaigns for Oakland city councilwoman and mayor, respectively, in the 1973 elections. While serving as the BPP chairperson in 1975, Elaine ran once more for city council. Even though Elaine and Bobby lost their campaigns (Elaine twice), academics have noted the BPP's enhanced political clout under Elaine's tenure leading the BPP from 1974 to 1977.[15] Through their political endeavors, Elaine and Bobby brought attention to the BPP's Intercommunal Youth Institute (IYI), later known as the Oakland Community School.[16]

The Oakland Community School

In 1973 Ericka expanded her BPP tasks, working as a language arts teacher for the BPP's IYI in Oakland. Her pedagogical approach was based on transforming the community culturally, psychologically, physically, and materially. The BPP organized its free educational programs with the development of the IYI in 1971. The IYI functioned "as an informal home-based community school" and a site of protection for the children of BPP members.[17] In the 1973–1974 academic year, the BPP purchased the IYI designated site, opened the school to the public, and changed its name to the Oakland Community School.[18] The OCS was a free, elementary-level institution serving primarily Black children from working-class backgrounds.[19] Once Brenda Bay, the IYI director, resigned, Huey asked Ericka to take over as the OCS director.

The school's assistant director, Donna Howell, previously of the Boston branch, worked alongside Ericka. The OCS addressed Point 5 of the BPP's Ten-Point Platform and Program, on having awareness of oneself and one's role in society.[20] It played a key role in the BPP's history of radical community education and grew into the largest and most enduring BPP community program.

The school was nontraditional in many ways. It had a low student-to-teacher ratio of ten students to one teacher.[21] According to Ericka and BPP scholar Angela D. LeBlanc-Ernest, "The student population ranged between 50 and 150 from 1974 to 1979, yet each continued to receive an education tailored to his or her specific needs and learning styles."[22] The OCS adopted a distinctive grading system that did not include placement in traditional age-based classes or the use of letter grades as the sole form of evaluation. Instead, teachers assigned students to levels based on their ages and furnished "carefully written academic and social evaluations" on their progress and needed improvement.[23] According to Robert P. Robinson, a scholar of urban education, the levels enabled students to maximize "the Each One Teach One model," which he argues "is reminiscent of the constructivist model, wherein students build each other's learning."[24] Pamela (Pam) Ward Pious, a former OCS teacher, preschool program director, and health officer, noted that students who performed well would assist their peers with their schoolwork and aid their teachers after they finished their assignments.[25] This practice promoted peer mentorship and collaboration.

As director, Ericka was responsible for directing the school's regular operations. She assisted in developing the curriculum, led staff meetings, provided staff training, and hired and fired instructors. "I just made sure that the school's programs served the children and that we were doing the best that we can to serve them," Ericka explained.[26] She wanted both students and teachers to learn in the educational process, with teachers sparking curiosity in students and cultivating a "sense of wonder for them as teachers."[27] This culture of shared learning was made possible because, in Ericka's words, "we taught [the curriculum] with an awareness that we didn't know everything."[28] The process encouraged an empowering and healthy learning environment.

Administrative and staff roles were assigned by ability, not by gender. Women played a central role in the school administration while men held executive positions "as head teachers, food service supervisors, and senior and teen program staff."[29] Ericka and LeBlanc-Ernest note that "it was not uncommon to see a male teacher brushing a child's hair or soothing tears. As well, it was common to see female staff making decisions that impacted facility use, programmatic details, and finances. No duty was beyond any person."[30] Overall, the school sought to destabilize power dynamics and hierarchies between men and women and between students and teachers.

The OCS offered students a unique holistic and cultural pedagogy. Its teachings attended to students' mental, physical, and spiritual needs. The Oakland public school system, on the other hand, was frequently viewed as a warehouse of white patriarchal knowledge that relied on memorization rather than the critical understanding of ideas based on the realities of race and class in America, although not all Oakland public schools lacked love and care for the whole child. To disrupt the dismal public school paradigm, Ericka joined the Association of Alternative Schools, a group that supported the OCS and teachers at alternative schools. Unlike the Oakland public school system, the OCS loved and cared for the whole child. Ericka recalled,

> We fed them, we loved them, and we hugged them. If their hair needed combed, we did it. If they were having trouble at home, we intervened. If they were creative, we supported them in that pursuit. If you love somebody, you care about all the parts of them, not just one part.[31]

The OCS emphasized the development of "all the parts" of a person, including their physical, social-emotional, cognitive, and linguistic abilities. The OCS instructors implemented a "culturally relevant curriculum" to accommodate the students' learning preferences and those of the teachers.[32] All students, including those with disabilities, benefitted from this approach, which "provid[ed] them concrete material assistance as needed and adapting to their educational needs," as pointed out by disability studies scholar Sami Schalk.[33] Pam, for instance, reflected on how she encouraged Joseph, an OCS student who experienced family trauma and frequent seizures, to draw pictures of what his seizures were like. "It's like the lights get turned off and you're in the dark and afraid," he told her. She learned that the more he talked about his health condition, the more accepting he became in "knowing that he was going to come out of darkness." He found solace in the tactile approach of sketching. When his medications started to be administered on time every day, something that had not been happening at home, combined with creative expression, he had fewer seizures; Pam claimed that "he was a less aggressive child [and] he wasn't angry all the time anymore."[34] She met a certain need for him, which offered him a positive perspective and enhanced his learning.

The OCS also grounded its curriculum in dialectical materialism, where students were challenged to think about complex ideas and interrogate phenomena. The curriculum included core academic areas, including math, reading comprehension, literature, speech, art, physical education, environmental studies, history, Spanish, physical education, natural sciences, the social sciences, language, and writing.[35] Teachers of some subject areas in particular, such as the visual and performing arts, theater, and dance, remained "highly conscious" of sociopolitical issues.[36] Students were encouraged to consider limitless possibilities. Dialectical materialism as a theoretical framework exemplified the school's motto, "The World Is Our Classroom," as it promoted imagination and innovation to help students draw connections between their own lives and the lives of others across the world.[37]

The OCS faculty were fervent believers in whole-body instruction. In the pupils, they recognized themselves. Their diversity mirrored that of the students.[38] The OCS martial arts, physical education, and math teacher Steve McCutchen recalled the close ties and mutual respect between the instructors and the pupils. "The teacher-student relationship was one where they would come to us and ask questions outside the classroom that may have been subject-related or may have been human relations issues," he remembered.[39] The ease with which students confided in their teachers demonstrated how involved teachers were in promoting the spiritual development of their students. It marked a departure from the traditional hierarchical nature of the student-teacher relationship. Although the staff found fulfillment in their educational work, their dual roles as teachers and parental figures consumed them. During the week, many teachers lived collectively in the dormitories with the students. "We worked hard at the school; not only did we teach the kids, we didn't leave them. We took care of their dorm life and got them ready for bed and then up the next morning," recalled former OCS teacher Haven Henderson.[40] Even with the intense labor demands, the staff's dedication to meet the needs of the OCS children never wavered. Initially the faculty consisted of BPP members, but over time, teachers from the Oakland public system began to work there as well. "Teachers and other staff from public school settings quit their jobs and took a pay cut to be at OCS," Ericka remembered.[41] The OCS emerged as the sought-after hub for teaching and learning due to its innovative and cutting-edge theories and practices.

Teachers eagerly embraced opportunities to grow as educators. Weekly meetings served as essential platforms for information sharing to enhance student learning and foster parental engagement. The staff presented their reports, tackled challenges related to cultural biases, and deliberated on student performance and strategies to close the gaps within the school. They also explored fresh concepts and students' conduct, seeking feedback from the group.[42]

However, there were disagreements and conflicts among the OCS faculty. Managing the school put Ericka under constant pressure, and sometimes she wasn't at her best. Pam recalled some harrowing experiences with Ericka as her supervisor. "Ericka is the only person in the Black Panther Party who threatened me with violence," she declared. According to the incident she described in our interview, the OCS cook berated his assistant in earshot of the students, who were seated in the dining area eating family-style. Pam confronted him over his mistreatment of women: "Brother, first of all you're disrespecting this sister, and you can't talk like that in front of the children. They can hear you." Her words inflamed his wrath even more; he threw a melon or another large fruit into a sink of water and splashed his assistant with it.[43] "The next thing I knew I was in Ericka's office with the two of them, wondering how I was there," Pam recalled. When Ericka confronted her about her involvement in the matter, she explained that the children heard his abuse. Ericka then admonished her, "If you can't mind your business, I'll have somebody take you out and take care of you."[44] Shocked, Pam responded with silence. In her threat, Ericka's warning clearly conveyed that she would resort to physical measures if Pam didn't stay out of the situation.

Another incident occurred when Pam's infant daughter was hospitalized for life-threatening asthma and severe allergies and placed under an oxygen tent. Like any mother, she was intensely worried about her daughter's health. Ericka would not allow her to be with her daughter at the hospital because she was needed at the school.[45] Her decision disappointed Pam. She had so much respect for Ericka that she was left in disbelief. She thought that Ericka would have understood why she wanted to be with her daughter through her health crisis because she had a child of her own who was the same age. She had no one to turn to for help. Elaine came to the rescue and intervened: "Let that woman go and be with her baby. She needs to be with her child," she told Ericka.[46] With Elaine's support, Pam was permitted to be with her daughter every day until her release from the hospital. "I lost trust in her," Pam remarked as she thought about Ericka's decision to keep her away from her daughter in her time of need.[47] Elaine's decision to allow Pam to be with her sick daughter during her urgent health crisis ran counter to Ericka's expectations that her staff adopt her same parenting style, which meant prioritizing BPP assignments ahead of your children's individual needs.

To Ericka, the larger movement took precedence over being fully present for one's children. While many questioned Ericka's choices, her missteps underscored how fallible humans can be. Ericka clarified that she acted under external influence, being prodded by others, and never intentionally prevented anyone from seeing their child.[48] Pam bore no animosity toward Ericka, recognizing the pressures she faced. Furthermore, Pam pointed out that a BPP comrade was mistreating Ericka, which she believed influenced Ericka's behavior toward the staff during this time. Rumors suggested that this BPP comrade was physically and sexually abusive toward her.[49] In her heart, Ericka expressed deep regret for her wrongdoings and acknowledged how her spiritual practice aided her in improving herself.[50]

She made sure that OCS students learned meditation and yoga, spiritual survival skills that she had cultivated in prison. Students learned proper breathing exercises, which taught them an "internal locus of control" and provided them with a way to center their energies.[51] The OCS educators established a room to meditate in 1979 for faculty and staff to "honor their own innate greatness."[52] The March 1979 OCS parent memo "Meditation as a Way to Attain a Disciplined Attitude" announced that all students and faculty would engage in a meditation practice each day. The memo used the analogy of rest and the body sleeping to illustrate to the parents the benefits of meditation:

> Think about deep sleep. When we sleep we are at peace. We awaken revitalized, reenergized. Our bodies need rest. Our minds need it even more. Meditation then is a way to still the mind. It is a way to calm down the stressful flutterings of our thoughts and give us some sense of peace. The more we meditate the more peaceful we become.[53]

The OCS staff thought that equating meditation with rest, renewal, and noticeable behavioral improvements in many children was the most effective way to communicate its value to parents. The memo shared that the OCS staff and students would sing a chant: "Om Namah Shivaya ('I Bow to the Inner Self')." They believed that repeating this sentence while in a meditative state "help[ed] still the mind more quickly."[54] In order for all children to participate in the meditation practice, the OCS staff advised parents to buy a mat or use their own resources to make one by stitching two pieces of durable cloth together.[55] By explaining how to sew a yoga mat together, they made it accessible to all OCS families, regardless of their socioeconomic status. The OCS emphasized that meditation was consistent with the school's philosophy "to show children how and not what to think."[56] According to another OCS memo, "Instructors do not give opinions in passing on information; instead, facts are shared and information discussed while conclusions are reached by the children themselves."[57] This practice helped students think critically, analyze the world around them, and express themselves freely.

Yoga helped students refocus their energy by using their bodies, which, along with meditation, was essential to students learning discipline and control over their whole body. These practices quiet the mind, reduce reactivity, and enable emotional regulation. To train students to regulate their emotions, Ericka introduced students to basic hatha yoga poses such as the tree pose.[58] She recalled her experience with Brian, a brilliant student with a learning disability who would sometimes get aggressive in the classroom because he was bored.[59] As a way to recenter him, she instructed Brian to do the tree pose.

"Brian, do you think you need to go do the tree pose?" Ericka asked.

"Uh huh, I better go do the tree pose right now."[60]

Brian left for the courtyard for five minutes. Ericka trusted that he was in the courtyard as he was instructed. Some of his peers could see him from the classroom and later told Ericka that he struggled to do the pose at first and would fall. Ericka knew that this was because he was imbalanced and still unfocused. Once he was able to balance himself in the pose, he came back to the classroom smiling and refocused. "I'm better now. I did the tree pose and I did it real good. You wanna see?" he said to Ericka.[61] He then showed the whole class how he did the tree pose. They clapped for him. He stayed focused for the rest of the day. Yoga supplemented any formal academic support he might have also needed.

Spiritual development was just as important as restorative justice, a liberating framework for repairing harm with "indigeneity as its birthright," as restorative justice practitioner and attorney Fania E. Davis reminds us.[62] Although OCS did not use the term "restorative justice," the youth committee modeled restorative justice practices in how it addressed students' concerns. As a liaison between the administration and the students, the Justice Board was a "peer-run committee of children, older children [in particular] fourth and fifth graders."[63] This committee, which was advised by Donna, held hearings for students in violation of school rules; the student and appointed board members would come together to form a balanced agreement to rectify the problem. In contrast to the criminal justice system, the Justice Board did not shun or stigmatize the student but embraced him or her with the creation of a carefully designed mutual agreement to repair the harm. This more loving practice was important to Ericka since she experienced the horrors of the prison system. Although the Justice Board was caring in its approach, former OCS student Gregory B. Lewis recalled the fear of having to go before the board to face his peers. "[The threat] was enough to keep me from acting out." He also noted that he never served on the Justice Board because of his forgiving disposition toward his peers. "I think they [my peers] were wise enough at the time to leave me off the committee. I would have probably been more lenient on some of my cohorts," he laughed.[64] He chose to pursue law and justice because of his OCS educational experiences.

The OCS offered a range of extracurricular activities that promoted social justice-oriented community work, physical fitness, the arts, and performance. Per the OCS instructor handbook, teachers employed a technique known as "directing," which meant that they provided students with "enough options in the form of rewarding activities" to show self-motivation, freedom of choice, and agency.[65] Some of these activities included martial arts, creative writing, calisthenics, math bowls, science fairs, field trips, language arts bees, theater, dance, poetry classes, art, vocal music, and a jazz band. The OCS's extension center, the Oakland Community Learning Center (OCLC), provided a variety of extracurricular activities and volunteer opportunities that tied the school to the community. Students engaged in physical activity at the start of the day to get them moving. Steve McCutchen taught the martial arts classes after school and during the day.[66]

Students had the opportunity to run for office on the OCS Youth Committee to collaborate in managing the Youth Store, the KIDS radio show, and the newsletter, for which students authored, edited, and illustrated the articles.[67] Activities engaged the students, parents, and the community. The OCS teachers, staff, the broader BPP membership, and parents raised funds for the school through fundraising initiatives, individual contributions, and support from county, city, and state agencies. Proposals for grants and other funding sources were also submitted by the Education Opportunities Corporation, OCS's nonprofit group made up of OCS administrators.[68] The success of the school and student participation in activities garnered so much attention that notable public figures paid visits to the students; the celebrities included Don Cornelius, the host of the television show *Soul Train*, writers James Baldwin and Maya Angelou, baseball player Willie Mays, and civil rights icon Rosa Parks.[69] Ronald "Money-B" Brooks, a former OCS student and part of the rap group Digital Underground, noted that these well-known individuals "were excited to come check us out just as much as we were to have them come."[70] Their visits left the OCS students with priceless memories and profoundly impacted their lives as change agents.

Activities and projects that addressed social change were part of Gregory's OCS experiences. He recalled a writing assignment from his English class that required students to hone their writing skills by composing and mailing letters to the president of the United States about issues impacting them.[71] They also wrote letters to political prisoners to express solidarity. By doing this, OCS teachers fostered a sense of civic engagement and community activism. Amber Landis-Reedy, a white student at the OCS, shared that the school was educationally liberating. "It was safe. It was loving. It was kind. It was gentle. Everybody there just had a passion for the struggle . . . from top to bottom," she remembered.[72] The OCS provided a warm and loving atmosphere. "As a child, everybody that you came in contact with was excited to teach you [and] excited to be in your presence. You were not a burden. You were not in the way," she declared.[73] Because the school had a beneficial impact on their lives, students recall their OCS experiences with pride and joy.

Ericka asserts that OCS students navigated the world with a strong sense of self and that they were "really calm and able to engage lots of different people, [and] able to retain information."[74] I believe that it was the focus on community education and spirituality working in tandem that contributed to the "strong sense of self" in former OCS students. The OCS was so popular, parents often enrolled their family members and children while still in the womb.[75] Political scientist Charles E. Jones and anthropologist Jonathan Gayles note that the OCS bolstered student learning so much that they "perform[ed] 3 to 4 years in advance of their public [school] peers."[76] Ronald remembered entering public school in Berkeley and Philadelphia ahead of his peers: "I always tested at a higher grade than whatever my age was. So we were learning things two and three grades ahead of what our age was."[77] OCS students were excelling by leaps and bounds. At the OCS, students' education extended beyond academics; it nurtured the whole person. The Alameda Board of Supervisors honored the OCS in 1976 "for its outstanding contribution to the education of poor and disadvantaged youth."[78] The next year, the California State Department of Education declared the OCS a model elementary school, and the California state legislature also honored the institution.[79]

Alameda County Board of Education

While managing OCS, Ericka kept a foothold in politics. In 1976 California state assemblyman Thomas H. Bates appointed Ericka to the Alameda County Board of Education.[80] The Alameda County Board of Education regulated the county's educational programming for children with disabilities and those living in juvenile institutions. At one of her first evening countywide board meetings, Ericka recalled that the board members, older white men, were asked to review many children's suspension and expulsion appeals. The members often automatically rejected the appeals. This appalled her. When they gave their testimonies, the white male board members doubted their honesty. Parents and children of color defending themselves likely made white male school board members feel threatened, thus, it never occurred to them to inquire more deeply about their cases. At this moment, Ericka was experiencing the white backlash from the Civil Rights Act of 1964 and the Voting Rights Act of 1965. From her own personal experience as a BPP member and a former political prisoner, she was aware that not all information written about a person was accurate, so she would interject during the hearing to ask important questions to the parents about their children. She identified with the parents and children's firsthand accounts and was aware that the school board historically did not consider systemic injustices in its decision making.

Her investigation uncovered deep-seated family issues. Many appeals involved mothers and their daughters navigating unique challenges, such as a young person having to work due to a parent's illness or incarceration. In some situations, parents could not afford bus fare to get their child to school, or they worked two jobs, leaving a void in their children's lives. Sometimes parental separation destabilized the family. Ericka ensured that the school board's conclusions regarding the appeals were well-informed. While holding this governmental post, she presented a progressive perspective and worked to protect underprivileged youth who were frightened at testifying in front of a predominately racist white male audience at the school board meetings and who had been suspended, expelled, arrested, or adjudicated to juvenile institutions. When she visited classrooms with disabled students, she noted a pattern of Black and Brown boys who should not have been present. They were misdiagnosed and not given proper support and instruction based on their learning needs. In these situations, she would collaborate with teachers to develop an individualized education plan for the student. She addressed inadequacies in the school system and juvenile detention centers, challenged discriminatory ideas, advised the school board to reconsider habitually expelling students, and suggested restorative justice training for school administrators.[81] Ultimately, she challenged the criminalization of Black and Brown youth and refused to let them enter the school-to-prison pipeline.

Ericka's participation in large-scale demonstrations advocating for the disability rights movement was a continuation of her work in education as the director of the OCS and a member of the Alameda County Board of Education. At a demonstration in San Francisco in 1977, Ericka was photographed delivering a speech in favor of "Section 504 of the Vocational Rehabilitation Act of 1973, thus barring discrimination against disabled people in all buildings and facilities receiving federal funds."[82] She referred to "the signing of 504, this demonstration, [and] the sit-in" as a "beautiful thing" in her remarks.[83] The significance of the historic event was explained in the article for readers: "The signing of the long-delayed implementation regulations was the significant victory [for] the handicapped and disabled."[84] Ericka's activism represents what Schalk brilliantly showcases about the BPP: that "disability rights and anti-ableism fit within their existing revolutionary ideology."[85] Schalk draws attention to the multitude of ways the BPP supported the demonstration, including supporting fellow members and disability rights activists Chuck Jackson and Brad Lomax as demonstrators, as well as feeding protesters, arranging for members to speak, and issuing media announcements and stories about the protests in the BPP newspaper.[86] Ericka's speech was important to the work of the BPP in championing the 504 demonstration. Her community engagement and advocacy were shaped by her own experience articulating the voice of the people. She returned to school to finish her bachelor's degree in diversified liberal arts with a focus on education at Antioch University West in 1979. Until 1980, Ericka served on the Alameda County Board of Education, after which she continued in her role as the OCS director until she left the BPP the following year.

Post–Black Panther Party Life

By the 1980s, the BPP had all but collapsed. Yet it was not its decline that compelled Ericka to leave, but the sexual violence she endured within the organization.[87] Given her past, she couldn't tolerate such a violation.

Ericka loved the BPP, but it harbored its own demons and darkness. Toxic members could be violent toward one another, and the drugs on the streets felt insurmountable. Huey's mental health deteriorated; he became addicted to drugs, exhibited violent tendencies, and ultimately died by violence.[88]

Six months after leaving the BPP, Ericka found work as an educator, first as a co-director of a church-owned Black private school for two years and then at a high school. In her downtime, she attended spiritual centers to deepen her inner work and found love again. She met Coulter Huyler, a Dutch English man, to whom she was married for six years.[89] In 1987 her youngest son, Yadav, was born from their union. She was able to be a full-time mother. "I could just be a mom and I enjoyed it."[90] During this period she might have been trying to make up for her absence in her children's lives, as some of them might have felt abandoned by her. It is not uncommon for children of political activists in the Black freedom movement to harbor some resentment. Balancing freedom work with family is precarious. As she dedicated herself to being a full-time mother to Yadav, Ericka remained engaged in community work. She aimed to weave her spiritual awareness into every aspect of her life, including parenting. Yadav does not remember a time where he was not deeply rooted in spiritual practice. Before he knew how to talk, he was in meditation environments with his parents. His earliest memories include playing with other children while also watching his parents meditate, chant, and engage in spiritual practice. He grew up surrounded by spiritual practices, influenced by both his parents, and witnessed his mother drawing on her spirituality as she reentered the workforce in 1989.[91]

In the 1990s, during the HIV/AIDS crisis, Ericka worked with women and children as a health educator. She found work as a practical support volunteer coordinator with the Shanti Project, a community organization known for its focus specifically on the LGBTQIA+ community, intravenous drug users, sex workers, and transgender people. She trained support volunteers at the Shanti Project to carry out care work through home visits, form connections with people, and provide emotional support. She also worked as an organizer at the AIDS Project-Contra Costa County in San Francisco, creating health care programs for women and children and people of color who engaged in intravenous drug usage.

She helped those who were HIV/AIDS positive and collaborated with nurses and doctors to spread awareness of the virus/disease among community organizations and in prisons. Her spiritual practices helped her work with those with HIV/AIDS; as she remembered, it took a lot of inner work and stamina to work with children and adults who were facing death. This experience allowed her to recognize the resiliency of children. However, after so many years, the deaths and the suffering of families began to take a toll on her. She then started working for the Mind/Body Institute in its Los Angeles and Northern California school sites, teaching resiliency skills to Black and Brown educators and their elementary, middle, and high school students in the inner city, taking on the role full-time in 1994.

The Mind/Body Institute offered mindfulness and relaxation programs to heal life-threatening illnesses. What made her work powerful in these positions was her daily meditation practice. Without such a practice, when she worked for the AIDS Project-Contra Costa, for example, she would not have been able to sit with a dying child or comfort a mother who recently completed drug recovery and learned that she and her newborn daughter were HIV positive. Her spiritual wellness practices kept her mentally healthy while doing this work. She went from the BPP, which she described as "all about war," to HIV/AIDS work, which is all about quality of life.[92] She then moved to working as an educator in the college setting, teaching classes in women's and gender studies at San Francisco State University and California State University, East Bay, and sociology and African American studies in the Peralta Community College District.[93] She completed a master's degree in sociology at California State University, East Bay, in 2010. She wrote her master's thesis on the BPP's OCS.[94] Four years prior, she found love with Lisbet Tellefsen, whom she has been with for over seventeen years. Ericka facilitated restorative justice workshops in schools and prisons and now lectures across the country.

As a trailblazer in education, Ericka has been recognized across the nation. In 2019 MetWest High School of the Oakland Unified School District honored Ericka by naming its ninth-grade academy campus the Ericka Huggins Campus.[95] It took the collective effort of the school community to name the campus after Ericka. According to Ericka, student feedback was considered when officials decided to name the campus in her honor.[96] When the students were invited to make a short list of potential people to name the campus after, Ericka placed first. The students and staff, who are majority of color, had developed a relationship with Ericka through her visits to the school, where she mentored students and discussed mindfulness techniques with them. Given her presence, MetWest considers Ericka an integral component of the school. Located in Oakland, California, MetWest is built in the city's radical tradition, and the BPP's history permeates the school. Free breakfast is provided for students, and a health clinic is located next to the school. The legacy of the BPP is reflected in the landscape of the school, as pictures of Huey P. Newton, Angela Y. Davis, and the Ten-Point Platform and Program adorn the walls.[97]

MetWest was founded in 2002 as part of an initiative to remedy "overcrowded and under-performing schools" within the Oakland Unified School District.[98] Through the initiative, MetWest launched "as one of the first 'new small autonomous schools.'"[99] With a focus on social justice, the school is designed to enhance student achievement via "real world learning" and a comprehensive internship program.[100] According to its website, "MetWest is one of forty public high schools" in the United States leading "a model of internship-based education."[101] The school's philosophy is one that promotes restorative practices to create healthy communities. Malik, who collaborated with Ericka on the BPP newspaper cadre and currently works as a MetWest High School restorative practices staff member for its other campus dedicated to civil rights and labor icon Dolores Huerta, explained that the process "starts in the classroom" through circles and conversations.[102] He added that students demanded restorative practices because "they wanted to feel safe."[103] Since the school is small, the teachers and staff are able to develop close bonds with the students, which enables them to take a proactive approach. "We can tell when people are not getting along, when they're having problems, when they're having difficulty. So we just try to deal with it immediately," Malik added.[104] Restorative practices have resulted in MetWest having the "lowest suspension rates" and the best attendance and exit exam scores among high schools within the Oakland Unified School District.[105] The school also prioritizes wellness and mindfulness in its community-building framework to develop its students as resilient and resourceful global citizens, as illustrated in the school vision.[106] Although many of its practices mirror those of the BPP's Oakland Community School, especially in its adoption of restorative practices and learner outcomes that foster social emotional intelligence, critical thinking, self-determination, and advocacy for social change, it showcases ties between community education and wellness that transcend the BPP's scope.[107]

Ericka believes in restorative justice and personal and spiritual transformation. She revealed that one of the agenda items at the formative meeting for the Black Panther Party National Alumni Association was to begin a healing process. "People said a lot of things and were not very kind to each other in that meeting. It was difficult," she reflected. She recalled that a BPP comrade told her that she never forgave her for forcing her to work through an injury. "I want you to know what I've been holding for thirty years about you. I wasn't feeling well, and I had an accident—my leg, or my ankle, was sprained—and you never let me go home and take care of it. You just kept me there working, and I've never forgiven you for that," she said to Ericka. To set things right, Ericka publicly apologized to her and everyone else in the room whom she had harmed. "I don't remember that, but I believe you to be telling me the truth, and I am so sorry from the bottom of my heart," Ericka meekly responded.[108] After the session, Ericka explained that the BPP members applauded her for accepting responsibility for her actions. Being a restorative justice facilitator, she felt strongly about asking for forgiveness and forgiving herself. In her life, she experienced trauma and contributed to the trauma of others. She did not always act in a caring, sisterly manner. Sometimes these failings were apparent in her leadership and other times in her parenting, but she took responsibility for harming others and continues to grow in her spiritual practice.

In 2010 Ericka entered a restorative justice dialogue with Larry Watani Stiner, former US organization member and one of the men convicted of conspiring to murder John and Bunchy.[109] She agreed to the dialogue on the condition that they employ "a both-and principle" to underscore that "humans are capable of the most heinous actions and the most lovely—all in one day."[110] By doing this, with honesty and openness, they intentionally considered the complexity of the human experience. Their conversations began through prison letters that continued over two years. In 2012 Ericka came to San Quentin State Prison for a face-to-face meeting with Watani. When they transitioned from letters to a face-to-face meeting, which lasted for five hours, they witnessed each other's emotions and feelings. "It was the most emotional engagement of my entire life. And it was also the most fulfilling and rewarding," Watani recalled.[111] Watani learned that he and Ericka "had both been on long, arduous journeys of the mind, heart, and spirit."[112] He considered their restorative dialogue a model for youth to address conflict resolution and foster peacemaking.[113]

Even though he did not murder John and Bunchy, he accepted responsibility, and apologized for his "participation in the warrior mindset that had contributed the[ir] deaths."[114] He explained how this mindset "finds justification in violence and accepts casualties of war over preservation of life."[115] Militarism and a combative orientation shaped this mindset, one that "COINTELPRO exploited to create distrust and to obliterate collaboration and unity among" the BPP and Maulana Karenga's US organization.[116] Even though they both knew that COINTELPRO murdered John and Bunchy, Watani grappled with his choices that day. He revealed to Ericka that on the day they were murdered, he walked over their dead bodies. At that moment, he did not extend care and concern for human life but instead treated them as disposable.

Decades had passed, but Ericka still needed answers. "How did you know they were dead?" Ericka asked. Watani remembered, "I could see John and Bunchy, but everything was moving quickly and in slo-mo at the same time. They looked so peaceful, like they were sleeping."[117]

To know that they were not in pain but seemed to be sleeping gave Ericka comfort and closure. Neither she nor Watani could change the past, but the information and exchange were powerful. Somehow, they both found resolve and clarity. Their restorative justice dialogue was necessary for healing, understanding, and repair.[118] Ericka sees restorative justice as an important pathway for social justice. Fania E. Davis writes, "We have reached a historical point in this country where it is clear that if we do not seek both justice and healing, injustice will keep replicating itself ad nauseum and we will find ourselves intoning the very same social justice demands generation after generation."[119] Ericka and Watani's participation in a restorative justice dialogue helped them break the vicious cycle of suffering. Ericka employed restorative justice and healing practices as pathways for healing and transformation.

The throughline in Ericka's life is service, wellness, and spirituality. She never strayed from her core beliefs. Ericka is now over seventy-five and remains committed to the Black political struggle. Over the years, her children have lauded her perseverance and resilience as she has devoted her life to the spiritual wellness of others. "One of the things I admire about my mom is that she's still involved and principled," Mai said.[120] Ericka's social justice work exemplifies the relationship between wellness, spiritual practices, and political resistance among radical Black women.

Black Panther Woman stands as a testament to social justice and abolition movements. Ericka's unwavering assertion of her humanity and identity in prison challenges readers to confront the brutality of mass incarceration. Her journey showcases the resilience of women, especially mothers, navigating the treacherous waters of prison politics, championing transformation both within and outside its confines. Ericka staunchly rejects the notion that there's anything restorative or redemptive about severing individuals from their communities and subjecting them to the harsh realities of incarceration. Her advocacy for Black humanity and the call to abolish prisons resonate deeply with the principles of the Black Lives Matter movement, spearheaded by Alicia Garza, Patrisse Cullors, and Opal Tometi; the Movement for Black Lives, a partnership of more than fifty organizations representing the needs and interests of Black communities nationwide; the #SayHer-Name movement, initiated by the African American Policy Forum; and Black Youth Project 100, developed by political scientist Cathy J. Cohen and Chicago activist Charlene A. Carruthers, among others. Indeed, her spiritual wellness practice foreshadowed the Black feminist ethos of Black Lives Matter and Black feminist love politics. The multifaceted nature of Ericka's experiences defies a straightforward narrative, challenging conventional historical storytelling.

The inventive ways Black people have confronted anti-Blackness require scholars to prioritize interdisciplinary perspectives. This book positions us to grasp the intricate bond between trauma and recovery, emphasizing the significance of wellness and its role in promoting social change. Ericka's journey—blending moments of spiritual awakening with political activism and groundbreaking self-care and care for others—offers insight into the complex challenges involved in not perpetuating the very practices and behaviors we aim to abolish. Her teachings on political activism intertwined with spirituality prompt us to champion compassion, wellness, and love.

ACKNOWLEDGMENTS

I am eternally grateful to the village of people who supported me during the making of this book. First and foremost, I would like to thank Mary Catherine Durant Lyles, my beautiful mother. Those who know me well are aware of our enduring bond, which will forever persist. She has supported me with unwavering consistency whether near or far. No matter where I am in the world, we communicate every day. She is not just a friend, but a confidante, an inspiring motivator, and a model of Black excellence for me. Her support through thick and thin, her insightful discussion of different sections of the book, her patient ear as she listened to me debate passages, and her ability to help me identify the perfect words to convey the spirit's power have all been priceless gifts. As my spiritual guide, she has also assisted me in processing my feelings about writing this book. Without her continuous support, I could not have finished this book, completed my doctorate, or survived academia. She means the world to me, and I will always love her. Being her daughter is a true blessing.

Second, I would like to acknowledge and thank Ken Gulley and the Gulley family for their heartfelt support. Ken has been a dear and close friend of mine since high school. Over the years, we have been there for one another. He read passages from the book, served as a soundboard, meticulously transcribed many of my subjects' interviews, and transported me to and from the airport. His labor means so much to me. I want to thank Ken, Ms. Gulley, Kim, and Wendy for their support and encouragement. I also want to express my gratitude to Kellie Carter Jackson and Natalie Léger for taking the time to read drafts and passages, generously offering feedback, and helping me talk through the book. Our sisterhood has encouraged and supported me tremendously. I also extend my gratitude to Nicole Burrowes, Cheryl D. Hicks, and Robyn C. Spencer-Antoine from my Sister Scholars writing group. I cherish the joy our sisterhood brings. It's like a breath of fresh air, filled with mutual support, encouragement, care, and concern.

I am indebted to the following readers during my book manuscript workshop: Stephanie Y. Evans, Barbara Green, LaKisha Michelle Simmons, Robyn C. Spencer-Antoine, Ula Y. Taylor, and Rhonda Y. Williams, whose books have helped shape my work. Thank you for your invaluable time, wise advice, insightful feedback, and considerable support. Their feedback immensely strengthened the manuscript. Special thanks to the following people: Eshe Sherley for her wonderful assistance in taking thorough and well-organized notes throughout the manuscript workshop; Ula Y. Taylor and Rhonda Y. Williams for the additional support they offered as I worked through sections of the manuscript; LaKisha Michelle Simmons for her wonderful remarks regarding my project and her tremendous support; Stephanie Y. Evans for meeting with me when I needed a pick-me-up and for her beautiful encouraging emails; as well as Rashida L. Harrison for her incredible support during this process and for helping me through various portions. The book manuscript workshop was made possible by funding from the Notre Dame Initiative on Race and Resilience and the University of Notre Dame's Institute for Advanced Study (NDIAS) 2021–2022 Faculty Fellowship. I would like to extend my thanks to my NDIAS colleagues for their support: Scott Alves Barton for your collegiality and friendship, Char Brecevic for your camaraderie, Jennifer Forestal for your feedback, John Golden for our meetings while I worked through the legal ramifications of Ericka's trial, Jason McLachlan and Rebecca Stumpf for your support, Claire Scott-Bacon for your sisterhood, Roy Scranton for your creative writing guidance, LaKisha Michelle Simmons for your counsel, friendship, and generosity, and Apryl A. Williams for your friendship and generosity.

I would like to thank the Black, Race, and Ethnic Studies 2022–2023 Grant Initiative through the City University of New York for their support of my publication, and the University of Michigan's Institute for Research on Women and Gender, where I was able to take on the role of remote visiting scholar from 2022 to 2024, which allowed me access to institutional library resources. I am particularly grateful for Harriet (Niki) Fayne, who held the position of provost at Lehman College during the period that I was granted the American Association of University Women's (AAUW) 2018–2019 American Postdoctoral Research Leave Fellowship. Harriet helped me to secure funding through the Chancellor's

Faculty Opportunity Fund through the City University of New York to bridge my salary wage difference, enabling me to accept the award. My AAUW fellowship period was extremely important in providing me with the time I needed to work on my manuscript. I would like to thank Ruth Wilson Gilmore for her support and the Center for Place, Culture, and Politics Faculty Fellowship and the New-York Historical Museum and Library through the Center for Women's History, Early Career Workshop.

Billy X Jennings provided invaluable assistance in my search for certain articles in the Black Panther Party newspaper. I have received assistance from numerous librarians over my journey. Thank you to Daniel DeKok at Lincoln University, Meredith Kahn at the University of Michigan, Melanie Locay at the New York Public Library, Janet Munch at Lehman College, Carolyn Picciano at the Connecticut State Library, Allen Ramsey at the Connecticut State Library, Breezy Silver at Michigan State University, and Lisa Timothy at the East Lyme Public Library. I am appreciative to have completed library archive work at the following institutions: the Huey P. Newton Foundation Special Collection at Stanford University, the Special Collections at Michigan State University, the Beinecke Rare Book and Manuscript Library that houses the Catherine Roraback Collection of Ericka Huggins Papers at Yale University, and the Connecticut State Library. Special thanks to everyone at Niantic Prison and the Department of Corrections that I worked with to secure archives for this project, including Paul Harrison, whose assistance was fundamental in providing me with a foundation on the history of Niantic. Thank you, Paul, for all the binders of history, emails, and conversations in person and by phone, and Janet S. York, for her time and conversation.

I appreciate the many invitations and opportunities from universities, organizations, and institutes to share my work. I want to especially recognize Maryam Aziz and the Black Research Roundtable at the University of Michigan. The opportunity to present my research at Queen's University Belfast, Northern Ireland, in February 2023 was made possible by Nik Ribianszky, Kieran Connell, Keith Breen, the School of History, Anthropology, Philosophy, and Politics, and the Mitchell Institute. This enabled Ericka and me to discuss the book's creation abroad. Additionally, I want to thank Martin Brady for his support.

I am thankful for the handful of editors, assistants, and helpful hands that have worked with me over the years, including Tiffany Ball, LaToya Faulk, Victoria Law, Kendra Lyimo, Charié Jewel Payne, Charlotte Ritz-Jack, Antonio Rodriguez, and Rachel Nishan. For her amazing editing of the book, Aurora Chang deserves special recognition.

The seeds of my project date back to my early years as a doctoral student at Michigan State University under the direction of Pero G. Dagbovie. His mentorship and guidance were foundational to my intellectual development. He taught me what it meant to be a historian and scholar. I thank him immensely. I want to also thank Geneva Smitherman during my graduate years for her support and encouragement. Stephane Dunn's mentorship throughout my time as a master's student was pivotal to my academic development at the Ohio State University. Our friendship has grown out of our mentorship relationship. She read the Sister Love Collective chapter and provided input, for which I am also grateful. Shelly Eversley and the Faculty Fellowship Publication Program (FFPP) gave me time and access to a network of scholars that allowed me to build on my work in the spring of 2015. With Shelly's help, I published my first journal article on Ericka Huggins with the *Women's Studies Quarterly*, and I learned so much working closely with her. Thank you for your incredible support and mentorship. I want to thank my FFPP comrade and writing accountability partner Lara Saguisag. I'm grateful for our friendship and weekly check-ins about the writing journey, academia, and work-life balance. I thank Jeanne Theoharis for her friendship and support of my work. She and Komozi Woodard have given me several opportunities to share my research at the Schomburg Center for Research in Black Culture, and I am grateful for that. I give special thanks to Ashley D. Farmer, my series editor, for her support of my work and feedback on both my book proposal and my manuscript as it neared completion, which enabled me to consider the deeper, more significant implications of my work.

I would like to thank colleagues, friends, and associates who read early drafts and offered feedback or advice: Melissa Coss Aquino, Say Burgin, Siobhan Carter-David, Adam Dell, LeConté Dill, Geraldine Friedman, David Goldberg, Katherine Greenstein, LaShawn D. Harris, Rashida L. Harrison, Amanda Hughett, Ollie A. Johnson, Amy Kesselman, Kimberly Thomas McNair, Olivia Loksing Moy, Eziaku Atuama

Nwokocha, Nik Ribianszky, Maria Salowich, LaToya L. Sawyer, Eldra Dominique Walker, and Jacqueline Wolf. I would like to thank those who have offered advice on oral history, including Scot Brown, Erik S. McDuffie, David Ritz, and Kelly C. Sartorius. I would like to express my gratitude to everyone whose work has inspired me: Charlene A. Carruthers, Patricia Hill Collins, Angela Y. Davis, Nicole R. Fleetwood, Marisa J. Fuentes, Farah Jasmine Griffin, Beverly Guy-Sheftall, Saidiya Hartman, Robin D. G. Kelley, Angela D. LeBlanc-Ernest, Talitha L. LeFlouria, Audre Lorde, Tracye A. Matthews, Alondra Nelson, Barbara Smith, and Robyn C. Spencer-Antoine. I am appreciative of my friends, supporters, those who have cheered me on, and my Lehman College community: Stefan M. Bradley, Nikki Brown, Charles Cange, Kefentse K. Chike, Shannon M. Cochran, Javiela Evangelista, K. T. Ewing, Robert Farrell, Tanisha C. Ford, Alyshia Gálvez, Keisha Goode, David Hyman, Tanisha M. Jackson, Bayyinah S. Jeffries, Tonisha B. Lane, Sarah Ohmer, Katondra Price, Ava Purkiss, Rosa L. Rivera-McCutchen, Monica Rivers, Nara Roberta Silva, Stephen Ward, and the anonymous reviewers.

I would like to thank the National Center for Faculty Development and Diversity (NCFDD) and my NCFDD writing partner, Geraldine Friedman, for her support and friendship, Kathryn Sophia Belle and the La Belle Vie Writing Group, the Association of Black Women Historians morning and evening writing groups, members of the Black Power Writing Group, and additional writing partners across time: Charles Cange, Sophia Hsu, Sarah Ohmer, Jason Payton, and Lisa ze Winters.

I want to thank those who gave interviews about their personal and political lives for the book, including JoNina Abron-Ervin, Charles Alexander, MaryAnn Andelson, Ronald "Money-B" Brooks, Walia Burnett, Alicia Caraballo, Connie Civita, Lisa Cowell, Geri DeLaRosa, Dázon Dixon Diallo, Emory Douglas, George Edwards, Malik Edwards, Carol Granison, Dorthula Green, LaReese Harvey, Haven Henderson, Lennox Hinds, Yadav Jelal Huyler, Mae Jackson, Amber Landis-Reedy, Gregory Lewis, Alprentice McCutchen, Steve McCutchen, Masai Minters, Muhammad Mubarak, Siwatu-Salama Ra, Delinah Rivera-Dowdy, David Rosen, Malik Shabazz, Nancy Shia, Cleo Silvers, Harold Taylor, Ivan Toro, Jan Von Flatern, Pamela (Pam) Ward Pious, John Williams, and Lauryn Williams. I want to thank

Delinah Rivera-Dowdy and Linda Sciongay for connecting me with Ivan Toro. I want to especially thank Angela Y. Davis for supporting the book, agreeing to an interview, and connecting me with Lennox Hinds, Lisbeth Tellefsen for her help when needed, Mai Huggins Lassiter for feedback on the portions of the book about her life, and Ericka Huggins for her generosity, time, and trust.

I am grateful to my therapist, Lee Jenkins, for helping me develop a deeper knowledge of self and providing emotional support as I was writing this book. I want to close by thanking my sister, Angela Marie Phillips-Tyler, for her love and support. She always has my back and has been a listening ear. I love her dearly. I thank my brother-in-law, Benjamin Joseph Tyler Sr., for his support, as well as my nephew, Benjamin Joseph Tyler Jr., and niece, Alycia Josephine Tyler, for allowing me to impart so much knowledge on the Black Panther Party. I express my gratitude to my aunts Diane, Joanne, Karen, and Carolyn for exemplifying Black feminism. I want to thank my Uncle Larry for his support of my work and attendance at my talk while I was in Chicago. As the book was nearing completion, my grandmother, Mary Frances Jenifer-Durant, transitioned. Being her namesake makes me incredibly proud. She allowed me to work on my book at her home during my AAUW fellowship, and for that, I am grateful. I would especially like to express my gratitude to my grandfather, Joseph Solomon Durant, whom I refer to affectionately as Papa. I have always looked to him as my "real" father. He always told me to go to the top. I owe my doctorate to him and my mother. He meant the absolute world to me, and I miss him dearly. I know he would be so proud. I shall always love him. To my mother and my Papa, I dedicate this book.

APPENDIX A

Ericka Huggins's Life Timeline

1948
January 5, 1948—Ericka Jenkins is born.

1963
August 28, 1963—Ericka attends the March on Washington at the age
of 15.

1965–1966
Ericka attends Cheyney State College, now Cheyney University of
Pennsylvania.

1966–1967
Ericka transfers to Lincoln University.
Ericka meets John Jerome Huggins Jr. at Lincoln University.
November 15, 1967—Ericka withdraws from Lincoln University to join the
Black Panther Party (BPP).

1968
Ericka's daughter, Mai, is born.

1969
January 17, 1969—BPP leaders John Jerome Huggins Jr. and Alprentice
"Bunchy" Carter are murdered on the UCLA campus.
May 20, 1969—George Sams accuses Alex Rackley of being an informant.
Warren Kimbro and Lonnie McLucas commit Rackley's torture and
murder under Sams's direction.
May 22, 1969—Ericka and other Connecticut BPP women, including
Frances Elsie Carter, Maude Louise Francis, Jeannie Wilson, Margaret
"Peggy" Hudgins, and Rose Marie Smith, begin their incarceration
at the Connecticut Correctional Institution for Women in Niantic on

conspiracy charges for murder, kidnapping, and conspiracy to murder BPP member Alex Rackley. Frances and Rose arrive in Niantic while pregnant, giving birth there.

May 29, 1969—On conspiracy charges for the murder, kidnapping, and plot to murder Alex Rackley, pregnant Loretta Luckes enters Niantic prison. Correctional officers transfer Maude and Jeannie to a juvenile detention home.

1970

January 19, 1970—Frances is released on bond.

January 21, 1970—Frances is found in contempt of court and sentenced to additional time.

February 16, 1970—Millie Rivera, a Puerto Rican teenager and artist, begins her incarceration.

June 12, 1970—Frances is released from Niantic.

July 19, 1970—Millie Rivera escapes Niantic with other incarcerated women.

September 10, 1970—Loretta Luckes is released from prison.

October 2, 1970—Peggy and Rose are released from Niantic. Ericka is placed in solitary confinement.

October 1970—After attorneys Stanley A. Bass, Catherine G. Roraback, David N. Rosen, and Charles R. Garry file a complaint for declaratory and injunctive relief with the US district court in New Haven to seek relief for Ericka and Bobby Seale from the oppressive conditions of pretrial confinement, the State of Connecticut releases Ericka from solitary confinement.

November 9, 1970—Correctional officers move Ericka out of administrative isolation to the general population.

December 1, 1970—Connie Civita begins her incarceration and soon joins Ericka and Millie's Niantic-based Sister Love Collective.

December 4, 1970—Millie, a fugitive on the run, is apprehended and brought back to prison, where she gives birth to a son. Ericka, with Millie Rivera, develops the Sister Love Collective, a Niantic-based clandestine organization to support women prisoners' spiritual, social, and health needs at Niantic. As a hairstylist, Connie joins Sister Love.

December 30, 1970—Connie is released from prison.

1971

May 1971—After numerous hearings, a Memorandum of Decision is
  submitted to the US district court in New Haven regarding Ericka and
  Bobby's case for declaratory judgment, an injunction, and other relief.
May 25, 1971—Ericka is released from Niantic and Bobby is freed from
  Montville Correctional Center.
Ericka begins working for the BPP newspaper cadre for two years as an
  editor.
July 23, 1971—Millie is released from prison.

1972

May 1972—Ericka accepts position on the Berkeley Community Development Council by election.

1973

Ericka becomes a language arts teacher at the Black Panther Party's
  Intercommunal Youth Institute (IYI) in Oakland, California, before
  becoming director of the BPP's Oakland Community School (OCS), an
  elementary school, for eight years.

1974

Ericka's second child, Rasa, is born.

1975

Insights and Poems, a collection of poems by Ericka and BPP co-founder
  Huey P. Newton, is published by City Lights.
Ericka joins the Association of Alternative Schools.

1979

Ericka completes her bachelor's degree in diversified liberal arts with a
  focus on education at Antioch University West.

1981

Ericka leaves the BPP.

1984

Peggy dies at the age of 36.

1987

Yadav, Ericka's youngest son, is born.

1990s

Ericka works as a health educator for institutions like the Mind/Body Institute, AIDS Project-Contra Costa County, and the Shanti Project.

2003

Ericka starts an appointment as a lecturer in women's and gender studies at California State University, East Bay, and San Francisco State University.

2008

Ericka begins her seven-year tenure as a lecturer in sociology and African American studies at Peralta Community College District.

2010

Ericka receives a master of arts in sociology at California State University, East Bay. Her thesis, "Countering the Effects of Multigenerational Race and Gender Trauma: A Prescriptive Educational Model," explores the Black Panther Party's Oakland Community School.

2011

Millie dies from a massive heart attack at the age of 57.

APPENDIX B

Glossary of Names

BPP = Black Panther Party
OCS = Oakland Community School
Niantic = Connecticut Correctional Institution for Women in Niantic

Walter Bremond	Head of the Black Congress Consortium. Bremond arrived at Ericka's home on the day she was arrested and cared for Ericka's daughter, Mai.
Ronald "Money-B" Brooks	Former BPP OCS student and member of the rap group Digital Underground.
Elaine Brown	Former BPP chairperson from 1974 until her resignation in 1977.
Stokely Carmichael (Kwame Ture)	Prominent civil rights activist, credited for coining and defining the term "Black Power."
Alprentice "Bunchy" Carter	Founder and deputy minister of defense of the BPP's Southern California chapter. Carter was slain on the campus of UCLA in 1969.
Frances Elsie Carter	One of the young BPP women imprisoned with Ericka while in Niantic, and sister of Peggy Hudgins. Frances was pregnant while incarcerated. She delivered her son, Osceola, while in prison.
Mr. & Mrs. Carter	Parents of Frances Elsie Carter and Peggy Hudgins. Owners of a barbershop in Bridgeport, CT, they repudiated their daughters' involvement in the BPP.
Connie Civita	Hairdresser in the Sister Love Collective at Niantic. Ericka wrote a poem, "for connie, a rollingstone," dedicated to her.
Altomae Davis	Ericka's maternal aunt. Altomae lived in poverty and nurtured a cohesive family unit of nine children.
Angela Y. Davis	Black Power activist and author. Although she left the BPP, she remained active in Black Panther Party defense.
Irene Davis	Ericka's maternal aunt. She nurtured Ericka's spiritual life and helped her address personal challenges.
Lula Davis	Ericka's maternal grandmother, who was a maternal force in the family. She experienced medical discrimination and died of uterine cancer after a fifteen-year battle.
Ossie Davis	Ericka's maternal grandfather. A tobacco farmer and the descendant of a freedman.
Reginald Davis	Ericka's maternal uncle. Known for his humor and natural ability to brighten the days of those around him.

Thelma Davis	Ericka's maternal aunt. Known for her bold fashion sense and self-assurance, she helped Ericka and her sister develop a sense of self-worth as Black girls.
Malik Edwards	BPP artist who worked with Ericka on the BPP newspaper cadre. He currently works at MetWest High School in Oakland as a restorative practices staff member.
Elizabeth Marie	Woman imprisoned at Niantic who was punished for communicating with the BPP women.
Maude Louis Francis	One of the young BPP women arrested and sent to Niantic with Ericka before being transferred to a juvenile detention home.
Charles Garry	Bobby Seale's lawyer and member of Ericka's legal team, a yoga enthusiast who sent books to Ericka while imprisoned.
Charles V. Hamilton	Civil rights activist and political scientist who advanced Black Power's intellectual growth. He co-wrote *Black Power: The Politics of Liberation* with Stokely Carmichael (Kwame Ture).
Donna Howell	Assistant director of the OCS.
Margaret "Peggy" Hudgins	Frances Carter's sister, and one of the young BPP women imprisoned with Ericka in Niantic. Her rheumatoid arthritis worsened during her incarceration. She died in 1984 at age 36.
Carolyn & Joan Huggins	John Huggins's sisters, who helped raise Mai and supported Ericka while she was incarcerated.
Elizabeth Huggins	John J. Huggins's mother, who nurtured and parented Mai, Ericka's oldest child and only daughter, while Ericka was incarcerated in Niantic.
Ericka Huggins	BPP leader, educator, and lifelong civil rights activist.
John Huggins Sr.	John J. Huggins's father, who took on a paternal role with Mai. He and his wife, Elizabeth, offered Mai and Ericka unconditional love and support.
John J. Huggins Jr.	Captain and later deputy chairman of the BPP's LA chapter. Huggins was murdered on the campus of UCLA in 1969 and laid to rest in his hometown of New Haven, Connecticut.
Mai Huggins	Daughter of Ericka and John Huggins. Mai was just 3 weeks old when her father was murdered, and her mother arrested.
Coulter Huyler	Father of Yadav, Ericka's youngest son.
Yadav Jelal Huyler	Ericka's youngest son with Coulter Huyler.
Demetrius "Jack" Granville Jackson III	Ericka's first boyfriend, whose young disabled brother's condition in a facility encouraged her college attendance with the hope of starting her own school. Theophilis, Demetrius's brother, died young due to his disability.
George Jackson	Prison activist, BPP member, and one of the Soledad Brothers accused of killing a correctional officer in 1970. His prison letters are published in his book *Soledad Brother*.
Cozette (Davis) Jenkins	Ericka's mother, who used stories to arm her children with information to navigate a white supremacist world.
Gervaze Joseph Jenkins Sr.	Ericka's father. He served in the military during World War II and was a dominating and controlling figure in the Jenkins household.

Gervaze Jenkins Jr.	Ericka's younger brother and a gifted musician.
Joseph Jenkins	Ericka's paternal grandfather, a frank man who prided himself on honesty and dignity.
Kyra Jenkins	Ericka's younger sister, known for her joyous personality and creative aptitude.
Sadie B. Jenkins	Ericka's paternal grandmother, a gentle woman. Ericka's parents resided with Mr. and Mrs. Jenkins in the early years of their marriage.
Joanne	Ericka met Joanne when transferred to general population at Niantic. They shared cell room walls and a heartfelt, spiritual connection.
Stewart H. Jones	US attorney the Connecticut. In 1968 he furiously responded to the Niantic Black Panther prison strike, ordering the women to be severely punished and isolated.
Amber Landis-Reedy	Former OCS student.
Gregory B. Lewis	Former OCS student.
Loretta Luckes	Imprisoned at Niantic and charged with murder and kidnapping. Luckes was pregnant at the time of her arrest.
Linda	Woman imprisoned at Niantic. Due to inadequate medical attention, Linda died after experiencing severe drug withdrawal.
Maria	Woman imprisoned at Niantic. Maria mentored other women in the drug recovery process.
Steve McCutchen	Martial arts and math teacher at OCS.
Mrs. Monk	Niantic prison matron who ordered Ericka to undo her pin curls the day before her trial.
Rasa Mott	Ericka's oldest son with Saturu Ned (James Mott).
Saturu Ned (James Mott)	Rasa's father and a member of the Black Panthers' funk band the Lumpen.
Huey P. Newton	Black Panther Party co-founder and minister of defense.
Officer O'Conner	Correctional officer at Niantic. Ericka forged a positive, friendly relationship with O'Conner during her time there.
Alex Rackley	BPP member alleged by George Sams to have been a police informant. Rackley is at the center of the 1970 New Haven Black Panther trials.
Millie Rivera	Co-founder (with Ericka) of the Sister Love Collective. She fled from prison and was pregnant by the time she was captured and returned.
Catherine "Katy" Roraback	Ericka's progressive feminist lawyer. At the time, she was the sole woman practicing criminal defense law in New Haven.
David Rosen	Member of Ericka's legal team. A recent law school graduate at the time of Ericka and Bobby's trial, he often visited them in prison with trial updates and obliged Ericka's requests in support of incarcerated women.
Bobby Seale	Black Panther Party chairman and co-founder. Bobby stood trial with Ericka in New Haven in 1970.
Officer Smith	Correctional officer at Niantic.

Rose Marie Smith	One of the other young women imprisoned with Ericka at Niantic. Rose was pregnant and likely delivered her baby in prison.
Larry Watani Stiner	Member of the US organization. He was convicted in 1969 of conspiring to murder John Huggins and Bunchy Carter. He and Ericka began corresponding in 2010 and engaged in a restorative justice dialogue.
Ivan Toro	Millie Rivera's brother, whom she visited when she escaped Niantic in 1970.
Jan Von Flatern	Political journalist who met Ericka while covering her trial. Their exchange of letters and drawings illustrates the importance of "sisterlove" and "peoplelove." She helped Ericka communicate with the outside world in support of other incarcerated women.
Officer Walsh	Correctional officer at Niantic, who used physical violence and intimidation against the BPP women.
Pamela (Pam) Ward Pious	Teacher at OCS.
Jeannie Wilson	One of the young BPP women arrested with Ericka and sent to Niantic before being transferred to a juvenile detention home.
John Williams	Connecticut-based Black Panther lawyer who founded New Haven's first public interest law firm, still in operation today as John R. Williams and Associates, LLC.
Janet S. York	Warden at Niantic during Ericka's incarceration. The prison was renamed the Janet S. York Correctional Institution in her honor.

Ericka Huggins's Family Tree

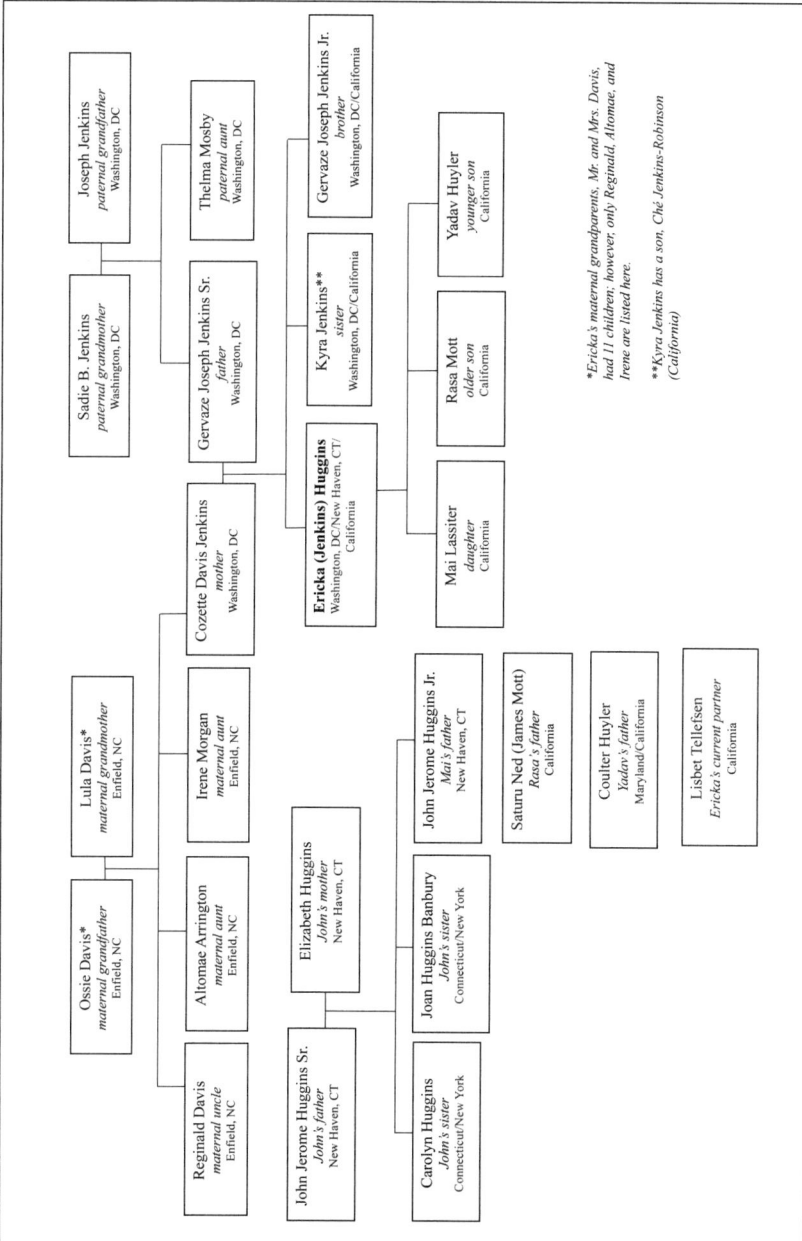

Joseph Jenkins
paternal grandfather
Washington, DC

Sadie B. Jenkins
paternal grandmother
Washington, DC

Thelma Mosby
paternal aunt
Washington, DC

Gervaze Joseph Jenkins Sr.
father
Washington, DC

Cozette Davis Jenkins
mother
Washington, DC

Gervaze Joseph Jenkins Jr.
brother
Washington, DC/California

Kyra Jenkins**
sister
Washington, DC/California

Ericka (Jenkins) Huggins
Washington, DC/New Haven, CT/
California

Yadav Huyler
younger son
California

Rasa Mott
older son
California

Mai Lassiter
daughter
California

Ossie Davis*
maternal grandfather
Enfield, NC

Lula Davis*
maternal grandmother
Enfield, NC

Irene Morgan
maternal aunt
Enfield, NC

Altomae Arrington
maternal aunt
Enfield, NC

Reginald Davis
maternal uncle
Enfield, NC

Elizabeth Huggins
John's mother
New Haven, CT

John Jerome Huggins Sr.
John's father
New Haven, CT

John Jerome Huggins Jr.
Mai's father
New Haven, CT

Joan Huggins Banbury
John's sister
Connecticut/New York

Carolyn Huggins
John's sister
Connecticut/New York

Saturu Ned (James Mott)
Rasa's father
California

Coulter Huyler
Yadav's father
Maryland/California

Lisbet Tellefsen
Ericka's current partner
California

**Ericka's maternal grandparents, Mr. and Mrs. Davis,
had 11 children, however, only Reginald, Altomae, and
Irene are listed here.*

***Kyra Jenkins has a son, Ché Jenkins-Robinson
(California)*

NOTES

INTRODUCTION

This chapter contains portions from Mary Frances Phillips, "The Power of the First-Person Narrative: Ericka Huggins and the Black Panther Party," *Women's Studies Quarterly* 43, nos. 3–4 (Fall/Winter 2015).

1 Ericka Huggins, author interview, February 20, 2010.

2 Huggins, *Oral History*.

3 Ericka Huggins, author interview, October 14, 2019.

4 Jones and Jeffries, "'Don't Believe the Hype,'" 37–39.

5 Alkebulan, *Surviving Pending Revolution*, 41; Hilliard and Cole, *This Side of Glory*, 211. During this time, the BPP implemented modifications to its programming initiatives; as pointed out by Robyn C. Spencer-Antoine, the BPP "expanded the range and scope of these programs and renamed them 'community survival programs.'" *Revolution Has Come*, 117.

6 Jones and Jeffries, "'Don't Believe the Hype,'" 29.

7 Newton, "Speech Delivered at Boston College: November 18, 1970," 160.

8 Ward Churchill and Jim Vander Wall note that John Huggins and Bunchy Carter's assassinations were "provoked by a carefully orchestrated COINTELPRO." *Agents of Repression*, 78. They also mention an agent whom the FBI promoted for his successful COINTELPRO operations against John Huggins, Bunchy Carter, and other BPP members including Geronimo Pratt and BPP supporters such as Jean Seberg. *Agents of Repression*, 370.

9 Ericka Huggins, author interview, May 23, 2017. Ericka recounts the incident where the police arrived at the apartment following the murders of John and Bunchy and protected Mai. Thompson's interview in Huggins, *Oral History*, 50–53.

10 Ericka Huggins, author interviews, May 23, 2017, April 11, 2016, December 17, 2018. In Ericka's oral history with Fiona Thompson, she recalls the episode of police violence after the state murders of John Huggins and Bunchy Carter. Huggins, *Oral History*, 49–55. In her interview with me, Ericka recalls that she was arrested on charges of malicious mischief. She mentions "aggravated assault" in her interview with Fiona Thompson. Huggins, *Oral History*, 49. Elaine Brown noted that they were charged with "conspiracy with the intent to commit murder." She added, "we were being held, we were told, to 'prevent a bloody retaliation' against the US Organization for the assassinations of John and Bunchy." Brown, *A Taste of Power*, 169. The *Los Angeles Times* reported that the Black Panthers were

detained on "suspicion of conspiracy to commit assault with a deadly weapon." Drummond, "Black Panther Aide."

11 Ericka Huggins, author interview, April 16, 2010; Huggins, *Oral History*, vii.

12 I am using the name of the prison as noted in Ericka and Bobby's Memorandum of Decision, produced from the hearings to remove them from solitary confinement in 1970. Memorandum of Decision, 1971, US District Court, Ericka Huggins prison file, Connecticut Department of Correction records, RG 017.

13 Approval for administrative segregation for Ericka Huggins, May 27, 1969, Ericka Huggins prison file.

14 Another woman associated with the BPP, Loretta Luckes, was also arrested in connection with Alex Rackley but was not placed in solitary confinement with Ericka and the rest of the BPP women.

15 Maude Louis Francis prisoner index card, 1969, Maude Louis Francis prison file, Connecticut Department of Correction records, RG 017; Jeannie Wilson prisoner index card, 1969, Jeannie Wilson prison file, Connecticut Department of Correction records, RG 017.

16 In Ericka's prison conduct log, a correctional officer writes, "E. Huggins refused to let me check her hair." Ericka Huggins prison conduct log, January 27, 1970, Ericka Huggins prison file.

17 In Ericka's prison conduct log, on January 18, 1970, correctional officers wrote that "E. Huggins refused tetracycline." The log does not state why the correctional officers were giving Ericka tetracycline, an antibiotic. Ericka's prison conduct log entry on August 26, 1970, records that "Ericka is keeping some kind of record as to when medications are being given to the three girls."

18 Huggins prison conduct log. In the June 4, 1970, entry a correctional officer wrote, "Panthers hostile this evening. Demanded to see some written (Or printed) set of rules saying their trays must be checked. E. Huggins had a lot of unflattering remarks to make about the administration and cottage staff." Ericka remembered that correctional officers were checking their food trays when they picked up their food because they believed they were sending things outside the prison. She wanted something in writing to verify that checking food trays was a Niantic rule. Ericka Huggins, author interview, August 11, 2020.

19 Ericka's entry date of May 22, 1969, and her transfer to the general population date of November 9, 1970, constitute the total number of days that have been calculated. This number also includes the time Ericka spent in medical segregation upon admittance. The date of her transfer to the general population was obtained from her conduct log. In my conversation with Ericka, she explained that she was moved from administrative segregation to solitary confinement one month after the other BPP women left. Ericka Huggins, author interview, October 14, 2019. According to the State Farm Record Book entry, Frances was released on bond on January 19, 1970. She went back to prison and was released again on June 12, 1970. For an explanation of Frances's return to Niantic, see chapter 3. Ericka Cozette Huggins prisoner index card, 1969–1970, Connecticut Department of Correction

records; Rose Marie Smith prisoner index card, Rose Marie Smith prison file, Connecticut Department of Correction records, RG 017; Frances Elsie Carter prisoner index card, 1969–1970, Frances Elsie Carter prison file, Connecticut Department of Correction records, RG 017; Margaret Hudgins prisoner index card, 1969–1970, Margaret Hudgins prison file, Connecticut Department of Correction records, RG 017; Maude Louise Francis prisoner index card; Jeannie Wilson prisoner index card; Loretta Luckes prisoner index card, 1969, Loretta Luckes prison file, Connecticut Department of Correction records, RG 017.

20 After spending a month in solitary confinement, Ericka was eventually released to the general population. Ericka Huggins, author interview, October 14, 2019. This was a result of a complaint for declaratory and injunctive relief filed in the Connecticut District Court by attorneys Stanley A. Bass, Catherine G. Roraback, David N. Rosen, and Charles R. Garry on behalf of Ericka and Bobby Seale. Complaint for Declaratory Judgement, Injunction, and Other Appropriate Relief, 1970, Ericka Huggins prison file. The author consulted attorney Lennox Hinds on the complaint for declarative and injunctive relief. Lennox Hinds, author interview, July 23, 2019.

21 Beale, "Double Jeopardy"; Collins, *Black Feminist Thought*; Guy-Sheftall, *Words of Fire*; Crenshaw, "Mapping the Margins"; Lorde, *Sister Outsider*; hooks, *Feminist Theory*; Smith, *Home Girls*; Moraga and Anzaldúa, *This Bridge Called My Back*; Angela Y. Davis, *Women, Race, and Class*; hooks, *Ain't I a Woman*; Bambara, *Black Woman*.

22 Jones and Guy-Sheftall, "Black Feminist Therapy," 205.

23 hooks, *Salvation*, 13.

24 Harrison, Phillips, and Jackson, "Introduction."

25 Huggins, "Global 1968."

26 Huggins, "Global 1968."

27 Ericka Huggins, author interview, January 29, 2016.

28 See Davis, *Angela Davis: An Autobiography*, 262; Umoja, "Straight Ahead," 17–21; Donovan, *Dope Is Death*; Holley, "How Acupuncture Became a Radical Remedy."

29 The Son of Man Temple supported other community programs that focused on health care, children's education, financial support for prisoners, and transportation services for senior citizens and to prisons for families with loved ones imprisoned. "Son of Man Temple Opens."

30 Miller and Thoresen, "Spirituality, Religion, and Health," 27.

31 Miller and Thoresen, "Spirituality, Religion, and Health," 27.

32 Lorde, *Burst of Light*.

33 Such a tenor was central to the story of the civil rights movement, perhaps best exemplified by the Southern Christian Leadership Conference, a Christian civil rights group whose first president was Dr. Martin Luther King Jr.

34 See Nelson, *Body and Soul*, 1.

35 Kelley, *Freedom Dreams*, 198.

36 See Evans, *Black Women's Yoga History*; Aziz, "Built with Empty Fists"; and Johnson, "Dancing Africa."

37 Solomon and Rankin, *How We Fight*, vii.

38 Solomon and Rankin, *How We Fight*, vii.

39 Rosemarie Freeney Harding's *Remnants* and Jan Willis's *Dreaming Me* engage activism and spiritual work and turn to spiritual approaches.

40 Spencer-Antoine, *Revolution Has Come*; Matthews, "'No One Ever Asks What a Man's Place in the Revolution Is'"; Farmer, *Remaking Black Power*; LeBlanc-Ernest, "'Most Qualified Person'"; Taylor, *Promise of Patriarchy*; Blain, *Set the World on Fire*.

41 These texts include Randolph, *Florynce "Flo" Kennedy*; Ransby, *Eslanda*; Theoharis, *Rebellious Life of Mrs. Rosa Parks*; Fujino, *Heartbeat of a Struggle*; Ransby, *Ella Baker*; and Lee, *For Freedom's Sake*.

42 See Nelson, *Body and Soul*, 1.

43 Huggins, *Oral History*, 68.

44 See Erikson and Newton, *In Search of Common Ground*. According to Kai T. Erikson's introduction, Huey P. Newton arrived at Yale University just as Ericka and Bobby's trial "was reaching its climax" (12). They were released from prison nearly four months later. See also Treaster, "Erikson and Newton Discuss Issues." As pointed out by Farmer, "Intercommunalism also brought about a new organizing mantra: survival pending revolution," discussed earlier in this chapter. Farmer, *Remaking Black Power*, 78.

45 Newton, "Intercommunalism," 187. For Huey P. Newton's full remarks on intercommunalism, see Erikson and Newton, *In Search of Common Ground*, 23–43. For more on intercommunalism, see Jeffries, *Huey P. Newton*; and Hayes and Kiene, "'All Power to the People.'"

46 Ericka worked with the Third World Women's Alliance in the mid-1970s to create the Coalition to Fight Infant Mortality. Ericka Huggins, author interview, February 20, 2010.

47 Springer, *Living for the Revolution*, 72.

48 Springer, "Interstitial Politics," 166.

49 Muñoz, *Cruising Utopia*, 1.

50 Thank you to feminist thought and queer theory scholar Tiffany Ball for her wonderful insights on this section.

51 Davies, *Left of Karl Marx*, 5.

52 Kelley, *Freedom Dreams*, 9.

53 Kelley, *Freedom Dreams*, 9.

54 Taylor, "Women in the Documents," 187.

55 Taylor, "Women in the Documents," 189.

56 Huggins, Kochiyama, and Kao, "Stirrin' Waters 'n Buildin' Bridges"; Huggins, "Two Interviews"; Huggins, "Conversation with Ericka Huggins"; Huggins, *Oral History*; and Huggins, interview by David Cline.

57 Hamlin, "Historians and Ethics," 496.

58 Taylor, "Women in the Documents," 187.

59 Ericka Huggins, author interview, February 20, 2010.

60 Ericka Huggins, author interview, February 20, 2010.
61 Farmer, *Remaking Black Power*.
62 Rodney, *Walter Rodney Speaks*, 113; Christian, "Black Intellectual/Activist Tradition," 130–31.
63 Ericka's understanding of knowledge production echoes what historian Crystal Marie Moten identifies as community intellectualism in Black women's economic-based activism. Moten, *Continually Working*.
64 Ericka Huggins, author interview, February 20, 2010.
65 BPP members were required to attend political education classes and read the works of thinkers including Malcolm X, Marcus Garvey, W. E. B. Du Bois, Kwame Nkrumah, and John Hope Franklin, among others. See "Black Panther Party Book List."
66 Spencer-Antoine, "Engendering the Black Freedom Struggle," 91.
67 See Shakur, *Assata*; Njeri, *My Life with the Black Panther Party*; Elaine Brown, *Taste of Power*; Perkins, *Autobiography as Activism*; Collier-Thomas and Franklin, *Sisters in the Struggle*; Gore, Theoharis, and Woodard, *Want to Start a Revolution?*; and Bukhari, *War Before*.
68 Gluck and Patai, *Women's Words*, 3.
69 Achebe, "Getting to the Source," 14.
70 Ahmed, "Affective Economies," 119.
71 Combahee River Collective, "Black Feminist Statement," 233.
72 When I decided to cut stories from earlier drafts of the manuscript at Ericka's request and faced the disparity between the type of book I wanted to write and the book Ericka wanted me to write, I encountered difficulties akin to those described by historian Nell Irvin Painter in her book *The Narrative of Hosea Hudson*.
73 Hamlin, "Historians and Ethics," 491.

CHAPTER 1. A SPIRITUAL CHILDHOOD

1 Ericka Huggins, author interview, February 28, 2020.
2 Ericka Huggins, author interview, February 28, 2020.
3 Gervaze J. Jenkins, 1940 United States Federal Census, Ancestry.com. The 1940 US census listed his highest completed grade as his first year of high school. His World War II army enlistment record noted grammar school as his educational background. Gervaze J. Jenkins, US, World War II Army Enlistment Records, 1938–1946, Ancestrylibrary.com. Ericka recalled that her father only completed the eighth grade. Ericka Huggins, author interview, February 12, 2022. His estimated birth year was 1911, according to the 1940 US census. According to his World War II army enlistment record, he was born in 1910. His birthdate is May 5, 1910, according to his Veteran Affairs BIRLS death file. Gervaze J. Jenkins, US, Department of Veterans Affairs BIRLS (Beneficiary Identification Records Locator Subsystem) Death Files, 1850–2010, Ancestrylibrary.com.
4 Mr. Jenkins's occupation was given as a driver in the 1928 Washington, DC, city directory. By then, he was eighteen. Gervaze Jenkins, US, City Directories,

1822–1995, Ancestry.com. In the 1940 US census, Mr. Jenkins, now thirty years old, was recorded as residing with his parents, his older sister Thelma Jenkins, and three lodgers his family had taken in. His occupation is listed as a chauffeur. Gervaze J. Jenkins, 1940 United States Federal Census, Ancestry.com.

5 Gervaze J. Jenkins, US, World War II Army Enlistment Records, 1938–1946.

6 "75 Selectees to Go to Camp Tomorrow." His enlistment date is July 20, 1942, according to his VA death file. Gervaze J. Jenkins, US, Department of Veterans Affairs BIRLS Death Files, 1850–2010.

7 Gervaze J. Jenkins, US, World War II Army Enlistment Records, 1938–1946. The specific location of his employment as a general office clerk is not specified on his World War II army enlistment record.

8 Ericka Huggins, author interview, January 21, 2022.

9 Mrs. Jenkins's father, Ossie Davis, was no relation to the famed actor.

10 Ericka Huggins, author interview, February 12, 2022. Ericka could not recall whether her grandfather or a different relative on her maternal side were descendants of a freedman.

11 Ericka Huggins, author interview, January 21, 2022.

12 Ericka Huggins, author interview, January 21, 2022.

13 Asch and Musgrove, *Chocolate City*, 273.

14 Austin, *Coming of Age in Jim Crow DC*, 41.

15 Asch and Musgrove, *Chocolate City*.

16 Asch and Musgrove, *Chocolate City*, 273–74.

17 Asch and Musgrove, *Chocolate City*, 274.

18 Ericka Huggins, author interview, February 12, 2022.

19 As reported in the *Evening Star* newspaper, Gervaze Jenkins and Cozette Davis were among the couples who applied for a marriage license. "Marriage License Applications."

20 Guglielmo, *Divisions*, 301.

21 According to Ericka, her father served as an army sergeant. Ericka Huggins, author interview, February 12, 2022. Mr. Jenkins was discharged from the army on November 1, 1945, according to his VA death file. Gervaze J. Jenkins, US, Department of Veterans Affairs BIRLS Death Files, 1850–2010. Ericka believes that her father secured employment as a file clerk for the Pentagon after leaving the army. Ericka Huggins, author interview, January 21, 2022.

22 In 1956 Mr. Jenkins, then forty-six years old, was one of three who "received work simplification proposal awards" from the army Adjutant General's Office. The details of the award and his requirements for receiving it are not documented in the article, "Capital Roundup."

23 Asch and Musgrove, *Chocolate City*, 280–81.

24 See Guglielmo, *Divisions*, esp. 297–343, for additional information on the experiences of Black soldiers in World War II.

25 Ericka Huggins, author interview, January 21, 2022.

26 Ericka Huggins, author interview, January 21, 2022.

27 Huggins, *Oral History*, 4.
28 Huggins, *Oral History*, 4.
29 Huggins, *Oral History*, 4.
30 Huggins, *Oral History*, 5.
31 Ericka explained that her paternal grandmother worked for the Treasury Department.
32 Ericka Huggins, author interview, February 12, 2022.
33 Ericka Huggins, author interview, February 12, 2022.
34 Huggins, *Oral History*, 2.
35 Huggins, *Oral History*, 5.
36 See Asch and Musgrove, *Chocolate City*, 286, and 285–87 for a discussion of the activism and lawsuit against Sousa Junior High, which was intricately connected to the *Brown v. Board of Education* ruling, serving as a "companion case."
37 Huggins, *Oral History*, 5.
38 Ericka Huggins, author interview, February 12, 2022.
39 Ericka Huggins, author interview, February 12, 2022. Some may interpret this lesson about blindness and paralysis as negative and potentially fueling internalized ableism.
40 Ericka Huggins, author interview, January 21, 2022.
41 Ericka Huggins, author interview, January 21, 2022.
42 Ericka Huggins, author interview, January 21, 2022.
43 Ericka Huggins, author interview, January 21, 2022.
44 Ericka Huggins, author interview, March 27, 2019.
45 Ericka Huggins, author interviews, April 28, 2019, January 21, 2022.
46 Ericka Huggins, author interview, January 21, 2022.
47 Ericka Huggins, author interview, May 31, 2022
48 Ericka Huggins, author interview, May 31, 2022.
49 Guglielmo, *Divisions*, 6.
50 Ericka Huggins, author interview, May 31, 2022.
51 Ericka Huggins, author interview, February 28, 2020.
52 Ericka Huggins, author interview, May 31, 2022.
53 Ericka Huggins, author interview, February 18, 2022.
54 Ericka Huggins, author interview, February 18, 2022.
55 James, "Mothering," 45.
56 Ericka Huggins, author interview, February 18, 2022.
57 Ericka Huggins, author interview, February 18, 2022.
58 Ericka Huggins, author interview, February 12, 2022.
59 Ericka Huggins, author interview, February 28, 2020.
60 Ericka Huggins, author interview, February 12, 2022.
61 Ericka Huggins, author interview, February 12, 2022.
62 Ericka Huggins, author interview, December 17, 2018; Hine, "Rape and the Inner Lives of Black Women," 383.
63 Ericka Huggins, author interview, December 17, 2018.

64 Ericka Huggins, author interview, February 28, 2020.

65 Gervaze J. Jenkins, US Department of Veterans Affairs BIRLS Death Files, 1850–2010.

66 Ericka Huggins, author interview, February 12, 2022.

67 Gervaze J. Jenkins, US Department of Veterans Affairs BIRLS Death Files, 1850–2010.

68 Both Ericka's parents and especially her father in his post-traumatic stress disorder experienced disability but may not have regarded it as such.

69 Ericka Huggins, author interview, May 31, 2022.

CHAPTER 2. BECOMING A BLACK PANTHER

This chapter contains portions from Mary Frances Phillips, "The Feminist Leadership of Ericka Huggins in the Black Panther Party," *Black Diaspora Review* 4, no. 1 (Winter 2014); and Mary Frances Phillips, "The Power of the First-Person Narrative: Ericka Huggins and the Black Panther Party," *Women's Studies Quarterly* 43, nos. 3–4 (Fall/Winter 2015).

1 For more on the political activism of young people, see Franklin, *Young Crusaders*; Devlin, *Girl Stands at the Door*; and de Schweinitz, *If They Could Change the World*.

2 Huggins, *Oral History*, 6–7; Ericka Huggins, author interviews, February 12, 2022, March 27, 2019.

3 Ericka Huggins, author interview, July 31, 2022.

4 The account of Ericka attending the March on Washington is condensed in Franklin's book *The Young Crusaders*, where he refers to her by her maiden name. In his narrative, he cites Euchner, *Nobody Turn Me Around*, 133–34.

5 Huggins, *Oral History*, 7.

6 Huggins, *Oral History*, 7.

7 Huggins, *Oral History*, 7–8.

8 Asch and Musgrove, *Chocolate City*, 1.

9 Huggins, *Oral History*, 8.

10 A disorder left him mentally disabled. Huggins, *Oral History*, 13–14.

11 Huggins, *Oral History*, 13.

12 According to Ericka, T was placed in a dormitory with children who had birth defects and those who were emotionally distressed and mentally disabled. Huggins, *Oral History*, 13.

13 Huggins, *Oral History*, 13.

14 Ericka Huggins, author interview, May 9, 2010.

15 Huggins, *Oral History*, 37.

16 Huggins, *Oral History*, 14.

17 Ericka Jenkins, Lincoln University transcript, Lincoln University Records, 1966–1967. On her transcript, Ericka's first name is listed as Erica, not Ericka. Ericka shared that throughout her life, her first name was often misspelled. Her mother

told her that she thought spelling her name "Ericka" would prevent others from spelling her first name incorrectly.

18 Ericka Jenkins, Lincoln University transcript.

19 For more on Ku Klux Klan violence on the campus of Lincoln University and student resistance during this time, see "Students Prepare for 'K' Invasion"; and Black, "Klan's Coming Stirs Campus." Ericka also discussed burned crosses on the lawn across from the Lincoln University campus in Huggins, *Oral History*, 14.

20 Hill, *Deacons of Defense*.

21 "June 1966 Meredith March." For more on Black Power, see Farmer, *Remaking Black Power*; Rhonda Y. Williams, *Concrete Demands*; Joseph, *Waiting 'til the Midnight Hour*; Conyers, *Engines of the Black Power Movement*; and Joseph, *Black Power Movement*.

22 Ericka Huggins, author interview, July 30, 2011. She also discussed these sessions in Huggins, *Oral History*, 18. Sutton, "Wall to Wall." Sutton mentions that Kwame Ture and Charles V. Hamilton wrote the book *Black Power* at Lincoln University. Charles V. Hamilton is listed as faculty in political science in Lincoln University's 1968 yearbook, *The Lion*, Lincoln University Special Collections.

23 Huggins, *Oral History*, 18.

24 Huggins, *Oral History*, 15.

25 Ture and Hamilton, *Black Power*, 44.

26 Ericka Huggins, author interview, July 30, 2011. Ericka expounds on the misappropriation of the term "Black Power" in Huggins, *Oral History*, 15.

27 Ericka Huggins, author interview, February 20, 2010.

28 Ericka was also a member of writing and drama student clubs.

29 Fried, "Black Student Congress," 4. Although in the article Fried criticized the BSC's leadership, he also praised it for its programming over the span of two years despite its small size. For descriptions of the BSC committees and programs, see "Black Student Congress Plans Ambitious Program"; and "Black Student Congress Sponsors Appearance of Jeremiah X," 1. According to Charyn Sutton in the article "Wall to Wall," the BSC was defunct by 1968. Sutton suggests that the BSC existed informally and formalized itself as a student organization shortly before Charles V. Hamilton left Lincoln University. Sutton claimed that the BSC was active as an organization for only one year. The articles "Black Student Congress" and "Wall to Wall" in the *Lincolnian* display a discrepancy over the life span of the BSC; "Black Student Congress" discusses the BSC programming over two years, while "Wall to Wall" explains that the organization existed for one year. Sutton charts the history of the organization, including its emergence and activities and its merge with the Student Government Association as the reason for its decline.

30 "Dr. Wachman Holds Second Discussion," 1. In their meetings with Lincoln University president Marvin Wachman, the BSC student activists also took issue with the administrator's decision to commemorate Presbyterian minister Francis Grimke by naming the new women's dormitory after him. In sum, because

of Grimke's biracial identity, the BSC students believed that he was not Black enough for selection as a namesake of a dormitory. Their concerns paralleled the racial politics that Ericka experienced as a member of the organization while a student.

31 Ericka Huggins, author interview, July 30, 2011.

32 Huggins, *Oral History*, 13.

33 For more on the story of how Ericka and John met at Lincoln University, see Huggins, *Oral History*, 15–16.

34 John Huggins, US, School Yearbooks, 1900–2016, Hopkins Grammar School, Ancestry.com. In memory of John Huggins, the school featured him in an article in the Hopkins Grammar School online student newspaper. In the article, John's mother, Mrs. Huggins, mentions that John was given a modest scholarship at Hopkins Grammar School because of his academic standing. Tellides, "John Huggins."

35 Tellides, "John Huggins."

36 Tellides, "John Huggins"; John Huggins, US, School Yearbooks, 1900–2016, Hillhouse High School, Ancestry.com.

37 Tellides, "John Huggins."

38 Tellides, "John Huggins."

39 Tellides, "John Huggins"; Ericka Huggins, author interview, April 16, 2010.

40 Huggins, *Oral History*, 16.

41 Ericka Huggins, author interview, June 6, 2022; Huggins, *Oral History*, 16.

42 Huggins, *Oral History*, 16–17.

43 Ericka Jenkins, Lincoln University transcript.

44 Spencer-Antoine, *Revolution Has Come*, 29.

45 Bloom and Martin, *Black Against Empire*, 2. For a history of the international chapter of the BPP, see Cleaver, "Back to Africa." For the Black Panthers within a broader international context, see Clemons and Jones, "Global Solidarity."

46 While Huey P. Newton and the Black Panthers were covered in *Ramparts* magazine, I could not find the specific story with the photograph in any of the 1967 and 1968 issues of the magazine. It has been over fifty years. Given the time, it is likely that Ericka misremembered the magazine title. Although I was not able to find the story, I was able to locate the AP photograph of Huey P. Newton that she referenced.

47 Ericka Huggins, author interview, July 30, 2011. Ericka also discussed *Ramparts* magazine and the story of Huey P. Newton in Huggins, *Oral History*, 17.

48 Ericka Huggins, author interview, February 12, 2022; Huggins, *Oral History*, 19, 9.

49 Huggins, *Oral History*, 19. Although she mentioned a Swahili class in her oral history with Fiona Thompson, Ericka's Lincoln University transcript does not list that she enrolled in this class. Ericka Jenkins, Lincoln University transcript.

50 Ericka Jenkins, Lincoln University transcript. The same day Ericka withdrew from Lincoln University, she received an honorable mention on the dean's list in the school newspaper, the *Lincolnian*, for receiving a 3.0 in the second semester of the

1966–1967 academic school year. *Lincolnian*, November 15, 1967. Her first name is listed incorrectly as Erika, not Ericka.

51 According to Ericka, the wedding was the last time John's parents and siblings would see him alive. Ericka Huggins, author interview, July 31, 2022.

52 In her interview with Fiona Thompson, Ericka explained that out of fear of arguing with her family about her decision to join the BPP, she did not make a detour to visit them on her way to California. Huggins, *Oral History*, 10. In Ericka's conversation with me, she mentioned that they did not stop at her mother's house because they did not have the gas money. Ericka Huggins, author interview, July 31, 2022.

53 Ericka Huggins, author interviews, April 16, 2010, February 12, 2022. For more on Ericka's mother's reaction to her dropping out of school to join the BPP, see Huggins, *Oral History*, 19.

54 Huggins, *Oral History*, 19.

55 Huggins, *Oral History*. 20.

56 My reference to the resentment that Ericka believed her family felt at this moment was taken from Ericka's interview with Fiona Thompson. In the interview she stated, "I just talked to her on the phone—I'm sure that hurt her, she made it known later in life. But that was what I felt called to do. It left my mother sad, and my sister and brother were very resentful because they had felt like I had abandoned them because I was kind of the glue in the dysfunctional family so if I was gone what were they all going to do? But I had to go." Huggins, *Oral History*, 10.

57 On the way to California, Ericka and John dropped off their friend Eddie in Santa Barbara; Eddie had tagged along for the ride to get to Hollywood to pursue his dream of being a blues singer. They drove John's car to California, but much of their trip was funded by Eddie, as he had more money for gas than Ericka and John did. They ended up in Los Angeles because they were fatigued and did not have enough money to get to Oakland. Ericka and John ended up in Venice Beach because they found an inexpensive apartment with a Murphy bed. Venice Beach was the only area they could afford. Ericka recalled horrific experiences working at a factory run by sexist and misogynistic white male foremen. She remembered that the factory segregated its workers by gender, with no women in leadership positions. Women workers were mostly Black and Latina. She recalled stories of a white male foreman who sexually assaulted and raped women. As a result of his sexual violence, some of the women ended up pregnant. Women placed cardboard blockers at their desks in front of their legs to protect themselves from sexual assault. Ericka Huggins, author interview, July 26, 2022. In her conversation with me, Ericka stated that she became a steward for the union to advocate for better working conditions, but in Thompson's interview, she mentioned that she "tried to become the steward of the Union." Nonetheless, Ericka advocated for a safe and proper working environment while employed at the factory. To learn more about Ericka moving to California and her experience working for an automobile factory during this time, see Huggins, *Oral History*, 23–24.

58 Ericka Huggins, author interview, July 7, 2017; Huggins, *Oral History*, 25.

59 Based in Los Angeles, the Southern California chapter included Black Panthers from cities throughout Southern California. I refer to it as the Los Angeles chapter. Black Panthers referred to it as the Los Angeles chapter or the Southern California chapter. For a history of the founding of the Los Angeles chapter, see Jeffries and Foley, "To Live and Die in L.A."

60 Ericka Huggins, author interview, February 20, 2010; Huggins, *Oral History*, 25.

61 According to Elaine Brown, the apartment on Century Boulevard was primarily Ericka and John's home. Brown, *Taste of Power*, 153.

62 Spencer-Antoine, "Communalism and the Black Panther Party," 92.

63 Spencer-Antoine, "Communalism and the Black Panther Party," 92.

64 "Black Panther Party Ten Point Platform and Program."

65 Huggins, *Oral History*, 30–31.

66 Huggins, *Oral History*, 30.

67 Huggins, *Oral History*, 31.

68 Huggins, *Oral History*, 31.

69 Porter, "Rainbow in Black," 372.

70 Matthews, "'No One Ever Asks What a Man's Place in the Revolution Is,'" 220.

71 Matthews, "'No One Ever Asks What a Man's Place in the Revolution Is,'" 220.

72 Elaine Brown, *Taste of Power*, 153. Ericka stated that she was not sure of the accuracy of Elaine's claim that John gave her a hatchet for self-protection.

73 Ericka Huggins, author interview, February 20, 2010.

74 Davis, *Angela Davis: An Autobiography*, 139. For more on the Black Panther Political Party, see pp. 138–41.

75 Elaine Brown, *Taste of Power*, 106. Historian Scot Brown posits that Maulana Karenga's US organization symbolizes Black racial identity: "The name 'US' actually stands for Black people . . . [meaning] 'US' as opposed to 'them,' the White oppressors," not "united slaves," as often assumed by the general public. See Scot Brown, *Fighting for US*, 2.

76 For a history on the Student Nonviolent Coordinating Committee, see Carson, *In Struggle*; Holsaert et al., *Hands on the Freedom Plow*; Hogan, *Many Minds, One Heart*; Zinn, *SNCC*; Monteith, *SNCC's Stories*; and Greenberg, *A Circle of Trust*.

77 Davis, *Angela Davis: An Autobiography*, 148. For information on the story behind the name change of the Black Panther Political Party to the Los Angeles Student Nonviolent Coordinating Committee and their history, see Davis, *Angela Davis: An Autobiography*, 141–62.

78 See Davis, *Angela Davis: An Autobiography*, 162–64; and Angela Y. Davis, author interview, July 3, 2019.

79 Angela Y. Davis shared with me that she eventually became a member of the BPP. Angela Y. Davis, author interview, July 3, 2019. See Davis, *Angela Davis: An Autobiography*, 166, for her account of her joining the BPP. Ericka remembered that she was present when John Huggins asked Angela Davis to join the BPP. Ericka Huggins, author interview, July 31, 2022.

80 Lenin, *State and Revolution*, 20.

81 Angela Y. Davis, author interview, July 3, 2019. In my interview, Angela shared that John occupied the highest-ranking position in the office where they both worked. See Davis, *Angela Davis: An Autobiography*, 166–67, for her experiences running the political education program and her reflections on teaching Lenin's *State and Revolution*.

82 Angela Y. Davis, author interview, July 3, 2019. In my interview with Angela Y. Davis, she commented that she had no hard feelings toward the BPP when she left it, and continued to support the BPP and worked to free BPP political prisoners. When the BPP office in Los Angeles was attacked, she helped organize community support, including UCLA's support for the Black Panthers. For a discussion of her departure from the BPP, see Davis, *Angela Davis: An Autobiography*, 168, 170. According to her autobiography, she mentions that the BPP did not explicitly force her to choose between membership in its organization and the Communist Party. Based on her statements in her autobiography and the information she shared with me in my interview with her, it can be inferred that the BPP expected individuals with dual membership to make a decision.

83 LeBlanc-Ernest, "From 'Babies for the Revolution' to Planned Parenthood."

84 Ericka Huggins, author interview, February 20, 2010.

85 LeBlanc-Ernest, "'Most Qualified Person,'" 309.

86 Spencer-Antoine, *Revolution Has Come*, 59. For more on the BPP and self-defense, see Spencer-Antoine, *Revolution Has Come*, 35–60.

87 For a discussion of BPP gender politics and ideology, see Farmer, *Remaking Black Power*, 50–92; and Matthews, "'No One Ever Asks, What a Man's Role in the Revolution Is,'" 267–304. For more on the history of the BPP's community programs, see Spencer-Antoine, *Revolution Has Come*, 61–87; Abron, "'Serving the People'"; and Hilliard, *Black Panther Party*. For charts on the BPP community programs, see Phillips and LeBlanc-Ernest, "Hidden Narratives"; and Jones and Jeffries, "'Don't Believe the Hype,'" 30.

88 Wilson, *Truly Disadvantaged*, 131.

89 Wilson, *Truly Disadvantaged*, 131.

90 See Churchill, "'To Disrupt, Discredit, and Destroy'"; Churchill and Vander Wall, *Agents of Repression*; and Churchill and Vander Wall, *COINTELPRO Papers*.

91 Churchill, "'To Disrupt, Discredit, and Destroy,'" 82. For more on the FBI, see Chard, *Nixon's War at Home*.

92 Churchill, "'To Disrupt, Discredit, and Destroy,'" 78.

93 LeBlanc-Ernest, "'Most Qualified Person,'" 310.

94 For more on women and political repression, see Spencer-Antoine, *Revolution Has Come*, 88–108.

95 Huggins, author interview, April 16, 2010; and Elaine Brown, *Taste of Power*, 162. For more on the High Potential Program and the murders of John and Bunchy, see Scot Brown, *Fighting for US*, 95–96.

96 On John as captain, see Huggins, *Oral History*, 27. Jeffries and Foley state that John rose to the rank of deputy chairman. "To Live and Die in L.A.," 267. For more on Bunchy, see "To Live and Die in L.A.," 261–63.

97 For more on the history of the US organization, see Scot Brown, *Fighting for US*; and Scot Brown, "Politics of Culture." Like other political organizations in Los Angeles, both US and the BPP shared office space directly next to one another in the Black Congress Building.

98 Huggins, author interview, April 16, 2010; and Huggins, *Oral History*, 27–29.

99 Huggins, author interview, April 16, 2010. For more on the COINTELPRO murders of John and Bunchy, see Scot Brown, *Fighting for US*, 91–99; and Scot Brown, "Politics of Culture," 240–41. Elaine Brown also recalls the events in Campbell Hall; see Brown, *Taste of Power*, 156–70. The following month after the murder of John and Bunchy, Lincoln University covered the story in the *Lincolnian*. In the story, the author does not mention that John was a former student at Lincoln. "Black Students Shot on UCLA Campus." UCLA alumnus J. Daniel Johnson, who presided over the meeting, provided an eyewitness account. See Levin, "Alum Continues Activism"; and Pool, "Witness to 1969 UCLA Shootings."

100 Huggins, author interview, April 16, 2010.

101 Churchill and Vander Wall, *COINTELPRO Papers*, 130.

102 Churchill and Vander Wall, *COINTELPRO Papers*, 130.

103 For more on the strategic ways the FBI attacked the BPP, see Churchill, "'To Disrupt, Discredit, and Destroy.'"

104 Anzaldúa, *Light in the Dark*, 35.

105 Huggins, *Oral History*, 32–33.

106 Elaine Brown, *Taste of Power*, 167–68.

107 The COINTELPRO report on the actions of law enforcement reported that Ericka and John's residence was surveilled the evening of January 17, 1979. It lists individuals whose names are redacted who were arrested at the residence or in the vicinity. John Huggins, Federal Bureau of Investigation FOI/PA #1334356-0 Section 001, FOI/PA# 1320481-0, pp. 52–56 of CD packet; see also pp. 68–71.

108 Angela Davis remembered hearing about the shooting of John and Bunchy and supporting Ericka through the process. In Davis's words, "One of the memories that is absolutely seared on my brain is hearing about the shooting at UCLA and the fact that John and Bunchy had been killed. And a few of us realized that we needed to find Ericka immediately. So we went to John and Ericka's house and once we arrived there, we discovered that the police were already there and that they were planning to arrest Ericka for some ridiculous charge like conspiracy to get back at the men who had killed John and Bunchy. But they took her to jail, and it was someone in our group who had to keep her daughter because their daughter was at that time a few months old, I remember she was an infant. . . . I can remember feeling so sad for Ericka. I knew how much she and John loved each other and both of them were incredible human beings." Angela Y. Davis, author interview, July 3, 2019; also see Davis, *Angela Davis: An Autobiography*, 169.

109 Walter Bremond with his wife took Mai. Ericka Huggins, author interviews, April 11, 2016, May 23, 2017. Scot Brown notes that following the murders of John and Bunchy, Bremond withdrew from the Black Congress. *Fighting for US*, 99.

110 Ericka Huggins, author interview, April 16, 2010.

111 Freed, *Agony in New Haven*, 65.

112 Ericka Huggins, author interview, May 23, 2017.

113 In Fiona Thompson's interview, Ericka recounts the solace she found in Sybil Brand from another incarcerated woman, which prompted her to express her emotions and shed tears. See Huggins, *Oral History*, 54–55. In the interview, she also recalls the relationship between the BPP and the US organization, the murders of John and Bunchy, and her arrest and violent treatment by the police. Huggins, *Oral History*, 45–55.

114 Ericka Huggins, author interview, April 16, 2010.

115 Angela Y. Davis, author interview, July 3, 2019.

116 Angela Y. Davis, author interview, July 3, 2019; also see Davis, *Angela Davis: An Autobiography*, 169–70.

117 Angela Y. Davis, "Letter to Ericka."

118 Newton, *Revolutionary Suicide*, 167–68.

119 Ericka Huggins, author interview, February 20, 2010.

120 Angela Y. Davis, "Reflections on the Black Woman's Role," 126.

121 In the anthology *He Never Came Home*, Ericka's daughter, Mai, recalls that her uncle took her and her mother to New Haven from Los Angeles by train. She explains that days later, her father's body was flown back to New Haven to place him to rest in his hometown and celebrate his life. Lassiter, "Life, After," 168. Ericka also recalls this in her interview with Fiona Thompson. Huggins, *Oral History*, 55.

122 For more on the history of the New Haven BPP chapter, including Ericka's arrival in New Haven, see Yohuru Williams, *Black Politics/White Power*, 124–45.

123 For more on Alex Rackley's interrogation, see Yohuru Williams, *Black Politics/White Power*, 140–42.

124 Lorde, "Master's Tools Will Never Dismantle the Master's House."

125 Ericka Huggins, author interview, October 14, 2019.

126 Frances Carter Hilliard, interview by Lewis Cole.

127 Spencer-Antoine, *Revolution Has Come*, 89.

128 Ericka Huggins, author interview, October 14, 2019. In Ericka's interview with Fiona Thompson, she discusses the New Haven chapter, Alex Rackley, George Sams, and COINTELPRO. Huggins, *Oral History*, 59–63.

CHAPTER 3. GENDERED PRISON VIOLENCE

1 State Farm for Women Record Book entry, 1969; Ericka Cozette Huggins prisoner index card, 1969–1970; Rose Marie Smith prisoner index card; Frances Elsie Carter prisoner index card, 1969–1970; Margaret Hudgins prisoner index card, 1969–1970; Maude Louise Francis prisoner index card; Jeannie Wilson prisoner index card. I use "Niantic" to refer to the York Correctional Institution because

Ericka refers to it as such in the poem "A Reflection on Niantic" in Newton and Huggins, *Insights and Poems*, 47.

2 On Maude's and Jeannie's prisoner index cards, the word "False" is handwritten next to their age and date of birth. While their ages and birthdates are unclear, the fact that they were both sent to juvenile detention homes a week after their imprisonment confirms that they were minors.

3 On December 1, 2017, I visited Niantic to view the grounds and the building(s) where Ericka was housed during her incarceration. I was taken to the basement of Davis Hall, where former correctional officer Paul Harrison believed Ericka came in upon her initial arrival. He informed me that the building was in the same condition as it was when Ericka was there in the late 1960s.

4 Ericka Huggins, author interview, October 14, 2019.

5 Quoted in Shakur, *Assata*, 83.

6 Shakur, *Assata*, 83–84. For more on Assata's experience and sexual violence in prison, see also Angela Y. Davis, *Are Prisons Obsolete?*, 61–63, 67–69, 77–83.

7 Given the prison's prohibition against zippers, the dress had buttons down the front.

8 Physical examination, 1969, Ericka Huggins prison file. Ericka's intake process details were based on Assata Shakur's autobiography and former Niantic correctional officers' descriptions, as Ericka struggled to recall specifics, providing a glimpse into her experience. Ericka's medical records show a physical examination on June 30, 1969, roughly one month into her incarceration. Other documents in her medical records include a memo regarding a dental filling, an injury from a badminton racket, and a headache from a "chalazion of the right upper lid."

9 According to journalist Andi Rierden, in 1968 Niantic was "under the jurisdiction of the state's newly created Department of Correction." She adds, "From then on, state farm matrons, as they had been referred to since the beginning, were now called correctional officers." Despite this, in 1969, when the Black Panthers were incarcerated at Niantic, correctional officers recorded Ericka's use of the term "matron" in a log detailing her activities. Moreover, during her interview with Lewis Cole, Frances Carter used "matron" when referring to prison authority. Ericka also used the term "matron" in my interviews with her. This suggests that Niantic continued to use the term "matron" despite being under the Department of Correction's authority. Reirden, "Prison Reaches Back"; Ericka Huggins prison conduct log; Frances Carter Hilliard, interview by Lewis Cole.

10 Rafter, *Partial Justice*, 13; Freedman, *Their Sisters' Keepers*, 58.

11 Rafter, *Partial Justice*, 14. For more on matrons, see Freedman, *Their Sisters' Keepers*, 58–64.

12 Rafter, *Partial Justice*, 14–15.

13 Rafter, *Partial Justice*, 15. To further support this line of reasoning, see Freedman, *Their Sisters' Keepers*, 58.

14 Rafter, *Partial Justice*, 15. To further support this line of reasoning, see Freedman, *Their Sisters' Keepers*, 58.

15 Rafter, *Partial Justice*, 15

16 Over the course of its history, Niantic has been known by many different names. Paul Harrison (former Niantic correctional officer and "in-house" historian), recalls this history in "It's all in the Name," email message to author, May 10, 2019. For more on the history of Niantic, see Rogers, "History of the Movement"; Rierden, *The Farm*; and Gander, "From Farm Pen to Penitentiary."

17 Welter, "Cult of True Womanhood," 152.

18 For more, see Angela Y. Davis, *Are Prisons Obsolete?*, 64, 70.

19 Rogers, "History of the Movement," 522.

20 Paul Harrison (former Niantic correctional officer and "in-house" historian), "Workers," email message to author, February 16, 2020.

21 Ericka Huggins, State of Connecticut Department of Correction waiver: Working of Unsentenced Inmates, Ericka Huggins prison file. Ericka signed the work waiver midway into the time of her imprisonment. On the form, the word "peace" is spelled incorrectly as "piece."

22 Huggins, waiver. Ericka spelled the word "should" as "shd" to use shorthand. She often used shorthand when writing in prison.

23 Huggins, waiver. I assumed that "Good Time" referenced some form of leisure denied to pretrial detainees who chose to work full-time.

24 Ericka Huggins, author interview, June 9, 2017.

25 Connecticut State Department of Correction, York Correctional Institution, https://portal.ct.gov. For more on the history of Niantic, see Rierden, *The Farm*; and Gander, "From Farm Pen to Penitentiary."

26 Rafter, *Partial Justice*, xxviii. While Rocky Neck State Park is located down the street from Niantic, the Samuel M. Peretz Park, managed by East Lyme, borders the prison. Niantic is surrounded by Bride Lake. See also Angela Y. Davis, *Are Prisons Obsolete?*, 70–72.

27 Ericka Huggins, author interview, May 6, 2017.

28 Connecticut Department of Correction, "Inmates in Connecticut's Correctional Institutions."

29 Connecticut Department of Correction, "Inmates in Connecticut Correctional Institution, Niantic, (p. 3)." While "Puerto Rican" is the language of the primary documents, it may not represent the full nature of the Latino/Hispanic diversity at Niantic.

30 After the age of two, the child was released to the family or remained in state care in a children's asylum. Rierden, "Prison Reaches Back."

31 Reirden, "Prison Reaches Back."

32 According to Paul Harrison (former Niantic correctional officer and "in-house" historian), in 1920 a maternity hospital opened with six babies. Roughly six months later, the number rose to sixteen babies and continued to increase over time, contributing to infant neglect. After a state investigation, new leadership, and over sixty babies to care for, a new baby hospital was built in 1928. Its name was later changed to Thompson Hall in 1933. Deliveries occurred at Fenwick Hall until

1948. As a result of a fire in Fenwick Hall in 1937, only Thompson Hall was available for deliveries. To meet the high demand for deliveries, the board of directors discussed planning arrangements for a new hospital until a vote to halt planning arrangements in 1953. From 1948 to the present, baby deliveries occurred at Lawrence and Memorial Hospital in New London, Connecticut. Paul Harrison, "The History of the Children of the Farm," email message to author, January 7, 2021.

33 Harrison, "History of the Children of the Farm."

34 Angel Memorial symbolizes Niantic's maternal and pediatric care practices. Its proximity allowed mothers in the general population to visit their children's gravesite. In 2002 imprisoned women led renovations at the site to promote remembrance, collective grief, and solidarity. Walsh, "Inmates Restore Children's Graves"; "York Inmates Toiling to Restore Children's Graves."

35 Walsh, "Inmates Restore Children's Graves." Paul Harrison (former Niantic correctional officer and "in-house" historian) estimated that Union Cemetery is two miles from Niantic.

36 Most likely Niantic dispensed diethylstilbestrol, a popular hormonal-based medication that could cause a rebound effect, reversing milk suppression. This medicine was banned in 1971 because of its link to breast cancer. Ericka was not informed by the Niantic medical staff of the dangerous side effects of the medicine she was taking. The author consulted Maria Salowich, RN, lactation clinician at Beaumont Hospital, Royal Oak, Michigan, on lactation suppression practices during this time. Maria Salowich, author interview, October 4, 2021.

37 Ericka Huggins, author interview, August 11, 2020.

38 Ericka Huggins, author interview, November 1, 2020.

39 Ericka Huggins, author interview, November 1, 2020.

40 Ericka Huggins prison conduct log, May 31, 1969. Contrary to what the correctional officer documented in Ericka's log, she was unable to "come for 4 p.m. meds" because she was detained in solitary. Nurses brought the medicine to her. Ericka believed that the medications referenced in the log entry were lactation suppression pills given to her within the first week of her imprisonment to dry up her breast milk. There is no history of lactation suppression pills given to Ericka in her medical records at Niantic.

41 Ericka Huggins, author interview, November 1, 2020.

42 Ericka Huggins, author interview, November 1, 2020.

43 Ericka Huggins, author interview, November 1, 2020.

44 Wolf, "What Feminists Can Do for Breastfeeding," 401–3.

45 Wolf, "What Feminists Can Do for Breastfeeding," 407.

46 Some physicians believed the false notion that urbanization debilitated women's bodies, preventing mothers from producing enough milk to feed their infant. For more on the history of breastfeeding, see Wolf, *Don't Kill Your Baby*; and Freeman, *Skimmed*.

47 Institute of Medicine, *Nutrition during Lactation*, 29–30. Initiated breastfeeding means breastfeeding once before you are discharged from the hospital. Wolf,

"What Feminists Can Do for Breastfeeding," 399. In 1972 breastfeeding rates started to rise because of the women's health reform movement, which challenged misogynistic medical birthing practices and advocated for maternal agency. This movement later shaped the reproductive rights movement.

48 For more on the benefits of breastfeeding, see American Academy of Pediatrics, "Breastfeeding and the Use of Human Milk," policy statements, 2005 and 2012.

49 American Academy of Pediatrics, "Breastfeeding" (2012). The World Health Organization and the Institute of Medicine also recommend breastfeeding within the first six months. The Centers for Disease Control suggest that breastfeeding decreases the risk of type 2 diabetes, breast cancer, ovarian cancer, and high blood pressure for women. Centers for Disease Control, "Breastfeeding," www.cdc.gov, accessed January 26, 2020.

50 Ericka Huggins, author interview, November 1, 2020.

51 Ericka Huggins, author interview, March 8, 2019.

52 The State of Connecticut defined "lascivious carriage" as wanton sexual acts that occurred without consent between unmarried persons. The offense "manifest danger of falling into vice" was a charge brought against women who were pregnant out of wedlock.

53 Freedman, *Their Sisters' Keepers*, 14.

54 Approval for administrative segregation for Ericka Huggins, May 27, 1969, Ericka Huggins prison file.

55 "Telephone Conversation with Francis [Frances] Carter."

56 "Telephone Conversation with Francis [Frances] Carter."

57 Miles, *All That She Carried*, xvii.

58 "Telephone Conversation with Francis [Frances] Carter."

59 "Telephone Conversation with Francis [Frances] Carter." For more on the inhumane conditions of the Black Panther women in Niantic, see "Defense of the New Haven Panther 14."

60 "Telephone Conversation with Francis [Frances] Carter."

61 The date May 26, 1969, would put Ericka in medical segregation for seventy-two hours. It is hard to figure out the actual day of her release from medical segregation because we do not know the time of her admission.

62 "Telephone Conversation with Francis [Frances] Carter."

63 Administrative segregation is called "administration isolation" in Ericka's prison conduct log, November 9, 1970.

64 Maude Louise Francis prisoner index card; Jeannie Wilson prisoner index card. The Connecticut State Library's State Farm for Women Record Book cites Maude and Jeannie's discharge dates as May 24 and May 26, 1969, respectively. It is speculated that Maude and Jeannie may have been sent back to Niantic at some point and then released on December 3, 1969, because two dates are noted under the release column on their prisoner index card.

65 Loretta Luckes prisoner index card.

66 Epps, "Trial of Bobby Seale."

67 Loretta Luckes was referred to as "an enemy of the people" in the BPP newspaper "for turning in a state's witness in the Alex Rackley case." According to their claim, she "allowed the state to indict Chairman Bobby Seale for a murder he did not commit." They continue by saying that she can be included in "the list of traitors and counter-revolutionaries . . . who have always sold out to the racist power structure at the expense of seeing their people free." "Loretta Luckes State's Witness."

68 Umoja, "Set Our Warriors Free," 431–33.

69 Complaint for Declaratory Judgement, 7. While this was mentioned in Ericka and Bobby's Complaint for Declaratory Judgement, likely all the BPP women experienced interruptions in their sleep due to excessive noise, walkie-talkies, and lights.

70 "Telephone Conversation with Francis [Frances] Carter."

71 Ericka Huggins, author interview, March 18, 2020. Frances Carter describes their living conditions in "Telephone Conversation with Francis [Frances] Carter."

72 Ericka remembered barred windows in her cell. The only building that has historically contained barred windows is the North Building, or the Prison Unit. The North Building is segregated from the other buildings on Niantic's campus because it was reserved for high-level prisoners. Given that Ericka was a political prisoner, she could have spent some time in the North Building, although her prison conduct log indicates that she spent the majority of her imprisonment in Thompson Hall. Thompson Hall served as the high-security building until the opening of the Janet S. York Correctional Institution, a maximum-security correctional facility, in 1994. With the opening of the Janet S. York Correctional Institution, Thompson Hall in addition to the rest of the east side of the campus shifted to minimum security. Thompson Hall as well as other buildings on the east side contain strong metal screens on the windows but no bars.

73 In an article in the Modern Times, breakfast is listed as served at 7:00 a.m., and the BPP women are described as being doubly locked in by 9:00 p.m. Dominski, "Panther Women."

74 Frances Carter Hilliard, interview by Lewis Cole, 45.

75 Frances Carter Hilliard, interview by Lewis Cole, 46.

76 Frances Carter Hilliard, interview by Lewis Cole, 46.

77 Frances Carter Hilliard, interview by Lewis Cole, 43, 46.

78 Frances Carter Hilliard, interview by Lewis Cole, 43.

79 Frances Carter Hilliard, interview by Lewis Cole, 47.

80 Frances Carter Hilliard, interview by Lewis Cole, 46.

81 Frances Carter Hilliard, interview by Lewis Cole, 27, 28.

82 Frances Carter Hilliard, interview by Lewis Cole, 28–29.

83 Frances Carter Hilliard, interview by Lewis Cole, 29.

84 Frances Carter Hilliard, interview by Lewis Cole, 47.

85 Frances Carter Hilliard, interview by Lewis Cole, 50.

86 Frances Carter Hilliard, interview by Lewis Cole, 50.

87 Frances Carter Hilliard, interview by Lewis Cole, 47. For Frances Carter's discussion of their interrogations, see pp. 47–48 of the interview.

88 Ericka Huggins, "interrogation," email message to author, June 21, 2021. Ericka learned later that another woman she did not know had taken the officers' deal, so they tried to see whether she would do the same.

89 Ericka Huggins, author interview, March 18, 2020.

90 Ericka Huggins, author interview, May 6, 2017.

91 Ericka Huggins, author interview, October 14, 2019.

92 Frances Carter Hilliard, interview by Lewis Cole, 48.

93 On September 22, 1969, correctional officers recorded Ericka's first entry in her commissary bank statement four months into her imprisonment. Commissary bank statement, Ericka Huggins prison file.

94 "Legal Aid and Educational Program."

95 There is no indication on Frances's prisoner index card of her delivery in prison. Unlike the files for other imprisoned women such as Millie Rivera, the file for Frances contains no documentation of her travels to and from the hospital, which would give some indication of when she likely had her baby.

96 During her interview with Lewis Cole, Frances provided a detailed description of her son's head at the moment of his birth. She asserted that his head was an oblong shape from "where he was stuck . . . for that long period of time." Frances Carter Hilliard, interview by Lewis Cole, 52.

97 Frances Carter Hilliard, interview by Lewis Cole, 54.

98 Ericka Huggins, author interview, May 25, 2020.

99 Dominski, "Panther Women."

100 Frances Carter Hilliard, interview by Lewis Cole, 52.

101 Guha, "Connecticut Lawmakers Push Back." In 2018 the First Step Act was passed; the act restricts shackling of pregnant women during childbirth in federal prisons.

102 Frances Carter Hilliard, interview by Lewis Cole, 53.

103 Frances Carter Hilliard, interview by Lewis Cole, 53.

104 According to Frances Carter's interview, her mother and sibling were not in the delivery room and were not able to see her and her baby until after her delivery. Frances Carter Hilliard, interview by Lewis Cole, 53. *Modern Times* reports that her family was not allowed to visit her at the hospital. Dominski, "Panther Women."

105 I concluded that Rose had her baby around the same time, based on the conversation about Rose in her Lewis Cole interview. Frances stated in the interview that Rose's baby went to the care of a white couple in the community, but she did not say why. Frances Carter Hilliard, interview by Lewis Cole, 58. There is no indication of Rose's delivery on her prisoner index card.

106 Loretta Luckes, prisoner index card.

107 As listed on her prisoner index card, she weighed 126 pounds when she entered Niantic. Frances Elsie Carter prisoner index card. In the interview, she mentioned

that medical professionals gave her drugs, including Thorazine, Librium, and sodium pentothal. Frances Carter Hilliard, interview by Lewis Cole, 54.

108 Frances Carter Hilliard, interview by Lewis Cole, 54.

109 Frances Carter Hilliard, interview by Lewis Cole, 53–54.

110 In the interview, Frances indicated that she was in solitary confinement for a month. Frances Carter Hilliard, interview by Lewis Cole, 56.

111 Frances Carter Hilliard, interview by Lewis Cole, 55.

112 Frances Carter Hilliard, interview by Lewis Cole, 56.

113 Frances Carter Hilliard, interview by Lewis Cole, 56.

114 While we do not know for certain whether Niantic laced prisoners' food with saltpeter during this time, Ericka and former correctional officers believed this to be true in the 1960s and 1970s. In addition, in prisons and in the military saltpeter was commonly believed to subdue sexual drive; however, it is important to note that some beliefs about it are merely urban legends. Most often, saltpeter is used in explosives and to cure food and retain its color. For more, see Helmenstine, "Saltpeter"; Sicard, "Saltpeter for Sex Drives"; Schwarcz, "What Is Saltpeter"; and *Encyclopedia of Food Microbiology*, 2nd ed., 2014, s.v. "saltpeter," www.sciencedirect.com.

115 Frances Carter Hilliard, interview by Lewis Cole, 56. The famous line is from a speech given by BPP veteran Fred Hampton, of the Illinois chapter, at a rally in support of the Chicago Eight. See Jakobi Williams, "'You Can Kill the Revolutionary,'" citation 6. Williams claimed that Fred Hampton plagiarized a preponderance of Dr. Martin Luther King Jr.'s speeches and sermons (80).

116 Frances Carter Hilliard, interview by Lewis Cole, 56.

117 Frances Carter Hilliard, interview by Lewis Cole, 56.

118 Frances Carter Hilliard, interview by Lewis Cole, 54.

119 Solomon and Rankin, *How We Fight*, xii.

120 Frances Carter Hilliard, interview by Lewis Cole, 55. The names of the officers are made up. While Frances tells this story in her oral interview with Lewis Cole, Ericka claims that she does not remember running from correctional officers.

121 For more on Frances Carter's experience in labor, see Frances Carter Hilliard, interview by Lewis Cole, 52–57.

122 "Message of Francis [Frances] Carter"; Aubyn Lewis, "Panther Asked to 'Sell-Out'"; Dominski, "Panther Women." Frances's prisoner index card lists that she was released on bail on January 19, 1970, and returned to prison on January 21, 1970.

123 Aubyn Lewis, "Panther Asked to 'Sell-Out.'"

CHAPTER 4. SURVIVING SOLITARY

1 Huggins, *Oral History*, 72; Freed, *Agony in New Haven*, 47, Garry and Goldberg, *Streetfighter in the Courtroom*, x–xi, 5–6.

2 Stearn, *Yoga, Youth and Reincarnation*, 10. He lists karma yoga, bhakti yoga, jnana yoga, and raja yoga (10–11). For more definitions on hatha yoga, see his Sanskrit glossary in the back of the book.

3 Joshua Clark Davis, "Five Myths about Hippies."

4 Evans, *Black Women's Yoga History*, 213.

5 Evans, *Black Women's Yoga History*, 13.

6 Evans, *Black Women's Yoga History*, 13.

7 The entry mentions that Ericka and several other BPP women went "to [the] office to see [the warden,] Mrs. [Janet S.] York at 2:30p [and] also went to exercise for ½ hour." All names but Ericka's are redacted in the entry. Ericka Huggins prison conduct log, February 5, 1970. In a letter to political journalist Jan Von Flatern, Ericka refers to her yoga poses as exercises. She mentions waking up early and doing sun salutations and a headstand/shoulder stand followed by meditation. She writes, "this morning I got up earlier than earlier and exercised. First, the sun salutations—for a sleeping sun—then a headstand/ a shoulderstand and on and on, then thots—almost meditation . . . the door opened, light came on, I remembered that I was in the prison camp." "Thots" is her shorthand for "thoughts." In the letter she notes meditating on John Huggins and her sister friends Kani/Connie and Jan. Jan Von Flatern, personal letters, February 11, 1971. According to the Complaint for Declaratory Judgement, Ericka and Bobby were "denied adequate and frequent exercise and access to available gymnastic facilities." Complaint for Declaratory Judgement, 7. This likely happened to all the BPP women.

8 Ericka Huggins, author interview, May 6, 2017.

9 Ericka Huggins, author interview, June 9, 2017.

10 Ericka Huggins, author interview, June 9, 2017.

11 Stearn, *Yoga, Youth and Reincarnation*, 17.

12 Ericka Huggins, author interview, January 29, 2016.

13 Stearn, *Yoga, Youth and Reincarnation*, 16.

14 Ericka Huggins, interview by Amy Kesselman.

15 Hicks, "Incomplete"; Parker, *Restorative Yoga*; Berila, Klein, and Roberts, *Yoga*.

16 Aziz, "Built with Empty Fists," 134. She also includes other types of embodied practices such as martial arts and dance as "movement arts."

17 Lorde, *Burst of Light*, 130, italics in original.

18 Ericka Huggins, author interview, April 16, 2010.

19 For more on Clark, see Gloria Clark Jackson, *Mark Clark*.

20 Ericka Huggins, author interview, November 11, 2015.

21 Ericka Huggins, author interview, November 11, 2015.

22 Ericka Huggins, author interview, November 11, 2015.

23 In 1972 the BPP distributed over six thousand bags of groceries and registered Oakland community residents to vote. For more, see Murch, *Living for the City*, 191–228; and Seale, interview; the Bay Area Television Archive also has footage of Seale packing groceries.

24 Ericka Huggins, author interview, May 25, 2020.

25 Huggins prison conduct log. Once Ericka was moved to the general population, correctional officers recorded in her prison conduct log that other imprisoned women fasted with her. Their names are redacted in the prison conduct log. By

the time Ericka was moved to the general population, the other BPP women were already released from Niantic.

26 Huggins prison conduct log.

27 Huggins prison conduct log.

28 Huggins prison conduct log.

29 Ericka Huggins, author interview, August 11, 2020.

30 Huggins prison conduct log.

31 Huggins prison conduct log.

32 Ericka Huggins, author interview, August 11, 2020. In my conversation with Ericka, she spoke in general terms about Niantic holding items from those imprisoned for petty offenses.

33 Ericka Huggins, author interview, October 14, 2019. Ericka's words are paraphrased. Her exact words are as follows: "We were put in that wing because our words were considered contraband, and our presence was considered that which would incite riot among the women."

34 Ericka Huggins, author interview, October 14, 2019.

35 Ericka Huggins, author interview, October 14, 2019.

36 Huggins prison conduct log. In the log, the person's name is blacked out; I named her Elizabeth Marie.

37 Huggins prison conduct log, December 31, 1969.

38 Huggins prison conduct log. By the length of the name blacked out, it seems to be a different person mentioned in the entry than the person referenced in discipline, which is why I listed a different name in the text. Based on the context in the log, I believe there is a typo in the entry. The entry reads, "—— looked for visiting at Panther's door." "Looked" was probably supposed to be "locked."

39 Huggins prison conduct log.

40 Huggins prison conduct log. The name was blacked out in the story in the prison conduct log; I named her Tammy. In the prison conduct log the date for this incident is noted as November 31, 1969. Given that the prison conduct log is dated chronologically, covering Ericka's imprisonment from 1969 to 1971, this is likely a typo and should be December 31, 1969.

41 Huggins prison conduct log, September 17, 1969.

42 Huggins prison conduct log.

43 Huggins prison conduct log. Ericka's first name was misspelled in this entry.

44 Huggins prison conduct log.

45 Huggins prison conduct log, September 19, 1969.

46 Ericka Huggins, author interview, August 11, 2020.

47 Huggins prison conduct log. Ericka's first name was misspelled in this entry.

48 Ericka Huggins, author interview, August 11, 2020. When I visited the prison in 2017, women imprisoned were still referred to as "girls" by the prison staff.

49 In her co-written book of poetry, *Insights and Poems*, Ericka includes poetry about her prison experiences.

50 "Report from New Haven."

51 "Report from New Haven."

52 "Report from New Haven."

53 Officer Walsh's name has been changed for privacy purposes. Officer Walsh, author interview, August 24, 2018.

54 Officer Walsh, author interview, August 24, 2018.

55 Ericka could not remember the exact details involving the officer's complaint about the cigarettes. Ericka Huggins, author interview, June 9, 2017. Frances mentioned that the prison staff told them they could not smoke. Frances Carter Hilliard, interview by Lewis Cole, 48.

56 Ericka Huggins, author interview, June 9, 2017.

57 Ericka Huggins, author interview, August 11, 2020.

58 Ericka Huggins, author interview, June 9, 2017.

59 Ericka Huggins, author interviews, June 9, 2017, March 18, 2020.

60 Ericka Huggins, author interview, March 18, 2020.

61 Ericka Huggins, author interview, June 9, 2017.

62 In the prison conduct log, the name of the woman who was boasting about biting one of the guards is blacked out. The fact that the name was so briefly blacked out and that there were no letters extending below the baseline to identify Peggy led me to believe that it was Rose. They spelled "guards" incorrectly in the entry. Huggins prison conduct log, February 16, 1970.

63 Frances Carter Hilliard, interview by Lewis Cole, 49.

64 Frances Carter prisoner index card.

65 Loretta Luckes prisoner index card. Loretta was released on September 10, 1970.

66 Margaret Hudgins prisoner index card; Rose Smith prisoner index card. "2 Women Panthers in Rackley Case Freed on Probation," *New York Times*, October 3, 1970, 57. Peggy passed away at the age of thirty-six; she lived for roughly fourteen years after her release. Her confinement worsened her arthritis, which negatively impacted her health and likely shortened her life. She was identified as divorced in her death index. Margaret C. Hudgins, Connecticut Death Index, 1949–2012, Ancestry.com.

67 I have opted to use the pseudonym "Ruth" for this individual.

68 Ericka Huggins, author interview, March 18, 2020. Ericka believed that Ruth was not who she claimed she was, and that she was part of an operation to set her up.

69 Ruth's exact arrival date and the day of her transfer to a different isolation room remain unknown. I determined Ericka's time in a smaller solitary cell room by taking into account the release date of October 2, 1970, for Peggy and Rose, the last of the Black Panther women released, as well as the date noted in the prison conduct log when Ericka was moved to the general population, November 9, 1970. This is a rough estimate.

70 According to historian Yohuru Williams, Bobby engaged in a hunger strike lasting ten days in opposition to a prison ban on "the wearing of long hair and beards." Yohuru Williams, *Black Politics/White Power*, 156.

71 Complaint for Declaratory Judgement, 2. The complaint for declaratory and injunctive relief was filed on behalf of Ericka and Bobby (whose name was redacted) by attorneys Catherine G. Roraback, David N. Rosen, Charles R. Garry, and Stanley A. Bass of New York. According to Ericka, once Angela Davis's attorneys filed an appeal against the ruling that kept Angela in solitary confinement on the grounds of "cruel and unusual punishment," Roraback, Garry, Rosen, and Bass used the same defense to get her and Bobby out of solitary confinement. Ericka Huggins, author interview, October 14, 2019.

72 Complaint for Declaratory Judgement, 2.

73 Complaint for Declaratory Judgement, 4–9.

74 Complaint for Declaratory Judgement, 7, 6, 8, 10, 11.

75 Memorandum of Decision, 1971, 3. See Memorandum of Decision for discussion of agreements and stipulations.

76 On November 9, 1970, Ericka was transferred to the general population. Prison conduct log. Her transfer took place prior to the December 1970 hearings and legal conference, where many of the significant concerns surrounding her and Bobby Seale's case were settled. Memorandum of Decision, 1971.

77 Huggins prison conduct log, October 31, 1970. Ericka is reported to have "resumed eating" in the next entry, on November 3. Given the order of the dates in the log, it was an error that the date 11–3 was written as 3–11.

78 Huggins prison conduct log, October 2, 1970, and October 17, 1970.

79 Ericka felt that she would have been okay without a television. She could not recall whether they had a record player.

80 Huggins prison conduct log, November 5, 1970. The name of the incarcerated woman communicating with Ericka is redacted in the prison conduct log entry.

81 The time until Ericka's release date was calculated using Peggy and Rose's release date of October 2, 1970.

CHAPTER 5. THE SISTER LOVE COLLECTIVE

1 Ericka Huggins prison conduct log. The Department of Corrections transferred Ericka to the general population roughly in the last six months of her incarceration. I calculated the period from Ericka's entry into Niantic on May 22, 1969, to her transfer to the general population on November 9, 1970, to determine the duration of her administrative segregation.

2 Ericka noted that she experienced all these feelings and more, especially the joy of being with her daughter, Mai. Ericka Huggins, email message to author, March 20, 2019.

3 hooks, Salvation; hooks, All about Love; hooks, Communion; Laura, "Intimate Inquiry."

4 hooks and Jhally, Cultural Criticism and Transformation.

5 White, Ar'n't I a Woman?

6 Berger, Captive Nation, 11.

7   Rooks, *Hair Raising*; Banks, *Hair Matters*; Byrd and Tharps, *Hair Story*; Bundles, *On Her Own Ground*; Battle-Walters, *Sheila's Shop*; Majors, "'I Wasn't Scared of Them'"; Jacobs-Huey, *From the Kitchen to the Parlor*; Prince, *Politics of Black Women's Hair*; Spellers and Moffitt, *Blackberries and Redbones*; Gill, *Beauty Shop Politics*; Majors, *Shoptalk*; Mbilishaka, "PsychoHairapy."

8   Kelley, *Race Rebels*, 8. For more on a hidden transcript, see Scott, *Domination and the Arts of Resistance*.

9   Ericka Huggins, email message to author, May 4, 2017.

10 Lampert, *Women Doing Life*, 83.

11 Gill, *Beauty Shop Politics*, 3–4.

12 Talvi, *Women behind Bars*, 127.

13 hooks, "Theory as Liberatory Practice."

14 Huggins, *Oral History*, 69.

15 Local press coverage of Ericka's trial was included in newspapers such as the *Hartford Courant* (Hartford, CT), the *Bridgeport Post* (Bridgeport, CT), and *The Day* (New London, CT). Numerous national newspapers, including the *New York Times*, *Boston Globe*, *Chicago Tribune*, and *Los Angeles Times*, covered her trial.

16 Huggins, *Oral History*, 69.

17 Lorde, "Age, Race, Class, and Sex," 115–16.

18 Ford explains that "soul style comprises African American and African-inspired hairstyles and modes of dress such as Afros, cornrows, denim overalls, platform shoes, beaded jewelry, and dashikis and other garments with African prints that became massively popular in the 1970s when 'Black is Beautiful' was a rallying cry across the African diaspora." Ford, *Liberated Threads*, 4.

19 Ford, *Liberated Threads*, 6.

20 As a result of these hardships, women prisoners have historically created their own beauty products. For information on homemade beauty products made by imprisoned women, see Komar, "Why Makeup Matters."

21 I am focusing on femininity as a form of love and care for the sake of my argument. This is not to say that some children might view femininity as discipline rather than care.

22 Millie had a passion for Asian-inspired art.

23 At the time of writing this book, Millie had already passed away. I conducted oral histories with Millie's daughter, Delinah Rivera-Dowdy, and brother Ivan Toro. Millie was closest to her brother Ivan. Overwhelmed with motherhood as a teenager, Millie's mother abandoned some of her children and almost gave Millie away. Ivan nevertheless spoke of life with his mother and siblings as playful and loving. However, the familial dynamic was disrupted by their mother's boyfriends. Millie and Ivan were forced to live on the streets during their childhood years due to the distress caused by their mother's lovers. He recalled that his mother's lovers "wanted to boss us around. They wanted to hit us." Despite this, Ivan was clear that they were not abused. Rather, they felt unloved, and the feeling of being

unwanted at home propelled them to spend most of their time out on the streets. Young Millie and Ivan would play and hang out on the streets in the late hours, unrestrained and unafraid. For fun, leisure, and recreation, they jumped over the rooftops of buildings in New York City and sometimes went to the movies or traveled to the neighborhood of Coney Island in Brooklyn. They were occasionally arrested by the police for shoplifting and taken into the juvenile justice system. They eventually began to live on park benches as they ceased making their late-night trips home. When they needed shelter, they occasionally spent a few days at the juvenile facility or in the homes of friends. In the early 1960s, Millie's mother moved her family from New York to Connecticut. Millie and Ivan were in their tween years. A confrontation with other kids at a mall in New Haven landed Millie in Long Lane School for Girls. Ivan explained that Millie "either was confronted, or something happened, and Millie had a knife with her, and she stabbed the girl." Although she was sixteen, Millie was tried as an adult and transferred from Long Lane to Niantic, where she met Ericka. Ivan Toro, author interview, September 27, 2019; Delinah Rivera-Dowdy, author interview, August 5, 2019.

24 Millie Rivera prisoner index card, Millie Rivera prison file, Connecticut Department of Correction records, RG 017. Although Millie is Puerto Rican, her color was marked as white on her prisoner index card. On February 16, 1970, she was taken into custody and given a $5,000 bond. She was charged with aggravated assault and theft.

25 Delinah Rivera-Dowdy, author interview, August 2, 2019.

26 Although Millie's prisoner index card indicated that she had tattoos on her ankles, left hand, and left hip, her daughter, Delinah, did not remember her having a tattoo on her hip; however, her brother Ivan suggested that due to her tough nature she may have burned the tattoo off. Delinah believes that her mother received several tattoos during her time incarcerated, including the heart tattoo and her love tattoo. She believes it's possible that she received her love tattoo while at Long Lane. She later covered her love tattoo with a dragon, as she adored Asian-inspired designs. Delinah Rivera-Dowdy, author interviews, August 2, 2019, August 5, 2019; Ivan Toro, author interview, September 27, 2019.

27 Ericka Huggins, author interview, May 9, 2019.

28 Ericka Huggins, author interview, May 9, 2019.

29 Ericka's commissary bank statement demonstrated how much she was able to contribute at any given moment to the Sister Love Collective. Commissary bank statement, Ericka Huggins prison file.

30 Apart from Millie Rivera and Connie Civita, the women's names in the Sister Love Collective are pseudonyms.

31 Camp, *Closer to Freedom*, 7.

32 Camp, *Closer to Freedom*, 7.

33 Camp, *Closer to Freedom*, 7.

34 Ericka shared that the topic that broke her heart was women and their children. Ericka Huggins, author interview, May 9, 2019.

35 Nadasen, *Household Workers Unite*, 3.

36 Ericka Huggins, author interview, April 16, 2010.

37 The woman Ericka fell in love with while incarcerated has been given a false identity to preserve her anonymity.

38 Ericka Huggins, author interview, July 7, 2017.

39 Ericka Huggins, author interview, July 7, 2017.

40 Connecticut Department of Correction, "Admissions and Releases." This research report on the admissions and releases in Connecticut correctional institutions lists Niantic as having no admissions between the ages of sixteen and eighteen in December 1970, the month Connie was imprisoned (7). It also lists no releases in December 1970 between the ages of sixteen and seventeen, with only one person at the age of eighteen released (11). In my interview with Connie Civita, she identified herself as sixteen years old when she was incarcerated. Connie Civita, author interview, May 13, 2017. On the front of her prisoner index card, the Connecticut State Jail Administration did not list any identifying information on Connie except for her name and prison number. The back of the prisoner index card indicates that she entered Niantic on December 1, 1970, and was released on December 30, 1970, with a $100 bond. If Connie was sixteen years old at the time of her admission and release, researchers excluded her from their report. Likely there are others also excluded.

41 Connie Civita, author interview, May 13, 2017.

42 Connie Civita, author interview, May 13, 2017.

43 Huggins, *Oral History*, 66–67. Ericka revealed to me during our interview that she and Millie found humor when discussing hair politics. "The white women will want their hair to be curly like mine and the Black women would want their hair to be straight like the white girls, and . . . [the Puerto Rican women] would want their hair any kind of way," Millie said to Ericka as they fell out laughing. Huggins, author interview, May 9, 2019.

44 Angela Y. Davis et al., *If They Come in the Morning*, 118. In 2017 Connie's daughter, Lisa Cowell, wrote to Ericka after coming across the poem to her mother, "for connie, a rollingstone," in Davis's anthology. On March 17, Ericka received Lisa's email providing an update on her mother's well-being. In the email, shared with me by Ericka, Lisa affectionately refers to her mother as "Aquarius Sister love," based on Ericka's reference to Connie in the poem.

45 Lorde, "Poetry Is Not a Luxury," 37.

46 Connie Civita, author interview, May 13, 2017.

47 Huggins, *Oral History*, 67.

48 Van Deburg, *New Day in Babylon*; Guillory and Green, *Soul*.

49 Springer, "Third Wave Black Feminism?"

50 Ericka Huggins, author interview, April 16, 2010.

51 Connie Civita, author interview, May 13, 2017.

52 Connie Civita, author interview, May 13, 2017.

53 Connie Civita, author interview, May 13, 2017.

54 Huggins prison conduct log.

55 Huggins prison conduct log.

56 Huggins prison conduct log.

57 It is unclear whether policing femininity is still a norm at Niantic. During my visit on December 1, 2017, I did not get the impression that this was still the case.

58 Huggins prison conduct log.

59 Huggins prison conduct log.

60 Connie remembered being at Niantic unsentenced for six months, but according to her prisoner index card, she was in prison for only one month. On December 1, 1970, she was incarcerated at Niantic, and on December 30, 1970, she appeared in court and was released that same day. Connie Civita prisoner index card. Connie attended Ericka's trial as often as she could. After Ericka's release from prison, they lost contact. Connie read about Ericka in *JET* magazine. She wrote to *JET*, claiming that she was the cousin of Huey P. Newton, in hopes that a connection to the famed Black Panther leader would be enough to persuade editors to put her in contact with Ericka. Her approach worked, as the editors sent her Ericka's address. She still has the letter that Ericka wrote in response to her. Looking back forty-six years later, Connie laughed as she referenced the lapse in time. "I'm a gray panther and proud of it," she declared. Connie Civita, author interview, May 13, 2017.

61 Huggins, *Oral History*, 67–68.

62 Ericka Huggins, author interview, June 9, 2019.

63 For more on patchwork, see Audin, *Patchwork and Quilting*; Shaw and Staples, *Clothing through American History*; and Square, "How Enslaved People Helped Shape Fashion History."

64 Ericka Huggins, author interview, March 8, 2019.

65 Ford, *Liberated Threads*, 5.

66 Ericka Huggins, author interview, June 9, 2017.

67 It's unclear whether there are any written regulations guiding the modesty code that correctional officers enforced.

68 Camp, *Closer to Freedom*, 68.

69 See Camp's theoretical framework pertaining to the "three bodies" of the formerly enslaved. *Closer to Freedom*, 62–68. Camp's explanation that the "third body was a source of pleasure, pride, and self-expression" characterizes the use of the body in the Sister Love Collective.

70 LeFlouria, *Chained in Silence*, 90.

71 LeFlouria, *Chained in Silence*, 88.

72 Huggins, *Oral History*, 68.

73 Huggins, author interview, May 9, 2019.

74 Linda is left nameless in Ericka's recollection of this story in Thompson's interview as well as my own. Huggins, *Oral History*, 68; Huggins, author interview, May 9, 2019. In my interview, Ericka explained that because of her isolation she was unable to figure out exactly where Linda was in the building, but could tell that

she was on a lower floor. Linda's loud screams, audible through closed windows, demonstrated that she was in excruciating pain. From her cell, Ericka witnessed the arrival of authorities as she initially saw flashing lights. She got up and saw out a window an ambulance with its sirens off and Linda's body being removed. In Thompson's interview, Ericka recalls hearing sounds downstairs and assumes that her body was taken away. "I'm sure her body was taken away." Huggins, *Oral History*, 68.

75 Huggins, *Oral History*, 68.

76 Huggins, *Oral History*, 68. Linda, according to Ericka, suffered from a "puncture of the lining of her intestines" and other peritonitis-related concerns, as stated in her interview with Thompson. The nature of the detective work of the Sister Love Collective remains unclear.

77 While members of the Sister Love Collective helped those women newly admitted, they also assisted all women imprisoned in Niantic.

78 Huggins, *Oral History*, 68. The methods by which the Sister Love Collective smuggled items to women in isolation remains unknown.

79 According to Ericka, she and Millie believed that cigarettes had a calming effect, and sugar replicated the effects of drugs.

80 Although the identities and anecdotes of Alice and Christine are fabricated, the narratives on how candy and cigarettes were smuggled offer some insight into how illicit activities likely happened at Niantic.

81 Ericka Huggins, author interview, May 9, 2019.

82 Ericka Huggins, author interview, May 9, 2019.

83 Huggins, *Oral History*, 68. In Thompson's interview, Ericka estimates that psychological counseling was not available as a form of drug treatment until the 1990s.

84 Huggins, *Oral History*, 69. False names have been given to the women to preserve their privacy.

85 Ericka Huggins, author interview, February 27, 2019. Ericka stated in Thompson's interview that the person I identify as Kimberly "nearly cussed," yet in my interview, she provided me with a more detailed description of what was said to the person I identify as Maria. Huggins, *Oral History*, 69.

86 Huggins, *Oral History*, 69.

87 Ericka Huggins, author interview, February 27, 2019. Her story represents women at large who benefitted from Maria's mentorship.

88 Huggins, *Oral History*, 69.

89 The donors to the women's bail fund operated by the Sister Love Collective remain unidentified.

90 In a letter to Jan Von Flatern dated January 28, 1971, Ericka mentions that she wrote a woman a poem and made a neckband for the birthday of a fellow imprisoned woman. She also notes that she, along with other imprisoned women, made her a card and signed it for her birthday. Jan Von Flatern, personal letters.

91 In another letter to Jan Von Flatern, dated February 2, 1971, Ericka wrote in all caps, "UNBELIEVABLE THINGS HAPPEN LIKE THESE ABSURD PEOPLE

TAKING BOOKS FROM SISTERS. BOOKS THAT AT ONE TIME BELONGED TO ME." Jan Von Flatern, personal letters. Ericka and Bobby's Connecticut District Court Memorandum of Decision stated that they could not share the Black Panther newspaper with those in the general population (3). The State of Connecticut banned what it described as "inflammatory" books and materials." Ericka and Bobby were required to keep this material in their cells away from other prisoners (3).

92 The work of Sister Love illuminates what historian Robin D. G. Kelley characterizes as infrapolitics. Kelley, *Race Rebels*, 9.
93 "Legal Aid and Educational Program."
94 National Bail Out collective, "Until Freedom Comes."
95 National Bail Out collective, "Until Freedom Comes."
96 Rodriguez-Cayro, "This Group Is Bailing Out Incarcerated Black Women."

CHAPTER 6. JOY ON TRIAL

This chapter contains portions from Mary Frances Phillips, "The Power of the First-Person Narrative: Ericka Huggins and the Black Panther Party," *Women's Studies Quarterly* 43, nos. 3–4 (Fall/Winter 2015).

1 Freed lists November 17, 1970, as the date jury selection started. *Agony in New Haven*, 29.
2 Ericka Huggins, author interview, April 14, 2019.
3 I learned that Ericka could slip out of her handcuffs from John Huggins's cousin, Ruth Wilson Gilmore. Ericka then offered more details on her experience.
4 Frances recalled that Peggy also slid in and out of her handcuffs during her travels back and forth to court when she was imprisoned and, like Ericka, commented on the "beautiful day." Frances Carter Hilliard, interview by Lewis Cole, 48.
5 Ericka Huggins, author interview, May 6, 2017.
6 Ericka Huggins, author interview, April 14, 2019.
7 Ericka Huggins, author interview, April 14, 2019.
8 Ericka Huggins, author interview, April 14, 2019.
9 Ericka Huggins, author interview, April 14, 2019.
10 Ericka Huggins, author interview, April 14, 2019.
11 Ericka Huggins, author interview, July 31, 2022.
12 Ericka Huggins, author interview, July 31, 2022.
13 Ericka Huggins, author interview, April 14, 2019.
14 Mrs. Huggins, John's mother, brought Mai to visit Ericka in prison once a week.
15 Ericka mentions that her daughter and the children of community supporters attended the trial; however, Jan Von Flatern, in her article published in the *Black Panther*, states that small children were prohibited from entering the New Haven courtroom. Von Flatern, "Ericka and Bobby Put the State on Trial."
16 See Gilyard, *Louise Thompson Patterson*; Spencer-Antoine, *Revolution Has Come*; and Springer, *Living for the Revolution* for more on how a life in struggle can produce personal joy and happiness while also advancing freedom and justice.

17 Ericka Huggins, author interview, April 14, 2019.

18 David Rosen, interview by Amy Kesselman, January 7, 2016. In his interview he suggests that "the jury pool had been tainted by all the publicity."

19 Freed, *Agony in New Haven*, 82.

20 Freed, *Agony in New Haven*, 83. Exemptions were offered to women caretakers and mothers with children sixteen years or younger in Connecticut. For more on exemptions, see Kesselman, "African American Activism."

21 Freed, *Agony in New Haven*, 119.

22 Freed, *Agony in New Haven*, 119.

23 State of Connecticut v. Ericka Huggins v. Bobby G. Seale, no. 15681, no. 15844, vol. 35, Superior Court New Haven, May 25, 1971, 13–14, New Haven Black Panther Trial Transcripts. The trial transcript indicates that it took four months to complete the jury selection (14).

24 Ericka Huggins, author interview, April 14, 2019.

25 Ericka Huggins, author interview, April 14, 2019.

26 Due to an injury preventing jury service, an African American woman selected as an alternate replaced an African American man, which resulted in a jury panel of five African American women, three white women, and four white men. For more on the jury, see Kesselman, "African American Activism."

27 David Rosen, interview by Amy Kesselman, January 7, 2016.

28 For more on the trial, see Freed, *Agony in New Haven*, 17, 134; "Is Justice Too Much Trouble?"; Kesselman, "African American Activism"; and State of Connecticut v. Ericka Huggins v. Bobby G. Seale, New Haven Black Panther Trial Transcripts.

29 Freed recommended Jan Von Flatern for employment at the Liberation News Service. For more history on the Liberation News Service, see Mungo, *Famous Long Ago*; Mungo, *Total Loss Farm*; Diamond, *What the Trees Said*; Wasserman, "Joy of Liberation News Service"; Slonecker, "Living the Movement"; and McMillian, *Smoking Typewriters*, 82–114.

30 Jan Von Flatern, author interview, May 20, 2017.

31 Jan Von Flatern, author interview, May 20, 2017.

32 Jan Von Flatern, author interview, May 20, 2017.

33 Poem printed in Freed, *Agony in New Haven*, 67.

34 The Panther Trial News Committee lists that it published the *Panther Trial News* weekly. The Yale Collection of American Literature, Beinecke Rare Book and Manuscript Library, has several of the publications.

35 "What's Really Happening." The twelfth day corresponds with Donald Freed's timeline of the trial in *Agony in New Haven*.

36 Jan Von Flatern, author interview, May 20, 2017.

37 Jan Von Flatern, personal letters from 1970 to 1971, with many letters undated. Most of the letters are from Ericka; however, there are some from others. In possession of the author. In one letter, Ericka shows affection for Jan Von Flatern and pours her love for her as well as John Huggins, Mai, New Haven chapter member

Marcia Robertson, and the women imprisoned with her. In a letter dated February 3, 1971, Ericka included Marcia Robertson in her group with Jan Von Flatern and Connie Civita. She wrote, "Jan—(Kani—Marcia)" [. . .] you/Kani/Marcia," which indicates that her feelings for Marcia paralleled her feelings for Jan and Connie. In the letters she thanked Jan for items such as stockings. In addition to letters, she wrote her poems.

38 Jan Von Flatern's personal letters. Ericka's birth month is January, which may have inspired her creativity in referring to Jan as January in some of her letters. In the letters, Ericka mentions and sends love to other sister friends/comrades in addition to Jan, Connie, and Millie.

39 Ericka Huggins, author interview, June 9, 2017.

40 Jan Von Flatern, author interview, May 20, 2017.

41 Hriji and Krishnamurthy, "What Is Romantic Friendship?"

42 Jan Von Flatern, author interview, May 20, 2017.

43 Ericka Huggins, author interview, April 28, 2019.

44 Jan Von Flatern, author interview, May 20, 2017.

45 Ericka Huggins, author interview, April 28, 2019.

46 Jan Von Flatern, author interview, May 20, 2017.

47 Jan Von Flatern, email message to author, July 1, 2017.

48 Jan Von Flatern, author interview, May 20, 2017.

49 In the words of Lauren Berlant, when we attach or desire, we are doing so to "a cluster of promises we want someone or something to make to us and make possible for us." *Cruel Optimism*, 23. Jan's attachment to Ericka and other women Ericka connected to or linked can be characterized by Berlant's theory.

50 Jan Von Flatern, author interview, May 20, 2017.

51 Haley, *No Mercy Here*, 3.

52 A further illustration that showcases the political import of love letters and spans the experiences of political prisoners is the correspondence between George Jackson and Angela Y. Davis. See Papers of Angela Y. Davis, 1937–2017 (inclusive), 1968–2006 (bulk), People v. Angela Y. Davis, 1962–1997, General trial files, 1970–1992, George Jackson letters to Davis, 1971, MC 940 57.19, Schlesinger Library, Radcliffe Institute. For an analysis of their letters, see Corrigan, "Theorizing Black Power in Prison"; and Rodríguez, "Radical Lineages."

53 Ericka Huggins, email message to author, June 14, 2017.

54 Ericka Huggins, author interview, June 9, 2017.

55 Fleetwood, *Marking Time*, 18.

56 She sometimes opened and/or closed the letters with the word "sisterlove."

57 Berger, *Captive Nation*, 8.

58 Jan Von Flatern, personal letters, January 15, 1970.

59 Jan Von Flatern, personal letters, February 11, 1971. Ericka mentioned that her public defender railroaded Isabel. In a letter dated May 8, 1971, Ericka discusses another woman whose lawyer does not advocate for her and asks whether Jan could get her another lawyer.

60 Jan Von Flatern, personal letters, undated letters. All names in letters have been changed for the purpose of privacy.

61 Jan Von Flatern, personal letters, undated letters.

62 John Williams and Ericka's lawyer Katy Roraback worked as partners for years after the completion of Ericka's trial in 1971. He represented many members of the Black Panther Party, including Bobby Seale. John Williams, author interview, August 6, 2019.

63 Jan Von Flatern, personal letters, undated letters.

64 Jan Von Flatern, personal letters, undated letters. In another undated letter, Ericka mentions that the sister of an imprisoned woman volunteered to take people back and forth for visits at Niantic. She includes her phone number and location of her residence in Stamford, Connecticut. In a letter dated May 19, 1971, Ericka mentions an imprisoned woman who would like her sister who lives in New Haven to visit her.

65 In the letters, Ericka requests lawyers for those in need for a range of crimes, including murder, forgery, prostitution, and shoplifting.

66 Jan Von Flatern, personal letters, January 17, 1971. Ericka uses "tho" as shorthand for "though" and "trans." for "transportation." In a letter on January 21, 1971, Ericka talks about a choker Millie made for her from a sheet and colored with a marker.

67 Ericka wrote to Jan to have her search for the prison location of a husband arrested in Bridgeport, Connecticut, whose wife, imprisoned at Niantic, could not locate as the state would not communicate his whereabouts with his wife. Jan Von Flatern, personal letters, February 11, 1971.

68 "Legal Aid and Educational Program."

69 "Washington State Free Bussing Program"; "Free Prison Bussing."

70 Jan Von Flatern, personal letters, undated letter.

71 Jan Von Flatern, personal letters, undated letter.

72 Jan Von Flatern, personal letters, undated letter.

73 Jan Von Flatern, personal letters, undated letter. The names have been changed for privacy. For Helen, Ericka lists contact information for a man in Waterbury, Connecticut, who has no phone. For Doris, Ericka lists contact information for her sister-in-law.

74 Jan Von Flatern, personal letters, undated letter. Perhaps given the context, Ericka reunited a family through a visitation in prison.

75 Jan Von Flatern, personal letters, March 24, 1971. Names have been changed for privacy and confidentiality.

76 Jan Von Flatern, personal letters, March 24, 1971. Ericka used "wd" as shorthand for "would."

77 Jan Von Flatern, personal letters, March 24, 1971.

78 Jan Von Flatern, personal letters, March 24, 1971. Ericka used "cd" as shorthand for "could."

79 In the letter, Ericka included Dorothy's parents' address and a phone number for her sister-in-law as a backup as her parents were without a phone. Moreover,

she mentions the names of Dorothy's relatives if Jan wished to visit them. She also mentions the option for Jan to visit Dorothy at Niantic. Ericka writes that in serious situations, such as the state threatening to separate a mother and child, she would contact Katy Roraback to ask her to find a top-notch lawyer for the case. Ericka Huggins, author interview, May 9, 2019.

80 Jan Von Flatern, author interview, May 20, 2017.

81 Jan Von Flatern, personal letters, January 19, 1971. Based on the context of the letter, I assume that this letter was not written to Jan.

82 In the letter, it is unclear what building Ericka is referring to; however, she suggests that she was in the same building as Millie.

83 Ericka Huggins, author interview, May 9, 2019.

84 Jan Von Flatern, personal letters, 1969–1971.

85 Ericka Huggins, author interview, August 21, 2023. Ericka did not provide precise details about the topics discussed during her conversations with David regarding his observations in the courtroom. David was perceptive and socially aware, and Charles Garry explained that he played a pivotal role during the trial. In his biography, *Streetfighter in the Courtroom*, Garry described David as "a brilliant young graduate of Yale Law School . . . [who] did much of the pre-trial work, and was invaluable in preparing the many motions" (188).

86 Ericka Huggins, author interview, August 21, 2023.

87 Millie Rivera prisoner index card, 1970–1971.

88 "Five Women Flee Prison." Millie was the only teenager in the group.

89 Millie was released from prison well before the Janet S. York Correctional Institution, a maximum-security facility building, was built in 1994 on the west side of the prison grounds. The west side is surrounded by a barbed wire fence.

90 Ivan Toro, author interview, September 27, 2019.

91 Millie was captured on December 4, 1970. Millie Rivera prisoner index card.

92 Betsy Lee Selmer prisoner index card, 1970, Connecticut Department of Correction records, RG 017. Betsy's index card lists her as "deceased in Boston" two months after her escape from Niantic.

93 Millie's work in Sister Love began when she was pregnant, as Ericka believes that when she met Millie, she was not yet full-term in her pregnancy. It is unknown how far Millie traveled when she escaped or her whereabouts when she was caught by authorities. Her daughter stated that her mom met her brother's father in Massachusetts during her escape. Delinah Rivera-Dowdy, author interview, August 2, 2019.

94 Charlton, "4 Women Flee Connecticut Jail."

95 Connecticut State Farm for Women, minutes, 16.

96 Jan Von Flatern, personal letters, 1971.

97 Jan Von Flatern, personal letters, February 24, 1971.

98 Jan Von Flatern, personal letters.

99 Jan Von Flatern, personal letters, February 24, 1971.

100 Jan Von Flatern, personal letters, February 24, 1971.

101 JanVon Flatern, personal letters, February 24, 1971.

102 Jan Von Flatern, personal letters, February 24, 1971.

103 Millie Rivera prisoner index card, 1970–1971.

104 Freed notes that Bobby Seale argued that the sign most often associated with Black Power was actually the "Power to the People" salute. Freed, *Agony in New Haven*, 52. For more on the Black Power salute, see Van DeBurg, *New Day in Babylon*; and Ogbar, *Black Power*.

105 There were many restricted items that people could not bring into the New Haven County Courthouse, but Ericka believed that she possibly carried a comb in her shoulder bag. Ericka Huggins, author interview, April 14, 2019.

106 She also made items for Mai.

107 Ericka Huggins, author interview, April 14, 2019.

108 Freed, *Agony in New Haven*, 225.

109 In his book, Donald Freed includes Charles Garry's affidavit, which states, "After reaching a verdict in the *Seale* case on Wednesday, May 19, 1971, the jury conducted no further deliberations on that day and began its deliberations in the *Huggins* case for the first time on Thursday, May 20, 1971, after concluding its deliberations and arriving at a unanimous verdict in the *Seale* case on Wednesday, May 19, 1971." Freed, *Agony in New Haven*, 318.

110 Ericka Huggins, author interview, April 16, 2010. Ericka paraphrased the juror's comments. She was unable to precisely recollect her statements as they were uttered.

111 Ericka Huggins, author interview, April 16, 2010.

112 Jan Von Flatern uses a passage from Donald Freed's report to describe what transpired with the jury. The jurors first acquitted Bobby and then deliberated on Ericka's verdict. Freed writes, "A fierce fight over Ericka began (screeching voices could be heard in the jury room). But when a stalemate on Ericka was unavoidable, then, as it seems, the minority 're-opened' the case of Bobby in order to bargain one against the other in hopes of breaking the spine of the Black majority." Despite this, the Black-majority jurors remained determined, and the jury was hung. Freed goes on to highlight the significant influence of women on the jury: "One Black woman stood up and said[,] 'That's not right,' when the foreman [of the jury] told the judge that there had been no agreement." A mistrial was declared. Their cases were ultimately dropped. See Von Flatern, "Victory for the People." This story is also accounted for in Charles Garry's affidavit. See point d. in Freed, *Agony in New Haven*, 318. According to Ericka, the male juror held out to the end and hung the jury; the judge sent him back and said, "Come up with a verdict one way or the other," and the jury hung again.

113 Ericka Huggins, author interview, April 16, 2010. Judge Harold Mulvey refused to try the case again due to its public notoriety.

114 Ericka Huggins, author interview, April 16, 2010. Although a mistrial was declared, the African American women and two of the white women jurors voted to acquit Ericka. The prosecutor requested a retrial but the judge supported the

defense, which advocated to have the indictments dismissed. Kesselman, "African American Activism," 42. For a viewpoint from Charles Garry on the trial and the preparations, see Garry and Goldberg, *Streetfighter in the Courtroom*, 181–216. Upon release, Bobby was extradited to Chicago to stand trial in the Chicago Eight trial. For a history of the Chicago Eight, see Hayden, Sossi, and Condon, *Voices of the Chicago Eight*.

115 Commissary bank statement, Ericka Huggins prison file. On May 18, 1971, a week before Ericka's release, she had $30.99 in her commissary. The statement ends after this listing. The words "Received above $30.99" are written underneath with Ericka's signature, along with a smiley face she drew. Likely this means that she received $30.99 at the time of her release from Niantic. For information on key events, main points raised by the prosecution and defense teams, and evidence presented in court that led to Ericka and Bobby winning their trial, see New Haven Black Panther Trial Transcripts; and Freed, *Agony in New Haven*.

116 For more on the Chicago Eight trial, see Wiener et al., *Conspiracy in the Streets*.

117 For more on the May Day protests, see Vaz, "Memories of May Day"; Taft, *May-Day at Yale*; and Chauncey, Hill, and Strong, *May Day at Yale, 1970*.

118 Jan Von Flatern, author interview, June 22, 2017.

119 Angela Y. Davis, author interview, July 3, 2019; Davis, *Angela Davis: An Autobiography*, 264.

120 George Jackson, *Soledad Brother*.

121 Angela Y. Davis, "Afro Images."

122 Angela Y. Davis, author interview, July 3, 2019.

123 Angela Y. Davis, author interview, July 3, 2019.

124 Angela Y. Davis, author interview, July 3, 2019. See also Evans, *Black Women's Yoga History*, 260.

125 Angela Y. Davis, *Angela Davis: An Autobiography*, 262.

126 Angela Y. Davis, *Angela Davis: An Autobiography*, 262.

127 Angela Y. Davis, author interview, July 3, 2019.

128 Evans, *Black Women's Yoga History*, 260.

129 For more on Angela Y. Davis's trial, see Aptheker, *Morning Breaks*; Angela Y. Davis, *Angela Davis: An Autobiography*; and Chakravarti, "Wanted."

130 Millie Rivera prisoner index card. Delinah Rivera-Dowdy, author interview, August 6, 2019.

131 Ivan Toro, author interview, September 27, 2019.

132 Delinah Rivera-Dowdy, author interview, August 2, 2019.

133 Ivan Toro, author interview, September 27, 2019.

134 Ivan Toro, author interview, September 27, 2019.

135 Alicia Caraballo, author interview, April 7, 2021.

136 Ivan Toro, author interview, September 27, 2019.

137 Delinah Rivera-Dowdy, author interview, August 2, 2019.

138 Jan Von Flatern, author interview, June 22, 2017.

139 Ericka Huggins, author interview, August 21, 2023.

140 Jan Von Flatern, author interview, June 22, 2017.

141 Jan Von Flatern, author interview, June 22, 2017.

142 In our oral history session, Jan thanked me for reconnecting her with Ericka. She shared with me that she had a delightful two-hour conversation with Ericka. Jan Von Flatern, author interview, June 22, 2017.

143 Ericka Huggins, author interview, November 10, 2022.

144 After Mai read this section of the manuscript, shared by Ericka with my permission, Mai added the words quoted. Received by Ericka via email on August 2, 2023.

145 Lassiter, "Life, After," 171.

146 When reflecting on growing up as a child of BPP members, Mai comments, "I saw a lot of people killed or imprisoned." Quoted in Lena Williams, "Revolution Redux?"

147 Lassiter, "Life, After," 171.

148 Elizabeth Huggins died on June 18, 2004, at the age of ninety-five. Her death notice was published in the *New York Times* on June 21, 2004.

149 Lassiter, "Life, After," 171.

150 For a history of the Lumpen, see Vincent, *Party Music*.

151 Huggins, "Biography." Mai began attending the OCS in the 1973–1974 school year. She entered the OCS directly from the BPP Intercommunal Youth Institute, which she attended from 1971 to 1973. See the epilogue for a discussion of IYI. In 1978 Ericka transferred Rasa from the nearby Child Development Center for toddlers to the OCS. Mai graduated from the OCS in 1980, and Rasa remained at the OCS until 1981, when Ericka left the BPP. Mai and Rasa are listed among enrolled students in the September 1979 OCS Handbook, Papers of the Oakland Community School. In Lena Williams's *New York Times* article "Revolution Redux?," Mai and Rasa, who were twenty-four and nineteen years old at the time of the interview, offer a snapshot of their young life in the BPP, highlighting their schooling experiences and political views. Maceo and Joju Cleaver, the children of Kathleen and Eldridge Cleaver, also discuss their experiences coming of age as BPP children.

EPILOGUE

Portions of the epilogue on the OCS were taken from Mary Frances Phillips, "The Feminist Leadership of Ericka Huggins in the Black Panther Party," *Black Diaspora Review* 4, no. 1 (2014): 187–221.

1 Davenport, "Reading the 'Voice of the Vanguard,'" 197.

2 For more on the BPP newspaper as an alternative to the mainstream press, see Davenport, "Reading the 'Voice of the Vanguard,'" 195.

3 For more on the role of women and gender in the BPP newspaper, see Lumsden, "Good Mothers with Guns."

4 Davenport, "Reading the 'Voice of the Vanguard,'" 197.

5 Ericka Huggins, author interview, May 9, 2019.

6 The BPP began using the name Black Panther Intercommunal News Service instead of the Black Panther Black Community News Service in 1971, when it began to focus on and expand its community programs. The first issue, published on April 25, 1967, featured the police murder of Denzil Dowell. For more on the history of the BPP newspaper, see Davenport, "Reading the 'Voice of the Vanguard'"; and Davenport, *Media Bias.*

7 According to Ericka, she originally intended to co-author a book with Angela Y. Davis that combined her poetry and Angela's prose, but the Communist Party intervened to stop the process, and the publication did not go forward as anticipated. Huey was informed in writing, by the Communist Party, that Angela would not be working on a book with the BPP. In Ericka's words, the Communist Party "was feeling as if this wasn't a way they wanted Angela to be represented." He then decided to collaborate with Ericka to write the book. Ericka Huggins, author interview, February 28, 2020.

8 For more on Dr. Phillip Shapiro, see the Phillip Shapiro Papers, Online Archive of California.

9 Ericka Huggins, author interview, February 28, 2020.

10 Ericka Huggins, author interview, February 28, 2020.

11 Newton and Huggins, *Insights and Poems,* 15.

12 Newton and Huggins, *Insights and Poems,* 47.

13 For more analysis on Ericka's poetry, see Washburn, "Pen of the Panther"; and Rocker, "Poetic Revolution."

14 Murch, *Living for the City,* 203; Spencer-Antoine, *Revolution Has Come,* 148; LeBlanc-Ernest, "'Most Qualified Person,'" 318.

15 For more on the political campaigns of Elaine Brown and Bobby Seale, see LeBlanc-Ernest, "'Most Qualified Person,'" 318; Murch, *Living for the City,* 191–228; and Spencer-Antoine, *Revolution Has Come,* 143–56. For the leadership of Elaine Brown as BPP chairperson, see Spencer-Antoine, *Revolution Has Come,* 173–76; and LeBlanc-Ernest, "'Most Qualified Person,'" 321–24.

16 Huggins and LeBlanc-Ernest, "Revolutionary Women," 169.

17 Huggins and LeBlanc-Ernest, "Revolutionary Women," 168.

18 Huggins and LeBlanc-Ernest, "Revolutionary Women," 170.

19 Huggins and LeBlanc-Ernest, "Revolutionary Women," 172.

20 "Black Panther Party Ten Point Platform and Program."

21 Huggins and LeBlanc-Ernest, "Revolutionary Women," 168.

22 Huggins and LeBlanc-Ernest, "Revolutionary Women," 170.

23 Huggins and Le-Blanc-Ernest, "Revolutionary Women," 176.

24 Robinson, "Until the Revolution," 192.

25 Pamela (Pam) Ward Pious, author interview, March 6, 2017. This language is paraphrased. Her exact words were as follows: "It wouldn't be uncommon for a child who was doing well in the classroom, when he or she finished their work to help somebody else who needed assistance, along with the staff." Pam's initial position involved working with newborns at the BPP's Child Development Center before

transitioning to an OCS assistant teacher. She later attained full teacher status and subsequently rose to become the preschool program director and the health officer.

26 Ericka Huggins, author interview, April 16, 2010.

27 Ericka Huggins, author interview, February 20, 2010.

28 Ericka Huggins, author interview, February 20, 2011.

29 Huggins and LeBlanc-Ernest, "Revolutionary Women," 172.

30 Huggins and LeBlanc-Ernest, "Revolutionary Women," 172.

31 Ericka Huggins, author interview, April 16, 2010.

32 Huggins and LeBlanc-Ernest, "Revolutionary Women," 173.

33 Schalk, *Black Disability Politics*, 42.

34 Pamela (Pam) Ward Pious, author interview, March 6, 2017. Pam did not share the name of the student. I gave him the name "Joseph" for narrative purposes.

35 Oakland Community School, "Overviews," Instructor Handbook, September 1978, Papers of the Oakland Community School. For more on dialectical materialism at the Oakland Community School, see Huggins and LeBlanc-Ernest, "Revolutionary Women," 173.

36 Ericka Huggins, author interview, February 20, 2011.

37 Huggins and LeBlanc-Ernest, "Revolutionary Women," 178.

38 Huggins and LeBlanc-Ernest, "Revolutionary Women," 172.

39 Steve McCutchen, author interview, September 16, 2016.

40 Haven Henderson, author interview, April 14, 2017.

41 Ericka Huggins, author interview, February 20, 2011.

42 Steve McCutchen, author interview, September 16, 2016.

43 Pamela (Pam) Ward Pious, author interview, March 6, 2017. Pam's words are paraphrased. Her exact words are as follows: "He got so mad that he took a melon or a pineapple, I don't remember which one now, threw it in a big sink of water and splashed this woman with it."

44 Pamela (Pam) Ward Pious, author interview, March 6, 2017.

45 At the time her daughter was hospitalized, Pam had not started her position as the OCS health officer, which included overseeing the children's medical needs, taking them to their doctor's appointments, and yearly dental examinations. She was an assistant in the preschool program.

46 Pamela (Pam) Ward Pious, author interview, March 6, 2017.

47 Pamela (Pam) Ward Pious, author interview, March 6, 2017. In our interview, Pam also told me about a letter Ericka received from a woman who had been shot in the legs during the L.A. shootout. According to Pam, the letter explained that a BPP comrade would frequently sneak in and attempt to get in bed with women who were sleeping on cots in the OCS building's meditation room. She recounted how she was certain that the assertion was accurate because the comrade had attempted to have sex with her. She continued by saying that when the comrade told Ericka about the circumstance, Ericka reacted by asking, "Now what am I supposed to do about this? I can't do anything about this." Pam was shocked at Ericka's response. Pam added that "this guy was just allowed to do this [sexually

assault women].” She wanted Ericka to protect the women staff at the OCS. The intense pressure Ericka was under to manage the school and perhaps the sexual violence inflicted on her by male comrades contributed to her inactivity regarding this situation. When I spoke with Ericka about the incident, she shared with me that she went to the BPP's Central Committee about the person and others who harmed women at night. She didn't say whether it had an impact or whether the sexual assaults had stopped.

48 Ericka Huggins, author interview, July 7, 2017.

49 Pamela (Pam) Ward Pious, author interview, March 6, 2017.

50 Ericka Huggins, author interview, July 7, 2017. More than forty years later, in October 2022, Pam joined Ericka on her book tour stop at the Eastside Cultural Center in Oakland, during the release of *Comrade Sisters: Women of the Black Panther Party*, co-authored by Ericka and BPP photographer Stephen Shames, which features reflections from women across ranks in the organization and stunning photographs of BPP women at work in the community programs.

51 Ericka Huggins, author interview, April 16, 2010.

52 Huggins and LeBlanc-Ernest, “Revolutionary Women,” 173. While meditation positively impacted many OCS students, some did not respond well. Former OCS student Ronald Brooks revealed how he detested meditation when he was just eight years old. Ronald “Money-B” Brooks, author interview, March 22, 2017. Former OCS student Amber Landis-Reedy added that meditation was hard for her. She was taught how to meditate at the school, but still found it challenging, which made her unhappy. She used meditation time as quiet time and admitted that she still has difficulties with meditation as an adult. Amber Landis-Reedy, author interview, August 31, 2016.

53 “Meditation as a Way to Attain a Disciplined Attitude,” parent memo, March 27, 1979, Papers of the Oakland Community School.

54 “Meditation as a Way to Attain a Disciplined Attitude,” parent memo.

55 “Meditation as a Way to Attain a Disciplined Attitude,” parent memo.

56 “Meditation as a Way to Attain a Disciplined Attitude,” parent memo. For more on this philosophy, see Huggins and LeBlanc-Ernest, “Revolutionary Women,” 170; and Robinson, “Until the Revolution,” 196–97.

57 “About the Oakland Community School,” memo, Papers of the Oakland Community School.

58 In the tree pose, you stand with your feet together, lift one foot so that you raise the heel of one foot off the floor, and carefully place that foot or lock that foot into the inner thigh of the other leg. Ultimately, you will stand on one leg with your arms stretched to the side.

59 The student has been given a false name to protect his privacy.

60 Ericka Huggins, author interview, April 16, 2010.

61 Ericka Huggins, author interview, April 16, 2010.

62 Fania E. Davis, *Little Book of Race and Restorative Justice*, 19.

63 Ericka Huggins, author interview, April 16, 2010.

64 Gregory B. Lewis, author interview, February 12, 2017.

65 Oakland Community School, "Approach to Learning," Instructor Handbook, September 1978, 2, Papers of the Oakland Community School.

66 For more on the history of martial arts at the OCS, see Aziz, "They Punched Back"; and Aziz, "Built with Empty Fists." Huggins and LeBlanc-Ernest briefly mention martial arts in "Revolutionary Women," 173.

67 Oakland Community School, brochure, 1977–1978, Papers of the Oakland Community School.

68 Huggins and LeBlanc-Ernest, "Revolutionary Women," 170–71. In the OCS handbook dated September 12, 1977, members of the Educational Opportunities Corporation were as follows: chief administrator, Phyllis Jackson; bookkeeper, Norma Armour; special services, Joan Kelley; and building maintenance, Rollin Reid. Oakland Community School, "Oakland Community School Structure," OCS Handbook, September 12, 1977, Papers of the Oakland Community School.

69 Charles E. Jones and Jonathan Gayles note other iconic politicians, athletes, and musicians who came to visit the OCS. Jones and Gayles "'World Is a Child's Classroom,'" 110. See also Huggins and LeBlanc-Ernest, "Revolutionary Women," 180. In my interview with Ronald "Money-B" Brooks, he remembered participating as a cast member in the school's play to honor Rosa Parks during her visit.

70 Ronald "Money-B" Brooks, author interview, March 22, 2017.

71 Gregory B. Lewis, author interview, February 12, 2017. Gregory was four years old when he began at the OCS, which was then called the Oakland Community Learning Center (OCLC). It is likely that he is referring to President Jimmy Carter for his English class assignment because he is seen in class photos from 1978 and 1979. Gregory B. Lewis, "Power to the Children." Gregory is featured in a 1977 OCS promotional video, https://www.youtube.com/watch?v=9dYsjDqUdro, accessed August 1, 2023.

72 Amber Landis-Reedy, author interview, August 31, 2016. Amber shared that she attended the OCS for two and a half years. She sent me a photograph of her math period evaluation from the 1976–1977 academic year. The evaluation named Joe Abron as her math teacher and Gwen Johnson as her homeroom teacher. It included her abilities with whole number operations, less than one operation, measurement, and problem-solving. She shared a photograph of the front cover of the OCS production "Come to Me, Let's Be Friends" from Sunday, March 27, 1977, at the OCLC. In addition, she shared a photograph of the purple first-place ribbon she won at the OCS math bowl on May 19, 1977. It named Joe Abron as the judge. She saved these mementos and spoke highly of the OCS, demonstrating how much she valued her time as an OCS student.

73 Amber Landis-Reedy, author interview, August 31, 2016.

74 Ericka Huggins, author interview, April 16, 2010.

75 Huggins and LeBlanc-Ernest, "Revolutionary Women," 177.

76 Jones and Gayles, "'World Is a Child's Classroom,'" 110.

77 Ronald "Money-B" Brooks, author interview, March 22, 2017. Although I am uncertain of Ronald's precise OCS enrollment dates, he is included among the students enrolled in 1979. Oakland Community School, "Student Enrollment," OCS Handbook, September 1979, Papers of the Oakland Community School. He is also pictured in the 1978 and 1979 class photos included in Gregory B. Lewis, "Power to the Children."

78 Jones and Gayles, "'World Is a Child's Classroom,'" 111.

79 Huggins and LeBlanc-Ernest, "Revolutionary Women," 177; Jones and Gayles, "'World Is a Child's Classroom,'" 111. For more on the history of the OCS, see Schalk, *Black Disability Politics*, 40–45; Robinson, "Until the Revolution"; Spencer-Antoine, *Revolution Has Come*, 183–86; Murch, *Living for the City*, 178–83; Huggins and LeBlanc-Ernest, "Revolutionary Women"; Jones and Gayles, "'World Is a Child's Classroom'"; and Perlstein, "Minds Stayed on Freedom," 261–70. Under contract with New York University Press, Robert P. Robinson is currently penning the first exhaustive study on the OCS, which will undoubtedly make a groundbreaking contribution to the existing scholarship on the BPP.

80 Thomas H. Bates spent twenty years in the assembly. He was elected mayor of Berkeley in 2002 and held the position for fourteen years. He retired from politics in 2016. Knobel, "Berkeley Mayor Tom Bates Retires."

81 Ericka Huggins, author interview, February 9, 2015. In our conversation, Ericka mentioned that in some juvenile detention facilities, young people were denied access to appropriate hair products such as hair oils or natural hair combs and were treated as criminals when they had such products in their possession, since those items were viewed as superfluous luxuries or weapons.

82 "Pressure Forces Califano to Sign."

83 "Pressure Forces Califano to Sign." For an analysis of more of Ericka's speech, see Schalk, *Black Disability Politics*, 34–35.

84 "Pressure Forces Califano to Sign."

85 Schalk, *Black Disability Politics*, 29.

86 Schalk, *Black Disability Politics*, 29. For more on the BPP and disability rights, see the chapters "We Have a Right to Rebel" and "Fighting Psychiatric Abuse" in Schalk's seminal book. See also the chapter "Race and Disability" in OToole, *Fading Scars*.

87 For the story on why Ericka left the BPP, see Huggins, *Oral History*, 99–102. Ericka left the BPP one year before the OCS closed.

88 It is important to note that Huey earned his PhD in 1980 in the History of Consciousness program at the University of California at Santa Cruz. He wrote his dissertation on the history of the FBI's political repression of the BPP, which was later published as his book *War against the Panthers*. For more on Huey's downfall, see Spencer-Antoine, *Revolution Has Come*, 168–70.

89 See Fiona Thompson's oral history, where Ericka mentions telling her mother that she was going to marry a white man. Huggins, *Oral History, 4*.

90 Ericka Huggins, author interview, June 20, 2016.
91 Yadav Jelal Huyler, author interview, March 20, 2019.
92 Ericka Huggins, author interview, July 20, 2016.
93 Huggins, "Biography."
94 Huggins, "Countering the Effects of Multigenerational Race and Gender Trauma."
95 The Ericka Huggins campus is located on a floor of MetWest High School that is shared with the Oakland Unified School District's Westlake Middle School due to space limitations.
96 Ericka Huggins, author interview, August 3, 2023.
97 Malik Edwards, author interview, August 4, 2023.
98 MetWest High School, "About Us," https://metwest.ousd.org, accessed August 3, 2023.
99 MetWest High School, "About Us."
100 MetWest High School, "About Us"; Malik Edwards, author interview, August 4, 2023.
101 MetWest High School, "About Us."
102 Malik Edwards, author interview, August 4, 2023. For a history of Dolores Huerta, see Peter Bratt's PBS documentary *Dolores*. For more on how restorative practices are employed in schools, see Costello, Wachtel, and Wachtel, *Restorative Practices Handbook*.
103 Malik Edwards, author interview, August 4, 2023.
104 Malik Edwards, author interview, August 4, 2023.
105 MetWest High School, "About Us."
106 MetWest High School, "Vision Statement," https://metwest.ousd.org, accessed August 3, 2023.
107 MetWest High School, "Schoolwide Learner Outcomes," https://metwest.ousd.org, accessed August 3, 2023.
108 Ericka Huggins, author interview, July 7, 2017.
109 Fania E. Davis, restorative justice practitioner and sister of Angela Y. Davis, connected Ericka and Watani for the restorative justice dialogue. For more on how they came together for the restorative justice dialogue, see Stiner, "Watani Stiner: Tending to Historical Wounds." See also Stiner, interview by Karin Stanford and Keith Rice, February 27, 2022. Larry Watani Stiner and his brother George Ali-Stiner as well as US member Donald Hawkins were charged with conspiracy for the murder of John Huggins and Bunchy Carter. According to Scot Brown, the alleged shooter, Claude Hubert-Gaidi, was never apprehended. Scot Brown, *Fighting for US*, 97.
110 KALW Public Media/97.1 FM Bay Area, "47 Years after Black Panther Killings." Watani shares his story in dialogue with Ericka in the *San Francisco Bay View*. In the story, he includes their initial exchange of letters in 2010. Stiner, "Watani Stiner: Tending to Historical Wounds."
111 Stiner, "Watani Stiner: Tending to Historical Wounds."
112 Stiner, "Watani Stiner: Tending to Historical Wounds."

113 Watani referred to his restorative justice dialogue with Ericka as "a truth and rec-
     onciliation forum as a model for our youth." "Watani Stiner: Tending to Historical
     Wounds."
114 Stiner, "Watani Stiner: Tending to Historical Wounds."
115 Stiner, "Watani Stiner: Tending to Historical Wounds."
116 Stiner, "Watani Stiner: Tending to Historical Wounds."
117 KALW Public Media, "47 Years after Black Panther Killings."
118 Watani recalled that he and Ericka participated in a restorative justice symposium
     at San Quentin State Prison months after their face-to-face meeting in the wake of
     the Sandy Hook Elementary School murders, to share their story with prisoners
     and guests. On January 11, 2015, more than four years after Watani Stiner began
     his restorative justice dialogue with Ericka, he was released from prison. "Watani
     Stiner: Tending to Historical Wounds."
119 Fania E. Davis, *Little Book of Race and Restorative Justice*, 41.
120 Lena Williams, "Revolution Redux?"

BIBLIOGRAPHY

PRIMARY SOURCE MATERIALS

Manuscript Collections
Ancestry.com. www.ancestry.com.
———. Connecticut Death Index, 1949–2012.
———. United States Federal Census, 1940.
———. US, City Directories, 1822–1995.
———. US, Department of Veterans Affairs BIRLS Death Files, 1850–2010.
———. US, School Yearbooks, 1900–2016.
———. US, World War II Army Enlistment Records, 1938–1946.
Connecticut Department of Correction. Records. RG 017. Connecticut State Library, Hartford.
Davis, Angela Y. Papers. Schlesinger Library, Radcliffe Institute, Harvard University. https://iiif.lib.harvard.edu.
Lincoln University. Records, 1966–1967. Lincoln University, PA.
———. Special Collections. Langston Hughes Memorial Library, Lincoln University, PA.
New Haven Black Panther Trial Transcripts. Documents Collection Center, Yale Law School Lillian Goldman Law Library. https://documents.law.yale.edu.
Oakland Community School. Papers. Department of Special Collections, Stanford University Libraries.
Roraback, Catherine. Catherine Roraback Collection of Ericka Huggins Papers. James Weldon Johnson Collection, Yale Collection of American Literature, Beinecke Rare Book and Manuscript Library, Yale University.
Shapiro, Phillip. Papers. Online Archive of California. Stanford University. https://oac.cdlib.org.
Von Flatern, Jan. Personal letters, 1970–1971. In possession of author.
York Correctional Institution. Records. Connecticut Department of Correction. https://portal.ct.gov.

Author Interviews and Published Oral Histories and Interviews
Brooks, Ronald "Money-B." Author interview, March 22, 2017.
Caraballo, Alicia. Author interview, April 7, 2021.
Civita, Connie. Author interview, May 13, 2017.
Davis, Angela Y. Author interview, July 3, 2019.
Edwards, Malik. Author interview, August 4, 2023.

Henderson, Haven. Author interview, April 14, 2017.

Hilliard, Frances Carter. Interview by Lewis Cole. Columbia University Black Panther Project, Alexander Street Press, 1990.

Hinds, Lennox. Author interview, July 23, 2019.

Huggins, Ericka. Author interviews, February 20, 2010–August 21, 2023.

———. "A Conversation with Ericka Huggins." Interview by Lisa Rofel and Jeremy Tai. *Feminist Studies* 42, no. 1 (2016): 236–48.

———. Interview by David Cline, June 30, 2016. Civil Rights History Project, Southern Oral History Program, Smithsonian Institution's National Museum of African American History and Culture and the Library of Congress.

———. Interview by Amy Kesselman, January 6, 2016.

———. *An Oral History with Ericka Huggins.* By Fiona Thompson, 2007. Oral History Center, Bancroft Library, University of California Berkeley. https://digitalassets.lib .berkeley.edu.

———. "Two Interviews with Ericka Huggins." By Tony Platt and Cecilia O'Leary. *Social Justice* 40, nos. 1–2 (2014): 54–71.

Huggins, Ericka, Yuri Kochiyama, and Mary Uyematsu Kao. "Stirrin' Waters 'n Buildin' Bridges: A Conversation with Ericka Huggins and Yuri Kochiyama." *Amerasia Journal* 35, no. 1 (2009): 140–67.

Huyler, Yadav Jelal. Author interview, March 20, 2019.

Landis-Reedy, Amber. Author interview, August 31, 2016.

Lassiter, Mai Huggins. "Life, After." In *He Never Came Home: Interviews, Stories, and Essays from Daughters on Life without Their Fathers,* edited by Regina R. Robertson, 167–73. Chicago: Bolden, 2017.

Lewis, Gregory B. Author interview, February 12, 2017.

McCutchen, Steve. Author interview, September 16, 2016.

Rivera-Dowdy, Delinah. Author interviews, August 2, 2019, August 5, 2019, August 6, 2019.

Rosen, David. Interview by Amy Kesselman, January 7, 2016.

Salowich, Maria. Author interview, October 4, 2021.

Seale, Bobby. Interview, n.d. Bay Area Television Archive. https://diva.sfsu.edu.

Shabazz, Malik. Author interview, September 17, 2019.

Stiner, Larry Watani. Interview by Karin Stanford and Keith Rice, *Black Power Hour,* February 27, 2022. Tom and Ethel Bradley Center, California State University, Northridge. https://www.youtube.com/watch?v=CM3LKRXH89w.

Toro, Ivan. Author interview, September 27, 2019.

Von Flatern, Jan. Author interviews, May 20, 2017., June 22, 2017.

Ward Pious, Pamela (Pam). Author interview, March 6, 2017.

Williams, John. Author interview, August 6, 2019.

SECONDARY SOURCE MATERIALS

Abron, JoNina. "'Serving the People': The Survival Programs of the Black Panther Party." In *The Black Panther Party Reconsidered,* edited by Charles E. Jones, 177–92. Baltimore: Black Classic Press, 1998.

Achebe, Nwando. "Getting to the Source: Nwando Achebe—Daughter, Wife, and Guest—A Researcher at the Crossroads." *Journal of Women's History* 14, no. 3 (2002): 9–31.

Ahmed, Sara. "Affective Economies." *Social Text* 22, no. 2 (2004): 117–39.

Alkebulan, Paul. *Surviving Pending Revolution: The History of the Black Panther Party.* Tuscaloosa: University of Alabama Press, 2007.

American Academy of Pediatrics. "Breastfeeding and the Use of Human Milk." Policy statement. *Pediatrics* 115, no. 2 (2005).

———. "Breastfeeding and the Use of Human Milk." Policy statement. *Pediatrics* 129, no. 3 (2012): e827. www.cdc.gov.

Anzaldúa, Gloria E. *Light in the Dark/Luz en lo Oscuro: Rewriting Identity, Spirituality, and Reality.* Edited by Analouise Keating. Durham: Duke University Press, 2015.

Aptheker, Bettina. *The Morning Breaks: The Trial of Angela Davis.* 2nd ed. Ithaca: Cornell University Press, 1997.

Asch, Chris Myers, and George Derek Musgrove. *Chocolate City: A History of Race and Democracy in the Nation's Capital.* Chapel Hill: University of North Carolina Press, 2017.

Audin, Heather. *Patchwork and Quilting in Britain.* New York: Bloomsbury, 2013.

Austin, Paula C. *Coming of Age in Jim Crow DC: Navigating the Politics of Everyday Life.* New York: New York University Press, 2019.

Aziz, Maryam K. "Built with Empty Fists: The Rise and Circulation of Black Power Martial Artistry during the Cold War." PhD diss., University of Michigan, 2020.

———. "They Punched Back: Martial Arts, Black Arts, and Sports in the Urban North and West, 1968–1979." *Journal of African American History* 106, no. 2 (2021): 304–27.

Bambara, Toni Cade, ed. *The Black Woman: An Anthology.* New York: Washington Square Press, 1970.

Banks, Ingrid. *Hair Matters: Beauty, Power, and Black Women's Consciousness.* New York: New York University Press, 2000.

Battle-Walters, Kimberly. *Sheila's Shop: Working-Class African American Women Talk about Life, Love, Race, and Hair.* Lanham: Rowman and Littlefield, 2004.

Beale, Frances. "Double Jeopardy: To Be Black and Female." In *The Black Woman: An Anthology*, edited by Toni Cade Bambara, 109–22. New York: Washington Square Press, 1970.

Ben-Moshe, Liat. *Decarcerating Disability: Deinstitutionalization and Prison Abolition.* Minneapolis: University of Minnesota Press, 2020.

Berger, Dan. *Captive Nation: Black Prison Organizing in the Civil Rights Era.* Chapel Hill: University of North Carolina Press, 2014.

Berila, Beth, Melanie Klein, and Chelsea Jackson Roberts, eds. *Yoga, the Body, and Embodied Social Change: An Intersectional Feminist Analysis.* New York: Lexington, 2016.

Berlant, Lauren. *Cruel Optimism.* Durham: Duke University Press, 2011.

Black, Carol. "Klan's Coming Stirs Campus." *Lincolnian*, December 1, 1965.

"Black Panther Party Book List." It's About Time Black Panther Party Legacy & Alumni website, n.d. www.itsabouttimebpp.com.

"The Black Panther Party Ten Point Platform & Program, October 1966, What We Want, What We Believe." Available at It's About Time Black Panther Party Legacy & Alumni website. www.itsabouttimebpp.com.

"Black Student Congress Plans Ambitious Program." *Lincolnian*, November 1, 1967.

"Black Student Congress Sponsors Appearance of Jeremiah X." *Lincolnian*, November 15, 1967, 1.

"Black Students Shot on UCLA Campus." *Lincolnian*, February 15, 1969.

Blain, Keisha N. *Set the World on Fire: Black Nationalist Women and the Global Struggle for Freedom*. Philadelphia: University of Pennsylvania Press, 2018.

Bloom, Joshua, and Waldo E. Martin Jr. *Black against Empire: The History and Politics of the Black Panther Party*. Berkeley: University of California Press, 2013.

Bratt, Peter, dir. *Dolores*. PBS documentary. Independent Lens. San Francisco: 5 Stick Films, 2017. DVD.

Brown, Elaine. *A Taste of Power: A Black Woman's Story*. New York: Doubleday, 1992.

Brown, Scot. *Fighting for US: Maulana Karenga, the US Organization, and Black Cultural Nationalism*. New York: New York University Press, 2003.

———. "The Politics of Culture: The US Organization and the Quest for Black Unity." In *Freedom North: Black Freedom Struggles outside the South, 1940–1980*, edited by Jeanne Theoharis and Komozi Woodard, 223–53. New York: Palgrave Macmillan, 2003.

Bukhari, Safiya. *The War Before: The True Life Story of Becoming a Panther, Keeping the Faith in Prison and Fighting for Those Left Behind*. New York: Feminist Press, 2010.

Bundles, A'lelia Perry. *On Her Own Ground: The Life and Times of Madam C. J. Walker*. New York: Washington Square Press, 2002.

Byrd, Ayana, and Lori Tharps. *Hair Story: Untangling the Roots of Black Hair in America*. New York: St. Martin's, 2001.

Camp, Stephanie M. H. *Closer to Freedom: Enslaved Women and Everyday Resistance in the Plantation South*. Chapel Hill: University of North Carolina Press, 2004.

"Capital Roundup." *Evening Star*, May 31, 1956.

Carson, Clayborne. *In Struggle: SNCC and the Black Awakening of the 1960s*. Cambridge: Harvard University Press, 1995.

Chakravarti, Sonali. "Wanted: Angela Davis and a Jury of Her Peers." *Political Theory* 49, no. 3 (2021): 380–402.

Chard, Daniel S. *Nixon's War at Home: The FBI, Leftist Guerillas, and the Origins of Counterterrorism*. Chapel Hill: University of North Carolina Press, 2021.

Charlton, Linda. "4 Women Flee Connecticut Jail; Caught Here after Wild Chase." *New York Times*, May 30, 1972, 22.

Chauncey, Henry "Sam," John T. Hill, and Thomas Strong. *May Day at Yale, 1970: Recollections: The Trial of Bobby Seale and the Black Panthers*. Westport: Prospecta Press, 2015.

Christian, Mark. "The Black Intellectual/Activist Tradition: Notes on the Past, Present, and Future." In *Black Identity in the 20th Century: Expressions of the US and UK African Diaspora*, edited by Mark Christian. London: Hansib, 2002.

Churchill, Ward. "'To Disrupt, Discredit, and Destroy': The FBI's Secret War against the Black Panther Party." In *Liberation, Imagination, and the Black Panther Party: A New Look at the Panthers and Their Legacy*, edited by Kathleen Cleaver and George Katsiaficas, 78–117. New York: Routledge, 2001.

Churchill, Ward, and Jim Vander Wall. *Agents of Repression: The FBI's Secret War against the Black Panther Party and the American Indian Movement*. 2nd ed. Boston: South End, 2002.

———. *The COINTELPRO Papers: Documents from the FBI's Secret War against Dissent in the United States*. 2nd ed. Boston: South End, 2002.

Cleaver, Kathleen Neal. "Back to Africa: The Evolution of the International Section of the Black Panther Party (1969–1972)." In *The Black Panther Party Reconsidered*, edited by Charles E. Jones, 211–54. Baltimore: Black Classic Press, 1998.

Clemons, Michael L., and Charles E. Jones. "Global Solidarity: The Black Panther Party in the International Arena." In *Liberation, Imagination, and the Black Panther Party: A New Look at the Panthers and Their Legacy*, edited by Kathleen Cleaver and George Katsiaficas, 20–39. New York: Routledge, 2001.

Cohen, Cathy J. "Punks, Bulldaggers, and Welfare Queens: The Radical Potential of Queer Politics." *GLQ* 3 (1997): 437–65.

Collier-Thomas, Bettye, and V. P. Franklin, eds. *Sisters in the Struggle: African American Women in the Civil Rights–Black Power Movement*. New York: New York University Press, 2001.

Collins, Patricia Hill. *Black Feminist Thought: Knowledge, Consciousness, and the Politics of Empowerment*. New York: Routledge, 2000.

Combahee River Collective. "A Black Feminist Statement." In *Words of Fire: An Anthology of African-American Feminist Thought*, edited by Beverly Guy-Sheftall, 232–40. New York: New Press, 1995.

Connecticut Department of Correction. "Admissions and Releases in Connecticut Correctional Institutions, December 1970." Research report, March 3, 1972. Connecticut State Library, Hartford.

———. "Inmates in Connecticut Correctional Institution, Niantic: A Profile." Research report 29, November 23, 1970. Connecticut State Library, Hartford.

———. "Inmates in Connecticut's Correctional Institutions: A Demographic Profile." Research document 13, December 17, 1969. Connecticut State Library, Hartford.

Connecticut State Farm for Women. Minutes, quarterly meeting of board of directors, January 18, 1964. In possession of author.

Conyers, James L. *Engines of the Black Power Movement: Essays on the Influence of Civil Rights Actions, Arts, and Islam*. Jefferson, NC: McFarland, 2007.

Corrigan, Lisa M. "Theorizing Black Power in Prison: The Writings of George Jackson and Angela Davis." In *Social Controversy and Public Address in the 1960s and Early*

1970s, 85–123. Vol. 9 of *A Rhetorical History of the United States*, edited by Richard J. Jensen. East Lansing: Michigan State University Press, 2017.

Costello, Bob, Joshua Wachtel, and Ted Wachtel. *The Restorative Practices Handbook for Teachers, Disciplinarians, and Administrators*. Bethlehem, PA: International Institute for Restorative Practices, 2009.

Crenshaw, Kimberlé Williams. "Mapping the Margins: Intersectionality, Identity Politics, and Violence Against Women of Color. In *Critical Race Theory: The Key Writings That Formed the Movement*, edited by Kimberlé Williams Crenshaw, Neil Gotanda, Gary Peller, and Kendall Thomas, 357–83. New York: New Press, 1995.

Davenport, Christian A. *Media Bias, Perspective, and State Repression: The Black Panther Party*. Cambridge: Cambridge University Press, 2010.

———. "Reading the 'Voice of the Vanguard': A Content Analysis of the Black Panther Intercommunal News Service, 1969–1973." In *The Black Panther Party Reconsidered*, edited by Charles E. Jones, 193–209. Baltimore: Black Classic Press, 1998.

Davies, Carol Boyce. *Left of Karl Marx: The Political Life of Black Communist Claudia Jones*. Durham: Duke University Press, 2008.

Davis, Angela Y. "Afro Images: Politics, Fashion, and Nostalgia." *Critical Inquiry* 21, no. 1 (1994): 37–45.

———. *Angela Davis: An Autobiography*. Chicago: Haymarket Books, 2021.

———. *Are Prisons Obsolete?* New York: Seven Stories, 2003.

———. "How Gender Structures the Prison System." In *Are Prisons Obsolete?* New York: Seven Stories, 2003.

———. "A Letter to Ericka from Angela." In *If They Come in the Morning: Voices of Resistance*, edited by Angela Y. Davis, Ruchell Magee, the Soledad Brothers, and other political prisoners, 123–27. San Francisco: Signet, 1971.

———. "Reflections on the Black Woman's Role in the Community of Slaves." In *The Angela Y. Davis Reader*, edited by Joy James, 111–28. Malden, MA: Blackwell, 1998.

———. *Women, Race, and Class*. New York: Vintage, 1983.

Davis, Angela Y., Ruchell Magee, the Soledad Brothers, and other political prisoners, eds. *If They Come in the Morning: Voices of Resistance*. San Francisco: Signet, 1971.

Davis, Fania E. *The Little Book of Race and Restorative Justice: Black Lives, Healing, and US Social Transformation*. New York: Good Books, 2019.

Davis, Joshua Clark. "Five Myths about Hippies." *Washington Post*, July 7, 2017. www .washingtonpost.com.

"Dean's List." *Lincolnian*, November 15, 1967.

"Defense of the New Haven Panther 14." *Black Panther*, October 15, 1969.

de Schweinitz, Rebecca. *If They Could Change the World: Young America's Long Struggle for Racial Equality*. Chapel Hill: University of North Carolina Press, 2009.

Devlin, Rachel. *A Girl Stands at the Door: The Generation of Young Women Who Desegregated America's Schools*. New York: Basic Books, 2018.

Diamond, Stephen. *What the Trees Said: Life on a New Age Farm*. New York: Delacorte, 1971.

Dillon, Stephen. *Fugitive Life: The Queer Politics of the Prison State*. Durham: Duke University Press, 2018.

Dominski, Joelle. "The Panther Women: A Talk." *Modern Times*, October 1, 1970.

Donovan, Mia, dir. *Dope Is Death*. Montreal: EyeSteelFilm, 2020. DVD.

Drummond, William J. "Black Panther Aide Lauds 2 Who Were Slain in UCLA Hall." *Los Angeles Times*, January 19, 1969.

"Dr. Wachman Holds Second Discussion with Students." *Lincolnian*, December 15, 1967.

Epps, Garrett. "The Trial of Bobby Seale." *Harvard Crimson*, April 28, 1970. www .thecrimson.com.

Erikson, Erik, and Huey P. Newton. *In Search of Common Ground: Conversations with Erik H. Erikson and Huey P. Newton*. New York: Norton, 1973.

Euchner, Charles. *Nobody Turn Me Around: A People's History of the 1963 March on Washington*. Boston: Beacon, 2010.

Evans, Stephanie Y. *Black Women's Yoga History: Memoirs of Inner Peace*. Albany: State University of New York Press, 2021.

Farmer, Ashley D. "Archiving While Black." *Chronicle of Higher Education*, July 22, 2018.

———. "In Search of the Black Women's History Archive." *Modern American History* 1 (2018): 289–93.

———. *Remaking Black Power: How Black Women Transformed an Era*. Chapel Hill: University of North Carolina Press, 2017.

"Five Women Flee Prison in Niantic; Screen Removed." *Hartford Courant*, July 21, 1970.

Fleetwood, Nicole R. *Marking Time: Art in the Age of Mass Incarceration*. Cambridge: Harvard University Press, 2020.

Ford, Tanisha C. *Liberated Threads: Black Women, Style, and the Global Politics of Soul*. Chapel Hill: University of North Carolina Press, 2015.

Franklin, V. P. *The Young Crusaders: The Untold Story of the Children and Teenagers Who Galvanized the Civil Rights Movement*. Boston: Beacon, 2021.

Freed, Donald. *Agony in New Haven: The Trial of Bobby Seale, Ericka Huggins and the Black Panther Party*. New York: Simon and Schuster, 1973.

Freedman, Estelle B. *Their Sisters' Keepers: Women's Prison Reform in America, 1830–1930*. Ann Arbor: University of Michigan Press, 2000.

Freeman, Andrea. *Skimmed: Breastfeeding, Race, and Injustice*. Stanford: Stanford University Press, 2020.

"Free Prison Bussing." *Black Panther*, October 31, 1970.

Fried, Morris. "The Black Student Congress." *Lincolnian*, March 1, 1968.

Fujino, Diane. *Heartbeat of a Struggle: The Revolutionary Life of Yuri Kochiyama*. Minneapolis: University of Minnesota Press, 2005.

Gander, Celeste A. "From Farm Pen to Penitentiary: How a Human Rights Framework Built Connecticut's Largest Female Prison." Undergraduate thesis, Trinity College, May 10, 2019.

Garry, Charles, and Art Goldberg. *Streetfighter in the Courtroom: The People's Advocate*. New York: Dutton, 1977.

Gill, Tiffany M. *Beauty Shop Politics: African American Women's Activism in the Beauty Industry*. Urbana: University of Illinois Press, 2010.

Gilmore, Ruth Wilson. *Golden Gulag: Prisons, Surplus, Crisis, and Opposition in Globalizing California*. Berkeley: University of California Press, 2007.

Gilyard, Keith. *Louise Thompson Patterson: A Life of Struggle for Justice*. Durham: Duke University Press, 2017.

Gluck, Sherna Berger, and Daphne Patai, eds. *Women's Words: The Feminist Practice of Oral History*. New York: Routledge, 1991.

Godrej, Farah. *Freedom Inside? Yoga and Meditation in the Carceral State*. New York: Oxford University Press, 2022.

Gore, Dayo F., Jeanne Theoharis, and Komozi Woodard, eds. *Want to Start a Revolution? Radical Women in the Black Freedom Struggle*. New York: New York University Press, 2009.

Gramsci, Antonio. *Selections from the Prison Notebooks of Antonio Gramsci*. New York: International Publishers, 1971.

Greenberg, Cheryl Lynn. ed. *A Circle of Trust: Remembering SNCC*. New Brunswick: Rutgers University Press, 1998.

Greene, Christina. *Free Joan Little: The Politics of Race, Sexual Violence, and Imprisonment*. Chapel Hill: University of North Carolina Press, 2022.

Guglielmo, Thomas A. *Divisions: A New History of Racism and Resistance in America's World War II Military*. New York: Oxford University Press, 2021.

Guha, Auditi. "Connecticut Lawmakers Push Back against Trump's Attack on Transgender Inmates." *Rewire.News*, May 22, 2018.

Guillory, Monique, and Richard C. Green, eds. *Soul: Black Power, Politics, and Pleasure*. New York: New York University Press, 1998.

Gumbs, Alexis Pauline. *Spill: Scenes of Black Feminist Fugitivity*. Durham: Duke University Press, 2016.

Guy-Sheftall, Beverly, ed. *Words of Fire: An Anthology of African-American Feminist Thought*. New York: New Press, 1995.

Haley, Sarah. *No Mercy Here: Gender, Punishment, and the Making of Jim Crow Modernity*. Chapel Hill: University of North Carolina Press, 2016.

Haley, Sarah, Shoniqua Roach, Emily Owens, and Keeanga-Yamahtta Taylor. "Confinement, Interiority, Black Feminist Study: A Forum on Davis's 'Reflection' at 50." *Black Scholar* 51, no. 1 (2021): 3–19.

Hamlin, Françoise N. "Historians and Ethics: Finding Anne Moody." *American Historical Review* 125, no. 2 (2020): 487–97.

Harding, Rosemarie Freeney, with Rachel Elizabeth Harding. *Remnants: A Memoir of Spirit, Activism, and Mothering*. Durham: Duke University Press, 2015.

Harrison, Rashida L., Mary Frances Phillips, and Nicole M. Jackson. "Introduction: Love Is Solidarity in Action." *Women's Studies Quarterly* 50, nos. 1–2 (2022): 12–24.

Hartman, Saidiya. *Wayward Lives, Beautiful Experiments: Intimate Histories of Social Upheaval.* New York: Norton, 2019.

Hayden, Tom, Ron Sossi, and Frank Condon. *Voices of the Chicago Eight: A Generation on Trial.* San Francisco: City Lights, 2008.

Hayes, Floyd W. III, and Francis A. Kiene III. "'All Power to the People': The Political Thought of Huey P. Newton and the Black Panther Party." In *The Black Panther Party Reconsidered*, edited by Charles E. Jones, 157–76. Baltimore: Black Classic Press, 1998.

Helmenstine, Anne Marie. "Saltpeter or Potassium Nitrate Facts." *ThoughtCo.*, March 1, 2022. www.thoughtco.com.

Hicks, Stephanie D. "Incomplete: Impeding the Settler Colonial Project through Yoga for Black Lives." In *Practicing Yoga as Resistance: Voices of Color in Search of Freedom*, edited by Cara Hagan, 118–32. New York: Routledge, 2021.

Hill, Lance. *The Deacons of Defense: Armed Resistance and the Civil Rights Movement.* Chapel Hill: University of North Carolina Press, 2006.

Hilliard, David, ed. *The Black Panther Party: Service to the People Programs: Dr. Huey P. Newton Foundation.* Albuquerque: University of New Mexico Press, 2008.

Hilliard, David, and Lewis Cole. *This Side of Glory: The Autobiography of David Hilliard and the Story of the Black Panther Party.* Chicago: Lawrence Hill Books, 1993.

Hine, Darlene Clark. "Rape and the Inner Lives of Black Women in the Middle West: Preliminary Thoughts on the Culture of Dissemblance." In *Words of Fire: An Anthology of African-American Feminist Thought*, edited by Beverly Guy-Sheftall, 380–87. New York: New Press, 1995.

Hogan, Wesley C. *Many Minds, One Heart: SNCC's Dream for a New America.* Chapel Hill: University of North Carolina Press, 2007.

Holley, Santi Elijah. "How Acupuncture Became a Radical Remedy in the Bronx: When Black and Brown Activists Created Lincoln Detox, They Also Helped Spread Eastern Medicine." *Atlas Obscura.* November 9, 2020. www.atlasobscura.com.

Holsaert, Faith S., Martha Prescod Norman Noonan, Judy Richardson, Betty Garman Robinson, Jean Smith Young, and Dorothy M. Zellner, eds. *Hands on the Freedom Plow: Personal Accounts by Women in SNCC.* Urbana: University of Illinois Press, 2010.

hooks, bell. *Ain't I a Woman: Black Women and Feminism.* Boston: South End, 1981.

———. *All about Love: New Visions.* New York: HarperCollins, 2000.

———. *Communion: The Female Search for Love.* New York: HarperCollins, 2002.

———. *Feminist Theory: From Margin to Center.* 2nd ed. Boston: South End, 2000.

———. *Salvation: Black People and Love.* New York: HarperCollins, 2001.

———. "Theory as Liberatory Practice." In *Teaching to Transgress: Education as the Practice of Freedom*, 59–75. New York: Routledge, 2020.

hooks, bell, and Sut Jhally, dir. *bell hooks: Cultural Criticism & Transformation.* Northampton, MA: Media Education Foundation, 1997. DVD.

Hriji, Sukaina, and Meena Krishnamurthy. "What Is Romantic Friendship? Deep and Lasting Connection Comes in Many Forms: We Need a New Vocabulary to Talk about Love." *New Statesman*, November 2, 2021. www.newstatesman.com.

Huggins, Ericka. "Biography." n.d. www.erickahuggins.com.

———. "Countering the Effects of Multigenerational Race and Gender Trauma: A Prescriptive Educational Model." MA thesis, California State University, East Bay, 2010.

———. "Global 1968: A World on Fire, Remembering 1968 and Looking to the Future." National Women's Studies Association, plenary session, Atlanta, GA, November 9, 2018.

Huggins, Ericka, and Angela D. LeBlanc-Ernest. "Revolutionary Women, Revolutionary Education: The Black Panther Party's Oakland Community School." In *Want to Start a Revolution? Radical Women in the Black Freedom Struggle*, edited by Dayo F. Gore, Jeanne Theoharis, and Komozi Woodard, 161–84. New York: New York University Press, 2009.

Institute of Medicine. *Nutrition during Lactation*. Washington, DC: National Academies Press, 1991.

"Is Justice Too Much Trouble?" *Chicago Tribune*, May 27, 1971.

Jackson, George. *Soledad Brother: The Prison Letters of George Jackson*. Chicago: Lawrence Hill Books, 1994.

Jackson, Gloria Clark. *Mark Clark: Soul of a Black Panther*. N.p.: Justice Publishing, 2020.

Jacobs-Huey, Lanita. *From the Kitchen to the Parlor: Language and Becoming in African American Women's Hair Care*. Oxford: Oxford University Press, 2006.

James, Stanlie M. "Mothering: A Possible Black Feminist Link to Social Transformation?" In *Theorizing Black Feminisms: The Visionary Pragmatism of Black Women*, edited by Stanlie M. James and Abena P. A. Busia, 45–56. New York: Routledge, 1994.

Jeffries, Judson L. *Huey P. Newton: The Radical Theorist*. Jackson: University Press of Mississippi, 2002.

Jeffries, Judson L., and Malcolm Foley. "To Live and Die in L.A." In *Comrades: A Local History of the Black Panther Party*, edited by Judson L. Jeffries. Bloomington: Indiana University Press, 2007.

Johnson, Elizabeth Jasmine. "Dancing Africa, Making Diaspora." PhD diss., University of California, Berkeley, 2012.

Jones, Charles E., and Judson L. Jeffries. "'Don't Believe the Hype': Debunking the Panther Mythology." In *The Black Panther Party Reconsidered*, edited by Charles E. Jones, 25–55. Baltimore: Black Classic Press, 1998.

Jones, V. Lani, and Beverly Guy-Sheftall. "Black Feminist Therapy as a Wellness Tool." In *Black Women's Mental Health: Balancing Strength and Vulnerability*, edited by Stephanie Y. Evans, Kanika Bell, and Nsenga K. Burton, 201–14. Albany: State University of New York Press, 2017.

Joseph, Peniel E. *The Black Power Movement: Rethinking the Civil Rights–Black Power Era*. Routledge: New York, 2006.

———. *Waiting 'til the Midnight Hour: A Narrative History of Black Power in America*. New York: Henry Holt, 2007.

"June 1966 Meredith March." SNCC Digital Gateway, n.d. https://snccdigital.org.

KALW Public Media/97.1 FM Bay Area. "47 Years after Black Panther Killings, a Cor-respondence Heals Old Wounds." September 21, 2016. www.kalw.org.

Kelley, Robin D. G. *Freedom Dreams: The Black Radical Imagination*. Boston: Beacon, 2002.

———. *Race Rebels: Culture, Politics, and the Black Working Class*. New York: Free Press, 1996.

Kesselman, Amy. "African American Activism in New Haven through Women's Eyes." Unpublished essay. Academia.edu.

Knobel, Lance. "Berkeley Mayor Tom Bates Retires after 14 Years: 'I Always Felt I Could Do the Right Thing.'" *Berkeleyside*, November 29, 2016. www.berkeleyside .org.

Komar, Marlen. "Why Makeup Matters to Women in Prison." *Racked*, January 3, 2018. www.racked.com.

Lampert, Lora Bex. *Women Doing Life: Gender, Punishment, and the Struggle for Iden-tity*. New York: New York University Press, 2016.

Laura, Crystal T. "Intimate Inquiry: Love as 'Data' in Qualitative Research." *Cultural Studies, Critical Methodologies* 13, no. 4 (2013): 289–92.

LeBlanc-Ernest, Angela D. "From 'Babies for the Revolution' to Planned Parenthood: The Transformation of the Black Panther Party Female Revolutionary." Lecture, Ohio State University, April 15, 2005.

———. "'The Most Qualified Person to Handle the Job': Black Panther Party Women, 1966–1982." In *The Black Panther Party Reconsidered*, edited by Charles E. Jones, 305–34. Baltimore: Black Classic Press, 1998.

Lee, Chana Kai. *For Freedom's Sake: The Life of Fannie Lou Hamer*. Champaign: Uni-versity of Illinois Press, 2000.

LeFlouria, Talitha L. *Chained in Silence: Black Women and Convict Labor in the New South*. Chapel Hill: University of North Carolina Press, 2016.

"Legal Aid and Educational Program." *CoEvolution Quarterly*, October 1974, 52.

Lenin, Vladimir. *State and Revolution*. N.p.: Leftist Public Domain Project, 2019.

Levin, Yael. "Alum Continues Activism 46 Years after Black Panther Shooting." *Daily Bruin*, October 13, 2015. https://dailybruin.com.

Lewis, Aubyn. "Panther Asked to 'Sell-Out.'" *Black Panther*, February 17, 1970.

Lewis, Gregory B. "Power to the Children: Writing from the Life of a Panther Cub." Unpublished manuscript.

Lorde, Audre. "Age, Race, Class, and Sex: Women Redefining Difference." In *Sister Outsider: Essays and Speeches by Audre Lorde*, 114–23. Freedom, CA: Crossing Press, 1984.

———. *A Burst of Light and Other Essays*. New York: Ixia Press, 2017.

———. "The Master's Tools Will Never Dismantle the Master's House." In *Sister Out-sider: Essays and Speeches by Audre Lorde*, 110–13. Freedom, CA: Crossing Press, 1984.

———. "Poetry Is Not a Luxury." In *Sister Outsider: Essays and Speeches by Audre Lorde*, 36–39. Freedom, CA: Crossing Press, 1984.

———. *Sister Outsider: Essays and Speeches by Audre Lorde*. Freedom, CA: Crossing Press, 1984.

"Loretta Luckes State's Witness Given Suspended Sentence by the State." *Black Panther*, September 19, 1970.

Lumsden, Linda. "Good Mothers with Guns: Framing Black Womanhood in the *Black Panther*, 1968–1980." *Journalism & Mass Communication Quarterly* 86, no. 4 (Winter 2009): 900–922.

Majors, Yolanda. "'I Wasn't Scared of Them, They Were Scared of Me': Constructions of Self/Other in a Midwestern Hair Salon." *Anthropology and Education Quarterly* 35, no. 2 (2004): 167–88.

———. *Shoptalk: Lessons in Teaching from an African American Hair Salon*. New York: Teachers College Press, 2015.

"Marriage License Applications." *Evening Star*, March 19, 1944.

Matthews, Tracye A. "'No One Ever Asks What a Man's Place in the Revolution Is': Gender and Sexual Politics in the Black Panther Party, 1966–1971." PhD diss., University of Michigan, 1998.

———. "'No One Ever Asks, What a Man's Role in the Revolution Is': Gender and the Politics of the Black Panther Party, 1966–1971." In *The Black Panther Party Reconsidered*, edited by Charles E. Jones, 267–304. Baltimore: Black Classic Press, 1998.

Mbilishaka, Afiya. "PsychoHairapy: Using Hair as an Entry Point into Black Women's Spiritual and Mental Health." *Meridians: Feminism, Race, Transnationalism* 16, no. 2 (2018): 382–92.

McMillian, John. *Smoking Typewriters: The Sixties Underground Press and the Rise of Alternative Media in America*. Oxford: Oxford University Press, 2011.

"Message of Francis [Frances] Carter." *Black Panther*, January 31, 1970.

Miles, Tiya. *All That She Carried: The Journey of Ashley's Sack, a Black Family Keepsake*. New York: Random House, 2021.

Miller, William R., and Carl E. Thoresen. "Spirituality, Religion, and Health: An Emerging Field." *American Psychologist* 58, no. 1 (2003): 24–35.

Monteith, Sharon. *SNCC's Stories: The African American Freedom Movement in the Civil Rights South*. Athens: University of Georgia Press, 2020.

Moraga, Cherríe, and Gloria Anzaldúa, eds. *This Bridge Called My Back: Writings by Radical Women of Color*. New York: Kitchen Table: Women of Color Press, 1983.

Moten, Crystal Marie. *Continually Working: Black Women, Community Intellectualism, and Economic Justice in Postwar Milwaukee*. Nashville: Vanderbilt University Press, 2023.

Mungo, Raymond. *Famous Long Ago: My Life and Hard Times with Liberation News Service*. Boston: Beacon, 1970.

———. *Total Loss Farm: A Year in the Life*. New York: Dutton, 1970.

Muñoz, José Esteban. *Cruising Utopia: The Then and There of Queer Futurity*. New York: New York University Press, 2009.

Murch, Donna Jean. *Living for the City: Migration, Education, and the Rise of the Black Panther Party in Oakland, California*. Chapel Hill: University of North Carolina Press, 2010.

Nadasen, Premilla. *Household Workers Unite: The Untold Story of African American Women Who Built a Movement*. Boston: Beacon, 2016.

National Bail Out collective. "Until Freedom Comes: A Comprehensive Bail Out Toolkit." N.d. www.nationalbailout.org.

Nelson, Alondra. *Body and Soul: The Black Panther Party and the Fight against Medical Discrimination*. Minneapolis: University of Minnesota Press, 2011.

Newton, Huey P. "Intercommunalism: February 1971." In *The Huey P. Newton Reader*, edited by David Hilliard and Donald Weise, 181–99. New York: Seven Stories, 2002.

———. *Revolutionary Suicide*. New York: Writers and Readers, 1995.

———. "Speech Delivered at Boston College: November 18, 1970." In *The Huey P. Newton Reader*, edited by David Hilliard and Donald Weise, 160–75. New York: Seven Stories, 2002.

———. *War against the Panthers: A Study of Repression in America*. New York: Harlem River Press, 1996.

Newton, Huey P., and Ericka Huggins. *Insights and Poems*. San Francisco: City Lights, 1975.

Nishida, Akemi. *Just Care: Messy Entanglements of Disability, Dependency, and Desire*. Philadelphia: Temple University Press, 2022.

Njeri, Akua. *My Life with the Black Panther Party*. Oakland: Burning Spear, 1991.

Oakland Community Learning Center. Promotional video, 1977. https://www.youtube.com/watch?v=9dYsjDqUdro.

Ogbar, Jeffrey O. G. *Black Power: Radical Politics and African American Identity*. Baltimore: Johns Hopkins University Press, 2004.

OToole, Corbett Joan. *Fading Scars: My Queer Disability*. Fort Worth: Autonomous, 2015.

Painter, Nell Irvin. *The Narrative of Hosea Hudson: The Life and Times of a Black Radical*. New York: Norton, 1994.

Parker, Gail. *Restorative Yoga for Ethnic and Race-Based Stress and Trauma*. Philadelphia: Singing Dragon, 2020.

Perkins, Margo. *Autobiography as Activism: Three Black Women of the Sixties*. Jackson: University of Mississippi Press, 2000.

Perlstein, Daniel. "Minds Stayed on Freedom: Politics and Pedagogy in the African-American Freedom Struggle." *American Educational Research Journal* 39, no. 2 (2002): 249–77.

Phillips, Mary Frances. "The Feminist Leadership of Ericka Huggins in the Black Panther Party." *Black Diaspora Review* 4, no. 1 (Winter 2014): 187–218.

———. "The Power of the First-Person Narrative: Ericka Huggins and the Black Panther Party." *Women's Studies Quarterly* 43, nos. 3–4 (Fall/Winter 2015).

Phillips, Mary Frances, and Angela D. LeBlanc-Ernest. "The Hidden Narratives: Recovering and (Re)Visioning the Community Activism of Men." *Spectrum: A Journal on Black Men* 5, no. 1 (2016): 63–89.

Pool, Bob. "Witness to 1969 UCLA Shootings Speaks at Rally." *Los Angeles Times*, January 18, 2008. www.latimes.com.

Porter, Ronald K. "A Rainbow in Black: The Gay Politics of the Black Panther Party." In *Sexualities in Education: A Reader*, edited by Erica R. Meiners and Therese Quinn, 364–75. New York: Peter Lang, 2012.

"Pressure Forces Califano to Sign 504 Regulations: Handicapped Win Demands—End H.E.W. Occupation." *Black Panther*, May 7, 1977.

Prince, Althea. *The Politics of Black Women's Hair*. London: Insomnia Press, 2009.

Rafter, Nicole Hahn. *Partial Justice: Women, Prisons, and Social Control*. 2nd ed. New Brunswick: Transaction Publishers, 1995.

Randolph, Sherie M. *Florynce "Flo" Kennedy: The Life of a Black Feminist Radical*. Chapel Hill: University of North Carolina Press, 2015.

Ransby, Barbara. *Ella Baker and the Black Freedom Movement*. Chapel Hill: University of North Carolina Press, 2003.

———. *Eslanda: The Large and Unconventional Life of Mrs. Paul Robeson*. New Haven: Yale University Press, 2013.

"Report from New Haven: Rose Smith Beaten by Pigs in Jail 2/16/70." *Black Panther*, February 28, 1970.

Rierden, Andi. *The Farm: Life inside a Women's Prison*. Amherst: University of Massachusetts Press, 1997.

———. "Prison Reaches Back to Its Farm Origins." *New York Times*, May 5, 1992. www.nytimes.com.

Robinson, Robert P. "Until the Revolution: Analyzing the Politics, Pedagogy, and Curriculum of the Oakland Community School." *Espacio, Tiempo y Educación* 7, no. 1 (2020): 181–203.

Rocker, Dominique Ashley. "A Poetic Revolution: Ericka Huggins, Narrative Resistance, and Erotic Power." MA thesis, University of California Los Angeles, 2020.

Rodney, Walter. *Walter Rodney Speaks: The Making of an African Intellectual*. Edited by Robert Hill. Trenton: African World Press, 1990.

Rodríguez, Dylan. "Radical Lineages: George Jackson, Angela Davis, and the Fascism Problematic." In *Forced Passages: Imprisoned Radical Intellectuals and the US Prison Regime*, 113–44. Minneapolis: University of Minnesota Press, 2004.

Rodriguez-Cayro, Kyli. "This Group Is Bailing Out Incarcerated Black Women in Time for Mother's Day and You Can Help." *Bustle*, May 9, 2018. www.bustle.com.

Rogers, Helen Worthington. "A History of the Movement to Establish a State Reformatory for Women in Connecticut." *Journal of Criminal Law and Criminology* 19, no. 4 (1929): 518–41.

Rooks, Noliwe. *Hair Raising: Beauty, Culture, and African American Women*. New Brunswick: Rutgers University Press, 1996.

Schalk, Sami. *Black Disability Politics*. Durham: Duke University Press, 2022.

Schwarcz, Joe. "What Is Saltpeter Used For and Is It True It Reduces Certain 'Carnal Urges'?" McGill Office for Science and Society. McGill University, March 20, 2017. www.mcgill.ca.

Scott, James C. *Domination and the Arts of Resistance: Hidden Transcripts*. New Haven: Yale University Press, 2009.

"75 Selectees to Go to Camp Tomorrow as Furlough Ends." *Evening Star*, July 19, 1942.

Shakur, Assata. *Assata: An Autobiography*. Chicago: Lawrence Hill Books, 1987.

Shames, Stephen, and Ericka Huggins. *Comrade Sisters: Women of the Black Panther Party*. Woodbridge: ACC Art Books, 2022.

Shaw, Madelyn C., and Kathleen A. Staples. *Clothing through American History: The British Colonia Era*. Santa Barbara: Greenwood, 2013.

Sicard, Sarah. "Saltpeter for Sex Drives, and the Urban Legend of the Military's Libido Manipulation." *Military Times*, September 22, 2021. www.militarytimes.com.

Simmons, LaKisha Michelle. *Crescent City Girls: The Lives of Young Black Women in Segregated New Orleans*. Chapel Hill: University of North Carolina Press, 2015.

Slonecker, Blake. "Living the Movement: Liberation News Service, Montague Farm, and the New Left, 1967–1981." PhD diss., University of North Carolina at Chapel Hill, 2009.

Smith, Barbara, ed. *Home Girls: A Black Feminist Anthology*. New Brunswick: Rutgers University Press, 2000.

Solomon, Akiba, and Kenrya Rankin. *How We Fight White Supremacy: A Field Guide to Black Resistance*. New York: Bold Type Books, 2019.

"Son of Man Temple Opens." *Black Panther*, July 14, 1973.

Spellers, Regina E., and Kimberly R. Moffitt, eds. *Blackberries and Redbones: Critical Articulations of Black Hair/Body Politics in Africana Communities*. Cresskill, NJ: Hampton Press, 2010.

Spencer-Antoine, Robyn C. "Communalism and the Black Panther Party in Oakland, California." In *West of Eden: Communes and Utopia in Northern California*, edited by Iain Boal, Janferie Stone, Michael Watts, and Cal Winslow, 92–121. Oakland: PM Press, 2012.

———. "Engendering the Black Freedom Struggle: Revolutionary Black Womanhood and the Black Panther Party in the Bay Area, California." *Journal of Women's History* 20, no. 1 (2008): 90–113.

———. *The Revolution Has Come: Black Power, Gender, and the Black Panther Party in Oakland*. Durham: Duke University Press, 2016.

Springer, Kimberly. "The Interstitial Politics of Black Feminist Organizations." *Meridians* 1, no. 2 (2001): 155–91.

———. *Living for the Revolution: Black Feminist Organizations, 1968–1980*. Durham: Duke University Press, 2005.

———. "Third Wave Black Feminism?" *Signs: Journal of Women in Culture and Society* 27, no. 4 (2002): 1059–82.

Square, Jonathan Michael. "How Enslaved People Helped Shape Fashion History." *Guernica*, December 14, 2020.

Stearn, Jess. *Yoga, Youth and Reincarnation*. New York: Bantam, 1965.

Stiner, Larry Watani. "Watani Stiner: Tending to Historical Wounds." *San Francisco Bay View*, September 27, 2017. https://sfbayview.com.

Stiner, Larry Watani, and Scot Brown. "The US-Panther Conflict, Exile, and the Black Diaspora: The Plight of Larry Watani Stiner." *Journal of African American History* 92, no. 4 (2007): 540–52.

"Students Prepare for 'K' Invasion." *Lincolnian*, December 1, 1965.

Sutton, Charyn. "Wall to Wall." *Lincolnian*, November 15, 1968.

Taft, John. *MayDay at Yale: A Case Study in Student Radicalism*. Boulder: Westview, 1976.

Talvi, Silja J. A. *Women behind Bars: The Crisis of Women in the US Prison System*. Emeryville, CA: Seal Press, 2007.

Taylor, Ula Y. *The Promise of Patriarchy: Women and the Nation of Islam*. Chapel Hill: University of North Carolina Press, 2017.

———. "Women in the Documents: Thoughts on Uncovering the Personal, Political, and Professional." *Journal of Women's History* 20, no. 1 (2008): 187–96.

"Telephone Conversation with Francis [Frances] Carter." *Black Panther Party*, January 24, 1970.

Tellides, Theodore. "John Huggins: A Hopkins Black Panther." *Razor* (student newspaper), n.d. www.therazoronline.com.

Theoharis, Jeanne. *The Rebellious Life of Mrs. Rosa Parks*. Boston: Beacon, 2013.

Thurma, Emily L. *All Our Trials: Prisons, Policing, and the Feminist Fight to End Violence*. Urbana: University of Illinois Press, 2019.

Treaster, Joseph B. "Erikson and Newton Discuss Issues in Conference at Yale." *New York Times*, February 5, 1971. www.nytimes.com.

Ture, Kwame, and Charles V. Hamilton. *Black Power: The Politics of Liberation*. New York: Vintage, 1967.

Umoja, Akinyele Omowale. "Set Our Warriors Free: The Legacy of the Black Panther Party and Political Prisoners." In *The Black Panther Party Reconsidered*, edited by Charles E. Jones, 417–41. Baltimore: Black Classic Press, 1998.

———. "Straight Ahead: The Life of Resistance of Dr. Mutulu Shakur." *Souls: A Critical Journal of Black Politics, Culture, and Society* 23, nos. 1–2 (2022): 4–35.

Van Deburg, William L. *New Day in Babylon: The Black Power Movement and American Culture, 1965–1975*. Chicago: University of Chicago Press, 1993.

Vaz, Megan. "Memories of May Day: A Look Back at Black Panther Protests at Yale." *Yale News*, February 18, 2022. https://yaledailynews.com.

Vincent, Rickey. *Party Music: The Inside Story of the Black Panthers' Band and How Black Power Transformed Soul Music*. Chicago: Lawrence Hill Books, 2013.

Von Flatern, Jan. "Ericka and Bobby Put the State on Trial." *Black Panther*, January 2, 1971.

———. "A Victory for the People: Jury Hangs the State; Ericka Is Free." *Liberated Guardian*, May 26, 1971, 3.

Walsh, Laura. "Inmates Restore Children's Graves." *Hartford Courant*, July 31, 2004.

Ward, Stephen. "The Third World Women's Alliance." In *The Black Power Movement: Rethinking the Civil Rights–Black Power Era*, edited by Peniel Joseph, 119–44. New York: Routledge, 2006.

Washburn, Amy. "The Pen of the Panther: Barriers and Freedom in the Prison Poetry of Ericka Huggins." *Journal for the Study of Radicalism* 8, no. 2 (2014): 51–78.

"Washington State Free Bussing Program." *Black Panther*, August 21, 1970, 6.

Wasserman, Harvey. "The Joy of Liberation News Service." *Serials Review* 16, no. 1 (1990): 49–58.

Welter, Barbara. "The Cult of True Womanhood: 1820–1860." *American Quarterly* 18, no. 2 (1966): 151–74.

"What's Really Happening at the Trial of Ericka and Bobby." *Panther Trial News* 2, no. 3 (December 13, 1970). Yale Collection of American Literature, Beinecke Rare Book and Manuscript Library.

White, Deborah Gray. *Ar'n't I a Woman? Female Slaves in the Plantation South*. New York: Norton, 1999.

Wiener, Jon, Tom Hayden, Jules Feiffer, and Richard Avedon, eds. *Conspiracy in the Streets: The Extraordinary Trial of the Chicago Eight*. New York: New Press, 2006.

Williams, Jakobi. "'You Can Kill the Revolutionary, but You Can't Kill the Revolution': A Reflection on Deputy Chairman Fred Hampton's Life and Legacy 50 Years after His Assassination." *Harvard BlackLetter Law Journal* 35 (2019).

Williams, Lena. "Revolution Redux?" *New York Times*, March 28, 1993.

Williams, Rhonda Y. *Concrete Demands: The Search for Black Power in the 20th Century*. New York: Routledge, 2015.

Williams, Yohuru. *Black Politics/White Power: Civil Rights, Black Power, and the Black Panthers in New Haven*. St. James, NY: Brandywine, 2000.

Willis, Jan. *Dreaming Me: Black, Baptist, and Buddhist—One Woman's Spiritual Journey*. Boston: Wisdom Publications, 2008.

Wilson, William Julius. *The Truly Disadvantaged: The Inner City, the Underclass, and Public Policy*. 2nd ed. Chicago: University of Chicago Press, 2012.

Wolf, Jacqueline H. *Don't Kill Your Baby: Public Health and the Decline of Breastfeeding in the 19th and 20th Centuries*. Columbus: Ohio State University Press, 2001.

———. "What Feminists Can Do for Breastfeeding and What Breastfeeding Can Do for Feminists." *Signs: Journal of Women in Culture and Society* 31, no. 2 (2006): 397–424.

"York Inmates Toiling to Restore Children's Graves." Associated Press. *New Haven Register*, July 31, 2004.

Zinn, Howard. *SNCC: The New Abolitionists*. 2nd ed. Chicago: Haymarket, 2013.

INDEX

ABOUT THE AUTHOR

MARY FRANCES PHILLIPS is Associate Professor of Africana Studies at Lehman College, City University of New York. She is a scholar-activist, a public intellectual, and a proud native of Detroit, Michigan. Her scholarly interests include the modern Black freedom struggle, Black feminism, and Black Power studies.